A MAGNA CARTA FOR ALL HUMANITY

The Magna Carta, sealed in 1215, has come to stand for the rule of law, curbs on executive power and the freedom to enjoy basic liberties. When the Universal Declaration of Human Rights was adopted by the United Nations in 1948, it was heralded as 'a Magna Carta for all human kind'. Yet in the year in which this medieval Charter's 800th anniversary is widely celebrated, the future of the UK's commitment to international human rights standards is in doubt.

Are 'universal values' commendable as a benchmark by which to judge the rest of the world, but unacceptable when applied 'at home'? Francesca Klug takes us on a journey through time, exploring such topics as 'British values', 'natural rights', 'enlightenment values' and 'legal rights', to convey what is both distinctive and challenging about the ethic and practice of universal human rights. It is only through this prism, she argues, that the current debate on human rights protection in the UK can be understood.

This book will be of interest to students of British Politics, Law, Human Rights and International Relations.

Francesca Klug is Professorial Research Fellow at the Centre for the Study of Human Rights, at the London School of Economics and has researched, written and lectured on human rights for twenty-five years. Professor Klug is a former Commissioner on the Equality and Human Rights Commission and advised on the model for incorporating the European Convention on Human Rights reflected in the UK's Human Rights Act.

If you read one book on rights this is it — a global citizen's guidebook to human rights, infused with the compassion and ethics which are the hallmark of Francesca Klug.

Baroness Helena Kennedy QC

Professor Francesca Klug, one of Britain's most distinguished authorities, offers an intellectual and personal exploration of the Universal Declaration of 1948 and the very idea of human rights.

Professor Philippe Sands, University College London

This is an outstanding account of how, in a fast moving world, human rights have developed into ethical values for pluralist societies. It draws on history, politics and law with all the authority and insight of an insider who helped to shape recent stages of the journey in the UK.

Sir Keir Starmer QC

A MAGNA CARTA FOR ALL HUMANITY

Homing in on human rights

Francesca Klug

Routledge
Taylor & Francis Group

LONDON AND NEW YORK

First published 2015
by Routledge
2 Park Square, Milton Park, Abingdon, Oxon OX14 4RN

and by Routledge
711 Third Avenue, New York, NY 10017

Routledge is an imprint of the Taylor & Francis Group, an informa business

© 2015 Francesca Klug

British Library Cataloguing in Publication Data
A catalogue record for this book is available from the British Library

Library of Congress Cataloging-in-Publication Data
Klug, Francesca.
    A magna carta for all humanity: homing in on human rights /
Francesca Klug.
        pages cm
    Includes bibliographical references and index.
    1. Human rights—Government policy—Great Britain.   2. Human rights—
Moral and ethical aspects.   I. Title.
    JC599.G7K58 2015
    323.0941—dc23
    2014049721

ISBN: 978-0-415-42373-1 (hbk)
ISBN: 978-0-415-42374-8 (pbk)
ISBN: 978-1-315-68996-8 (ebk)

Typeset in Bembo
by Apex CoVantage, LLC

Printed and bound in Great Britain by
TJ International Ltd, Padstow, Cornwall

To Mick and Tania to whom I owe everything.

This Universal Declaration of Human Rights "may well become
the international Magna Carta for all men everywhere."

Eleanor Roosevelt

"I have always acted on the level of humanity."

René Cassin

CONTENTS

COPYRIGHT INFORMATION

PREFACE AND ACKNOWLEDGEMENTS

When I first came across the 1948 Universal Declaration of Human Rights (UDHR) twenty-five years ago I was startled. I had rarely read a document more lyrical and inspirational. The fact that it was drafted by state delegates to the United Nations – not necessarily the first place you would look for stirring prose – and is now the most translated document in the world, made it all the more intriguing and surprising. Exploring further, I came to appreciate that the European Convention on Human Rights (ECHR) was a direct descendent of the UDHR, incorporating many of its standards and values. My journey of discovery in uncovering far more of this story forms the kernel of this book.

Shortly after it is published there will be a large national celebration hosted by the UK government – not for my book, you understand! The bunting will be out for the 800th anniversary of the English Magna Carta which has become totemic in these islands for ushering in 'the rule of law.' Just what the Barons of Runnymede, who mainly considered the 'Great Charter' a failure after it ceased to be operational in 1215 (a tale briefly recounted in the Introduction) would make of this birthday party, is hard to tell. What is certain, is that Eleanor Roosevelt, the mover and shaker behind the UDHR, would be shocked to discover that withdrawal from its progeny, the ECHR, has now been put on the agenda by senior politicans in the same country which spawned the iconic Magna Carta that she took such inspiration from (it should be noted that there is no equivalent appetite amongst political leaders in Northern Ireland, Scotland, or Wales).What does this tell us? Are human rights palatable in a mature democracy like England only as long as they are contained in an ancient document which no longer has any direct legal impact? Are they useful only as a benchmark by which to judge the rest of the world, especially our enemies or rivals, but dangerous when applied to us? These questions will be addressed throughout the book.

Before I became acquainted with post-war international human rights treaties, I had previously understood the phrase human rights to be synonymous with civil liberties, an issue of great importance. In so far as I thought about the *idea* of human rights, I understood it to be an extension of the 'natural rights' philosophy that developed out of the European Enlightenment, manifested in the debates and pamphlets, Bills of Rights and Declarations which are still familiar from that era. But as I delved further, I realised that the post-war human rights project reflected in the UDHR was partly intended as a 'corrector' to the perceived 'failures' of the Enlightenment, a theme I explore in some depth in Section I of the book.

In discussions with the late Professor Kevin Boyle, I came to appreciate that the UDHR was at least partly an attempt to craft an *ethic* to aid human beings throughout the world to live peaceably with one another, following a catastrophic war which impacted on most of the globe. In Section I I attempt to sketch the contours of that ethic. The drafters drew not just on what is sometimes called 'Enlightenment values,' but on a mosaic of insights and ethical precepts from many faiths, philosophies and belief systems. To some degree they followed the lead of the Lebanese delegate, Dr Charles Malik, who advised them to mine the 'wisdom and light from all time', whilst simultaneously learning from the more immediate 'barbarous acts which have outraged the conscience of mankind'.[1]

Also explored in Section I are the other more prosaic factors which were in play, and the many contradictory currents, not least the fact that virtually the whole of sub-Saharan Africa was still living under colonial rule at the time of the UDHR drafting and was therefore unrepresented at the UN. But the defects and distortions this produced only speak to a partial truth. The legacy of the UDHR lies not just in the fact that it inspired some of the world's greatest liberation leaders like Nelson Mandela, who spoke of its galvanising effect, but that today, all over the globe, campaigns and struggles adopt the language and values of human rights. These are the movements which shine a light in dark corners; campaigns crafted out of the simple notion that every human being is of equal worth and value and should be treated with equal dignity and respect. As the decades have passed the centre of gravity for human rights thinking has navigated away from the West and is all the richer for it.

The UDHR is not mainly addressed to states but to 'every individual and every organ of society'[2]; it aims to make 'duty bearers' out of us all. It asserts that peace and progress depend on us understanding that we are 'all members of the human family'.[3] When the chips are down, in other words, it is our common humanity that we must privilege. When the Human Rights Act (HRA), which incorporates the values and standards in the ECHR, was introduced as a bill of rights in 1998, it seemed that this ethic of universal human rights would loom much larger in our legal and public life. To some degree it has, but its impact has also produced a political and philosophical backlash the nature of which is explored in Section II, alongside proposals for the HRA's replacement and for the curtailment of the ECHR in the UK.

As indicated, after a brief introduction on the Magna Carta, the book is divided into two largely self-contained sections. The first mainly focuses on the development and ethic of universal human rights and the second 'homes in' on the reception given to universal human rights 'at home.' Following both sections I have included an Anthology of some of my already published and unpublished articles, chapters and lectures which, in each case, I have selected to amplify my argument; sometimes because they were written without the hindsight that I am now able to benefit from. Virtually all this material is not readily available; other more accessible articles and books are listed in a Select Bibliography alongside the main publications which have influenced the ideas in this book, all of which were invaluable to my thinking whether I concurred with their central argument or not.

My purpose in writing this book is three fold.

First, as I come towards the end of my academic career, I hope this book might contribute to an understanding, and perhaps appreciation, of the ethic encapsulated in the idea of universal human rights, as I see it. I wrote every page with a new generation of students and activists in mind. Unlike my parents, I grew up in a country which had seemingly made its peace with the compromises to national sovereignty that subscribing to an international or regional human rights treaty like the ECHR inevitably entails. Withdrawal from such a framework, crafted from the ashes of the Second World War, was once unthinkable. Now that this is potentially on the cards, it seems to me all the more important that we understood what it is we might be about to lose.

Second, this book is an attempt at an interdisciplinary treatment of human rights. I have had the privilege of teaching on the multi-disciplinary MSc at the LSE Centre for the Study of Human Rights where I am based. When I was a student, degrees in human rights did not exist. I have long harboured the hope that in time the study of human rights might achieve greater recognition as a discipline in its own right, similar to gender, peace or race and ethnic studies. This is a shot at a modest contribution in that direction.

Third, I have been asked by a number of people over the years to catalogue the steps that led to the adoption of the HRA in the UK, a country which had hitherto rejected bills of rights as 'alien' to the British constitution. In attempting to do so, I have drawn from my own experience as an occasional advisor to the previous government on bills of rights to track the story of how the particular model in the HRA was adopted.

Whilst the responsibility for the ideas and arguments in this book is entirely mine, I am conscious that they are the product of discussions and engagements that stretch back over many decades, involving a large number of people who I have been privileged to know and work with, some of whom are referenced in the text or footnotes. Included amongst them are the women and men I worked with or campaigned alongside at the extraordinary Anti-Apartheid Movement and the Runnymede Trust, in the Migrants Action Group and the Women Immigration and Nationality Group (WING) and at Liberty, the British Institute of Human Rights and Justice. In more recent years, students, researchers and colleagues at Essex University, King's College London and the LSE have challenged and inspired me to think critically and delve deeply. Special thanks go to Helen Wildbore, Amy Williams and Breony Allen who have all worked with me at the Human Rights Futures Project at the LSE and whose meticulous research and legal scholarship are reflected in many pages of this book. Breony forensically scrutinised the whole manuscript, spotting errors, correcting mistakes and supplying references with characteristic tact and thoroughness. Zoe Gillard and Sara Ulfsparre at the LSE Centre for the Study of Human Rights provided unstinting practical support, making it possible for me to write at long distance whilst always feeling welcome when returning to my home base.

My editors at Routledge, Nicola Parkin and her assistant Peter Harris, provided invaluable advice throughout as did Emily Davies, Production Editor. I am equally indebted to Heidi Bagtazo, my former Routledge editor, whose idea it was to include in this book an anthology of my previously published work after I failed to provide any material at all over a period of several years from signing the original publication contract!

I have benefitted greatly from feedback and encouragement from both colleagues and friends who read the manuscript and imparted invaluable comments, both broad and specific. Shami Chakrabarti, the Director of Liberty, has been an inspiration to me for many years and I am enormously appreciative and touched by her thoughtful and generous foreword. Sir Rabinder Singh and my brother Dr Brian Klug read the first section and have both been hugely influential on my thinking over the years through many conversations and their own incisive writings. It was Brian, together with my friend and early mentor Nony Ardill, who encouraged me both to get started and keep going when I intermittently dried up. Jonathan Cooper, barrister and Director of the Human Dignity Trust, and my esteemed colleague Professor Conor Gearty from the LSE, both took time out from their extremely busy work schedules to read the whole draft. The richness of their forensic feedback and loan or procurement of crucial material were indispensible to the development of the text. Grateful thanks is also owed to Tom Blackmore, grandson of Sir David Maxwell-Fyfe (who played a major role in the drafting of the ECHR) for providing me with unpublished letters and guiding me to other material for inclusion in this book.

I am blessed with many good friends from different generations, whose warmth, good humour and insatiable appetite for fun nourished me during the intense and lonely process of writing, sometimes in person but more often remotely through emails, texts and calls. These include my 'Parkholme Road pals,' the 'caravan crowd' and 'New Year chums' and my friends in domestic and international human rights organisations, barristers' chambers and at the LSE. I am indebted to the beautiful village of Hayfield in the High Peaks, Derbyshire, where I drafted the whole manuscript inspired by a magnificent view of the Snake Path, '20 trees,' three donkeys and numerous sheep and cows. Above all I simply could not have embarked on this endeavour, let alone completed it, without the love and support of my fantastic daughter Tania and my rock and partner Mick. Not only did he prove to be an unfailingly good natured sounding board when despair crept in but he discovered his inner house husband, plying me with endless dinner trays, cups of tea and mugs of coffee throughout the 11 months it took to research and write this book. Only our lovely Red Setter dog Ruby proved to be a more faithful companion to me whilst I wrote in my attic office.

The personal influences that have shaped this book precede my birth. Like all people who come from immigrant families, the experience of migration echoes down several generations. The insider–outsider perspective which often comes with such a background can enrich the whole of life – it certainly has mine! As far as I am aware there is no-one in my extended family whose near ancestors hail from the same country that they live in now. All four of my Yiddish-speaking grandparents came to the East End of London and Hackney at the turn of the twentieth century from Russia and Poland. They did not come on luxury liners and they brought with them stories of pogroms, poverty and persecution, to varying degrees, which my parents continued to relay. I was still very young when my mother recounted how, at the end of the war, she had been contacted by the Red Cross to meet her first cousin who had survived Auschwitz along with his wife, unlike most of the rest of their families.

When my three older brothers explained to me the genesis of the civil rights, Anti-Apartheid and anti-colonial movements that were gaining such momentum in my early childhood, these folded into the stories I had learnt about my own family. This no doubt led me to work for the Anti-Apartheid Movement and Runnymede Trust in my twenties, to be involved in anti-deportation and anti-racist campaigns and eventually to be appointed Director of the Civil Liberties Trust, the charitable arm of Liberty, in 1989. When I later became an academic and worked with others on the HRA it was, for me, partly a means of putting into practice the respect for the stranger – 'for we were strangers once'[4] – I had learnt from my family's story as a child. This was why, twenty-five years ago, the UDHR struck such a chord the first time I encountered it. I only hope I have done justice to this remarkable 'Magna Carta for all Humanity' in writing this book.

Francesca Klug
January 2015

Notes

1   *Preamble*, UDHR.
2   Ibid.
3   Ibid.
4   Leviticus 19:34.

FOREWORD

Francesca Klug has been at the forefront of human rights thinking in the United Kingdom for more than twenty-five years, and it's a pleasure and privilege for me to have known her and her work for the last seventeen. This ambitious, important and timely book is a fitting culmination of that impressive body of work, drawing on history, politics, law and – as always with this author – ethics, going back to the Magna Carta as we prepare to celebrate its 800th anniversary.

Klug tells us that she completed the first section during a bombardment of Gaza which killed more than 2,000 people last year. I write this foreword just days after jihadi gunmen took seventeen lives in Paris. Umpteen civil wars and national wars of independence, two world wars, a cold war and a 'war on terror' have not, it seems, diluted our capacity for cruelty. Nor however – as acts of Parisian hero-ism first by a Muslim policeman and then a shop-worker of the same faith demonstrate – have they extinguished the conscience, reason and empathy which Klug so powerfully articulates as the basis for human rights the world over, including 'close to home'.

The history and scholarship to be found here are of course beyond question. Yet this is so much more than an essential academic text, coming as it does at a time when the UK Conservative Party has vowed to repeal the Human Rights Act 1998 and replace it with a 'British Bill of Rights'. This move is in truth nothing more than the flimsiest of figleaves for privileges, rather than real freedoms, that will emasculate domestic and international judges currently charged with rights protection. It will include this pledge in its manifesto for what is likely to be an extremely close, contested and potentially toxic 2015 General Election with an agenda increasingly set by the xenophobic right.

This contribution is vital in telling the stories of both the journey from Magna Carta to post-war international human rights documents and the genesis and benefits of the Human Rights Act during the author's working life (although her own enormous role is characteristically underplayed for the careful reader to decode). It points up many of the historical ironies and logical contradictions of current anti-human rights comment and debunks many of the myths that have arisen, more by design than accident (as Klug very clearly explains).

We first receive an important analysis of both the inspiration and limitations of the Magna Carta and its legend. This is so important as we prepare to watch a range of politicians (including the most vociferous opponents of fundamental rights and freedoms as protected by the Human Rights Act and European Convention on Human Rights) wrap themselves in the Great Charter as well as the Union Jack.

We then witness the birth of the Universal Declaration on Human Rights after the horrors and terrors of the Holocaust and the Blitz. Klug's painstaking revelation of drafting negotiations reveals how hard it can be to craft international instruments that some find so easy and convenient to destroy or reject.

The very British, and indeed Conservative, parentage of the European Convention is then unpacked, though never one to over-egg an argument, Klug is clear about 'the many parents and step-parents' of the Convention and ultimately the Human Rights Act that gives its best effect at home in the UK.

At this point the author moves from meticulous historical research to the direct and fascinating personal experience which makes her story of the Human Rights Act particularly unique. For few will have witnessed its gestation so closely, or indeed contributed so much to its birth. She is also well placed to examine the vested interests pitted against our modern Bill of Rights (for that is what the HRA is) and the political and media onslaught it has received from the first.

Nonetheless, this book is in the end as uplifting as it is informative, explaining the great strengths of our Human Rights Act in balancing parliamentary sovereignty and the rule of law and its genius in appropriately involving each limb of the Constitution in protecting the vulnerable.

Further, the book's great generosity and vision in attributing human rights progress to so many people from different walks of life, political persuasions, nationalities and generations reminds us that there is always the potential and instinct to make such progress once more. In that respect *A Magna Carta for All Humanity* is both great testament to, and a reflection of, the woman herself. It is both academic and accessible. It has a long memory but never rambles or fails to reveal the acute pertinence of long-passed milestones to present forks in the road. It is clear in its values and opinions but never shrill or dogmatic in that clarity. The wisdom of ages provides hope for tomorrow.

Shami Chakrabarti
Liberty House, London
January 2015

ABBREVIATIONS

ACHPR	African Charter on Human and Peoples' Rights
AU	African Union
CoE	Council of Europe
CoM	Committee of Ministers
ECHR	European Convention on Human Rights
ECOSOC	United Nations Economic and Social Council
ECtHR	European Court of Human Rights
EHRC	Equality and Human Rights Commission
EU	European Union
HRA	Human Rights Act
ICC	International Criminal Court
ICCPR	International Covenant on Civil and Political Rights
ICESCR	International Covenant on Economic Social and Cultural Rights
ILO	International Labour Organisation
IPT	Investigatory Powers Tribunal
NIHRC	Northern Ireland Human Rights Commission
OHCHR	Office of the High Commissioner for Human Rights
UDHR	Universal Declaration of Human Rights
UN	United Nations
UNCHR	United Nations Commission on Human Rights
UNHCR	UN Refugee Agency
UNHRC	United Nations Human Rights Council

INTRODUCTION

The Magna Carta: marvel or myth?

The inventor of the World Wide Web, Sir Tim Berners-Lee, announced in March 2014 that 'an online Magna Carta is needed to protect and enshrine the independence' of the Internet. He was not the first or the last to cite this medieval English document in calling for a written constitution or 'a bill of rights'.[1]

When the Universal Declaration of Human Rights (UDHR) was adopted by the United Nations in 1948 as the first leg of an international bill of rights,[2] Eleanor Roosevelt, the mover and shaker who drove the entire project, expressed her hope that it would become 'the international Magna Carta' for all human kind.[3] Yet, when it was sealed in 1215 the Magna Carta was largely seen as a failure. It was initially legally valid for no more than three months and was never properly implemented. The so-called Great Charter was originally called 'great' because of its large size, not because of its lofty intention. Historians have noted that immediate contemporaries made no great claims for it at all.[4]

The Charter, like many historic documents down the centuries, was the product of a political crisis. It was the result of a sustained and bitter conflict between a medieval King of England and his barons. Contemporary accounts tell us that King John of England was a fearsome monarch. 'All men bore witness that never since the time of Arthur was there a King who was so greatly feared in England, in Wales, in Scotland and in Ireland.'[5] He tried to throw off the restraints of those who wielded power in the court of his predecessor, his elder brother Richard I, and rule in his own way. Discontent about taxes for foreign adventures now focussed on the monarch himself. William Sharp McKechnie, an early twentieth-century authority on the Magna Carta, described how 'the whole administration of justice, along with the entire feudal system of land tenure' were 'degraded into instruments of extortion.'[6]

On 15 June 1215 a five day summit between King John and his barons began in a field known as Runnymede, located between Staines and Windsor. The King acceded to most of the barons' long list of grievances; the armed forces they had mustered no doubt concentrating his mind. His main purpose was to avert insurrection, and on the day the Charter was sealed the barons reaffirmed their oaths of allegiance to the King.[7] But this outbreak of peace did not last long, and soon both sides were preparing for war.

Neither King John nor the barons could possibly have contemplated that 800 years later a major birthday celebration would be planned in their honour by the British government in homage to the concessions that were wrung out of the King those few fateful days at Runnymede.

The Magna Carta was revived and re-issued in 1216 and 1217, but the text was substantially modified to water down some of the provisions that most threatened the sovereignty of the monarch, in particular the so-called 'sanctions clause' (61) which appointed a group of twenty-five barons to monitor enforcement of the Charter. In 1225, after John's death, his son Henry III confirmed both the Magna Carta and its shorter companion, the 'Forest Charter', and it was this fourth version that was to become the standard issue. The 'charters of liberties', as they were originally known, were included in collections of both the common and cannon law until the nineteenth century when successive parliamentary revisions of statute law, particularly in 1823, 1863 and 1879, repealed chapter after chapter. Today only three (and a half) chapters or clauses remain on the statute book.[8] Yet what still stands has enjoyed a longer life than any other English enactment[9] and has taken on a symbolic significance that far exceeds any legal effect.

Although many people in the UK may only be vaguely aware of the Magna Carta, its symbolic status has endured. Regardless of the actual words of the text, its impact or legacy, the Magna Carta has come to stand for 'the rule of law', limits to monarchical or executive power and basic liberties.

Whilst the Magna Carta's remaining legal provisions have been superseded by more modern statutes, it lives on, in historian J. C. Holt's words, as 'propaganda' as much as law.[10] At a ceremony to kick-off the countdown to the 800th anniversary, Lord Neuberger, former chair of the Magna Carta Trust and president of the Supreme Court, described the medieval document as the foundation of modern liberties:

> It enshrined such noble concepts as freedom under law, democracy and the importance of limited government; it was a pre-cursor to many of the freedoms and liberties that humanity rightly expects their governments to respect today.[11]

Yet most of the Magna Carta addressed specific grievances, rather than general principles, which have no relevance outside the feudal society they were drafted in. As the former Lord Chief Justice, the late Lord Bingham, pointed out with characteristic forthrightness in a speech delivered at St Alban's Cathedral in June

2010, many of the Charter's clauses are of local, particular or feudal interest only and 'about as interesting as our rules for recycling rubbish are likely to be to our descendants 800 years from now.' But he went on to assert that 'this yellowing parchment, soon to celebrate its 800th birthday, can plausibly claim to be the most influential secular document in the history of the world.'[12]

Central to the symbolic importance of the Charter, and expressed in terms that have resonated down the generations, are clauses 39 and 40 (in the original 1215 version) which are still on the statute book and worth reproducing in full.

> 39. No free man shall be seized or imprisoned or stripped of his rights or possessions, or outlawed or exiled, or deprived of his standing in any other way, nor will we proceed with force against him, or send others to do so, except by the lawful judgment of his peers or by the law of the land.
>
> 40. To no one will we sell, to no one will we deny or delay right or justice.[13]

These commitments were undoubtedly groundbreaking for Feudal England, but claims that they directly ushered in our current rights to jury trial (clause 39) or habeas corpus (clause 40) are overblown. Lord Bingham was at pains to point this out in his 2010 lecture:

> Establishment of a charter of human rights in the sense understood today was not among [the barons] objectives. Chapters 39 and 40 were important not as conferring rights on the subject but as imposing a restraint on the King.[14]

It was their own interests and privileges that the barons were seeking to protect, not the rights of the mass of their fellow countrymen (let alone countrywomen) or the liberties of future generations. The immediate impact was to establish the principle of legitimate constraints on monarchical rule. In the long run, 'the Charter provides a *building block* which has been crucial in developing our modern notion of the Rule of Law.'[15]

So how has the Magna Carta achieved such iconic status that the Ministry of Justice is planning a major international conference in 2015 to boast of its historic achievements? Three factors combined have contributed to what Holt refers to as 'the myth of the Magna Carta',[16] all of which, when present in current human rights laws, are the subject of much debate and criticism. That the same features (which will be explored further on) are lauded as 'totemic' when applied to this ancient document, but 'dangerous' when apparent in its modern equivalents, is one of the conundrums this book will explore.

A 'living instrument'

Much of the Magna Carta was an early model of what can be described as 'open textured drafting', avoiding the pitfalls of too much precision. Holt has demonstrated how 'the history of the document is a history of repeated re-interpretation'[17] to ensure that it conformed to new social and political conditions. Its adaptability 'was its greatest and most important characteristic.'[18] The Charter was a political document, as much as a legal one, produced to fix a specific medieval crisis, confirming as well as weakening crown privileges. Yet clauses 39 and 40 have survived 800 years because they were written in sufficiently open terms to be adaptable to fit evolving circumstances. The Magna Carta owes its continual existence to legislators and lawyers, keen to exploit the looseness of its language.

A series of parliamentary petitions submitted by the infant House of Commons during the reign of Edward III formed the basis of the six Acts of statutory interpretation of the Great Charter, passed between 1331 and 1352. These went far beyond its original intention. This is when the phrase 'lawful judgement of his peers' began its journey of evolving into the jury system we know today. This, and not before, was when the 'law of the land' was interpreted as 'due process of the law'.

It was these six Acts, as much as the Charter itself, which established the Charter's status as the precursor of modern liberties. Neither the Charter nor the six Acts ended monarchical tyranny when it reasserted itself in the centuries that followed, but they provided historic legitimacy to the claim that ancient freedoms were being sacrificed in the process. By the seventeenth and eighteenth centuries, according to constitutional historian Joyce Lee Malcom, 'the original articles in the Magna Carta had been stretched and interpreted to embrace an expanded list of individual rights.'[19]

It was in this period that the Magna Carta came into its own, as Anthony Arlidge QC and the former Lord Chief Justice, Lord Judge, have argued in another recent book to mark the 800th anniversary.[20] English Kings still exercised powers of arbitrary arrest and imprisonment in the seventeenth century, and the courts were scarcely independent, but the Act which abolished the Star Chamber in 1641 quoted from the six interpretative statutes, as well as clause 39, to reassert the liberties that were perceived as sealed by the Magna Carta.

In the 1628 debate on the *Petition of Right* (forced on King Charles I, much as the Magna Carta had been wrung out of King John) the House of Commons, led by Sir Edward Coke MP, cited the Great Charter to establish grounds for the writ of habeas corpus, although this was scarcely historically accurate. It was eminent lawyers such as Coke, a former Chief Justice, who restored the Magna Carta as a document of political importance, culminating in Blackstone's famous Commentaries of 1759.

By this time, the Magna Carta was being exploited and developed by lawyers, not so much to *establish* new legal principles but to *reassert* them, regardless of whether they had ever existed in the (somewhat mythical) past. Coke's famous assertion that the Magna Carta was 'such a fellow that he will have no sovereign' is hardly how King John saw it in 1215.[21] It was hardly how Charles I saw it either. Before losing both his head and the crown, he prayed in aid the Magna Carta to support the status quo and his version of the historic customs of Britain.[22] Such was the Great Charter's by now legendary status, combined with its elasticity, that it could be asserted by the powerful and powerless in equal measure. As Lord Bingham put it in his 2010 lecture, the Magna Carta was 'as influential for what it was widely *believed* to have said as for what it actually did'.

Universal application

Closely allied to the Charter's flexibility has been its evolving universality. It began its life as anything but a universal human rights charter in the meaning we give to such terms today. The Magna Carta was devised mainly in the interests of the landed classes of medieval England, a small proportion of the population of this island, even in the thirteenth century.

Clause 1 asserts that the liberties in the Charter were granted by King John to 'all freemen of my kingdom and their heirs forever'. McKechnie concluded that 'only a limited class could . . . make good a *legal* claim to share in the liberties secured' by the Charter which historian Nicholas Vincent estimates as roughly 10–20 per cent of the population.[23]

Enforcement was initially entrusted to a committee of twenty-five aristocrats, further mocking claims that the Magna Carta was the foundation of modern democracy. The famous reference to the 'judgment of peers' or 'equals' in clause 39 is also not quite as it sounds to the modern ear. The 'peers' of a crown tenant were fellow crown tenants and the point was that they should not be tried by their *inferiors*, which is quite a different principle to the random selection of fellow citizens that forms the basis of the modern jury system. In this respect English custom did not differ significantly from the feudal system commonly in place in other parts of Europe. What the Magna Carta was asserting here was a return to historic practices.[24]

Many of the Charter's clauses had no value except to landowners. 'Freemen' were distinguished from 'villeins' or serfs (for example in clause 20), with the latter excluded from many of the benefits conferred on others by the Magna Carta.[25] If villeins were protected at all, it was not as the subject of legal rights but because they were a valuable asset to the lords who presided over them. 'The villein was deliberately left exposed to the worst forms of purveyance,' from which clauses 39 and 40 'rescued his betters'.[26] Coke's seventeenth-century claim that villeins were protected by clause 39, 'is not well founded,' according to McKechnie, who concluded that the Charter viewed them 'as chattels attached to a manor, not as members of an English Commonwealth'.[27] The Common Law left a serf 'subject to arbitrary eject-ment by his Lord'[28] and the Magna Carta did nothing to alter this. A century ago McKechnie concluded that 'the baronial leaders are scarcely entitled to the excessive laudation they have sometimes received.'[29]

The narrow reach of the original Magna Carta was not confined to the exclusion of serfs and many town dwellers. Unsurprisingly, given its medieval pedigree, the Charter further singled out women and Jews for distinctly non-universal treatment, regardless of their social status. Women were forbidden from giving testimony in court that might lead to the arrest or imprisonment of the accused except in relation to the death of their husbands, in line with the already existing medieval law. Forced marriages were regulated, but not abolished, although 'disparagement' – that is, forced marriage with someone not an equal – was prohibited. The barons argued that an English heiress was 'disparaged' if she was married to anyone not English born, but 'the sale of heiresses went on unchecked.'[30]

Jews, who were totally reliant on royal patronage for their status, which could be withdrawn at will, were explicitly treated as a group apart from the 'freemen' in the original text of the Magna Carta. The contrast with the fourteenth-century Scottish Declaration of Arbroath is unmistakable, with its assertion that 'there is neither weighing nor distinction of Jew and Greek, Scotsman or Englishman.' According to McKechnie, in England 'the feudal scheme of society had no place for Jews. They shared the disabilities common to aliens in a form unmitigated by the protection extended to other foreigners by their sovereigns and by the church.'[31]

Whatever Jewish people owned was, by royal prerogative, not under the protection of law. When Jewish men died their widows and heirs had no legal right to their property. The King generally helped himself to a third of what, if anything, was accrued. According to McKechnie: 'Jews became the mere . . . chattels of the Crown, in much the same way as the villeins became the serfs or chattels of their Lords.'[32] Whilst this may not be an accurate analogy in many regards, it reflects the powerlessness of both groups in medieval England which was, if anything, further underlined in the original Magna Carta. A passage from the mid-twelfth-century revision of the written record of law, known as the *Leges Edwardi Confessoris*, declared that 'the Jews themselves and all their possessions are the king's . . . if someone detains them or their money the king shall demand them as his own property.'[33] Prohibited from most trades other than money lending, Jews were sometimes protected by King John from violent attacks by their Christian neighbours; however, he also arrested them en masse when he wanted to extort money from them, leading many to flee overseas. When the barons captured London on 17 May 1215 they demolished Jewish houses and used the materials to strengthen the city's defences. Yet they were aiming as much at the King as they were at Jews in the two clauses (10 and 11) they inserted into the Magna Carta to regulate the interest paid by the heirs of 'one who has borrowed from the Jews'. These clauses were omitted in the reissue of 1216, probably not to protect Jews but, rather, to enhance sources of wealth for the King. Jews were increasingly required to wear distinguishing clothes from 1222, and later many were effectively required to live in ghettos. In 1290 they were permanently banished from England by Edward I.

Yet by the seventeenth century Coke was boldly asserting that from the outset the Charter applied to the whole realm. In a similar vein, the former prime minister Lord Chatham (or William Pitt the Elder) insisted in the House of Lords in 1770 that the barons 'did not confine [the Magna Carta] to themselves alone, but delivered it as a common blessing to the whole people'. The nineteenth-century historian Sir Edward Creasy went so far as to declare that the Charter guaranteed 'full protection for property and person to every human being that breathes English air'.[34] If serfs, burghers, women, Jews and people not born on English soil are excluded, this might be a fair description. McKechnie was already dispelling this

myth of universal application 100 years ago, directly warning against such 'anachro-
nistic' interpretations of the Charter. It was primarily 'a baronial manifesto, seeking
chiefly to redress . . . private grievances . . . and mainly selfish in motive'.[35]

Whilst it would therefore be wildly historically inaccurate to bestow universal
intentions on the multiple authors of the Charter, the principles established in
the few clauses that remain on the statute book were nevertheless loosely enough
phrased to allow for increasingly generous interpretations in the centuries that followed. Today a phrase such as 'to no-one will we deny justice' has come to be
understood as the very foundation of our modern, inclusive justice system. Mirror-
ing those present-day politicians who complain that current human rights treaties
have been given a meaning that was never intended by their original authors, in the
early days the mediators chosen to referee the ongoing dispute between the barons
and King John insisted in writing that the words of the Charter must be read 'in a
restricted sense'.[36] The drafters 'did not themselves envisage this continuous process
of re-interpretation'.[37] Yet if they had been taken at their word and a narrow, literal
reading had been maintained throughout the centuries, the Magna Carta would
never have become the inclusive, iconic document that still has resonance today. It
would probably have had no more shelf life than any other medieval manuscript, let
alone become the source of a major national celebration in 2015 to commemorate
its 800th birthday.

A 'sacred text'?

Without the looseness of its drafting and the consequential re-interpretation of
two of the Charter's surviving clauses to uphold principles such as equal treatment
before the law and universal justice, it is also doubtful that the Magna Carta would
have achieved the status of '*fundamental* law' that some constitutional lawyers have
bestowed on it. In the late nineteenth century the renowned legal historian Frederic
William Maitland wrote: 'this document becomes, and rightly becomes, a sacred
text, the nearest approach to an irrepealable "fundamental statute" that England
ever had.'[38] More than a hundred years later Lord Bingham described the Magna
Carta as 'all but [a] sacrosanct instrument' with a 'venerability conferred by several
centuries of constitutional tradition'.[39]

These are bold statements in the context of Britain's constitutional arrangements. Unlike most other democracies, the UK famously lacks a codified constitution which is protected from actual or implied repeal and which acts as a
'higher law', interpreted by judges who can strike down legislation that does not
conform with it.[40] What Britain has instead is an accumulation of statutes, conventions, judicial decisions and treaties which collectively are sometimes (inaccurately)
referred to as 'the unwritten British Constitution'. The UK also has the Human
Rights Act 1998 (HRA), to which all other legislation is required to conform, but
only 'where possible'. In contrast to many other bills of rights around the world
the domestic courts cannot overturn Acts of Parliament under the HRA, and
hence parliamentary sovereignty is maintained.[41] This also means that no single

parliament can bind its successors so that Members of Parliament (MPs) and Peers are free to legislate, or repeal legislation, virtually at will. The fact that most of the Magna Carta has been taken off the statute book a long time ago in itself belies the boast of Maitland and others that it is a 'fundamental statute' that cannot be overturned. Yet the original text suggests that this permanence was precisely what the barons sought. In the very first clause, which is one of only three to remain on the statute book, it is declared:

> We have also granted to all the free men of our realm for ourselves and our heirs *in perpetuity*, all the liberties written below, to have and hold to them and their heirs from us and our heirs.
>
> *(my emphasis)*

Holt has described how, despite having no *formal* legal status as a 'higher law' in the manner of bills of rights or written constitutions, 'the Charter was used as a yardstick of legality against which new measures could be assessed and accepted or rejected.'[42] This role developed fairly rapidly and reasserted itself periodically down the centuries as was implicit in the original purpose of the Charter; 'for such a grant of liberties in perpetuity could not be made effective except by treating it as a fundamental law.'[43]

In keeping with the Charter's role, not just as law but 'also propaganda',[44] this feature of pre-eminence took on a political character when the Magna Carta 'became the political property of radicals', from the Levellers' struggle for liberty in the seventeenth century to John Wilkes's battle for free speech in the eighteenth century and the Chartists campaign for democracy in the nineteenth century.[45] Claims to 'English liberties' and the so-called rights of 'free-born Englishmen' had meanwhile become 'mainstream' so that 'even Tory political ideology underscored a fundamental patriotism derived from this historical tradition,'[46] a theme which is recognisable to this day. However, with the promotion of 'natural law' theories by John Locke, Thomas Paine and other Enlightenment thinkers, reliance on 'ancient liberties' was overshadowed by new currents championing rights and reason. Yet this did not mean the demise of the symbolism of the Magna Carta. For such radicals the Charter was cited, not in defence of the common law or Parliament, but *against* both as they operated at the time. From the point of view of such dissenters Parliament could be as arbitrary as the King had been, and the common law had been used not for freedom but to enforce draconian laws.

Unsurprisingly perhaps, the Magna Carta took on a similarly symbolic role in the fight of the American settlers against both the English King and the British Parliament. Here the 'due process' principles that had been 'read into' clauses 39 and 40 of the original 1215 version were fused with 'natural rights theories' to become embedded in the bills of rights that were drafted by state after state in the late eighteenth century. In this way clauses that had been written to prevent King John from imprisoning or executing opponents according to his arbitrary will became reformulated as a legally enforceable individual right not to be 'deprived of life, liberty, or property, without due process of law'.[47]

Perhaps it is a reflection of the relatively modest grip that the Magna Carta has had on the popular imagination in the UK in recent decades that it was the American Bar Association which funded and erected a monument at Runnymede in 1957 to acknowledge the heritage of the Magna Carta, close to the subsequent John F. Kennedy memorial. The 800th anniversary may lead to a revival of interest. But notwithstanding the naming of the Race Relations Charity in 1968 as the Runnymede Trust, there is scant evidence that the Magna Carta has played any significant role in galvanizing modern-day campaigns for justice and fair treatment in the UK.

This is no doubt in part because its legal remedies have been superseded by a range of statutes and case law that address modern concerns for equality and justice which a medieval document could not be expected to even conceive of. The disputes between a King and his English barons on a field outside Windsor 800 years ago seem very remote from the struggles of a modern, diverse democracy (currently) composed of four nations and citizens who stem from all parts of the world. The Magna Carta would seem to have nothing to offer if you are disproportionately more likely to be stopped and searched by the police because of the colour of your skin or religious affiliation. It has not even been relied upon by those terror suspects who have been subject to Orders[48] which control their freedom of movement without the due process protections that the Magna Carta had been assumed to guarantee 800 years ago.

Today such seekers after justice in the UK, to the extent that they have faith in the law at all, are far more likely to cite the 2010 Equality Act, or the 1998 Human Rights Act (HRA). Failing these, they might seek redress at the European Court of Human Rights (ECtHR). But such avenues are not as completely remote from the Magna Carta as it might seem at first glance, at least in symbolic terms. The 1950 European Convention on Human Rights (ECHR) is inspired by, reflects (and in many cases reproduces) the civil and political rights in the UDHR, adopted two years earlier. Both treaties were drafted in the wake of the Second World War and their standards and principles reflect the trauma of that event and the racism and persecution which preceded it. Yet despite the lapse of 750 years since the Great Charter was drafted, Eleanor Roosevelt hoped that:

> this Declaration may well become the international Magna Carta for all men everywhere. We hope its proclamation by the General Assembly will be an event comparable to the proclamation in 1789 [of the French Declaration of the Rights of Citizens], the adoption of the Bill of Rights by the people of the US, and the adoption of comparable declarations at different times in other countries.[49]

This widely quoted statement reflects the reality that each of these iconic documents – as distinct as they are – were linked, one with the other, by the inspiration, and sometimes the words, of the charters that preceded them. If Mrs Roosevelt were to return to modern Britain she would probably be amazed at the venom directed at the ECHR – the close descendant of the 'international Magna Carta' – by the same ministers and politicians who are intent on galvanizing the whole population to commemorate the Magna Carta in 2015. This is also the year of the next UK general election, which falls just a month before the 800th birthday celebrations. The Conservative Party's manifesto will commit to repealing the HRA, introduced by the last Labour government in the form of a bill of rights which incorporates the standards – but not the case law – of the ECHR. The Tories will promise to replace it with a bill of rights which they will claim is more 'British' in character and less tied to 'European law'. They may also seek to curtail the 'binding' nature of judgments by the ECtHR itself. All of this will be explored in detail later in the book.

Setting aside the Eurosceptic rhetoric which drives these proposals, the reasons given for opposing the HRA are often very similar to the reasons that the Magna Carta has stayed relevant for eight centuries. First, the rights in the HRA, similar to those in the Magna Carta, are broadly expressed. The HRA incorporates most of the rights in the ECHR which many senior Conservative ministers frequently criticize for its loose drafting, leading to interpretations which can stray from the apparent 'original intentions' of the drafters. Their motive, the lament goes, was to stop the Nazis from behaving like King John, not to allow gypsies and travellers to maintain their way of life or transgender people to alter their birth certificates, let alone allow prisoners to vote in elections. On this logic the due process provisions in the Magna Carta would still only extend to the landed aristocracy and would have no relevance to modern life.

Second, the HRA is criticized for its universal application. In line with international human rights law, everyone subject to the jurisdiction or control of the British state is covered by the HRA from soldiers serving in Afghanistan to Iraqi prisoners detained by British troops. In a globalized world, where the state's reach is not confined by geography, this developing inclusiveness is scarcely different to the revision to the Magna Carta under Edward III when the term 'no free man' was altered by statute in 1354 to become 'no man of whatever estate or condition he may be'. It is that universal reach which saved the Great Charter from irrelevance in the centuries that followed.

Finally, the HRA is attacked for weakening parliamentary sovereignty by requiring judges to interpret all legislation to conform with it or, where this is not possible, empowering them to 'declare' that a statute is not compatible with its terms. Like the Magna Carta, there is no power for the courts to overturn an Act of Parliament under the HRA, but just like the Magna Carta again, most constitutional lawyers recognize it as a type of 'fundamental law'.[50] Or at least they did until the Prime Minister committed his party to repeal it.[51] A major reason why the same political leaders on the one hand laud the Magna Carta as a constitutional document which Parliament is honour bound to adhere to, and on the other hand abjure the HRA for having the same de facto status, is differential impact. The sections of the Magna Carta that have survived are 'harmless confirmations of rights and privileges conveyed by other instruments.'[52] In other words, if the UK foreign suspects detained indefinitely without trial in Belmarsh prison, after the events of 9/11, could have relied on the Magna Carta to free them, the courts would not have had to issue a

Declaration under the HRA that such indefinite detention was discriminatory and disproportionate and therefore unlawful.[53] It is the HRA's legal effect which most directly distinguishes it from the Magna Carta and makes it such a fiercely opposed target for repeal.[54]

Is this backlash against the HRA a reassertion of the spirit of the Magna Carta and the common law against European infiltration or are its government opponents behaving more like King John did 800 years ago after sealing the deal, recoiling from a rights Charter that impinges on their freedom to legislate at will? To begin to consider this questions we need to journey back in time.

Notes

1 Quote in *The Guardian*, 12 March 2014. Another recent example was at a conference *A New Magna Carta? A Constitution for the 21st Century* held on 11 December 2014 at the House of Commons under the auspices of the Political and Constitutional Reform Committee, chaired by Graham Allen MP, and King's College Centre for Political and Constitutional Studies.

2 The 1948 UDHR, together with the UN's *International Covenant on Civil and Political Rights* and *International Covenant on Economic, Social and Cultural Rights*, both ratified in 1976, are in combination known as the International Bill of Rights.

3 Eleanor Roosevelt, *Speech on the Adoption of the Universal Declaration of Human Rights*, 9 December 1948, France. Her full quote is reproduced in the text below.

4 J. C. Holt, *Magna Carta* (Cambridge: Cambridge University Press, 1992), 21.

5 A contemporary chronicler quoted by William Sharp McKechnie, in *Magna Carta: A Commentary on the Great Charter of King John* (Glasgow: James MacLehose and Sons, 1914), 24.

6 Ibid., 22.

7 See Nicholas Vincent (ed), *Magna Carta: The Foundation of Freedom 1215–2015* (Law Society and Bar Council, London: Third Millennium Publishing, 2014) for a beautifully illustrated account of the events leading to, and following, the issuing of the Magna Carta.

8 These embody, with slight amendment, four of the original provisions: parts of clause 1 on the freedom of the church, clause 13 on the rights of the city of London and clauses 39 and 40, reproduced in the text below. See Vincent et al., *Magna Carta*, 15.

9 According to Holt, *Magna Carta*, 1.

10 Ibid., 21.

11 Lord Neuberger quoted in *The Lawyer*, 12 November 2010.

12 Lord Bingham, *Magna Carta Lecture*, St Albans Cathedral, 11 June 2010.

13 Both were incorporated into clause 29 in 1225.

14 Lord Bingham, *Magna Carta Lecture*.

15 Ibid.; my emphasis.

16 Holt, *Magna Carta*, 9.

17 Ibid., 18.

18 Ibid., 2.

19 Joyce Lee Malcom, 'Magna Carta in America: Entrenched', 120–135. *Magna Carta: The Foundation of Freedom 1215–2015*, 122.

20 Anthony Arlidge and Igor Judge, *Magna Carta Uncovered* (Oxford, UK: Hart Publishing, Oxford 2014).

21 The catchphrase that has echoed down the ages which most encapsulates this formula is: 'Be you never so high, the law is above you,' coined by Dr Thomas Fuller in 1733.

22 Quoted in H. Butterfield, *The Englishman and His History* (Cambridge: Cambridge University Press, 1944), 68.

23 McKechnie, *Magna Carta*, 115; Vincent et al., *Magna Carta*, 72.

24 McKechnie, *Magna Carta*, 37.

25 Ibid., 116.
26 Ibid., 118.
27 Ibid., 119.
28 Ibid.
29 Ibid.
30 Ibid., 213.
31 Ibid., 230.
32 Ibid.
33 Referenced by *The Magna Carta Project* (University of East Anglia, 2014), chapter 10, p. 2, http://magnacarta.cmp.uae.ac.uk.
34 Sir Edward Creasy, *The Rise and Progress of the English Constitution* (New York, D Appleton and Company, 1885).
35 McKechnie, *Magna Carta*, 119.
36 Ibid., 43.
37 Holt, *Magna Carta*, 14.
38 In F. Pollok and F. W. Maitland, *History of English Law*, vol. 1 (Cambridge: Cambridge University Press, 1898), 173.
39 Bingham, *Magna Carta Lecture*.
40 Written constitutions are generally only capable of amendment or repeal through special procedures, such as a two-thirds majority in parliament.
41 Since the *European Communities Act 1972*, the EU's European Court of Justice can overturn legislation which is held incompatible with EU law, and UK domestic courts are required to comply with such rulings. The UK is also subject to international law, notably the European Convention on Human Rights (ECHR), but the European Court of Human Rights (ECtHR) can only *declare* that UK law is incompatible with the ECHR, and it becomes a matter for the UK government, not the domestic courts, to determine how to proceed.
42 Holt, *Magna Carta*, 14.
43 Ibid.
44 Ibid., 21.
45 Ibid., 17.
46 Justin Champion "From *Liber Homo* to 'Free-born Englishman': How Magna Carta Became a 'Liberty Document 1508-1760's" in *Magna Carta: The Foundation of Freedom 1215–2015*, 116.
47 Malcolm, "Magna Carta in America: Entrenched," 132.
48 Otherwise known as TPIMS, these Orders can be placed on terror suspects by the Home Secretary if officials decide there is insufficient evidence to charge them or they cannot be deported. In January 2012 TPIMS replaced Control Orders, which were introduced by the New Labour government to control the movement of terrors suspects in the wake of 9/11. In their original form they were compared to house arrest.
49 Roosevelt, *Speech on the Adoption of the Universal Declaration of Human Rights*, December 1948. The full title of the 1789 Charter Roosevelt referred to is the *French Declaration of the Rights of Man and the Citizen*.
50 For example, see discussions and descriptions in Philip Alston, ed., *Promoting Human Rights through Bills of Rights* (Oxford: Oxford University Press, 1999).
51 See, for example, *Prime Minister's Questions*, House of Commons, 1 December 2010 and 16 February 2011.
52 Holt, *Magna Carta*, 1.
53 *A and Others v Secretary of State for the Home Department* [2004] UKHL 56.
54 A similar point is made about the drivers of opposition to the ECHR by the former Conservative Attorney General, Dominic Grieve, in 'Why Human Rights Should Matter to Conservatives', lecture at University College London, 3 December 2014.

Human rights

A time-traveller's guide

Introduction

The meaning of the phrase *human rights* is contested territory in modern Britain. Few people will be unfamiliar with the term, but whereas for some it connotes a precious idea about the equal worth and dignity of all human beings, for others it conjures up relentless demands and an abuse of freedom by the least deserving. There are connotations not only of rebellion and revolution in the term *human rights* but also of double standards and Western imperialism. To some ears human rights are synonymous with civil liberties whilst for others they convey a broader vision of a good society. Like any enduring idea, human (or fundamental) rights have a back story dependent on time, place and context. To say that the concept has evolved throughout the centuries is an understatement. So what would those we think of as the pioneers of earlier struggles make of current human rights debates were they to appear in our present day?

First stop: in search of 'British values'

If time-travelling medieval English barons were to land in modern Britain, they would probably be pretty chuffed right now. Back in the day, it must have seemed as if they had failed miserably in their attempts to restrain King John. No sooner had John conceded the Magna Carta on 15 June 1215, but Pope Innocent III annulled it, releasing the King from his oath to obey it. The Great Charter was legally valid for no more than three months, and England was effectively plunged into a civil war. To top it all, knowing King John would never be restrained by the Magna Carta, in a measure of desperation, the barons offered the crown of England to Prince Louis of *France*!

Yet 799 years to the day David Cameron, the Prime Minister of the United Kingdom, writing in the *Mail on Sunday*, cited this product of aristocratic *English* dissent as the font of '*British* values' which will be compulsorily taught in English state schools. In the context of a vexed debate about the curriculum and governance of some Birmingham schools with a large majority of Muslim pupils, it is this medieval document that the government ear-marked to come to the rescue.[1]

Eleanor Roosevelt would presumably be far less cheerful to discover that the Universal Declaration of Human Rights (UDHR), which she designated as a Magna Carta for all humanity, has not been assigned a comparable heroic status. She would undoubtedly be disconcerted to discover that 'human rights' have mysteriously been replaced by 'precious liberties' in the English school curriculum and that the government apparently does not consider the UDHR, or its progeny the European Convention on Human Rights (ECHR), to be emblematic of the country's values. She would probably be perplexed that a medieval charter which has nothing to say about most of the values the Prime Minister cited as signifiers of national identity in the same newspaper article, is preferred to a UN declaration created to foster the 'freedom, tolerance' and 'social responsibility' that the Prime Minister designated as specifically 'British'. How discomforting, as well, for Sir David Maxwell Fyfe, the former Conservative Home Secretary who was instrumental in drafting the ECHR and who, as a prosecutor at the post-war Nuremberg trials, proclaimed that 'some things are surely universal: tolerance, decency, kindliness . . . they are the inalienable heritage of mankind.'[2]

It is interesting to reflect on the speed with which the Magna Carta has been hoisted to pole position, and universal human rights virtually relegated out of sight, in the government's search for common norms in a diverse society. Only twelve years earlier, when Tony Blair's administration began this quest following the catastrophic terrorist attack on New York's twin towers on 9/11, the UK's Human Rights Act (HRA), which incorporates much of Fyfe's ECHR, was specifically cited as 'a key source of values that British citizens could share'.[3]

When I wrote 'Human Rights: A Common Standard for All Peoples?' (the first of the anthology pieces reproduced here) for the Foreign Policy Centre think tank in 2002, we were at the start of several outbreaks since the dawn of the twenty-first century of government-inspired quests to define 'British values'. It was only six months since 9/11, but already Muslims in Britain were being required to demonstrate that they did not support the attacks, prompting a debate on 'Britishness' which was even then under way. My short piece was published in a booklet that was specifically called *Reclaiming Britishness*. It reflected on the then current debate about whether it is meaningful, let alone constructive in a diverse society, to confer a specific nationality on basic values which many people around the globe comfortably share. It was then still relatively common for commentators to observe that defining 'Britishness' is not a very British thing to do and to wonder whether the government might cite internationally defined 'human rights values [to] provide the core of what can unite the diverse communities which make up the UK?'[4]

By 2009 the government-inspired project to define 'Britishness' appeared to take on a more specifically New Labour tinge when the former Prime Minister Gordon Brown wrote the introduction to a book on *Being British*. He claimed that whilst 'liberty might be seen as a universal value . . . in its uniquely British incarnation', which has evolved over the centuries through the 'common law . . . the combination of duty and liberty, of rights and responsibilities, lives and breathes each day.'[5]

For a set of principles that are said to be timeless, or at least 800 years old, it is fascinating how quickly they can evolve at the hands of the state. New guidelines on 'promoting fundamental British values' in maintained schools, published by the Department for Education in November 2014 in the wake of the furore regarding Birmingham (and a few other) schools, mentions nothing about 'rights and responsibilities', which were a stock New Labour phrase. Instead schools in England will be expected to 'actively' promote 'democracy, the rule of law, individual liberty and tolerance of those with different faiths and beliefs' which 'also means challenging opinions or behaviours in school that are contrary to fundamental British values'.[6] No explanation is given as to what makes these values specifically '*British*', leading Abdool Karim Vakil, lecturer in European history at King's College London, to comment:

> Muslims are happy to sign up to common values of justice, fairness, equality and democracy, but understood as values that all of us need to strive to live up to and make a reality, not as the already achieved preserve of some primordial British population that the not-quite-British enough must be civilised into.[7]

Next stop: rediscovering 'Enlightenment values'

A whole host of time travellers, including the English 'natural rights' proponents John Locke and Tom Paine, the German philosopher Immanuel Kant and the French radicals Rousseau and Voltaire, would be intrigued by this debate were they to turn up in modern Britain. They would certainly recognize those principles that the government is now requiring its schools to promote. They sound remarkably similar to the so-called Enlightenment values of justice, liberty, freedom of religion, free speech and tolerance (or 'toleration' to use an Enlightenment-era term) which they championed so assiduously in their day.[8] By the end of the eighteenth century, democracy, as a principle in itself, was added to the mix.[9]

These time travellers could be forgiven for wondering, therefore, why these 'values' are now being repackaged as specifically 'British' when the Enlightenment is fairly understood as a pan-European project. The apparent association between these 'values' and the Magna Carta might surprise them even more, given that beyond a common respect for 'the rule of law' there is not a great deal that links them (and even here there is a distinction between the 'natural rights' promoted by Enlightenment thinkers as the basis of a 'just law' and the more procedural 'legality' of the Great Charter). Tom Paine, for instance, whilst campaigning for democracy and rights in Britain (for which he was charged with seditious libel, leading to his lifelong exile from British shores) wrote somewhat disdainfully of the disproportionate stature granted the Magna Carta. If the barons deserved a memorial at Runnymede, he argued, surely Wat Tyler, the leader of the 1381 Peasants Revolt, warranted a monument in Smithfield.[10]

There is considerable historical dispute about whether the Enlightenment denotes an era spanning from roughly the mid-seventeenth century to the end of the eighteenth century (when 'the terror' following the French revolution created its own backlash) or a set of timeless ideas that still invigorate Western society today. Liberal commentators and authors such as Richard Dawkins, Martin Amis and the late Christopher Hitchens, who would presumably support the latter stance, have strongly asserted the need to protect so-called Enlightenment values since 9/11 (and the 7/7 London bombings on 7 July 2005) from what they, and many other commentators, call 'Islamism'.[11] The implicit allegation is that liberal values are under significant pressure and need reclaiming. According to author Dan Hind, the phrase 'enlightenment values' roughly quadrupled in the British press in the years after the 9/11 attack, but this did not prevent Dawkins from worrying that 'the Enlightenment is under threat, so is reason, so is truth.'[12] For Amis, 9/11 was 'a day of de-Enlightenment', inaugurating a 'bipolar' confrontation between 'the West' and 'an irrationalist . . . system' in a new 'age of religion',[13] whilst for Hitchens, 9/11 demanded an assertion of 'some very important Enlightenment principles'.[14]

It is interesting to reflect, therefore, on why the current government is insistent on re-casting these Enlightenment values as specifically 'British' when many would agree with the Enlightenment critic John Gray that 'the Enlightenment is part of the way we live and think.'[15] Presumably it is its pan-European association that a largely Eurosceptic government wants to avoid in a project aimed at bolstering British identity.

Regardless of the rights and wrongs of the practices of the specific Birmingham schools that led to the state reasserting 'fundamental British values' – and they have been cleared of any allegations of links to 'violent extremism' – the incident highlighted a familiar paradox. How do you demand tolerance as a mark of acceptance when the implicit message is that the expression of certain views and practices will not be tolerated? This question is as striking as it is familiar. It was in the Enlightenment era that this paradox was most apparent, only it was then European Jews rather than European Muslims who were the target community. The historian Adam Sutcliffe puts it like this:

> The idea of tolerance can only be defined in opposition to a contrasting notion of intolerance . . . In our own era Islam rather than Judaism is much more frequently cast as the inverse of enlightened toleration, in contrast to which 'western' values are defined and reinforced. During the Enlightenment era, however, Judaism was the ubiquitous agnostic partner of reason.[16]

This paradox is perhaps best reflected in the writings of Voltaire who, whilst insisting that individual Jews should be tolerated, persistently expressed hostility towards Jews as a group. In an article on 'Tolerance' Voltaire, with no apparent awareness of the irony of his words given the essay's title, famously wrote: 'It is with regret that I discuss the Jews: this nation is, in many respects, the most detestable ever to have sullied the earth.'[17] Voltaire searched for a notion of nationhood that Sutcliffe describes as 'in some sense both historical and fixed' whereas Jews who stood as an 'anomalous "non-national nation" exposed the tenuousness of eighteenth century (and later) notions of national identity'.[18] As Sutcliffe puts it, 'the Jews did indeed represent the Enlightenment's primary "unassimilable Other."'[19]

The pluralism of modern British society is a long way from the Janus-like quality of Enlightenment thinking, of which Voltaire is only the most extreme example,[20] but parallels with our own time are not without foundation. It is not necessary to agree with Max Horkheimer and Theodor Adorno when they linked the Enlightenment reverence for truth, science and reason to the growth of totalitarianism,[21] or with Gray's assertion that the 'race science' on which Nazism drew heavily was rooted in Enlightenment thinking,[22] to appreciate the problem. When the Prime Minister says 'we need to be far more muscular in promoting British values and the institutions that uphold them,'[23] and that 'it isn't enough simply to respect these values in school . . . they're not optional; they're the core of what it is to live in Britain,'[24] this can sound like demanding uniformity in the name of tolerance. There are echoes in Cameron's 'muscular liberalism' of Rousseau's famous dictum in *The Social Contract*, written in 1762, that 'whoever refused to obey the general will shall be compelled to it by the whole body: this in fact only forces him to be free'; although the Prime Minister would no doubt flinch at the comparison. But when new rules were floated to give the Secretary of State for Education the power to close a school or dismiss its governors where 'conduct' is deemed as 'undermining fundamental British values', it is not surprising that a spokesperson for the Muslim Council of Britain interpreted this to mean that 'conservative Muslim beliefs [could be] deemed incompatible with British values.'[25] This didn't feel much like 'liberal tolerance' to him!

At the heart of this issue lie two connected problems. First, at the very minimum, so-called British values will inevitably remain highly contested. As Professor Homi Bhaba has pithily observed, 'nations, like narratives, lose their origins in the myths of time.'[26] Britain has its self-delusions like any other country, described by the historian Joanna Bourke as 'a quaint assumption that we are a peaceable people, engaging in armed conflicts half-heartedly and only when threatened by aggressors' whilst 'there is still considerable reluctance to acknowledge the atrocities committed during the age of empire.'[27] When asked on a BBC discussion programme to nail down 'British values' in the wake of the Birmingham schools furore, the Eurosceptic Conservative MEP Daniel Hannan responded that you could do worse than the inscription in the monument to the Magna Carta at Runnymede: 'Freedom under the law'.[28] But in an impassioned piece that echoes the young Tom Paine, the radical journalist Owen Jones described the government's agenda as 'dangerous' if 'one side claims its values are those of the nation as a whole'. His take on the Magna Carta – 'an English rather than British document' – is that it 'meant diddly squat to average English subjects, most of whom were serfs'.[29] American historian Eric Foner has gone further:

> British freedom was anything but universal. Nationalist, often xenophobic, it viewed nearly every other nation on earth as 'enslaved' – to popery, tyranny or barbarism. . . . British freedom was the linear descendant of an understanding of liberty derived from the Middle Ages, when 'liberties' meant formal privileges such as self-government or exemption from taxation granted to particular groups by contract, charter, or royal decree. . . . The medieval understanding of liberty assumed a hierarchical world in which individual rights in a modern sense barely existed, and political and economic entitlements were enjoyed by some social classes and denied to others.[30]

Of course this version of history is as contested as any other, although the awarding of compensation in 2013 to more than 5,000 Kenyans tortured during Britain's colonial rule and the Prime Minister's acknowledgement in the same year of the 'monstrous' 1919 Amritsar massacre in British India of peacefully protesting Sikhs, provides evidence of Foner's assertion that British freedom was a rationed commodity. The second interconnected problem is that even when values such as 'liberty' and 'tolerance' are presented as 'universal' they can, as Gray has warned, sound like 'the universalising project of *Western* cultures'.[31] This was flawlessly reflected in the response of the former president of the European Union Herman Van Rompuy to the Turkish request for entry to the EU in 2009 when he said 'the universal values which are in force in Europe, and which are also fundamental values of Christianity, will lose vigour with the entry of a large Islamic country as Turkey [*sic*].'[32]

For a book aimed at homing in on universal human rights this critique may sound surprising. But the kernel of my argument is that post-war human rights should not be understood as a straightforward continuation of the Enlightenment project of universalizing a Western preoccupation with rationality and individual liberties, as is frequently presumed. To the contrary, it was in large measure an attempt to 'correct' the failures of that project in the aftermath of the Second World War.

Fast forward to the Universal Declaration of Human Rights

For theorists such as Paul Gordon Lauren, who wrote *The Evolution of Human Rights* in 2003, and Lynn Hunt, who published *Inventing Human Rights* in 2007, post-war human rights have evolved out of the 'natural rights' precedents of the Enlightenment era, almost 'as a seamless web without significant intellectual bumps in the road'.[33] Similarly, Gray asserts that the 'provenance' of universal human rights is 'manifestly that of the Enlightenment',[34] whilst the renowned moral philosopher Alasdair MacIntyre sees in post-war human rights a continuation of the failed 'Enlightenment Project'.[35]

How do we test these assertions, which are directly or indirectly reflected in the bulk of everyday discourse on human rights, if not by starting with the seminal text from which virtually all subsequent post-war human rights standards and treaties have flown? The UDHR, drafted in 1948 under the auspices of the United Nations, has been translated into more languages than the Bible. Johannes Morsink, the political philosopher who produced a forensic analysis of the UDHR, has compared its significance to the Qur'an, the Bhagavad Gita, the Bible and *The Communist Manifesto*.[36] It has spawned at least fifty international human rights instruments which make reference to it, and many domestic constitutions cite the UDHR as a source of inspiration or even as a higher authority to which they must conform.[37] It is because of its ubiquitous impact that Morsink has called the UDHR the 'moral lingua franca of our age'.[38] To assess whether the UDHR was, in essence, the continuation of an abruptly interrupted Western Enlightenment project to 'universalize' liberal values of freedom and tolerance or a significant leap in a new direction, it is necessary to time travel ourselves and imagine the world as it was when the UDHR was drafted and before.

If the 'Enlightenment continuity theorists' are correct, it might be expected that the idea of fundamental rights would have had a hegemonic pull throughout the Western world from the late eighteenth century onwards. But before the UDHR the term 'human rights' was not even in common use. 'Natural,' 'fundamental' or 'inalienable' rights were more usual phrases, even in countries with bills of rights such as France and the US. These iconic documents reflected the Enlightenment world view that every individual, as children of God, possessed 'natural rights' from the moment of their birth. Parroting the French Declaration of the same name, Paine was unusual in writing about 'the rights of man'[39] (to which the feminist writer Mary Wollstonecraft famously retorted with her 1792 classic *A Vindication of the Rights of Woman*). After the 'terror' took hold in France, the backlash against French revolutionary ideas grew even stronger in Britain than it had been when Whig MP Edmund Burke, widely seen as the intellectual founder of modern Conservatism, famously wrote *Reflections on the Revolution in France* in 1790, to which Paine's *Rights of Man* was a response.

During the course of the nineteenth century, Western debates on the 'natural' or 'inalienable' rights of 'man' were eclipsed by struggles for extending the franchise and campaigns to improve social and economic conditions and for trade union rights. In the twentieth century the fault line was increasingly between capitalism and socialism not Burkites versus Painites. Even moral philosophers, unless they were Kantians, became sceptical of the assertion that fundamental moral principles can be 'discovered' through pure reason.

It was only during the Second World War that interest in 'fundamental' rights revived a little in political and philosophical discourse, particularly in the UK, France and the Americas. One product of this is on my bookshelf. It is a small booklet by the famous British author H. G. Wells – a Penguin Special – written early in the Second World War, which I was completely unaware of until I began my own journey of discovery on the development of human rights thinking, twenty-five years ago. Its title is *The Rights of Man; Or, What Are We Fighting For?* and it includes a *Declaration of Rights* (in several versions) to present to then Prime Minister Neville Chamberlain. Whilst recalling the Magna Carta and the 'various Bills of Rights, Declarations of the Rights of Man and so forth' that had been drafted 'at various crises in the history of our communities', the new Declaration would 'go far beyond that assertion of individual liberty that has hitherto satisfied our ancestors'. Included were a range of social and economic rights to be added to traditional liberties which together would become 'the fundamental law for mankind throughout the world'.[40]

The booklet sold thousands of copies and was translated into thirty languages with articles about it appearing around the globe. Wells sent a copy of this Declaration to his friend, the US president Franklin D. Roosevelt, who corresponded with him about it. When Roosevelt made his State of the Union address to Congress on 6 January 1941 he concluded it with his famous appeal for a world founded upon 'four essential freedoms' that people 'everywhere in the world' should enjoy: freedom of speech and worship and from want and fear. Asserting that 'freedom means the supremacy of human rights everywhere,' the universalism of the presidential message struck an unusual chord in an annual speech aimed at a domestic audience. Roosevelt concluded that this was not a distant dream but:

> a definite basis for a kind of world attainable in our own time and generation. That kind of world is the very antithesis of the so-called new order of tyranny which the dictators seek to create with the crash of a bomb.

In the course of that year Roosevelt repeatedly returned to his 'four freedoms' theme, and in January 1942, at the third St James's Conference in London, the Allied powers belatedly included the protection of human rights among their official war aims, stating that victory was essential 'to preserve human rights and justice' everywhere.[41] A reference to the 'four freedoms' was eventually to make its way into the Preamble of the UDHR.

From 1943 pressure grew from nongovernmental organizations (NGOs) and prominent intellectuals for the protection of human rights to be included in any post-war peace settlement, with Protestants, Catholics and Jews in America combining to make this call in the widely distributed pamphlet *A Pattern for Peace*. In the same year the American Institute of Law produced its own version of an International Bill of Rights and the International Labour Organisation (ILO) did likewise, both of which eventually filtered into the drafting process of the UDHR.

In England René Cassin, the French law professor and resistance member who fled to Britain early in the Second World War, started corresponding with colleagues in North America 'on the state of the movement in America, towards an International Declaration of Human Rights'.[42] This was not simply a question of intellectual interest amongst academic lawyers but a very personal project for a Jewish exile who was acutely aware of the mortal peril his extended family was in under Nazi-occupied France, regardless of how integrated or patriotic they were. His biographers Jay Winter and Antoinette Prost put it like this:

> Cassin entered the inter-Allied circle which framed war aims not only in terms of punishing the Nazi criminals, but also in terms of enacting a new human rights regime which would make anything like the Hitler regime impossible in the post-war world.[43]

Cassin launched a Free France Commission in the UK. Its responsibilities included drafting an International Declaration of the Human Rights and Duties of Man and Citizen, which was intended to compliment France's iconic 1789 Declaration with an international code that would include 'duties'. Cassin's biographers point out that the *Beveridge Report,* published in the UK in 1942 whilst Cassin was living there, had established that social and economic rights would be on the agenda in the post-war world, directly influencing Cassin's thinking along with Wells's *Draft Declaration.* The preface of the final Free France document established that its aim was to 'help citizens to become conscious of the rights they have and the duty to defend and respect the rights of others'.[44]

If this project and Wells's draft represented a shift away from the Enlightenment focus on individual freedom to a more collectivist and communitarian outlook, the Cambridge academic lawyer and refugee Hersch Lauterpacht's influential *International Bill of the Rights of Man*, published in 1945, was in part a restatement of the 'natural rights' tradition on a universal scale.[45] As the war was coming to a close in 1945, the American Jewish Committee drew up its own version of an International Bill of Rights whilst at the Inter-American Conference on War and Peace. Twenty-one countries from the Americas declared their strong support for such an instrument to be included in the forthcoming UN Charter.[46] All of this material, with its different orientations, influenced the Declaration when it came to be drafted.

Cassin, Lauterpacht and other exiles from Nazism were amongst the first to argue for the proposed new international architecture to be grounded on a much firmer human rights footing than the abortive League of Nations, which the Allies agreed to replace with the United Nations at the Tehran Conference in 1943. The League had demonstrably failed to safeguard even those minorities it had partly been established to protect at the end of the First World War. A series of 'minority clauses' and treaties covering specific countries and regions were supposed to guarantee basic rights and freedoms to all the inhabitants of the affected territories, potentially marking an unprecedented interference with national sovereignty in the handful of states involved. Attempts to extend these guarantees to all League member states through a general Convention failed.

In 1933 the League was served with a petition drafted by the Committee of Jewish Delegations for a German Jew, Franz Bernheim, who had been dismissed from his job in Upper Silesia because of his ethnic origin. This was in breach of the 1922 bilateral treaty between Poland and Germany, supervised by the League. Bernheim's dismissal was part of the purge of all Jewish employees from a range of professions and jobs. His petition also objected to the officially organized boycott of Jewish shops, lawyers and doctors which he sought to have declared null and void. The legal issues raised with the League were submitted to a panel of three jurists who found against Germany, following which Bernheim was awarded compensation and the Jews of Upper Silesia received some temporary protection. However, the limited reach of the 'minority clauses' and treaties was soon exposed. Germany blocked an attempt to engage the League in the persecution of Jewish people within its own borders, insisting this was a matter for domestic jurisdiction only. On 3 October 1933 German foreign office delegate Von Keller, expounding on the German state philosophy of the Volkstum, which defined national identity not by residence or citizenship but by race, argued that the 'Jewish problem' fell outside the scope of the 'minority clauses'.

Representing Haiti, the jurist and diplomat Antoine Frangulis, supported by Czech, Greek and Irish delegates, maintained that the route to protecting minorities lay in the establishment of a universal convention for safeguarding the human rights of *all* people. This found no favour amongst the colonial powers, for obvious reasons, and there was apprehension about alienating Germany further. A much weaker French resolution was supported unanimously, but three days later Hitler announced Germany's withdrawal from the League. Japan followed suit in the same year, followed by Italy in 1937. When the Second World War broke out in 1939 it was clear that on every one of its objectives the League had failed.

All this was very much in the minds of the various forces that put pressure on the fledgling UN to include the protection of human rights in its founding Charter. At the San Francisco Conference in April 1945, where the terms of the Charter were agreed, the war was still raging but was drawing to a close. A month prior to this a US State Department official, Alice McDiarmid, had drafted a paper spelling out the disappointment of 'various governments and private organisations' with the lack of emphasis on human rights at the Dumbarton Oaks conference the previous year, where the basic structure of the post-war international edifice was agreed. 'Religious groups have been particularly emphatic in demanding that the Charter be strengthened in the field of human rights' she wrote.[47]

By the beginning of the San Francisco Conference the broad outline of the US State Department's position on human rights was clear. Key details had, however, been deliberately left vague due to resistance by some other governments compounded by domestic concerns about American vulnerability regarding rampant racial discrimination and segregation in the South.[48] An unholy alliance between the UK and the Soviet Union at Dumbarton Oaks, both with their own reasons to be concerned about incursions into 'national sovereignty', was aimed at watering down references in the Charter to respecting human rights. This resistance did not prevent Guildhaume Myrddin-Evans, the British delegate at San Francisco, from presenting a view of Britain's pre-eminent role in bringing freedom to the world that would make the current UK government proud.

> In matters affecting the liberty of the individuals [*sic*], in matters of social progress, in humanitarian and other fields . . . we can claim that our country has been a pioneer – and we intend to remain in that position.[49]

In an unprecedented step, more than forty civic and religious organizations were invited to attend the San Francisco Conference by the US government. They pushed hard to persuade reluctant delegates to include the safeguarding of human rights as one of the UN's founding goals. Legal historian Brian Simpson records that 'behind this enthusiasm for human rights lay the knowledge of the atrocities committed during the war,' although the full extent of NGO influence is a matter of some historical dispute.[50] The American Jewish Committee insisted that 'international machinery is needed,' to confront states which violate the human rights of its citizens 'because the two other methods of coping with the problem: intervention by one state and international agreement by treaty have been tried and found unsuccessful'.[51]

Walter White, representing the National Association for the Advancement of Colored People (NAACP), would have spoken for many of those present when he warned that safeguarding national sovereignty to the extent that was sought by the Allies would prevent the new body from speaking out against atrocities such as the Nazi's racial policies and persecutions. The UN would have been as hamstrung as its predecessor; a precedent that in the end the states represented at San Francisco chose not to replicate.

At a press conference midway through the conference Edward Strettinius, the US Secretary of State, put it like this:

> The people of the world will not be satisfied simply to return to an order which offers them only worn out answers to their hopes. They rightly demand the active defence and promotion of basic human rights and fundamental freedoms. It is a matter of elementary justice that this demand be answered affirmatively.[52]

In the end seven references to human rights were inserted into the UN Charter, including the requirement that a Commission 'for the promotion of human rights' should be established.[53] But to the disappointment of the many NGOs and human rights activists who had lobbied for an international bill of rights, there was no commitment to draft one. Morsink describes the UDHR, drafted by the UN Commission on Human Rights (UNCHR), which first met in January 1947, as 'an extension and an explication of these Charter references to human rights'[54] with some of the same language repeated in the Preamble to the Declaration.

It is unlikely that any of these human rights references would have survived if they hadn't been balanced, or some might say neutralized, by Article 7(2). This provision, reflecting mutual American and Soviet ambitions to limit interference in their domestic affairs, denied the UN the authority to 'intervene in matters which are essentially within the domestic jurisdiction of any state' and affirmed that there was no requirement on 'Members to submit such matters to settlement under the present Charter'. This unresolved tension between 'sovereignty' and 'universal human rights', enshrined in the Charter, has haunted the UN ever since. Simpson has observed that

> on a strict view of the founders' intention, the Charter of the United Nations, settled after a war which had witnessed the most appalling violations of

human rights, was drafted in a way which, had it been in force in the 1930s, would have seemed to exclude any action over the oppression of the Jews in Nazi Germany.[55]

The purpose of delving though this background to the drafting of the UDHR is to establish how completely different the world of 1945 was to seventeenth- and eighteenth-century Europe. The idea that somehow the drafters of the Declaration were picking up the pen from where Locke, Paine, Kant and Voltaire left off to have another go and make their ideas stick this time just doesn't wash. As I suggest in the second anthology piece, 'The Universal Declaration of Human Rights: 60 Years On', a lecture delivered at Chatham House on 8 December 2008 to mark the 60th anniversary of the UDHR:

> Critics and supporters alike generally presume it [the UDHR] is fundamentally a creature of the western Enlightenment, repackaged for the mid-20th century, with pretensions − substantiated or otherwise − to universality. Yet this is to miss the distinguishing features of the Declaration, reflecting the circumstances in which it was drawn up and the diverse philosophies and backgrounds of the drafters.[56]

There are two main factors to bear in mind if we are to heed Cassin's biographers, who challenge us 'to understand [the UDHR] from the standpoint of those who lived the moment in order to see what it meant to its creators'.[57] First there is the question of *who* drafted it. Second there is the precise circumstances in which they did so.

In terms of authorship, the scene is set by Dr Charles Malik, the academic philosopher from Beirut who represented Lebanon at the San Francisco Conference and went on to play a prominent role in the development of the Declaration.

> You are dealing in the United Nations with 57 sovereign states with a bewildering variety of cultures, histories, backgrounds, systems of government and legal practices. The principle of sovereign equality, enshrined in the UN Charter between all states, small and big, renders impossible the imposition of a bill of rights from above . . . Meeting around a table month after month and year after year, the nations are bound to learn from one another.[58]

Of course this process should not be sentimentalized. First, fifty-seven states is a very small number compared to the 193 represented at the UN today. The drafting procedure was, first and foremost, a self-evidently elite endeavour. Second, virtually the whole of sub-Saharan Africa was unrepresented at the UN due to colonization (which in itself was a significant source of debate and tension in the drafting process). Third, self-interest and geopolitical considerations surfaced throughout. But to read the primary-source material, as I have, is to be struck by the seriousness with which the delegates addressed their task, sometimes appearing to forget they were state delegates at all and being prepared, as Malik put it 'to learn from one another' even when they disagreed.[59]

The process began by considering the various proposals for an international bill of rights dispatched by NGOs, lawyers and academics, including Lauterpacht's and Wells's drafts and others submitted by Chile, Cuba, Panama, the Catholic Association for International Peace and the American Federation of Labour. Scholars have differed about whose influence was greatest, but no single authorship has been assigned to the UDHR because of the multiple inputs into the final product. Eleanor Roosevelt, wife of the American president, was elected president of the UNCHR; Malik, vice president; and the Chinese Confucian P. C. Chang was made rapporteur.

Cassin, who in 1968 was awarded the Nobel Peace Prize for his role in crafting the Declaration, sat on the Commission's drafting committee as the French representative, along with delegates from Australia, Chile, China, Lebanon, the Soviet Union, the UK and the US. Their writ was to work with the secretariat to produce a first draft. Dr John Humphrey, the Canadian who headed the secretariat, played much more than a supporting role. As a socialist, Humphrey found common cause with many of the Latin American delegates to the UN and was assisted by a former American UN relief worker, an Indian lawyer and a Confucian philosopher. Over time there was input from many other nations, including Egypt, India, Eastern and Western European states, Mexico, the Philippines, New Zealand and Iran, representing an array of religious and philosophical outlooks. Malik was a Christian but there were ten Islamic states represented at the UN, all of which contributed to the debates on the draft in the General Assembly.

There were no states which voted against the adoption of the UDHR in Paris on 10 December 1948. Only Saudi Arabia abstained, along with South Africa, the Soviet Union and five other Soviet satellite states. They made for an interesting combination. Malik's conclusion was that the UDHR was:

> Constructed on a firm international basis wherein no regional philosophy or way of life was permitted to prevail. The Secretariat's draft outline was a synthesis not only of all the hundreds of suggestions that had been made by governments, private organisations, and individuals, but also of law and practice in all the various United Nations.[60]

Undoubtedly Malik is smoothing over the edges here, but even so, to recalibrate this process as the straightforward imposition of Western Enlightenment values onto the delegates involved in drafting and debating the Declaration is a straightforward anachronism. It was the immediate past and the pressing present that was uppermost in their minds, not eighteenth-century Europe. This leads to the second major factor which needs to be appreciated to make sense of the UDHR and all the treaties, declarations and human rights movements which have emerged from it. The Declaration was not developed as an intellectual idea but was crafted out of the catastrophic events the drafters themselves, however elite they were, had all just lived through or witnessed, albeit in different ways. Cassin put it like this:

> Our declaration represents the most vigorous, the most essential protest of humanity against the atrocities and the oppression which millions of human beings suffered through the centuries and in particular during and after the two world wars.[61]

This is what provided a common thread to the multiple differences between the drafters and shaped their thinking and vision of a better world. A lack of appreciation of the significance of this life-changing context is a crucial factor in explaining the 'category error' of conceptualizing post-war human rights developments as simple continuations of the Enlightenment project. In my UDHR 60th anniversary lecture I put it like this:

> Notwithstanding the triumph of the defeat of fascism, the identity of Europe as the so-called 'crucible of civilisation' had been deeply shaken by the events of the 1930s and 1940s which had taken root on European soil. The collapse of the Weimar Republic in Germany had exposed democracy as a weak defence against a ruthless demagogue determined to exploit its loopholes and capable of rousing citizens effectively to disenfranchise themselves. 'Enlightenment values' of liberty and justice had been reviled and betrayed by Hitler's Germany and Stalin's Russia alike, apparently two ends of a political spectrum, uniting in their disdain of individual rights and freedoms. The dream of Soviet style communism as liberation, which had ignited a generation, was looking tarnished at best and preposterous at worst. But it was the specific nature of the persecution and suffering which gave birth to the UDHR that demonstrated, if any demonstration were needed, that tyranny cannot be conquered by restraints on governments alone. Across Europe Jews, Gypsies, homosexuals, disabled people, trade unionists and political opponents had been dehumanised and massacred in their millions, with the active collaboration or passive acquiescence of thousands of their fellow citizens.

The historian Samuel Moyn, in his landmark study of 'human rights in history', unusually dismisses as 'myth' the widely held view that 'human rights were a direct response to the worst crimes of the century' rather than 'the more recent invention of the contemporary utopian imagination', decades later, when 'human rights were called upon to serve brand new purposes'.[62] It is perfectly true that the word 'Holocaust' is not used in the debates on the UDHR, but it would have been surprising if it had been as the term was not in common usage until the 1960s. On the other hand there are numerous references to Nazism, Hitler, fascism and the 'monstrous crimes' that had been committed during the war. The language used and broad focus strikes me as unremarkable at a time when racism and anti-Semitism had not yet received anything approximating the degree of analysis they have now. But in a sense, relying on the precise terms and phrases used is to miss the point. A close reading of the many drafts and debates on the UDHR gives an unmistakable sense of the influence of time and place on the delegates who time and again demonstrated their awareness of the link between the terrible global events they had just witnessed and their unique task to craft a specifically *universal* Declaration of *human* rights. Almost as if she could have predicted that one day the absence of specific terms would be employed to cast doubt on the drafters' purpose, the Polish delegate Miss Kalinowska observed:

> In Nazi Germany monstrous crimes had indeed been committed without a definition existing in the world of what it had been decided to call 'genocide' and in spite of the fact that that type of crime had not been legally recognised. In the same way, it seemed of little use to define what was meant by 'fascism' each time the word was mentioned. During the war waged against fascism, the Allies knew very well what the word meant.[63]

Critiquing John Rawls, the esteemed American legal theorist who 'updated the social contract theories of the Enlightenment' with his proposition that justice that can be conceived from 'a veil of ignorance' in the 'original position', Morsink suggests that it was the very opposite of ignorance that informed the UDHR.[64] From my own reading of the 'travaux preparatoires', it was, in fact, the profound knowledge of what human beings are capable of doing to each other – including majorities to minorities of many kinds and not just states to citizens – that played an unmistakable role in shaping the debates and in drafting the Declaration (along, of course, with other geopolitical factors discussed in this section). This is what drove the realization that such perversity could not be put right *only* through applying the principle of reciprocity or an updated version of the so-called golden rule – do unto others what you would have done to you. Reciprocity is an important human rights principle, but *on its own* it doesn't cut it. The International Court of Justice amplified this point when commenting on adherence by states to the 1948 Genocide Convention, another UN treaty which emanated from the same catastrophic events, asserting that:

> In such a Convention States do not have any interests of their own, they merely have, one and all, a *common interest*, namely the accomplishment of the high purposes which are the raison d'etre of the Convention.[65]

In the very first session of the UNCHR's drafting committee Cassin, whose own sister and twenty-five other relatives had just been murdered in death camps, pointed out that 'in the period just passed there was wholesale denial of the right to life in a very light-hearted manner which outraged the conscience of all mankind,'[66] words that were soon to be reproduced in the preamble to the Declaration. A sense of moral purpose, in other words, had to be inculcated in human beings if such 'barbarous acts'[67] were to be prevented from happening again. A significant motivation for the drafters, therefore, was to create 'something good, an international bill of rights . . . out of this abomination'.[68] This went beyond providing protections against a direct recurrence of the events that had just passed, on my reading, but involved employing insights from this catastrophe to try to shape a better future.

Legal rights or *human* rights?

For some human rights campaigners, the UDHR was a damp squib from its very conception. Many activists and lawyers felt bitterly disappointed that after the protracted struggle to have human rights included in the Charter, the first human rights measure the UN produced was − as they saw it − a mere Declaration rather than a legally enforceable treaty. Lauterpacht, for example, 'argued vehemently' that both Cassin and the UNCHR 'had betrayed the principle of human rights' by 'choosing an unenforceable declaration instead of a convention'.[69]

The Commission met for nearly two years and there was considerable debate amongst the delegates on this issue from the start. The UK, Australia and India took the view that the drafting committee should immediately proceed to produce a binding Convention, albeit there was disagreement between them on how it should be enforced. The UK proposed that implementation should lie with the UN itself, whereas Australia favoured an international court. By the second session the UK delegate, Charles Duke, summoned 'history' as evidence that 'Declarations imposing no juridical obligation had remained inoperative for centuries.'[70] It is interesting to reflect how characteristic this was for Britain, despite initial misgivings about the human rights provisions in the UN Charter, to support 'only those things which are enforceable in the near future'.[71] It is also reasonable to infer that this push for a legally enforceable charter is a measure of how seriously the UK took the project to establish international human rights standards in this early period, a theme I return to in Section II.

In May 1948 the delegates decided not to proceed with a binding Covenant at this point. Cassin defended it as 'a way to move ahead' in that member states would be called 'gradually to bring their legislation into conformity with' the Declaration.[72] The US had initially strongly supported a legally enforceable treaty, proclaiming leadership in the field of human rights in terms reminiscent of their British cousins (it is remarkable how many godparents 'freedom' has). But with a growing anti-Communist climate and increasing nervousness about how a binding treaty might rebound on the legalized racism and segregation in many states, the American government soon cooled off. A new unholy alliance between America and the Soviet Union sealed the deal.

It was to be another eighteen years before the UN adopted the two legally enforceable international Covenants on 16 December 1966. Together with the UDHR these comprise the International Bill of Rights that had been lobbied for so determinedly during and immediately after the war. By then the Cold War was in full flow, reflected in the separation of economic, social and cultural rights from civil and political rights which were united in the UDHR but were now incorporated into two distinct treaties – the twin International Covenants on Civil and Political Rights (ICCPR) and Economic, Social and Cultural Rights (ICESCR). It was not until 1976 that they were ratified, with the US refusing to do so until 1992, when it committed to the civil and political rights charter only. The terms of these treaties reflect the combination of politics and principle, calculation and the common good that would be expected from any protracted process involved in drafting a legally enforceable instrument by an expanding group of nations. But they also reflect the ethical framework established by the UDHR, as do all the instruments that the Declaration spawned.

How to conceptualize this framework has been much debated. In my unpublished lecture 'Human Rights: Philosophy, Politics or Law?' – the third anthology piece reproduced here – I observe that, however they are described, it is an error to think of human rights as whatever international law says they are, as some legal scholars tend to do. This would be to recreate a form of 'legal positivism' which the human rights framework was partly conceived to resist. In other words, if human rights can only be asserted through the law and its interpretation by judges – including international law – this would negate one of the original purposes of human rights, which was to develop norms by which to *evaluate* law. Professor Costas Douzinas, who has written extensively on the legal philosophy of human rights, asks us to think of them as 'a hybrid category of liberal law and morality'.[73] As I see it, they must be 'capable of legal expression' but at root human rights are 'a set of ethical values that derive from human struggles and the lessons human beings have learnt about how to make life liveable'.[74] It is these 'values' which must drive the law, not the reverse. Otherwise we will have replaced the divine right of kings with the divine right of judges.

Sir Rabinder Singh, the respected judge and writer, put it like this in a paper delivered to a conference on the Magna Carta in London in June 2014:

> The concept human rights is not primarily a legal one: it is a moral concept. It is about how human beings ought to live in relation to each other, a relationship of mutual dignity and respect. Sometimes human rights have been recognised and given effect in law, often not. But they have still been there even when violated or denied in the most grotesque form.[75]

I will return to this claim that human rights 'are already there' before they are recognized in law further on. But to argue this is not to deny for a moment that the UDHR represented a watershed in legal terms, let alone the many enforceable treaties which it was midwife to. Commemorating the 60th anniversary of the UDHR in 2008, the former UN High Commissioner for Human Rights (UNHCRC) Louise Arbour observed that 'it is difficult to imagine today just what a fundamental shift the Universal Declaration of Human Rights represented when it was adopted 60 years ago'.[76] Before 1948 international law was mostly concerned with relations between states, not between individuals and their own governments. Attempts to include specific human rights provisions in the Covenant of the League of Nations were unsuccessful beyond labour rights (in Article 23). The International Labour Organisation (ILO), established in 1919 as an agency of the League of Nations, was unique as the first international body mandated to improve workers' rights on a global scale, but before the birth of the post-1948 human rights edifice it suffered from working in isolation. In the world before the establishment of the UN, nation states had almost limitless sovereignty to treat their citizens as they wished. It has, for example, often been remarked that the Nazi's pre-war racial policies were in accordance with 'the rule of law' in that they were perfectly legal under Hitler's Nuremburg laws.[77]

International humanitarian law, the cousin of international human rights law which regulates war crimes through the Geneva Conventions and other measures, at that time contained no provisions for crimes committed by a state against its own citizens. Heralding a new era, the Charter that established the Nuremburg Tribunal, which tried Nazi war criminals after the war, was drafted to include not only traditional war crimes and crimes against peace, but also (in paragraph 6(c)), 'Crimes Against Humanity'. Although this term was not new, the opprobrium which attaches to this legal and moral category is one all states are now eager to avoid.[78] The systematic persecution of one racial group by another, such as occurred in Apartheid South Africa, was recognized as a crime against humanity by the 1973 International Convention on the Suppression and Punishment of the Crime of Apartheid,[79] contributing to the international isolation and eventual demise of the South African regime. Israel was outraged when a UN Fact Finding Mission on the Gaza Conflict of 2008–2009 accused both Israeli and Palestinian forces of war crimes and 'possibly crimes against humanity'.[80] All of these developments flow from the human rights machinery established in the wake of the Second World War and reflect its legal and moral framework.

Today, the UDHR is considered by most international lawyers as 'the legal baseline for modern international human rights law'.[81] It has been cited so often in case law throughout the past six decades that it is generally accepted that some of its provisions are themselves now part of 'customary international law' and the 'general principles of law' binding on states.[82] There has been a related explosion of human rights mechanisms at a regional level, directly flowing from the UDHR. The African Charter on Human and Peoples' Rights (ACHPR), for example, ratified by fifty-three African states, specifically requires the African Commission for Human and Peoples' Rights to draw inspiration from the Declaration when interpreting the ACHPR (Article 60). Likewise the 1950 European Convention on Human Rights (ECHR) repeatedly cites the UDHR in its preamble, which in turn informs European Court of Human Rights case law. There is a similar provision in the 1969 American Convention on Human Rights enforced by the Inter-American Court. Although their effectiveness is variable, to say the least, the creation by the UN of a series of mechanisms throughout the past six decades to

monitor and expose state violations of internationally agreed human rights norms
is unprecedented in human history, as are quasi-judicial bodies such as the UN's
Human Rights Committee. When the International Criminal Court (ICC) was
eventually established by the Rome Statute in 2002, it must have seemed as if the
demands of the activists who were disappointed in 1948 by the non-enforceable
UDHR had finally been met.

Had I been alive back then I may well have been one of 'the disappointed'. But
with the benefit of hindsight I think we have reason to be grateful that there was
no consensus to proceed immediately to draft a legal treaty, even if the reasons were
inauspicious. The Cold War was already dampening post-war idealism – 1948 was
the year of the Berlin blockade – and with India gaining independence in 1947
after a long struggle, imperial powers such as Britain and France were fearful that
they would not be able to hold on to their extensive empires much longer. They
had no incentive to be held to account by a legally enforceable human rights treaty.
As Cassin's biographers have put it, 'what is most surprising about the Declaration
is that it happened at all.'[83]

So instead of focussing on legal rights, the delegates were required to think
deeply about how the world had arrived at this point and what it would take for
human beings to recognize their common humanity and treat each other with the
respect and dignity they warrant. They were asking the kinds of questions associated
with moral philosophy and religious ethics – they were, in other words, concentrating as much if not more on the 'human' as the 'rights'. As Morsink has pointed out,
'the juxtaposition of these two words' is 'crucial'. Whilst 'most books about human
rights tell us a great deal about what a *right* is (a justified claim that can activate the
duties of others)' they 'frequently fail to tell us about the import of the adjective
human'.[84] Yet it was on the 'human' that the drafters were frequently focussed and
in particular on how to develop a framework that would both reflect what they saw
as the intrinsic worth of human beings and encourage them to actively respect this
in others. Cassin thought it 'essential' that 'before defining concrete rights such as
the right to life etc to define . . . values which were higher than life itself'.[85] Whilst
Eleanor Roosevelt, believing all along that 'the declaration would not be legally
binding,' argued that this lack of legal force 'made it all the more necessary so to
phrase the preamble that it would exercise . . . the greatest possible force of moral
persuasion'.[86]

The use of the word 'rights' in this non-legally binding document has therefore
to some degree clouded understanding of its purpose. The drafters may just as well
have used the term 'ethical demands', adopted by the esteemed Indian economist
Amartya Sen's, or 'core human entitlements', preferred by the American philosopher Martha Nussbaum, who between them pioneered the human rights–allied
'human capabilities approach'.[87] The UDHR determined that it is our common
humanity, not our citizenship or other legal status, which is the source of both our
equal worth and our eligibility for those 'core human entitlements' which facilitate

human flourishing. This was the basis for the Declaration's 'faith' in the 'dignity and worth of the human person and the equal rights of men and women'.[88]

Rights or righteousness?

According to Malik, the drafters saw their basic task as being to provide 'the answer to the question "How does the world conceive of man's essential worth and dignity at the middle of the twentieth century?"'[89] He observed at the very first session of the HRC that they were in want of 'the advice of poets, prophets and philosophers' to guide them in this endeavour as much as politicians and diplomats.[90] Although the delegates were a bit short on poets, to some degree the freedom that thinking beyond the boundaries of the law gave them allowed prophets and philosophers to hover over all their deliberations. Quite literally, when it came to the submission to the drafters by UNESCO![91] This was another new UN agency which created a 'virtual symposium', many decades before the invention of the Internet, to collect the thoughts, via a questionnaire, of such 'prophets and philosophers' as Mahatma Ghandi, Aldous Huxley and Harold Laski. These were presented to the UDHR drafters, with a forward by the Catholic philosopher Jacques Maritain, to assist them with their deliberations.[92]

To mark the 60th anniversary of this extraordinary symposium in 2007, I was asked to address a conference in Belfast organized by the Northern Ireland Human Rights Commission (NIHRC) and the Irish School of Ecumenics titled Rights and Righteousness: Religious Pluralism and Human Rights. My paper, 'Rights and Righteousness: Friends or Foe?' is the fourth anthology piece reproduced here.[93] Northern Ireland (NI) was a singularly appropriate place to hold this conference as it had until recently suffered sustained trauma from human rights abuses by both the state and paramilitaries. Many of the British government's worst human rights violations during a prolonged period took place in the context of the NI 'troubles', as they were euphemistically called, leading to a number of landmark cases at the ECtHR (discussed further in Section II). With this backdrop, the Labour government incorporated the rights in the ECHR into NI law and established the NIHRC as part of the 1998 Good Friday peace settlement. The schisms in NI had extended to human rights which were perceived by many Unionists and Loyalists as a specifically 'Republican issue' benefiting Catholics only. Here was a conference which sought to challenge that characterization by specifically tying the discourse of human rights to that of religion, a field of interest to all the main communities in NI, devout or not. From this point of view, the title of my Penguin book *Values for a Godless Age*, published in 2000 to coincide with the introduction of the UK's Human Rights Act, appeared very ill judged. But the point of this title was not to portray human rights as essentially secular but, like the NI conference, to explore any links or parallels between the ethics of post-war human rights and the profound insights that have guided the world's major religions.[94]

The chair of the Nobel Committee, when awarding Cassin the Peace Prize in 1968, optimistically compared the UDHR to the 10 Commandments in its anticipated impact.[95] This kind of comparison reflected the sentiments that a number of the participants in the UN debates on the Declaration took the opportunity to express, particularly from Catholic Latin America. The Uruguay delegate, for example, affirmed that 'relations between people were determined not only by legal standards but also by social and moral principles'[96] whilst his Chilean counterpart stated that the Declaration should be a 'charter' of 'not only legal form but real human content'. It 'should not be just a Bill but rather a true spiritual guide for humanity'.[97] For the Bolivian delegate 'there was no intention of claiming that human beings were perfect. The draft declaration was designed to set a goal for mankind. It should inspire men to transform into realities the principles it proclaimed.'[98] Cassin himself described the UDHR as a 'moral' document[99] and insisted that 'the concept of human rights comes from the bible.'[100]

The religious leaders who in recent times have critiqued human rights as a concept that 'can undermine morality' and lead to 'self-centred demands', referenced in 'Rights and Righteousness: Friends or Foe?' would presumably have been surprised to learn of Cassin's characterization of human rights as essentially biblical. He was, in particular, referring to the commandment – for that is what it effectively is – that all human beings 'should act towards one another in a spirit of brotherhood' in the first Article of the UDHR. This, Cassin said, 'corresponded to' the iconic injunction in Leviticus in the Hebrew Bible to 'love thy neighbour as thyself', famously quoted by Christ as a foundational value, and the parallel reference to 'the stranger that dwelleth with you' who 'shall be unto you as one born among you, and thou shalt love him as thyself; for ye were strangers in the land of Egypt.'[101] Cassin's claim of the direct and conscious input of biblical ethics into the UDHR has been supported by Bishop Carlos Belo, the East Timorese recipient of the 1996 Nobel Peace Prize. Commemorating the 50th anniversary of the UDHR, he wrote that the assertion in the very first sentence of the Declaration's Article 1 that 'all human beings are born free and equal in dignity and rights' is of 'divine origin' in that it reflects the notion that human beings are created in the image of god, as declared in Genesis.[102] Likewise Professor Khaled Abou El Fadl, an authority on Islamic law, maintains that from an Islamic perspective 'a commitment in favour of human rights is a commitment in favour of God's creation and ultimately, a commitment in favour of God.'[103]

There is a growing literature affirming the link between human rights and religious ethics.[104] In 'Human Rights: Philosophy, Politics or Law?' I discuss wellworn parallels between the human rights idea of the essential dignity and worth of every individual human being and the Babylonian Hammurabi Code (dating back to about 1772 BC), the Koranic references to 'justice', 'mercy' and 'goodness' and the Christian idea of 'natural law' as developed, for example, by Saint Augustine in the fourth century and Thomas Aquinas in the thirteenth century. The latter evolved the Catholic concept of a 'just war' (and by implication an 'unjust war'). From this there was a short, but significant, leap to the 'natural rights' theories of the Enlightenment developed by Hugo Grotius, Thomas Hobbes and John Locke, amongst others. The Christian theologian Roger Ruston has argued that 'an examination of the origins of the natural rights theories reveals a close connection with the universal claims of the Christian gospel itself. Christian theology . . . posits a global "community" of human beings upon which universal rights may be based.'[105] Islamic scholar and law professor Hossein Mehrpour has similarly argued that 'apart from that aspect of religion which consists of the important duty to spiritually guide and instruct, there are no serious differences or contradictions in their social aspects and application between religious teachings and human rights.'[106]

Theologian Max L. Stockhouse would disagree only to the extent that he thinks 'human rights need god' to ground claims of inherent dignity in a higher force.[107] This, the UDHR drafters decided not to do, although a number of Latin American delegates thought this a mistake. The different convictions and ideologies which delegates brought to the drafting process caused tensions throughout, despite their sense of common purpose, with more than 1,400 votes on virtually every clause of the text. Amendments to tie human rights to 'nature' in the UDHR preamble and bring God into Articles 1 and 16 (on marriage) were rejected. Ultimately the drafters determined that no 'higher being' or pre-existing state of nature was *required* to validate what they chose to call 'human rights'. But neither was the framework they adopted to be viewed as in any way incompatible with belief in God or the theological precepts on which, as we have seen, they purposefully drew.

Natural rights *or human* rights?

It might seem paradoxical that whilst the UDHR, sometimes referred to as the 'new universal ethics',[108] is a document bent on 'moral persuasion', as Eleanor Roosevelt put it,[109] it makes no mention of a 'higher being', whilst the bills of rights that emanated from the 'rationalist' Enlightenment do indeed call on the 'creator' for validation. The 'natural rights' revolutionaries, in revolt against the established church and any vestige of 'the divine right of kings', nevertheless turned to their maker for legitimization of their cause. Many of them were Christians, and those who were not were generally 'deists' rather than atheists, believing in a higher force which could be discovered through reason and observation. So the 1776 American Declaration of Independence asserted that 'we hold these truths to be self-evident, that all men are . . . endowed by their *creator* with certain inalienable rights' (my emphasis) whilst the 1789 French National Assembly adopted the Declaration of the Rights of Man and the Citizen 'under the auspices of the Supreme Being'. Yet you would be hard pressed to characterize the thrust of iconic 'natural rights' charters like the American Bill of Rights or the French Declaration as anything other than measures intended to protect the individual citizens of their respective countries against the vagaries of the state (especially if you were a white, male citizen). If there was a moral framework to articulate it is to be found in Article 4 of the French Declaration:

> Liberty consists in the freedom to do everything which injures no one else; hence the exercise of the natural rights of each man has no limits except

those which assure to the other members of the society the enjoyment of the same rights.

This is as clear an articulation as any of the 'harm' and 'neutrality' principles which are said to be at the core of Western liberalism. The latter presumes that the state should be 'neutral' between competing conceptions of what is good or right for individuals, whilst the former affirms the right of individuals to choose their own path in life up to the point that they 'harm' the right of others to do likewise. Only then is the state entitled to intervene.[110]

Nearly 100 years later this framework was further developed by the doyenne of Liberalism, John Stuart Mill, who declared in *On Liberty*:

> The only freedom which deserves the name is that of pursuing our own good in our own way, so long as we do not attempt to deprive others of theirs or impede their efforts to obtain it.[111]

As we saw earlier, critics like MacIntyre and Gray have derided the 'failed' project of the Enlightenment and its 'wake', whether illustrated by Mill's refinement of the 'harm' and 'neutrality' principles,[112] or by the 'individual rights and freedoms perspective' of more recent American legal theorists such as Rawls or Ronald Dworkin. For MacIntyre the project of providing a *rational* vindication of morality has decisively failed. As Morsink puts it: 'He regards the opening philosophical clauses of the Universal Declaration . . . not as possible grounds for a common morality but as inchoate fragments of a failed Enlightenment tradition.'[113] For Gray, it is the *universalizing* of the 'morally neutral state' that is 'indefensible' and a 'wholly inadequate response' to the 'value-pluralism' as it is actually lived in different traditions around the world today.[114]

It was precisely because the drafters of the UDHR were trying to face up to the 'failure' of so-called Enlightenment values to address the diversity which the Enlightenment's 'toleration' paradoxically struggled to accommodate, let alone respect, that the framework on which they based their Declaration differed in certain vital respects from that of their Enlightenment forebears. Accepting Alan Gerwith's neat definition of *human* rights as 'moral rights which all persons equally have simply because they are human',[115] there is a categorical leap between the Enlightenment vision of *individual liberties* (what I have elsewhere called the 'first wave' of rights) and the post-war era of *human rights* (which I have called the 'second wave').[116] I elaborate on this distinction further in 'Human Rights: Above Politics or a Creature of Politics?' (the fifth anthology piece in this volume).[117]

This is not to say that there isn't obvious overlap, or a sense in which the drafters consciously saw themselves as emulating the renowned Charters which preceded them.[118] Although most of the delegates were not comfortable with pinpointing a single, transcendent source of human rights, they still presented them as 'inherent' or 'existing' regardless of whether they are reflected in law, as we saw Singh argue earlier. The words 'inherent', 'inalienable', 'born' and 'endowed' – standard terms in the 'natural rights' lexicon – are all present in the Preamble or Article 1. To 'reaffirm faith in fundamental rights', as the drafters do in the Preamble, is to make the claim that these rights already existed. In common with its Enlightenment precursors, the UDHR is shot through with the assumption that rights do not have to be defined in 'positive law' for human beings to have a 'moral claim' to them. Eleanor Roosevelt quoted Abraham Lincoln to make the obvious point that there is a crucial difference between setting down what rights every human *should* be able to assert and the enforcement of them, in the hopes that this 'might follow as soon as circumstances should permit'.[119]

But it is a mistake, as the moral philosopher Carl Wellman puts it, to impute from this that the UN Charter, or for that matter the UDHR which expanded on it, 'presupposes any traditional natural rights theory'.[120] As Wellman observes, 'the drafters with very different religious convictions and ethical beliefs could agree that human rights are fundamental moral rights without committing themselves to any implicit or explicit theory of their foundations.'[121] Morsink, the pre-eminent expert on the drafting of the UDHR, cautions us 'not to approach even these key Enlightenment terms (inalienable, inherent, born) within the framework of the Western rationalist tradition'.[122] These 'linguistic similarities' should not confuse us[123]: 'The drafters of the 1948 document did not blindly follow Enlightenment precedent but staked out their own independent course.'[124] Whilst they felt a 'kinship with the American and French revolutionaries' they 'clearly saw themselves as standing on the shoulders of these eighteenth century predecessors and as making huge improvements on the work begun earlier'.[125]

There is no denying that the following statement in the UDHR Preamble is pure Locke or Paine and resonant of the American Declaration of Independence: 'Whereas it is essential, if man is not to be compelled to have recourse, as a last resort, to rebellion against tyranny and oppression, that human rights should be protected by the rule of law.' There are even echoes of those medieval barons at Runnymede in that assertion. But it is a mistake to conclude from sentiments such as these, as the esteemed political theorist Bikhu Parek does, that the UDHR 'takes a statist view of human rights and emasculates their universalist and critical thrust' or that the rights in it 'are addressed to the state which alone is deemed to have the obligation to respect and realise them'.[126] In fact the word 'state' is only used three times in the Declaration, which was 'a statement not of unbridle individualism but of the moral force of associative life, without which human development is impossible'.[127] This was consistent with Cassin's vision which Morsink tells us did *not* encompass the UDHR acting as 'a mere offshoot of the eighteenth century tree of rights'.[128] Yet assumptions like Parek's are not uncommon, as we saw, and they have led to a blurring of the distinct contribution of the UDHR.

Not only was the state not the only addressee in the UDHR but, in direct contrast to 'first wave' bills of rights, there are three sectors that are appealed to in the Declaration, all referenced in the Preamble. The first is all human beings everywhere whose 'common understanding of these rights and freedoms is of the greatest importance for the[ir] full realisation'. The second is that of educators around the globe, who along with 'every individual and every organ of society . . . shall strive by teaching and education to promote respect for these rights' and the third is nation states which 'have pledged themselves to achieve . . . the promotion of, respect for and observance of human rights'. The renowned human rights scholar Louis Henkin has presented the layers of responsibility in international human rights in the following terms:

> Beneath the responsibilities of government for individual rights are political principles governing the relations of the individual to political authority and beneath those political principles appear to be moral principles governing relations between individual human beings.[129]

This multi-layered audience reflects the different questions which the UDHR drafters posed when compared to their Enlightenment forebears. They were not only asking how human beings can escape state tyranny and gain control over their own lives, but how a sense of mutual moral responsibility can be inculcated in all human beings everywhere. This was now understood to be indispensable to prevent flagrant breaches of human rights that were not just conducted by remote states but by tangible human beings, whether under orders or otherwise, and which can take place in multiple locations wherever there are gross imbalances of power. As Simpson has observed: 'Those who had experienced occupation knew, though this could not always be said . . . that under German occupation . . . those who ill-treated the population were, not infrequently, their own fellow citizens.'[130] This complex reality contributed to what the Sudanese human rights scholar Abdullahi A. An-Na'im has called 'the particular conception of freedom and social justice that was articulated in the Universal Declaration of Human Rights'[131] and it is quite a stretch from the 'natural rights' perspective of the Enlightenment.

Exploring the human rights ethic

To avoid clashing over whether human rights could be grounded in a higher – or deeper – foundation, the drafters of the UDHR developed a *framework* from which they could *explain*, rather than source, the rights they went on to declare. They presented Article 1 as a categorical statement establishing the ethical framework from which the subsequently declared 'rights' would flow:

> All human beings are born free and equal in dignity and rights. They are endowed with reason and conscience and should act towards one another in a spirit of brotherhood.

There was considerable debate about the contents of this initial article, including whether it would be better placed in the Preamble. It was retained as a first statement in the body of the text because, in the Syrian delegate's terms, 'Article 1 was the cornerstone of the draft declaration.' Likewise the Belgium delegate affirmed that 'Article 1 was important as a first article of a solemn document, since it affirmed a principle which in some measure summed up the Articles that followed.' Cassin, who was largely responsible for the first article, asserted that the Declaration had to begin with a statement of the framework within which all the rights that followed were contained, and the Cuban delegate, Perez Cisneros, said it could be labelled 'Essential Principles'.

There were failed attempts by the Chinese delegate to further 'de-Enlightenment' the draft. Chang complained that the reference to 'born' was 'reminiscent of Rousseau and the theory that man was naturally good'. But the Indian delegate, Mrs Menon, supported the text, declaring that 'although different countries had different beliefs and political systems, they shared the same ideals of social justice and freedom . . . lessons could be learnt from the democracies of both the East and West.'[132]

Reason **and** *conscience*

The reference in Article 1 to 'reason and conscience' was strongly debated. Do these terms denote human capacities which enable us to *know* that we should 'act towards one another in a spirit of brotherhood' or are they conceived as essential human characteristics which, along with human dignity, *justify* the 'rights' which follow?[133] Given that the drafters sought to avoid essentialist theories about the basis of human nature, they were presumably asserting that we are *capable* of *knowing* how to act towards one other in a manner which respects our 'inherent dignity' and 'equal and inalienable rights'.[134]

On either interpretation, the significance of adding 'conscience' to 'reason' is as great as combining 'human' to 'rights' in signifying the departure from an Enlightenment project of declaring 'natural rights' against the state. The strong implication is that reason alone does not allow human beings to discover what is 'right' and 'wrong', but reason aligned with the human conscience can. Compassion, empathy and the capacity to care about the fate of those you do not know, or cannot even imagine being in a similar situation to, and who cannot reciprocate because of the disparity between you, takes the human rights framework beyond the reciprocity of the Golden Rule as generally interpreted (for example, by Kant) and closer to the biblical injunction to 'love the stranger.'

Dignity

The explicit inclusion of 'dignity' alongside 'rights' signifies another departure from 'first wave' treaties. There is no mention of 'dignity' in the Enlightenment bills of rights but there are five such references in the UDHR. No definition of dignity is provided, but it has several implications for the intent and purpose of the Declaration and the many treaties it spawned, which are further discussed in 'Human Rights: Above Politics or a Creature of Politics?'

First, it signifies the Kantian principle that no human being should ever be instrumentalized or become a means to an end. This is a direct challenge to the utilitarian approach famously championed by the late-eighteenth-century British philosopher Jeremy Bentham and further refined by Mill. Utilitarianism has come to dominate social policy in Western democracies in that – simply put – the consequences of an action or decision is generally said to determine its worth. Its kernel principle, 'the greatest good for the greatest number', might be an inevitable, and even desirable, democratic tenet, but the human rights framework is based on the insight that it can be necessary to curtail majoritarianism from becoming a justification for riding roughshod over the rights of minorities and the dignity of the individual. The drafters had just seen with their own eyes where majoritarianism can lead if taken to extremes. In its early period in power, the Nazi party relied on its democratic mandate to extinguish the freedom – and eventually the life – of whole groups of German citizens, including disabled people, Communists, gay men, lesbians and Jews.

As significantly, the adoption of dignity as a framework value denoted a recognition that human beings have more complex needs than to be free from restraint, which was the main preoccupation of Enlightenment revolutionaries. The concept of inherent dignity illuminates the obvious point that the freedom to choose your own path in life is hollow if in reality you have few choices. Or as the author Anatole France famously put it: 'The law, in its majestic equality, forbids the rich as well as the poor to sleep under bridges, to beg in the streets, and to steal bread.'[135]

If human dignity is to be respected, therefore, it follows that the state has to do more than refrain from interfering or oppressing. It has to ensure that the basic requisites of human dignity are provided for, including the fundamental wherewithals of life. This, more than the principle of equality, was the route into so-called second-generation economic, social and cultural rights in the UDHR. Entitlements to work, social security, trade union membership, an adequate standard of living and health, rest and leisure are unusually fused with the civil and political liberties of freedom from torture, fee speech, a fair trial and so on, reflecting Franklin D. Roosevelt's vision of 'four essential freedoms'. Paine – whose *Rights of Man* uniquely came as close to proposing a welfare sate funded through progressive taxation on landed property as could be imagined 150 years before it was introduced in the UK – would no doubt have felt vindicated if he had shown up for the adoption of the UDHR sixty-six years ago. This new departure led the Philippines delegate, Carlos Romulo, to observe that the 'Declaration recognized rights which were perhaps not even contemplated in the Magna Carta, the 1789 Declaration of the Rights of Man or the American Declaration of Independence'.[136]

The value of dignity is also the route in contemporary international human rights law to the doctrine of 'positive obligations' on states to protect individuals from the abuse of rights by other human beings, discussed further in 'Human Rights: Philosophy, Politics or Law?' This has widened the protection of fundamental rights instruments to encompass the prevention and investigation of crime and terrorism, domestic violence and child abuse (as discussed further in Section

II). The 'second wave' concept of dignity, therefore, has had the effect of not only affirming the right of individuals to make their own life choices, provided they do not harm others, but of establishing a basic ethical framework necessary for human beings to flourish.

Liberty and *equality*

Voltaire, Rousseau and their comrades would be struck by the dictum in the very first article of the UDHR that 'all human beings are born free and equal'; a symbolic reaffirmation of an old idea which had been mocked to obliteration in the heart of supposedly democratic Europe. But the drafters were acutely aware that when their forebears wrote the principles of liberty and equality into the French and American Declarations[137] their vision was stymied by the prejudices of their era. To a significant degree the Enlightenment tracts were largely reaffirming a principle that can be traced back to the Magna Carta; that no one is above the law, which should be applied equally to all. Women were largely absent in the minds of the men who drew up these iconic documents in their own image to enhance their own freedom, although females were not directly discriminated against, as they had been in the Magna Carta. Not so black slaves! To obtain equal human rights you have to be counted as human in the first place. Cassin is recorded as 'repeatedly' saying that 'the slave trade was never so intense as during the Enlightenment'.[138]

The 1791 slave revolts, which led to the abolition of slavery in the French colony of Saint-Domingue (now Haiti), were an immediate test of the ideology of the white supporters of the French Revolution – a test they failed very badly indeed. Perhaps even more shockingly, in the new American constitution of 1787 slaves were counted as three-fifths of a human being for representation purposes. The result was that for nearly a century the Americans who most needed the 1791 Bill of Rights were not even eligible for its protection, in defiance of one of the Bill's founding principles – the safeguarding of minorities against the will of the majority. In revolutionary America it was slave owners who were perceived as the 'minority' whose 'rights' in defence of their 'property' needed 'protecting'. In 1864, following the Civil War, the Thirteenth Amendment abolished slavery except as punishment for a crime. But this did not overturn the notorious 1857 case of *Dred Scott v Sandford*, where the US Supreme Court ruled that constitutional rights did not apply to feed slaves. As the *Harper's Weekly* of the day put it: 'The court has decided that free negroes are not citizens of the United States.'[139]

It was with all this in mind, not to mention the calamitous events that had just occurred in supposedly democratic Europe, that the Declaration's drafters went considerably further than their Enlightenment ancestors and conceived of equality in different terms. Slavery and the slave trade were specifically 'prohibited in all their forms' in an article of their own (Article 4). The second article of the UDHR was entirely devoted to addressing discrimination on a range of specified grounds in a manner that has become very familiar in modern anti-discrimination law, but was pioneering at the time. It was eventually to lead to individual, legally enforceable UN conventions on race, gender, children and disability.[140] A distinction is made, in Article 7, between 'equality *before* the law' and 'equal protection' *of* the law, defined as protection 'against any discrimination in violation of this Declaration and any incitement to such discrimination'.

The Preamble makes specific mention of 'the equal rights of men and women', one of a few non-gendered phrases inserted under the influence of a female Indian delegate, Dr Hansa Jivraj Mehta, which sits side by side with words like 'man' and 'brotherhood' in other parts of the Declaration. This led the UN Commission on the Status of Women, whose Danish chair was invited to participate (though not vote) in the debates, to propose that a note be added to the Preamble to indicate that the masculine sex applies without discrimination to women. Perhaps unsurprisingly, this was not even discussed. The women's commission also proposed a more radical marriage clause than the one that was eventually adopted. Yet none of this prevented its chair, Bodil Begtrup, from remarking that 'the world had developed' since the French Declaration of the Rights of Man which 'made no mention of the rights of women and did not even imply them'.[141]

Of course the UDHR delegates had their own versions of national shame to hide, not to mention blind spots and prejudices. This meant, for example, that disability and sexual orientation received no specific mention in the categories against which discrimination was prohibited, despite such groups being specifically targeted by the Nazis. It was to take jurisprudence by a body like the European Court of Human Rights decades later before these groups were to receive specific protection.

The issue of empire probably caused more discomfort to the drafters than any other. By the time the UDHR was adopted on 10 December 1948 a number of the delegates represented states which had only just gained independence, including Burma, India, Lebanon, Pakistan and the Philippines. Most of sub-Saharan Africa, and many other nations, remained under the colonial rule of some of the most powerful UN states, with many brutal liberation struggles only just beginning or still to come. Race and gender discrimination were legal almost everywhere, race hatred and segregation were rampant in many parts of the US and Apartheid was just getting underway in South Africa, leading to that country's abstention from both Article 7 and the UDHR as a whole. The text of the Declaration, despite its far-reaching equality and non-discrimination references, subtly reflects aspects of this global reality.

The interests of the Western powers were frequently in play. When the Syrian delegate, Abdul Kayaly, argued for a 'minorities clause', claiming that 'in Africa, the indigenous populations were still prohibited from using their own languages in primary and secondary schools and were not even allowed to establish universities', he, along with his Byelorussian colleague, was slapped down by Ernest Davies, representing the UK. Their 'conception of the policies of the British empire . . . was rather out of date' Davies insisted, in that 'there had been considerable progress in the colonies towards self-determination.'[142] The US, acutely aware of its own domestic situation, also successfully opposed the inclusion of a 'minority groups' clause, with Eleanor Roosevelt arguing that 'provisions relating to rights of minorities had no place in a declaration of human rights'.[143]

Britain also resisted attempts to explicitly include people living under colonial rule, unsuccessfully this time. Cassin worked hard to ensure that his government supported the principle of equal rights between people in French colonies and those in 'metropolitan France'. The UDHR was applicable to 'everyone or to no one' he liked to say.[144] Early drafts contained no reference at all to the colonies. It was under pressure from the USSR and Allied states that the anti-discrimination article explicitly ruled out making a 'distinction' based on the status of a country or territory, 'whether it be independent, trust, non self-governing or under any other limitation of sovereignty'. An Egyptian amendment to include 'peoples' living under colonial rule in the Preamble was also accepted.

A stronger version of the equality clause, Article 7, which would have condemned 'advocacy of national, racial and religious hostility . . . or hatred' was rejected (although Article 20, prohibiting incitement to 'national, racial or religious hatred', *was* included in the legally enforceable 1966 ICCPR). The British delegate, Geoffrey Wilson, even opposed the reference to protection from 'incitement to . . . discrimination' in Article 7 on the grounds that:

> In the United Kingdom, where human rights had certainly been respected as much as in any country, there had never been any need for legislation to compel the authorities to take action against incitement to discrimination. The force of public opinion had always proved sufficient.[145]

This was nearly twenty years before the first Race Relations Act in the UK was introduced, in an era of rampant racism and discrimination. Landlords had no hesitation in exhibiting 'No Blacks, No Dogs, No Irish' signs, and there were openly displayed bans on Jews joining certain private clubs and 'Jewish quotas' existed in some schools. It was over fifty years later that the inquiry into the racist murder of the south London student Stephen Lawrence declared the Metropolitan Police 'institutionally racist'; such can be the self-belief in 'English liberties'.

But for all these limitations, there is no question that the UDHR represented a quantum leap in terms of the scope attached to equality. The old notion of being 'equal *before* the law' was now explicitly bolstered in Article 7 by the 'equal protection *of* the law', signalling the necessity for states to outlaw discrimination, including among private individuals. This approach was to change the way human rights defenders came to view the principle of liberty. Once people are told they are not free to choose who to rent their house to or who to hire and fire if their choice is based on racial or sexual discrimination, for example, then freedom takes on a new and more complex meaning. The Enlightenment ideal of a 'neutral' state interfering only when individuals face 'harm' was replaced by the vision of a state obliged to take steps to protect people from such harm occurring in the first place.

Individualism or mutualism?

Had the 'first wave' rights revolutionaries turned up at the UN when the UDHR was discussed they would have probably been pretty shocked at one aspect of the debate – the attention given to which duties individuals owe to the state, the community they live in and their fellow human beings. After all, Paine tells us that this question was relatively easily disposed of in revolutionary France:

> When the Declaration of Rights was before the National Assembly, some of its members remarked that if a Declaration of Rights was published, it should be accompanied by a Declaration of Duties. The observation discovered a mind that reflected and it only erred by not reflecting enough. A Declaration of Rights is, by reciprocity, a Declaration of Duties also. Whatever is my right as a man, is also the right of another and it becomes my duty to guarantee as well as to possess.[146]

This was not good enough for some of the natural rights proponents' sternest critics who would also have been surprised if they had appeared at the UN in 1948. For Jeremy Bentham, who became a harsh critic of the French Revolution in his lifetime, and Karl Marx who was a lukewarm supporter, individual rights were a route to dangerous individualism. As discussed in 'Human Rights: Philosophy, Politics or Law?' Bentham not only dismissed 'natural and imprescriptible rights as . . . nonsense upon stilts', but condemned them as bursting the cords that bind 'selfish passions', whilst Marx declared that 'none of the so-called rights of man . . . go beyond egoistic man.'[147]

Yet the drafters of the UDHR were at times intensely preoccupied with the responsibilities human beings owe to each other, the wider society and the international community. As with the philosophers and writers who contributed to the UNESCO symposium that was intended to influence their deliberations,[148] this was one of the most protracted conversations the UDHR drafters engaged in. Various cross-cutting themes contributed to this focus, including the communitarian philosophies of the East, religious sensitivities to the need for human obligations to sit alongside rights, Soviet and socialist anti-individualism (echoing Marx) and 'statist' concerns not to unleash too radical a document on the world which the governments that the delegates represented would come to regret.

In the very first session of the UNCHR in January 1947, Malik asserted that when we say 'human rights' we are 'raising the fundamental question: what is a man? Is he merely a social being like a bee or an ant? Is he merely an animal with biology governing his destiny? Is he just an economic being, a rational calculator of self interest?'[149] Malik's chief concern was to protect the autonomy of the individual in the light of Communist collectivism, arguing in opposition to Yugoslavia's prioritization of 'the social principle' that 'the human person's most sacred and inviolable possessions are his mind and his conscience.'[150] Disagreeing with his Lebanese colleague, the UK representative Mr Dukes argued that it would be 'useless to try to define the liberties of the individual without taking account of his obligations towards the State'. The social democrat Cassin took the view that 'the human being was above all, a social being' and warned against 'the danger of putting too little importance upon social rights'.[151] For China, Chang advised against producing a document which would be 'out of time with the spirit and atmosphere of the post war era',[152] subsequently asserting:

> The aim of the United Nations was not to ensure the selfish gains of the individual but to try and increase man's moral stature. It was necessary to proclaim the duties of the individual, for it was a consciousness of his duties which enabled man to reach a high moral standard.[153]

The drafters were exercised about every aspect of this 'high moral standard'. What priority should be given to the issue of human responsibilities? Should they be aired in the Preamble at the beginning of the draft, as Egypt, the UK and the USSR wanted, or at the end of the Declaration, as preferred by Roosevelt and Chang? Should the duty of the individual to the state be asserted in the UDHR, or is this inappropriate in the world's first human rights declaration? What is at the root of this debate, the requirements of governments or the social nature of human beings which inevitably puts limits on their individual rights? Should there be a list of duties enumerated as proposed by Cuba and Egypt, or is it sufficient to assert in a general sense the necessity for legitimate restraints on individual rights rooted in the responsibilities humans owe to each other? In 'Rights and Righteousness' I discuss the contours of this debate in more detail, the end product of which was Article 29, the penultimate article of the Declaration, which was largely drafted by Cassin: 'Everyone has duties to the community in which alone the free and full development of his personality is possible.'

This wording expresses two intertwined ideas that were exhaustingly explored by the delegates. First, that individuals have responsibilities as well as rights and that these are to the community which they are a part of, rather than to the state whose legitimacy, as the Preamble states, depends on 'human rights' being 'protected by the rule of law'. When the twin UN covenants were drafted a few years later, their Preambles likewise asserted that 'the individual' has 'duties to other individuals' as well as 'the community to which he belongs'.

The second significance of Article 29 – reflecting the considered views of the drafters – is the assertion that individuals do not exist in the world as isolated beings. In contrast to Rawls's 'original position', they live in societies, or more specifically, communities, which *alone* provide the means through which they can develop their personality and hence their humanity.

Humans as social beings

In Morsink's view, 'the deep reasons behind the principle of the correlation of rights and duties' in the UDHR is 'that a person is essentially a social being and that rights and duties are both grounded in that same communal soil'.[154] So significant is this emphasis on the 'social' nature of human beings in the Declaration that the word 'alone' in Article 29 'may well be the single most important word in the entire document for it helps us answer the charge that the rights set forth in the Declaration create egoistic individuals who are not closely tied to their respective communities'.[155] What would Marx make of that? Or of Gerwith's thesis in *The Community of Rights* that 'the concept of human rights . . . entails a mutualist and egalitarian universality.' How? Because 'each human must respect the rights of others while having his [*sic*] rights respected by all others . . . By the effective recognition of the mutuality entailed by human rights, the society becomes a community.'[156]

This is an important enhancement of Paine's assertion of *implied* duties in *Rights of Man*. Gerwith is surely onto something when he claims that the old binary division between the autonomous individual and the collective is broken down – or more accurately is no longer relevant – to the vision for a good society and better world summoned by 'second wave' human rights. But what Gerwith's observation doesn't quite capture in his emphasis on mutuality is the human capacity for empathy, compassion and imagination which the UDHR drafters relied on in asking 'every individual' to consider their 'conscience'. It was Chang's introduction of the Confucian concept of 'two-man mindedness' which led to this crucial addition, asking us to recognize the common humanity of people we will never meet and can never be in a reciprocal relationship with. It requires a leap of imagination, and a warm heart, to conjure the lives of others which the UDHR asks us 'to keep constantly in mind'.

The former UN Special Rapporteur on discrimination and minorities, Erica-Irene Daes, has commented on the significance of Article 29, linked in its second clause with 'limitations' in the exercise 'of rights and freedoms' that must be 'determined by law'. These must be 'solely' for the purpose of securing 'due recognition and respect for the rights and freedoms of others' and for meeting 'the just requirements of morality, public order and the general welfare in a democratic society'. Thomas Jefferson and his fellow 'founding fathers' who drafted the American Declaration of Independence and Bill of Rights would never have contemplated such restrictions on individual autonomy being inserted into their text. The specific limitations included can be debated, but the UDHR has to be understood as a product of the more collectivist time in which it was written and the communitarian influences of its drafters. It bore the marks of Latin American socialists, European social democrats, Marxist Soviets, a Chinese Confucian, Middle Eastern Muslims, Lebanese and European Christians, a Hindu and a Jew. The consequence for Article 29, Daes has concluded, is that: 'this provision is of a moral nature in the sense that it lays down a general rule for individual behaviour in the community to which the individual belongs.'[157]

Humans as responsible beings

The general grounds for limiting individual rights in Article 29 – such as protecting the rights and freedoms of others and public order – are found in some form in most of the binding treaties which flow from the Declaration, including the ECHR. It is through such qualifications that the ECtHR has developed the 'doctrine of proportionality' – or the 'don't use a sledgehammer to crack a nut' principle – discussed in 'Human Rights: Philosophy, Politics or Law?' Such limitation clauses simultaneously set boundaries on how far governments can go in restricting rights whilst establishing acceptable confines to individual entitlements. This in turn provides a guide as to where the exercise of valued liberties might hurt others; for example, by inciting racial hatred through freedom of speech or pruriently encroaching on others' privacy through a hidden camera lens. In this sense the obligations of individuals to others and to the broader society in which they live are broadly established.

As discussed further in Section II, this human rights approach to individual responsibilities has permeated UK law through the 1998 HRA,[158] although you would scarcely know this if you believed everything you read in the newspapers. Notwithstanding this developing framework, the philosopher Onora O'Neill, now chair of the UK's Equality and Human Rights Commission, had formerly bemoaned the lack of discussion of duty bearers in rights instruments and that 'the Declaration is so opaque about allocating the obligations of justice'.[159] For O'Neill it was a 'scandal' not knowing 'whether these universal rights are matched and secured by universal obligations'.[160] But Morsink is surely right to suggest that this would have involved a very long list given that the UDHR addressed in the Preamble 'every individual and every organ of society': 'We have human rights "against the whole world" because the whole world is full of duty-bearers'.[161]

In the decades that have followed the adoption of the UDHR this insight has become increasingly reflected in international law. Not in the anarchic way imagined by those who bemoan the creation of a so-called 'compensation culture' where everyone is suing everyone else for breaches of their 'rights', but in a manner which recognizes the responsibilities that come with power. The concept of 'individual responsibility' is, admittedly, generally more developed and more direct in international humanitarian law (e.g. the Geneva Conventions) and international criminal law (e.g. The Rome Statute which established the ICC) than in most of the human rights treaties spawned directly by the UDHR, partly reflecting the nature of conflict and crime. In the post-war firmament, the 1946 Nuremberg Tribunal kicked this off by affirming the doctrine of 'individual responsibility' for war crimes, under orders or otherwise:

> International law imposes duties and liabilities on individuals as well as upon states. . . . Crimes against international law are committed by men, not by abstract entities, and only by punishing individuals who commit such crimes can the provision of international law be enforced.[162]

Likewise, the 1948 UN Genocide Convention, drafted contemporaneously to the UDHR and adopted just the day before, asserted that: 'Persons committing genocide . . . shall be punished, whether they are constitutionally responsible rulers, public officials or private individuals' (Article 4).

The 1984 UN Convention on Torture similarly requires states to criminalize an act 'by any person' which constitutes complicity or participation in torture (Article 4). The 1998 Rome Statute also refers explicitly to both 'public officials and private individuals' as potentially liable for the human rights crimes that it is within the jurisdiction of the ICC to try. It explicitly refers to the doctrine of 'individual responsibility'. A number of paramilitary group members have been tried at the ICC. After years of debate about whether 'non-state actors' can be human rights violators according to international human rights norms, former UN high commissioner for human rights and Irish president Mary Robinson declared her position when she deemed the 9/11 attacks to be a 'crime against humanity'.

The private sphere

Contrary to common assumptions, it is not just in the public sphere that individual responsibility is addressed under international human rights law. Morsink corrects Nussbaum on this presumption when she claims that her 'capabilities approach', referred to earlier, is better suited to addressing domestic injustices than 'traditional rights talk'. She claims that the latter 'has neglected these issues' because 'rights language is strongly linked with the traditional distinction between the public sphere, which the state regulates, and a private sphere which it must leave alone.'[163] From Wollstonecraft onwards, the argument that the 'rights of man' were precisely what they said on the tin, and no more, has resonated with women. There is a persuasive feminist critique that Enlightenment liberties were crafted in the image of males in the public sphere and that, at their worst, they have enhanced the freedom of men to do what they want in their private lives, often at the expense of women and children.[164] There is a lot of mileage in this argument, but largely as a result of feminist lobbying, international law has come a fair way over the decades to address this critique.

Andrew Clapham, author of *Human Rights in the Private Sphere*, argues that 'the developments surrounding the international human rights of women have led to a complete reappraisal of the way in which the public/private divide has been constructed to delimit human rights law.'[165] After years of protest about the insufficient weight given to the crime of rape under international humanitarian law, the Statute of the International Criminal Tribunal for Former Yugoslavia, established in the wake of the atrocities committed in Bosnia and elsewhere in the early 1990s, declared that 'systematic rape', and 'sexual enslavement' in times of war was a 'crime against humanity', second only to the crime of genocide. The Statute of the 1994 International Tribunal, established to prosecute perpetrators of the Rwandan genocide, likewise declared rape as a 'crime against humanity' in affirming the doctrine of 'individual responsibility'. Mass rape as an instrument of war continues unabated, but the attention now given to it by human rights defenders is on a scale that might even have made Wollstonecraft feel vindicated.

UN treaties spawned by the UDHR, in particular the race, gender, disability and children's conventions, explicitly cross the public/private divide. The 1984 UN Convention on the Rights of the Child, in particular, focuses on the fate of children in the family, repeatedly acknowledging 'the rights and duties' of parents and carers. After the UDHR, it is probably the most well-known and culturally influential human rights charter in the world. As legally enforceable treaties are conducted between states, most of the responsibilities incumbent on parents – for example 'recognition of the principle that both parents have common responsibilities' for their children in Article 1 – are represented as 'positive obligations' on states to ensure these are implemented. This is the route through which victims of crime and terror are entitled to protection from their abusers under international human rights law, which in turn has led to significant advances for victims and witnesses in the UK (discussed further in Section II).

The 2006 UN Convention on the Rights of People with Disabilities is also directed partly at the private sector, requiring states to 'ensure that private entities that offer facilities and services . . . to the public, take into account all aspects of accessibility for persons with disabilities'. There is likewise a growing body of 'soft law', which is politically and morally persuasive rather than legally enforceable, that directly addresses corporate power in the context of ever-increasing globalization. Examples include Draft UN Norms on the Responsibilities of Transnational Corporations with Respect to Human Rights, which have yet to be formally adopted, and the 2011 Guiding Principles on Business and Human Rights, known as the Ruggie Principles, aimed at implementing the UN's 'Protect, Respect and Remedy' framework. Whilst the American Bill of Rights still largely operates on a traditional individual-versus-state nexus, this stark public/private divide has long since ceased to be the only working model in international human rights law.

Conflict resolution

At the root of the mischaracterization of human rights as essentially individualistic or egoistic lies the failure to appreciate that the post-war human rights framework was partly designed with an eye to the worldwide conflict which all the delegates had just lived through. The very first sentence of the UDHR Preamble asserts that:

> Recognition of the inherent dignity and of the equal and inalienable rights of all members of the human family is the foundation of freedom, justice and peace in the world.

One of the primary goals of the UDHR, therefore, was to find new ways to address tensions and conflicts between individuals and groups within diverse societies; just like the one in the Birmingham schools explored at the beginning of this section. Whilst being fingered as potential violators, states are also given a prime role as *protectors* in human rights law. Using human rights values as a framework through which to umpire disputes and differences, governments – or more usually domestic courts – are charged with refereeing competing rights and interests. This is the practical purpose, the utility if you like, of human rights, which has been met with varying degrees of acceptance and success, frustration and appreciation.

In 'Rights and Righteousness' (the fourth anthology piece) I present examples where this framework, essentially rooted in the UDHR but finding legal expression in later treaties, has been used to address conflicts between individuals and communities. These include an inflammatory Islamaphobic poster displayed by a member of the British National Party and the controversy over the ill-fated holy bull Shambo, who lived in a Hindu temple and was slaughtered after testing positive for tuberculosis. Other case law from the ECtHR, and Britain's own domestic courts interpreting the HRA, illustrate how this framework for deciding between individual freedoms and the interests of the wider community can play out in practice. Health and safety factors, such as those affecting Shambo, led the ECtHR to uphold the decision of a health authority to prevent a nurse from wearing a crucifix when she was on duty, whilst the same judges found that a British Airways dress-code ban on a flight attendant sporting a crucifix at work was neither necessary nor proportionate, in that no similar considerations were in play.[166]

These decisions by the ECtHR are complicated by the application of the doctrine of 'a margin of appreciation', developed by the Court to address the way in which the rather abstract rights in the ECHR should be applied in practice in states with different cultural mores and legal systems, even within Europe. This doctrine is a response to the argument which has been ongoing in the UK (as explored in Section II) that it is undemocratic for a regional or international court to determine certain questions that should be left to elected, and therefore accountable, national politicians. So when an Islington registrar refused to conduct same-sex civil partnership ceremonies because of her religious beliefs, and a sex therapist, employed by a private company, refused to advise same-sex couples, the ECtHR ruled that their dismissal was in accordance with government legislation and policies designed to secure the rights of others (same-sex couples) which, like the freedom to manifest religious beliefs, is equally protected by the ECHR. Accordingly, the Court allowed the UK a wide 'margin of appreciation' in striking the balance between these competing rights.[167]

A decision by the majority of judges at the ECtHR in July 2014 to uphold the ban on face coverings in public in France, clearly aimed at Muslim women wearing the *burqa* or *niqab*, was also upheld on 'margin of appreciation' grounds. But this case exposed the pitfalls of a supposedly universal human rights system deferring to a different set of values. The UK human rights group Liberty strongly condemned the judges' decision, which highlighted the differences between French Enlightenment values and the universal human rights framework. The Court acknowledged that 'a large number of actors, both international and national, in the field of fundamental rights protection have found a blanket ban to be disproportionate.'

However, the majority of the judges gave greater weight to the explanatory memorandum of the bill which banned 'the wearing of the full veil' because, according to the memorandum, it is 'a sectarian manifestation of a rejection of the values of the Republic'. They also took note of a parliamentary commission which found the *burqa* to be 'at odds with the values' expressed in the maxim 'liberty, equality and fraternity' and therefore 'a flagrant infringement of the French principle of living together'. Taking all these factors into consideration, the ECtHR determined that the ban did not fall outside the 'margin of appreciation' granted to states to make such decisions.[168] In deferring to the French government, therefore, the court prioritized Enlightenment-based reasoning over both the human rights arguments of the groups which opposed the ban and the liberties of the women affected. The distinction between universal human rights and 'Enlightenment values' has rarely been given a more vivid outing in the modern era.

The clash between these two perspectives was even more evident in the so-called cartoon controversy that engulfed Europe and the Middle East in 2005–2006 (explored in 'Freedom of Expression Must Include the Licence to Offend?'[169] the last of the anthology pieces in this section). The European editors who published the Danish cartoons that suggested an association between Islam and terrorism explicitly sought to make a stand against self-censorship in the name of what they saw as a threat to the supreme 'Enlightenment value' of free speech. They maintained that any right to freedom of expression worth its sorts *must* include the licence to offend – license in the sense of liberty rather than legal permission.

The editors thought they were standing up for human rights, but the UN Office for the High Commissioner for Human Rights (OHCHR) – the custodian of the UDHR and its progeny – suggested otherwise. The OHCHR argued that *self-restraint* can be necessary to prevent the demonization or denigration of minorities in certain contexts and is *not* necessarily inconsistent with a free and uncensored press. As the hate speech which preceded the Nazi Holocaust, the Rwandan genocide and the Bosnian massacres demonstrated, free speech – the cornerstone of a democratic society – can also be used to deny, or even obliterate, the rights of others in certain contexts. This may not have been clear in the Europe of the Enlightenment, but the post-war human right to free expression encompasses the *totality* of this perception.

What we understand today, on the basis of 'lessons learned', is that appropriately applied, the exercise of free speech can involve *refraining* from speaking – or indeed drawing – when it is not the state or other sources of power that are being attacked but vulnerable individuals whose core identity is at stake. This approach derives from human rights treaties, such as the ECHR, which *explicitly* refer to the responsibilities attached to exercising free speech (in contrast to the American Bill of Rights).[170] In other words, what lay behind the request for self-restraint by the then UN High Commissioner Louise Arbour was a conception of the 'common good' embedded in the moral universe plotted by 'second wave' rights. The phrase 'common good' has two elements to it, of course, 'common' and 'good.' It is a term sometimes used synonymously with national or public interest, but a human rights conception of the 'common good' is not whatever the state, or the majority, determines is in their interest.

There *is* a 'common good' in maintaining free speech in a democracy, of course, and this has been strongly asserted by the ECtHR. A legal *ban* on the cartoons would therefore have been disproportionate in a democracy. But, as we have seen, a human rights approach routed in the ethics of the UDHR seeks to avoid manifesting rights in a way that is exterior to human beings or rides roughshod over human dignity, as the cartoonists did in the name of free speech.

The esteemed American legal theorist Ronald Dworkin was wrong, therefore, to use the analogy of 'trumps held by individuals' to explain human rights, at least outside North America.[171] To claim a human right is not to play the winning hand but to assert our own humanity whilst simultaneously endeavouring to respect the equal worth and dignity of our 'neighbour', and indeed 'the stranger'. For we are 'all members of the human family', as the first paragraph of the UDHR reminds us.

The meaning of 'universal'

The radicalism of this assertion in 1948 by a body of state representatives – that we are all from one 'human family' – is impossible to overstate. It was the forerunner to the 1970s slogan: 'One race, the human race'. But this was not just a catchphrase. It was the central meaning given to the term 'universal' by the Declaration. During the drafting process, at the Third Committee, the decision was made to change the title of the Declaration from 'international' to 'universal' to intentionally shift the focus from one of relationships between *states* to relationships between the *men, women* and *children* of the world to whom the UDHR was directly addressed.

This doesn't mean that the paradox – bordering on hypocrisy – of the assertion that all human beings inhabit 'one family' was entirely lost on all of the drafters. None of them could be said to be wide-eyed idealists, but many had vested interests in not facing up to the degree to which the countries they represented were complicit in preventing such an aspiration from remotely being realized.

Ignoring the contradictions of his own position, the Soviet delegate made this point forcefully. Dismissing the reference to 'brotherhood' in Article 1 of the draft as 'too far divorced from the realities of the modern capitalist world', Mr Pavlov pointedly declared:

> The relations between the United Kingdom and Malaya, between the Netherlands and Indonesia, between different groups in Spain, between the rich and the poor everywhere, could not be described as brotherly unless the brothers referred to were Cain and Abel.[172]

Yet over time the universalism of the Declaration was to inspire the radicalism which the UDHR drafters both flirted with and feared. The imperial powers had no interest whatsoever in the Declaration becoming a weapon to be used against them, of course. But even if the draft hadn't specifically included the 'non-self-governing' territories 'without distinction', as we saw earlier, the aspirations of this first document addressed to 'all peoples and all nations' drove its own logic. By the time the International Covenants which formed the other two legs of the International Bill of Rights were adopted nearly two decades later, lobbyists engaged in anti-colonial struggles succeeded in inserting 'the right to self-determination' of 'all peoples' into their very first article. For Malik:

> The issues of the fundamental liberties of man – those qualities of existence . . . without which he would have no dignity whatever – were turned into issues of how people should liberate themselves from foreign rule and of how the masses should raise their standard of living.[173]

It is impossible to miss the lament in his voice at this change of focus, as he saw it. But Malik was certainly not the only scholar to question whether the 'right to self determination' was a human right at all. Moyn has argued that anti-colonialists 'capture[d]' the post-war human rights project, installing 'self-determination as the first of all human rights', and that it was not until the 1970s, with 'the death of other utopian visions and their transfiguration into a human rights agenda', that the international human rights project *started* to enjoy a 'startling spike in cultural prestige'.[174] He may be right, but even so this does suggest that the centre of gravity for human rights developments was fast moving from the north to the south and the west to the east, embracing the 'universal model' that the drafters notionally sought.

This outcome is perhaps less surprising than it might seem when the 'second wave' of human rights is no longer confused with the European Enlightenment but understood as a project in its own terms. A project which, in Cassin's words, was intended to stress 'the fundamental principle of the unity of the human race' because Hitler had 'started by asserting the inequality of men before attacking their liberties'.[175] For Malik, too, it was an article of faith that 'the human person is more important than the racial, national or other group to which he may belong.'[176] With this in mind, even 'the right to take part in the government of his county' in Article 21 was not limited to citizens but applied to 'everyone', precisely 'to draw in those people living in the colonies'.[177]

Singh is probably right, therefore, when he argues that 'the most important word in human rights charters' may be 'everyone'. This, he persuasively pointed out in his lecture to the Magna Carta conference in London in June 2014, is what distinguishes universal human rights instruments from what preceded them:

> In truth most legal systems have differentiated between human beings and accorded them rights by reference to their status. Certainly at the time of the

Great Charter it would have been unthinkable that everyone was entitled to certain basic rights.[178]

Virtually every article in the UDHR, and the treaties it bequeathed, begins with the word 'everyone'. But it is a 'solidaristic' rather than 'individualistic' take on universalism. Cassin explained his use of the phrase 'all members of the human family' in Article 1 not only as a means of avoiding the gendered term 'man' but also to stress 'the inherent equality of human beings'. This in turn linked with 'the idea of solidarity' which 'should be made explicit in Article 1 to convince the world that the United Nations firmly believed in their essential brotherhood'.[179]

In Morsink's words: 'The human rights they proclaimed were to them the moral cement that binds together the increasingly pluralistic societies of the modern world.'[180]

Morsink's point is that the cosmopolitanism promoted by the Declaration was neither individualistic nor monochrome. In emphasizing our common humanity it explicitly did not seek to deny ethnic, religious or national variations; indeed, it prohibited discrimination against such characteristics. It did not discount the existence of different nations and ways of life; the Declaration was in fact predicated on 'all nations' striving to 'promote respect' for the values it upheld. Neither was this an attempt to create one world government. Far from it! Especially in the legally enforceable Covenants, states were given the primary responsibility to uphold the rights they enshrined. There was a revolutionary entitlement to 'seek and enjoy in other countries asylum from persecution' (Article 14), but there was no obligation on states to grant it and certainly no restrictions placed on immigration controls.

It was the paradox of this universalistic framework which relies on nation-states for its fulfilment that contributed to the scepticism expressed by the esteemed political theorist Hannah Arendt, herself a refugee from Nazism, about the capacity of the Declaration to fulfil its goals. Her experience had taught her that there was one fundamental right, 'the right to have rights', which is only apparent 'when millions of people emerge who had lost and could not regain these rights'. Consequently:

> The right that corresponds to this loss . . . cannot be expressed in the categories of the eighteenth century . . . the right to have rights or the right of every individual to belong to humanity should be guaranteed by humanity itself. It is by no means certain that this is possible.[181]

Arendt did not live to see this, but politics and philosophy scholar Seyla Benhabib maintains that while states 'remain the most powerful actors' there has been a 'crucial transformation' brought about by the UDHR and its progeny from 'international to cosmopolitan norms of justice'.[182] At the level of a norm, it is plausible to argue that in comparison to the pre-war era of the League of Nations, explored earlier, there is clearly now a greater expectation that individuals will be protected because of their humanity rather than their citizenship status. However Benhabib rightly warns that 'this discourse of inclusion and exclusion about Islam' is 'repeating some of the well-known tropes of a dogmatic Enlightenment that could only tolerate otherness by forcing it to become like itself. In nation states . . . the cosmopolitan promise of human rights threatens always to be sacrificed for consolidating a homogenous nation.'[183]

For entrenched critics of the human rights framework who assert that it has never been more than a beefed-up version of Western liberalism with a universal veneer, it is no surprise that it is breeding a new 'intolerance in the name of tolerance'. Especially in the wake of 9/11 and more recent examples of so-called Islamist terror, resorting to the old 'Enlightenment' trope of 'muscular liberalism' to require conformity to Western values merely demonstrates that the shine has come off the veneer. From this perspective the facade of 'universalism' has never been more than a sham. This is not just at an ideological level. The 'right to have rights' – reflected in UDHR Article 6, which affirms 'everyone has the right to recognition everywhere as a person before the law' – is as fragile as it ever was, as the swelling number of stateless and internally displaced people dispiritingly demonstrates. There are few more graphic depictions of Arendt's prediction that those who have lost 'the right to have rights' will not regain them through declarations and treaties than boats brimming with migrants fleeing war and terror drowning in the Mediterranean Sea with the world turning away. This is made all the more grotesque when the spotlight shines for weeks on such tragedies when luxury liners hosting Western tourists meet a similarly grim fate. United in death they are not united in the value that appears to be put on their lives.

Universalism or cultural imperialism?

Criticisms of universal human rights as a form of Western imperialism began before the ink was dry. The provenance of such attacks is obviously relevant. Saudi Arabia presented a 'culturally relativist' objection to terms such as 'dignity and rights' because these terms 'had different meanings in different countries';[184] the Soviet Union argued that universal norms could be a threat to individual *states* which 'must be able to have certain indispensable rights';[185] and South Africa objected to the whole idea of 'universality in the concept of equality'.[186]

All three of these countries abstained in the adoption vote on the UDHR, as we saw, and their representatives were clearly expressing their governments' worldviews dressed up as theoretical objections to universalism. When the Iranian delegate argued that 'any attempt to set up a Court . . . to pass judgment on violations of human rights would constitute an infringement of the sovereignty of states'[187] he spoke for all governments everywhere that opposed 'universality' on the grounds that it limited their own sovereign powers. His objections were not materially different to those of the UK government today.

Criticisms from 'civil society' are of a different nature and are also as old as the UDHR itself. Reminding the delegates of the turmoil caused to non-Western cultures by colonialism, the American Anthropological Association (AAA) warned, even before the draft was complete, against providing a Declaration that was 'conceived only in terms of the values prevalent in the countries of Western Europe and America'. They pointed out that the Enlightenment-era charters were much simpler to write because they were not universal in reality, but were addressed to citizens in particular states.[188]

Many academics and commentators have echoed some or all of the AAA's characterization of 'second wave' human rights; not all of them opponents by any means. Human rights scholar Michael Freeman has asserted that 'the concept of human rights . . . is legally international, philosophically universal and historically Western,'[189] whilst Jack Donnelly has insisted that 'it is simply not true that all people at all times have had human rights ideas and practices.'[190] African scholar Asmarom Legesse has accused Western liberal democracies of writing 'most of their values and codes of ethics into the Universal Declaration';[191] An-Na'im has referred to the 'clearly secular Western origins of human rights';[192] and Antonia Cassese, the former UN Yugoslavia Tribunal judge, has questioned how 'the West succeeded[ed] in imposing its philosophy of human rights' on the UDHR.[193]

Critiques of the presentation of human rights as 'universal' have tended to involve a three-pronged attack: that they are deceptively ideological, politically manipulable and generally hypocritical. The 1993 Vienna World Conference on Human Rights asserted that 'all human rights are universal, indivisible, interdependent and interrelated' but not everyone was persuaded by this rhetoric. It was in the 1990s, just after the fall of the Berlin Wall when it seemed as if 'we were all human rights defenders now,' that the attack on human rights as an ideological imposition of Western, Christian values on the East came to a head in the so-called 'Asian values debate'.[194] The then Malaysian prime minister Dr Mahatir Mohammed maintained that the end of the Cold War provided Western powers with the opportunity to impose a new hegemonic world order through the vehicle of promoting democracy and human rights. As the leader of a state with a less than pristine human rights record he would say this wouldn't he? But his perspective received backing from sectors of civil society across the region, from radical socialists to religious conservatives. As Freeman put it at the time:

> What appears from the Western perspective to be a noble campaign for universal human rights is interpreted, from an Asian perspective, as cultural imperialism.[195]

The force of the argument that human rights are 'deceptively ideological' is even stronger when allied with the second criticism that they have been politically manipulated to provide cover, not just for interference, but also for intervention. When Western societies invade and bomb in the name of liberating another people to defend 'democracy and freedom,' as has repeatedly occurred in the past decade, this is heard as indistinguishable from the project to promote human rights. Despite the best efforts of the drafters of the UDHR, the moral force of human rights becomes not just blunted but inverted. Killing people to protect their human rights is a hard line to square.

There is a serious debate to be had about how to reconcile the limitations on national sovereignty inherent in the 'second wave' human rights project with the right to self-determination, an understandably valued principle, particularly in countries with a long history of struggle against imperialism. This is the context, of course, for the inevitable suspicion of Western motivations even when 'intervention' is called for by some marginalized or persecuted minorities themselves – as in Bosnia, Kosovo, Rwanda and Libya and, more recently, Syria, where the UN estimates that nearly 200,000 people have died in the current onslaught. Born out of the international community's anguish regarding the UN's failure to prevent the Rwandan genocide in 1994 and the Srebrenica massacre the following year, there is an argument that the 'responsibility to protect' all human beings anywhere from mass-atrocity crimes is, or should be, an emerging human rights norm. The salient questions are when should this norm be triggered, on whose authority and by what proportionate means?

It was, in fact, the African Union (AU) which first pioneered the concept, in its founding statute, that there is a responsibility to intervene in crisis situations if a state is failing to protect its population from mass-atrocity crimes.[196] But the germ of this idea goes back to the debates we visited earlier, during the Second World War, when human rights activists and academics were frantically trying to craft declarations which, in their impotence to stop the annihilation of unprotected minorities in their midst, they fervently hoped would prevent such horrors from reoccurring. This was the 'never again' impetus that drove them to demand that the fledgling UN adopt an international bill of rights. As a consequence, an embryonic version of 'the responsibility to protect' was inserted into a new French Declaration of Rights that Cassin and his colleagues in *Free France* drafted in 1943: 'If a nation, if a community of any kind, violates human rights, all of humanity must give total help to the oppressed.'[197]

At the beginning of the millennium the Canadian government established the International Commission on Intervention and State Sovereignty to develop guidelines for intervention which were presented to the UN and partly reflected in the General Assembly's Outcome Document of the 2005 World Summit.[198] The report supported 'military action' but only 'as a last resort', and on the authority of the Security Council, where a state 'manifestly fails to protect its citizens' from 'genocide, war crimes, crimes against humanity, and ethnic cleansing'. It is widely agreed that the report, whilst covering new ground, ultimately failed to resolve many complex issues and contradictions that arise from the intractably difficult dilemma of when and how to 'intervene' without causing as much, if not more, civilian misery or deaths. In reality, given the power blocks that continue to dominate our polarized world, authority from the Security Council is anyway exceedingly unlikely to be forthcoming in most circumstances, and Cassin's pledge remains as unachievable now as it was in 1943.

To many human rights *critics* from all regions of the world, this impotence is welcome insofar as the 'responsibility to protect' norm is, in practice, yet another smoke screen for Western imperialism, and one that is ripe for political manipulation.

Many human rights *supporters* are equally sceptical that military intervention can ever be a proportionate route to human rights protection, given the number of lives that are likely to be lost or destroyed in the process. Despite examples such as Sierra Leone and the Ivory Coast, where intervention saved vulnerable communities and many lives, the growing cynicism about 'human rights interventions' is largely a product of the disastrous consequences of the Iraq invasion and the ongoing conflicts in Afghanistan and Libya. This disillusionment has been compounded by accumulating evidence of Western powers – in particular the US – violating the most basic human rights standards through practices such as indefinite detention without trial and torture or inhuman and degrading treatment, such as in Guantanamo Bay and secret locations around the globe.[199] The rampant hypocrisy of Western governments citing human rights norms to evaluate other states but presenting 'exceptionalist' grounds for exempting themselves and their allies from the same standards, comprises the third layer of criticisms levelled at pretentions to universalism. As Gray has brilliantly observed:

> In a curious turn the world's pre-eminent Enlightenment regime has responded to terrorism by relaxing the prohibition on torture that was one of the Enlightenment's true achievements.[200]

But for *defenders* of *universal* human rights, there remains a credible argument that they are not so much a route to double standards as an ethical framework capable of being effectively employed to *expose* the hypocrisy of Western, and other, states.

Global human rights movements

To some degree theoretical debates about universalism have been overtaken by facts on the ground, most notably the structures and movements which have been inspired by the UDHR in the decades that have followed its adoption. They have not all been hewn from the same identikit, but have evolved to reflect different religious and cultural norms around the globe, whilst recognizably adopting the human rights framework as their baseline. The regional human rights mechanisms spawned by the UDHR described earlier (and further explored in Section II) are themselves a product of acknowledged variations in interpreting universal human rights norms.[201] Of particular interest for the purposes of the 'universalism debate' are developments in Africa. The dearth of African representation in the drafting of the UDHR did not mean that the continent turned its back on the project. Quite the contrary. The communitarian African Charter on Human and Peoples' Rights, adopted in 1981 by the Organisation of African Unity (replaced by the AU in 2001), is unique in enumerating the duties owed by individuals to other individuals, the family and the state in an enforceable regional human rights instrument. The stature of the African Charter grew with the ratification of a protocol in 2004 to establish The African Court of Human and Peoples' Rights to supplement the African Commission in interpreting and enforcing the Charter. The Court has already ruled against Burkina Faso, Senegal and Tanzania, but this has not neutralized the very understandable criticism that, to date, *every* prosecution at the *International Criminal Court* has been against an African.[202]

The Charter's Preamble specifically takes into consideration 'the virtues' of Africa's 'historical tradition and the values of African civilization which should inspire and characterize . . . the concept of human and peoples' rights'. The text fuses individual and collective rights from this tradition with values and norms from UN treaties, adherence to which is cited in the Preamble. Although concerns were expressed that it might, this approach did not stop the African Commission from passing a resolution in May 2014 on 'the protection against violence and other human rights violations' suffered by people 'on the basis of their real or imputed sexual orientation or gender identity'.

It was the African Charter which was appealed to by the UK-based human rights organization Redress in lodging a complaint (together with the Sudanese Human Rights Initiative and three other local bodies) to the African Human Rights Commission on behalf of Meriam Ibrahim in June 2014. Imprisoned and sentenced to death for apostasy and adultery after she married a Christian Sudanese, a man of the same faith as her mother, Ibrahim was released on appeal following global protests. Perhaps this is an illustration of what An-Na'im – Sudanese himself – meant by 'the way out of the vicious cycle of the universality-relativity debate' is 'to go deeper into the local context of each issue in order to find sustainable points of mediation'?[203]

Given the African Charter's emphasis on duties and 'peoples' rights, if the 'second wave' human rights framework were a duplication of the Western Enlightenment 'neutral value system' model we discussed earlier, it is difficult to see how the Charter would be welcomed as a legitimate member of the human rights 'family'. Conversely, why would the African Union have adopted and expanded its human rights apparatus if it were merely a route to Western imperialism through 'soft power'?

More significant still than Charters and Courts is the activism and protests explicitly conducted in the name of human rights in all parts of the globe, including Burma, India, Israel, Pakistan, Palestine, South Africa, the Sudan, Zimbabwe and across Latin America. Flourishing human rights groups exist in all those places and more, which apply international human rights standards to frame their work but which have adapted their emphases and means of operating to specific local contexts. Perhaps the most unexpected eruption of this nature was the so-called Arab Spring in 2011. The flame lit by twenty-six-year-old Mohamed Bouazizi, who set himself alight in a small town in Tunisia, spread like wildfire and reflected a range of social and political demands. Some aspects of the protests were as recognizably human rights inspired as the Velvet Revolutions in Eastern Europe, which saw the demise of the Soviet Union in the late 1980s. In neither case could they be pigeonholed as nationalist, Marxist or Islamist revolts, but demonstrations which welcomed participants from all these affiliations and none, in defiance of state oppression and for dignity and equality as well as rights and freedoms. In the glow of optimism that greeted this dissent, badly tarnished now, the then UN High Commissioner for Human Rights, Mary Robinson, asserted that:

> The wide protests for dignity, democracy and human rights in the Arab world reinforces that the Universal Declaration of Human Rights in not a Western Agenda but embodies the values we need to live together in peace and justice.[204]

Now activists jailed for protesting against the corruption of their revolt by the new authorities in Egypt are frequently described by commentators as donning a human rights mantle in support of their defiance. In countries where it is still very difficult for human rights groups to openly organize, such as Iran or China, some opponents nevertheless adopt this framework in their clandestine work, most recently in Hong Kong. The development of the Internet, blogs and social networking has had a huge impact on globalizing resistance and enabling human rights practices to take on different forms in different regions, whilst still recognizably sharing a common ethical framework. This includes respecting each individual's dignity and humanity whilst opposing all forms of discrimination, demonization and degradation. In my book *Values for a Godless Age* I called this global grass-roots phenomenon the 'third wave of rights' but in 2000, when it was published, it was only just beginning.

Today, barely a week goes by without a new global debate on human rights, often in the sphere of cultural differences and the compatibility of a human rights framework with religious traditions and beliefs, especially concerning women's rights and discrimination or persecution on grounds of sexual orientation.[205] For every religious conservative who complains that a Western secular blueprint, damaging to their deeply held faith and traditions, is being foisted on them in the name of human rights, there are women or minorities who protest that liberal sensitivities to different religions and cultures are denying them basic human dignities and sometimes putting them in mortal danger. Algerian American international law professor Karima Bennoune, in her book *Your Fatwa Does Not Apply Here*, puts it like this:

> While the Western Right sometimes advocates international crimes and bigotry in response to Muslim fundamentalist violence, the Western (and global) left often refuses to recognise the reality of that violence and the actual danger posed by its ideology.[206]

She quotes one Algerian feminist activist as stating: 'The international human rights organisations have been my enemies for thirty years.' This is not, it seems, because they have been imposing their Western imperialist values on her but because, as Bennoune sees it, 'the international human rights movement has all too often failed to grasp what is at stake in the fight against fundamentalism.'[207]

A commonly proposed resolution to such human rights impasses, outside the law, is the one suggested by Bulgarian scholar Yanaki Stoilvov in answer to his own question 'Are Human Rights Universal?'

> The achievement of at least a minimum core understanding of the value and significance of human rights is a prerequisite for their universal nature . . . without tolerance for the cultural, religious etc peculiarity in the content of rights and in the mechanisms of their realisation, even what is believed to be a common core might easily be lost.[208]

As a broad principle this argument might makes a lot of sense. But in practice we cannot escape the dilemmas that such an approach fails to resolve. For gay men imprisoned for loving each other in Uganda or child brides in Pakistan, settling on a 'minimum core understanding of the value' of human rights in the name of 'tolerance' of 'cultural' or 'religious' practices can mean coming full circle and bumping straight into the mirror image of the Enlightenment debate on 'toleration' we discussed earlier. Instead of requiring 'the other' to conform to a 'liberal culture', 'tolerance' can become a vehicle for demanding obedience to a non-liberal culture, even when the dignity, and sometimes safety, of marginalized and vulnerable human beings depend on us not trading their humanity to salvage a 'minimum common core'.

John Gray, who is so clear-sighted in naming the intolerance embedded within the Enlightenment value of 'toleration', seems a little less sure footed when he argues in the face of contemporary value conflicts in the UK, regarding some conservative religious practices, that 'the best we can hope for is tolerance.'[209] But what is the answer when young women ask us to 'speak out' and support them in *not* tolerating practices like forced marriages or female genital mutilation (FGM), which may not kill them but will destroy any chance to determine their own path in life? Malala Yousafzai, who was shot in the head at the age of fifteen by the Pakistani Taliban for going to school and has received sanctuary in the UK, told the Girl Summit in London in July 2014, in support of a victim-led campaign against FGM, that:

> We should not be followers of those traditions that go against human rights. We are the human beings and we make the traditions. Traditions are not sent from God. We have the right to change cultures and we should change it.[210]

Her statement stands as a strong response to Gray's assertion. The UDHR suggests that the route to respect for the human dignity and equal worth of *every* human being is not just tolerance as such, but to both love thy neighbour *and* the stranger (who can be your son or daughter if they are different from you). In other words, to keep attuned to the cries of those who are like us, and not like us, and to try to muddle our way through the sometimes intractable dilemmas a *universal* framework – that is simultaneously predicated on respect for *pluralism* and *commonality* – invariably throws up.

In spite of its inclusivity, I have personally often felt quite uncomfortable with the term 'universal'. To my ear, any set of ideas with the label 'universal' attached to it has a whiff of missionary Evangelicalism or Enlightenment dogmatism about it. But I have equally often asked myself, what would a *non*-universal declaration of human rights have looked like? Who would have been 'let off'? Religious lit-eralists who do not share its norms and so do not permit others in their family or community to do so either? Conservative authoritarians who see human rights values as inimical to theories about intrinsic good and evil? Marxist-Leninists who still maintain that 'the rights of man' threaten the 'collective'? Is not the purpose of a universal framework to throw down the gauntlet to such individu-als and groups and challenge them to express their beliefs in a manner which respects every human being in their orbit? Unlike some ideologies or religions, human rights do not require people to abandon their other belief systems; only to *manifest* them in a way that respects the dignity and equal worth of others. We saw that clearly in the previous section on rights and righteousness where several religious leaders and theologians insisted on the compatibility of univer-sal human rights norms with their deeply held faith and traditions. In fact, as we have seen, the human rights framework would be unrecognizable without the direct input of those same faiths and traditions; to present them as mutually exclusive is meaningless.

For the drafters of the UDHR, universalism did not mean forcing or threaten-ing or even hectoring others into submission to a common way of life and value system. It simply meant that over and above any and other consideration, every human being is of equal worth. It meant that all states (and increasingly other loci of power) should be held to account if people are treated otherwise and that the UN itself should act when governments fail.[211] Although most of us would say this is stating the obvious, in reality it is equally clear that some deaths and indignities cause more attention and anguish – let alone remedial action – than others. This was at the heart of the riots and demonstrations in the US following the deaths of two unarmed black men in 2014. In both cases grand juries determined that the white policemen who shot them should not be prosecuted. The loss of these men's lives, the protesters were saying, should attract the same level of sanctity and scrutiny as anyone else's.[212]

Universalism was anyway not intended to be just about the *victims* of rights viola-tions but also about who has responsibility to prevent them. If universalism means anything it means girls in Nigeria have as much of a right to education, to choose who to marry and what to wear as the men from Boko Haram who abducted them. And if, as is apparent, their government is not doing enough to protect them, it becomes the responsibility of us all to press their government to do so, as the locally based and globally supported Bring Back Our Girls campaign has asserted. This is where Bentham's whole approach breaks down when he insists that human rights are 'nonsense' without identifiable duty-holders. As we saw, human rights violations are everybody in the world's business; to that extent we are all duty-holders with a responsibility to speak out and take action where we can. That is what the 'universal' in the UDHR encompasses, and in 1948 that was even more of a radical idea than it is now.

Conclusion: inspiration or foundation?

Amongst academics, the claim that human rights are 'universal' has caused some consternation. If all people everywhere and at all times are said to possess something called 'human rights', it follows – so the logic goes – that there must be something essential about the human condition to justify this assertion.

As we saw, for our Enlightenment ancestors the problem of 'foundations' was solved by claiming rights to be 'natural'. But after the drafters of the UDHR ducked the quest for an 'objective foundation' for human rights, theoreticians have struggled to find alternative reductive ways of explaining why humans have rights; sometimes arguing from an essentialist belief in specific attributes of human nature, although usually denying that is what they are doing.

Some of these theories are briefly touched upon in 'Human Rights: Philosophy, Politics or Law?' Not mentioned there is H.L.A. Hart's 'choice theory',[213] and Joseph Raz's 'interest theory'.[214] The human capacity for reason remains a strong contender for 'justifying' rights. Rawl's 'rational' discovery of fundamental rights from the 'original position', discussed earlier, is challenged by Morsink, who also contests other 'rationalist' approaches to human rights, such as those of Gerwith and Jurgen Habermas,[215] for stressing 'the route of reason at the expense of conscience'.[216] Morsink persuasively asserts that 'simply wanting to be rational is not what makes a human being a moral creature.'[217] His alternative offering is the 'doctrine of inherence' based on 'classic moral intuition', which he denies is a version of 'full blown essentialism' but which he partly derives from a textual analysis of the UDHR. This convinces him that 'this doctrine of inherence reverberated throughout the adoption debates'.[218] As he sees it, the drafters 'worked with the idea that (unless blocked) human beings have an operative moral conscience that tells them when they are about to engage in a gross violation of human dignity or when others have done so'. The inclusion of 'conscience' alongside 'reason' in the UDHR is therefore crucial because our

> conscience puts us in touch with a realm of moral values and inherent rights which the drafters articulated in the articles. This realm is an objective one in that ordinary people from all walks of life and from any of the world's cultural milieus can (unless blocked) enter it.[219]

This theory is as difficult to prove as it is attractive. What it doesn't really attempt to answer is why 'the dictates of our conscience' should arrive at the precise list of entitlements found in the UDHR. Why, for example, should the Declaration include what Isaiah Berlin memorably called 'positive' as well as 'negative' liberties in his famous 1958 essay on 'two concepts of liberty'?[220] Nussbaum's capabilities theory, also referred to earlier, takes us some of the way to answering this question. Based on a distinct set of ten 'central human functional capabilities' that she alleges human beings share everywhere, she acknowledges that in this universal foundation her framework is 'similar to the international human rights approach'.[221] Other theorists today, such as Benhabib, Donnelly, Habermas, Sen and Charles Beitz,[222] turn to a form of 'discourse theory' to explain how rights have evolved and developed. Sen, for example, has taken Nussbaum to task on the grounds that such a 'canonical list' of capabilities, and the weight she assigns to them, cannot be chosen outside a further specification of context, and therefore her method involves 'a substantial diminution of the domain of public reasoning'.[223] His approach is based on dialogue and discourse:

> In practical applications of human rights, such debates are, of course, quite common and entirely customary, particularly among human rights activists . . . A theory of human rights can, therefore, allow considerable internal variations, without losing the commonality of the agreed principle of attaching substantial importance to human rights.[224]

My colleague Professor Conor Gearty has described Sen's (and by implication other) discourse theories as a form of 'passive foundationalism' which is 'emblematic' of the 'drift' from 'truth to discovery that has been occurring in recent years'.[225] I welcome this drift. When I first came across the 'anti-foundationalism' of the late American philosopher Richard Rorty, referenced further in 'Human Rights: Philosophy, Politics or Law?' I found his line of argument immensely refreshing. For Rorty:

> The idea of a universally shared source of truth called 'reason' or 'human nature' is for us pragmatists just the idea that such discussion *ought* to be capable of being made conclusive. We see this idea as a misleading way of expressing the hope, which we share, that the human race as a whole should gradually come together in a global community.[226]

I am partly persuaded by Rorty's argument that the quest to prove that human rights derives from the essence of humanity which, as rational beings, we are capable of 'discovering', is a fruitless task. The challenge, he argues, is '*doing* human rights' which for Rorty involves 'increasing our ability to see the similarities between ourselves and people very unlike us as outweighing the differences' and for this we simply need 'imagination'.[227]

For Rorty, human rights are a 'social construction',[228] a starting point I try to develop in 'Human Rights: Above Politics or a Creature of Politics?' American philosopher Charles Beitz, influenced by Rorty, maintains that it is the 'practice' of human rights as 'the constitutive norm of a global practice', which theorists like himself should seek to conceptualize, rather than objectively justify.[229] This approach allows for disagreements in the interpretation of human rights standards to be charted in that 'it is not part of . . . practice that everyone who accepts and acts upon the public doctrine [of human rights] must share the same reason for doing so.'[230]

It is this human rights *practice*, now in evidence all over the globe, which is at least a partial response to sceptics who, like Bentham, long ago argued that fundamental rights were 'nonsense'[231] unless prescribed by law. It is also a response to MacIntyre's insistence that to claim that 'human rights' exist is as delusional as believing in 'witches and in unicorns'.[232] But what drove these criticisms of human rights as illusions, beyond the legal positivism already described, is a rejection of the proposition that (outside of religion) there can be a higher value system, a basic morality which could successfully shape a framework for making life more liveable for us all.

So whilst pointing to the reality of 'a global practice' might provide an answer to the universalism critique just discussed, it cannot provide a satisfactory response to human rights sceptics querying the basis of their *ethical* dimension or *why* we should accept them, even if we can understand their internal logic. As Morsink points out, 'human rights practice' – in all its complexity and variations – cannot, on its own, explain the *moral* imperative that is the motor of human rights.

Gearty attempts to answer this question with what he calls 'a new kind of foundationalism' which 'puts giving and compassion' at 'the heart of the human story'. He traces this 'intuition to help others' to an 'evolutionary dynamic' which means 'we are not persuaded by our brains to care; we care because of what we are have become/are becoming. We start with feelings and end with reason, rather than the other way round.'[233]

The nub of my argument in this section is that to *understand* what *kind* of ethic drives human rights, recognizable in many human rights movements throughout the globe, you have to start with the basic text, the UDHR, and the *argument* it seeks to make. It is far from ideal or utopian in its conception or its scope. But it without doubt established the foundations of what we today mean by human rights, which is why I have delved in some detail into the roots of the values it projects. Every charter and treaty that has followed in the Declaration's wake, every organization that has subsequently adopted 'human rights' in its title, displays its stamp. Notwithstanding the plurality that has blossomed under its umbrella, there is a common thread. This is crucial to address Gearty's warning that whilst 'the "human rights movement" can capture a lot of idealistic space across the globe' it has 'to have some substantive content without which it risks total subversion'.[234]

What the labyrinthine human rights system established during the past sixty-plus years has plainly *not* achieved, however – if this needs saying – is ending human rights abuses. Surveying the world as it now is, it is difficult to claim it is any less volatile or murderous than it was sixty-six years ago. All we can say at this level is that there is far more transparency and accountability than in previous epochs. In centuries past it was simply unthinkable to conceive of an internationally agreed framework to hold governments to account for the way they treat the very people they are meant to protect and represent. With the establishment of the ICC, impunity for gross human rights violations is no longer a given, although it is still unimaginable to envisage the head of state of a major world power being brought before the court, even setting aside the fact that neither the US nor Russia have ratified the Rome Statute.

What is unquestionable is that far less happens out of the daylight now. Today, almost no one can say about virtually any atrocity anywhere that 'they didn't know'. This is what Gearty refers to as 'the visibility project' of human rights movements whose goal is 'to get us to *see* people truly *as* people and therefore – *each of them* – as *entitled* to right treatment *on account of their humanity*'.[235] This project has, of course, been hugely enhanced by the wonders of our technologically connected world. But it is significantly a product of the global human rights standards and structures that idealists and pragmatists crafted together after the Second World War and in the decades that have followed.

It is not necessary to have personally studied the UDHR, therefore, or even to be aware of it, to encounter its basic norms in the connected world we now inhabit. Like the Magna Carta, its effect has been symbolic as much as real. Evidence that international human rights norms have filtered down to community and street level, which in turn has fuelled their further evolution, is now well documented. Historian Jean Quataert argues in her study of human rights mobilization in global politics that: 'By the last third of the twentieth century the language of human rights had become an increasingly effective medium by which to press a moral claim.'[236]

Perhaps if the past sixty-odd years had not been an age of failed utopias the UDHR would by now be no more than a set of tame aspirations trapped in the era they were written, drowned out by other more effective strategies for human flourishing. But with the cruelties and perversions we have witnessed in the name of nationalism, Marxism, religious literalism and even liberalism, the ethic outlined in the UDHR continues to empower and inspire, whilst the norms themselves evolve to reflect new struggles. Benhabib observes that:

> Confronted with the greatest world-economic meltdown since the Great Depression of the 1930s, we still don't know how to achieve human dignity, precisely because we have not attained economic emancipation. Yet neither have the utopian schemes of really-existing socialism, which have lacked full respect for full human rights and democratic liberties, proved viable.[237]

As the preamble to the UDHR reminds us, there is a revolutionary aspect to human rights. It is about struggle as much as it is about standards and sentiment. The renowned ethicist Mary Midgley sees human rights as the modern expression of resistance in the streets; its legitimacy coming from its use by people in life-threatening situations pressing their claims through this medium. She has described the ethical sensitivities encouraged by human rights as an 'immense enlargement of our moral scene'.[238] This 'human rights practice' that Midgley describes provides at least a partial response to claims expressed by theorists from Rawls to Stoilvov that agreement on fundamental rights can only be found from acceptance of 'a minimum core'. As Benhabib observes, human rights standards 'define both a minimum to be maintained and a maximum to be aspired to'. With new 'struggles' they will evolve further:

> Precisely because they emerge out of such struggles and learning processes, human rights documents cannot simply embody an 'overlapping consensus' or 'minimum conditions of legitimacy'; they give voice to the aspiration of a profoundly divided humanity by setting 'a common standard of achievement for all people and all nations'.[239]

For Gearty this means that 'human rights' have become 'a lively and progressive feature of our democratic polity' in which 'the statement "these are our human rights" [is] best understood to be part of an argument'.[240] To my mind characterizing human rights as 'an argument' is the most persuasive and credible way of defending them, but this still begs the question: What *kind* of argument is it?

It is easier to say what it *isn't*. I have sought in this section to distinguish 'universal human rights norms' from the Enlightenment values which they are often conflated with. As much as the Enlightenment, whether defined as an era or an idea, was a source of liberation and illumination to many, it also failed to provide the sustenance for tolerance and pluralism for which it is fabled. Many of the distinguishing features of the UDHR reflect this insight, which is why a close reading of the text is essential to appreciate its contribution.

Claims to *human* rights should also not be confused with claims to *legal* entitlements, even though a defining characteristic of human rights is, arguably, that they must be *capable* of legal expression in some form. This is not a pedantic point, but a category error. As Gearty and Douzinas point out, 'the term is a combined one: the "human" refers to morality and ethics and the treatment that individuals are entitled to expect' whilst it is only 'rights' which 'refers to their legal provenance'.[241] In other words, human rights are not a euphemism for law but a means for judging its legitimacy.

In this section I have tried to piece together the 'human rights argument' by tracing the factors which drove NGOs and academics, resistance fighters and politicians, lawyers and ethicists to demand a new universal human rights framework, even as millions were being slaughtered in Europe and throughout the world. With the help of eminent scholars such as Morsink and the text of some of the original debates, I have attempted to sketch the questions the UDHR delegates were asking, and why, and from this have made a stab at conveying the human rights ethic they crafted. The great legal theorist Louis Henkin sums it up well:

> We should reject any claims of human rights as a total ideology . . . but if human rights may not be sufficient, they are at least necessary. If they do not bring kindness to the familiar they bring – as religions have often failed to do – respect for the stranger.[242]

Yet human rights are not just about what is happening now and how we should behave, but about 'what kind of world we reasonably ought to want to live in'.[243] They encourage us to question and to probe, but do so through the lens of the human rights ethic. Nothing brings the human rights framework into focus more clearly than contrasting the language, style and message of a human rights organization with an overtly ideological body covering the same terrain. For all the differences and debates among activists, human rights have become a 'lingua franca' or 'Esperanto' of struggles around the world, so that there is now a recognizable

> language of human rights, a language that speaks for people and that manages, by forcing people to be visible to everyone, first to make it possible for others to speak on their behalf and then for them to speak for themselves.[244]

This is what I understand Nelson Mandela to have sought to convey when he spoke of the galvanizing effect of the UDHR, adopted just a few months after Apartheid was formally introduced into South Africa:

> For all the opponents of this pernicious regime the simple and noble words of the Universal Declaration were a sudden ray of hope at one of our darkest moments. During the many years that followed, this document . . . served as a shining beacon and an inspiration to many millions of South Africans. It was proof that they were not alone, but part of a global movement against racism and colonialism and for human rights and peace and justice.[245]

It is remarkable, in many ways, that Mandela, widely acclaimed to be the greatest political leader of his generation, was inspired and motivated by the UDHR. It would have been perfectly understandable if he had seen it as limp and impotent as he witnessed the barriers coming down and oppression flaring up in his own homeland. One way of interpreting the inspirational and empowering effects of the UDHR is to conceive of it as 'the wisdom of the ages'. Its relevance continues, Benhabib suggests, through the treaties and campaigns bequeathed by the Declaration which have likewise reflected and amplified struggles and 'lessons learned' in the decades that have followed:

> The 1948 Universal Declaration, and the era of human rights that has followed it, reflect the moral learning experiences not only of Western humanity but of humanity at large. The world wars were fought not only in the European continent but also in the colonies, in Africa and Asia. The national liberation and anti-colonisation struggles of the post-World War 2 period, in turn inspired principles of self-determination. The public war documents of our world are distillations of such collective struggles.[246]

In this description Benhabib echoes Malik, who in January 1947 appealed to his fellow UDHR drafters in these terms:

> We must gather our wisdom and light from all time . . . we must . . . have the proper historical perspective and grounding . . . We must also free ourselves of too exclusive a subservience to legalism, politics and diplomacy. . . . We require, I submit. . . . vision and sensitivity [which] belong pre-eminently to the prophet, unity [from] the philosopher and simplicity [from] the poet.[247]

Personal reflections

I cannot conclude this section without some personal reflections. The journey we have been on with our time travellers, in trying to come to grips with human rights, is one I started on twenty-five years ago. This was when I first came to understand that the Universal Declaration of Human Rights – and all that has flown from it – was a consequence of 'lessons learned' and insights gained from the terrible global events which preceded its drafting, including the clinical mass murder of millions of human beings. Men, women and children massacred – not because they were at war or in conflict with anyone but because of characteristics they could not change: their ethnicity, their disability, their sexual orientation or their religion. It was partly because this annihilation, and other 'barbarous acts which have outraged the conscience of mankind', did not just take place at the hands of the state, the army or the security services but required the collaboration or indifference of almost as many people as were murdered, that the drafters knew they had to craft a document which would speak to all people everywhere. They stood on the shoulders, as they acknowledged, of those who had preceded them in trying to distil the wisdom of their own post-war era, and by no means did they rely only on the insights and philosophies of the West. What they crafted was, in Cassin's words, 'something new . . . the first document about moral value adopted by an assembly of the human community'.[248] It was certainly the first such Declaration that applied to everyone everywhere, that placed humanity over citizenship and that made 'duty-holders', in the ethical sense, out of us all.

Since that time there have been many more attempted genocides and 'crimes against humanity' in different parts of the world. It has often been observed that if the UDHR had not already been adopted it is doubtful that it would be now. But what struck me when, twenty-five years ago, I first came to understand what lay behind the text of the UDHR is that here was something that had the potential to benefit people all over the world into the future which drew insights and wisdom from the terrible suffering of human beings that had preceded its drafting. It became personally important to me, as someone with extended family who were caught up in what has become known as the Holocaust or Shoah, to understand what universal human rights are, explain them and support their development as they become shaped by new generations experiencing their own terrible ordeals. Now it is other people in different parts of the world whose anguished cries are only occasionally heard, in states such as the Central African Republic, Iraq, North Korea, Nigeria, the Ukraine, Sri Lanka, the Sudan and Syria. By the time this book is published this list of countries may change again.

The bombardment of Gaza by the Israeli government, taking place as I write in the summer of 2014, has a particular significance for me. The attempted Nazi genocide of the Jewish people, killing nearly two-thirds of European Jews, was also the catalyst for the UN's support for the partition of Palestine in 1947, leading to the creation of the state of Israel the following year, just seven months before the UDHR was adopted. Sixty-six years later and the Israeli government regularly resists all condemnation emanating from the international human rights framework that developed directly out of such well-documented suffering. When the many Israeli human rights groups apply international human rights standards to protest against the occupation of Palestinian lands, or the blockade of Gaza, they are frequently accused of betrayal. Yet all they are doing is using the same ethical framework which arose from that darkest of periods and applying it, as 'a common standard of achievement for all peoples and all nations' everywhere, as the UDHR proclaims.

To my mind, the 'wisdom' distilled in the ethic of human rights was evident when the then UN High Commissioner for Human Rights, Navi Pillay, condemned the catastrophic impact of Israel's offensive, which at the time of writing has taken the lives of more than 1,400 civilians, of whom nearly 500, shockingly, are children.[249] This raised 'concerns about respect for the principles of distinction, proportionality and precautions in attack' the High Commissioner said. Targeting civilians 'may amount to war crimes and crimes against humanity' she asserted, and 'the actions of one party do not absolve the other party of the need to respect its obligations under international law.' Whilst Hamas, although self-evidently unable to inflict remotely comparable damage, carried out 'indiscriminate attacks' which 'endanger the lives of civilians in Israel', her point was that this could not possibly justify the deaths of so many defenceless Palestinians who had nowhere else to go:

> All these dead and maimed civilians should weigh heavily on all our consciences. I know that they weigh heavily on mine. All our efforts to protect them have been abject failures.[250]

Like many others brought up in a Jewish family, I was told stories of lives hanging in the balance dependant on whether people spoke up or remained silent, took action or pretended not to see, not just during the Second World War but in the centuries of persecution and pogroms that took place in many parts of Europe before it. Even if this made no difference to the outcome, I came to understand that 'speaking out' provides solace and solidarity. By the time this book is published the situation in Gaza may have changed and the media spotlight will have moved on. But it seems to me that it is not credible to write on the ethic of human rights without 'speaking out' when atrocities are carried out in your name – or in anyone's name. That is what I understand to be the central message of the Universal Declaration of Human Rights. All the rest is commentary.[251]

Notes

1 'Be More British Cameron Tells UK Muslims', *Mail on Sunday*, 15 June 2014. Governors of ten Birmingham non-faith schools with overwhelmingly Muslim pupils were accused of a so-called 'Trojan horse conspiracy' to impose conservative Muslim practices on the schools. Whilst the original letter alleging such a conspiracy was almost certainly fabricated, two separate investigations into the affair published in July 2014 were highly critical of the governance of the schools but differed in the degree to which they saw this as a co-ordinated agenda. Defenders of the schools suggested that both reports contained many inaccuracies and exaggerations of practices that legitimately reflected the schools' intake.

2 Quoted by Tom Blackmore, grandson of Sir David Maxwell Fyfe, in the *UK Human Rights Blog*, 9 November 2010. Maxwell Fyfe's take on human rights is discussed in more detail in Section II of this book.

3 'Secure Borders, Safe Haven: Integration with Diversity in Modern Britain', *White Paper*, CM 5387, 2002, 3.

4 Francesca Klug, 'Human Rights: A Common Standard for All Peoples?' Phoebe Griffith and Mark Leonard (eds) in *Reclaiming Britishness: Living Together after 11 September and the Rise of the Radical Right* (London: Foreign Policy Centre, 2002), 20–33.

5 Mathew d'Ancona, ed., *Being British: The Search for the Values that Bind the Nation* (UK: Mainstream Publishing, 2009), 29.

6 'Guidance on Promoting British Values in Schools', Department for Education, 27 November 2014. Education is devolved in Northern Ireland, Scotland and Wales.

7 Abdool Karim Vakil, 'British Values and the British Muslims', *Open Democracy*, opendemocracy.net, 20 June 2014.

8 For example, John Locke, *Letter Concerning Toleration* (1689). See Richard Tuck, 'Scepticism and Toleration in the Seventeenth Century', in *Justifying Toleration: Conceptual and Historical Perspectives*, ed. Susan Mendus (Cambridge: Cambridge University Press, 1988), 21–35.

9 For example, Tom Paine's *Rights of Man, Part One* (1791; London: Penguin, 1984) was more focussed on the principle of democracy than fundamental rights.

10 Cited in Christopher Hitchens, *Tom Paine's Rights of Man* (London: Atlantic Books, 2007), 114.

11 This theme is discussed more fully in Madeleine Bunting, 'The Convenient Myth That Changed a Set of Ideas into Western Values', *The Guardian*, 10 April 2006.

12 Quoted by Dan Hind in 'The Threat to Reason: Fact Fantasy and the Politics of Enlightenment', lecture to the Royal Society of Arts, London, November 2007.

13 Martin Amis, *The Second Plane – September 11: Terror and Boredom, the Liberal Case against Islamism* (New York: Knopf, 2008), 9–13.

14 Simon Cottee and Thomas Cushman, eds, *Christopher Hitchens and His Critics: Terror, Iraq, and the Left* (New York: New York University Press, 2008), 63.

15 John Gray, *Enlightenment's Wake* (London: Routledge, 2007), xvi.

16 Adam Sutcliffe, *Judaism and Enlightenment* (Cambridge: Cambridge University Press, 2003), 225.

17 Voltaire, *Dictionaire Philosophique* [1764], 517–18.

18 Sutcliffe, *Judaism and Enlightenment*, 242.

19 Ibid., 254.

20 Other Enlightenment scholars who denigrated the superstitiousness and backwardness of ancient or contemporary Jews, or both, include Pierre Bayle, Denis Diderot and Montesquieu. This should not be confused with support for the persecution of Jews which they generally opposed. Even Locke, who specifically argued for the toleration of Jews, was also an ardent supporter of mass Jewish conversion.

21 Theodor W. Adorno and Max Horkheimer, *Dialectic of Enlightenment* (London: Verso, 1944).

22 John Gray 'A Clash of Ideologues: The Enlightenment versus Islamism', *The National UAE Newspaper*, 2 July 2010.

23 Cameron, 'Be More British Cameron Tells UK Muslims' *Mail on Sunday*, 15 June 2014. Here the Prime Minister was echoing his 'muscular liberalism' speech he gave in Munich in the first year after he was elected, 5 February 2011.

24 Ibid.

25 *The Guardian*, 20 June 2014. The issue of the 'compatibility' of 'conservative Muslim beliefs' with human rights will be explored further in the discussion on the French 'niqab ban' case at the ECtHR, *SAS v France* (2014), ECHR 695.

26 Homi K. Bhaba, 'Narrating the Nation', in *Nation and Narration*, ed. Homi K. Bhaba (Routledge, 1990), 1.

27 *The Guardian*, 24 June 2014.

28 'The Big Question', BBC 1, 15 June 2014.

29 *The Guardian*, 16 June 2014.

30 Eric Foner, *The Story of American Freedom* (USA: Picador, 1998), 6.

31 Gray, *Enlightenment's Wake*, 269 (my emphasis).

32 Quoted in *The Guardian*, 21 November 2009.

33 Johannes Morsink, *Inherent Human Rights: Philosophical Roots of the Universal Declaration* (Philadelphia, PA: University of Pennsylvania Press, 2009), 25.

34 Gray, *Enlightenment's Wake*, 215.

35 Alasdair MacIntyre, *After Virtue: A Study in Moral Theory* (London: Duckworth, 1981), 39.

36 Morsink, *Inherent Human Rights*, 1.

37 See, for example, the 1978 Spanish Constitution Article 10(2) and the preamble to the 1987 Haitian Constitution. William A. Schabas has collected *The Travaux Preparatoires* of the UDHR in three volumes (Cambridge: Cambridge University Press, 2013).

38 Morsink, *Inherent Human Rights*, 1.

39 Paine, *Rights of Man*. The French Declaration of the Rights of Man and Citizen was adopted in 1789.

40 H. G. Wells, *The Rights of Man: Or, What Are We Fighting For?* (London: Penguin Special, 1940), 13, 17, 61.

41 Jan Burgess, 'The Road to San Francisco: The Revival of the Human Rights Idea in the 20th Century', *Human Rights Quarterly* 14 (1992): 448.

42 Letter from René Cassin to Henri Laugier, 1 September 1942, quoted in Jay Winter and Antoine Prost, *Renee Cassin and Human Rights: From the Great War to the Universal Declaration* (Cambridge: Cambridge University Press, 2013), 230.

43 Ibid., 135.

44 Ibid., 162–5.

45 Hersch Lauterpacht, *International Bill of the Rights of Man* (Oxford: Oxford University Press, 2013 [1945]).

46 See Johannes Morsink, *The Universal Declaration of Human Rights: Origins, Drafting and Intent* (Philadelphia, PA: University of Pennsylvania Press, 1999), 1–2, for a fuller description of these developments and, generally, for a forensic analysis of the drafting of the UDHR. For Britain's role, see A. W. Brian Simpson, *Human Rights and the End of Empire: Britain and the Genesis of the European Convention* (Oxford: Oxford University Press, 2001), chapters 3–5.

47 Quoted in Kirsten Sellars, *The Rise and Rise of Human Rights* (Stroud, UK: Sutton, 2002), 4. See also Burgess, 'The Road to San Francisco', for a detailed account of this period.

48 James Loeffler, '"The Conscience of America": Human Rights, Jewish Politics, and American Foreign Policy at the 1945 United Nations San Francisco Conference', *Journal of American History* (September 2013): 415. See also Burgess, 'The Road to San Francisco', 474.

49 Loeffler, '"The Conscience of America"', 6.

50 Simpson, *Human Rights and the End of Empire*, 264. Sellers (*The Rise and Rise of Human Rights*, 10), takes the view that the NGOs 'acquired an exaggerated sense of their own importance' whilst Morsink (*The Universal Declaration of Human Rights*) and Loeffler ('"The Conscience of America"') suggest that their influence was more substantial than this.

51 Loeffler, '"The Conscience of America"', 415.

52 Quoted in Sellers, *The Rise and Rise of Human Rights*, 268.

53 Article 68 says the Economic and Social Council (ECOSOC) 'shall set up commissions in economic and social fields and for the promotion of human rights'. The UNCHR was replaced by the United Nations Human Rights Council in 2006.

54 Morsink, *The Universal Declaration of Human Rights*, 3.

55 Simpson, *Human Rights and the End of Empire*, 268.

56 Francesca Klug, 'The Universal Declaration of Human Rights: 60 Years On', *Public Law* 2 (2009): 210.

57 Winter and Prost, *Renee Cassin and Human Rights*, 237.

58 Habib C. Malik, ed., *The Challenge of Human Rights: Charles Malik and the Universal Declaration* (Oxford: Charles Malik Foundation and the Centre for Lebanese Studies, 2000), 87–8.

59 Their initial mandate was as independent members, but from the summer of 1947, ECOSOC (see note 53) required them to serve as state delegates.

60 Malik, *The Challenge of Human Rights*, 120.

61 Quoted in Winter and Prost, *Renee Cassin and Human Rights*, 250.

62 Samuel Moyn, *The Last Utopia: Human Rights in History* (Cambridge, MA: Belknap Press, 2010), 83. See also Marco Duranti, 'Holocaust Memory and the Silences of the Human Rights Revolution', www.academia.edu/8187184, 2013, for a thoughtful development of this thesis.

63 Schabas, *Travaux Preparatoires*, vol. 3, 2519. See note 37. Miss Kalinowska was responding in support of a Soviet amendment to the right to free expression, but her narrow point here seems to be that meanings can be inferred or understood with or without specific terms. It is noteworthy here that the fact that she referred to 'monstrous crimes' and 'genocide' without specifically mentioning the victims – who included Jews, gypsies, homosexuals and disabled people – does not mean that they were not in the drafters' minds.

64 Morsink, *Inherent Human Rights*, 121. See John Rawls, *A Theory of Justice* (Cambridge, MA: Harvard University Press, 1971). His theories were further developed in *The Law of Peoples* (Cambridge, MA: Harvard University Press, 1999).

65 Quoted in Morsink, *Inherent Human Rights*, 131 (my emphasis).

66 'Summary Record of the Second Meeting of the Drafting Committee', ECOSOC paper E/CN.4/AC.1/SR. 2, 13 June 1947.

67 The full quote is: 'Whereas disregard and contempt for human rights have resulted in barbarous acts which have outraged the conscience of mankind', UDHR Preamble, second paragraph.

68 Morsink, *Inherent Human Rights*, 132.

69 Winter and Prost, *Renee Cassin and Human Rights*, 249.

70 Morsink, *The Universal Declaration of Human Rights*, 17.

71 'Summary Record of the Second Meeting of the Drafting Committee'. See also Simpson, *Human Rights and the End of Empire*, chapters 4 and 5.

72 ECOSOC paper E/CN/4/147, 16 June 1948.

73 Costas Douzinas, 'Human Rights and the Paradoxes of Liberalism', *Open Democracy*, 7 August 2014.

74 Francesca Klug, 'Human Rights: Philosophy, Politics or Law?' unpublished lecture, Centre for the Study of Human Rights, LSE, Certificate in International Human Rights Law and Practice, October 2013.

75 Rabinder Singh, 'The Development of Human Rights Thought from Magna Carta to the Universal Declaration of Human Rights', in The Rev. Robin Griffith-Jones and Mark Hill QC, eds, *Magna Carta: Religion and the Rule of Law* (Cambridge: Cambridge University Press, 2015).

76 Quoted in Mashood Baderin and Manisuli Ssenyonjo, eds, *International Human Rights Law Six Decades after the UDHR and Beyond* (Farnham, UK: Ashgate, 2010), 4.

77 Dr Bienenfeld, the representative of the World Jewish Congress, repeatedly drew the drafters' attention to this point. Morsink, *The Universal Declaration of Human Rights*, 50.

78 The Rome Statute, which established the ICC in 2002, defines 'crimes against humanity' as 'particularly odious offenses in that they constitute a serious attack on human dignity or grave humiliation or a degradation of human beings'.

79 The UN Apartheid Convention came into force in 1976. The 'crime of Apartheid' was also declared 'a crime against humanity' in the Rome Statute.

80 The United Nations Fact Finding Mission on the Gaza Conflict, known as the *Goldstone Report*, was established in April 2009 by the UN Human Rights Council (UNHRC) in the aftermath of Israel's 'Operation Cast Lead', reporting on 15 September 2009. Some of its findings, in particular that the Israeli security forces targeted civilians as a matter of government policy, have subsequently been retracted by the Chair but continue to be supported by the other panel members – Professor Christine Chinkin, Desmond Travers and Hina Jilani. The report recommended that both sides openly investigate their own conduct and if they failed to do so, that the allegations be brought to the ICC.

81 Baderin and Ssenyonjo, *International Human Rights Law*, 3.

82 See, for e.g., Ian Brownlie, *Principles of Public International Law*, 7th ed. (Oxford: Oxford University Press, 2008), 559.

83 Winter and Prost, *Renee Cassin and Human Rights*, 237. See also Simpson, *Human Rights and the End of Empire*, for a detailed analysis of the impact of Empire on the imperial powers' approach to human rights, in particular Britain.

84 Morsink, *Inherent Human Rights*, 172.

85 'Summary Record of the 2nd Meeting of the Working Group on the Declaration on Human Rights', ESOSOC paper E/CN.4/AC.2/SR/2, 5 December 1947.

86 Morsink, *The Universal Declaration of Human Rights*, 295.

87 Amartya Sen, 'Elements of a Theory of Human Rights', *Philosophy and Public Affairs*, 32 (2004): 319. Martha Nussbaum, *Women and Human Development: The Capabilities Approach* (Cambridge: Cambridge University Press, 2000) and *Frontiers of Justice: Disability, Nationality, Species Membership* (Cambridge, MA: Belknap Press, 2006). The capabilities approach is discussed further in 'Human Rights: Philosophy, Politics or Law?' and further on.

88 Preamble to the UDHR, 4th paragraph.

89 Malik, *The Challenge of Human Rights*, 132.

90 ECOSOC paper E/CN.4/SR.9, 1 February 1947.

91 UNESCO stands for the United Nations Educational, Scientific and Cultural Organization, established in 1946.

92 UNESCO, ed., *Human Rights: Comments and Interpretations: A Symposium* (New York: Columbia University Press, 1949). It is unclear what impact their deliberations had on

the UDHR draft, as the contents of the Symposium are not detailed in the *Travaux Pre-paratoires*, but many of the themes, particularly on responsibilities and community, overlap.

93 Reproduced and updated as Francesca Klug, 'Rights and Righteousness: Friends or Foe?' in *Strategic Visions for Human Rights: Essays in Honour of Professor Kevin Boyle*, ed. Geoff Gilbert et al. (London: Routledge, 2011). It was the late Kevin Boyle who started me on the journey of understanding the 'ethic of human rights'.

94 Francesca Klug, *Values for a Godless Age: The Story of the UK's New Bill of Rights* (London: Penguin, 2000).

95 Aase Lionaes, speech at the Nobel Peace Prize Award Ceremony, 1968. Her full quote is reproduced in the 'Conclusion' to Section II.

96 'Draft International Declaration of Human Rights', UN Transcript E800 of the 96th meeting of the Third Committee, 7 October 1948.

97 'Summary Record of the Second Meeting of the Drafting Committee'.

98 UN Transcript, 98th meeting of the Third Committee, 9 October 1948 (see note 96).

99 Morsink, *The Universal Declaration of Human Rights*, 33.

100 Quoted in Micheline R. Ishay, *The History of Human Rights from Ancient Times to Globalisation* (Berkeley: University of California Press, 2004), 19.

101 René Cassin, 'From the Ten Commandments to the Rights of Man', in *Of Law and Man: Essays in Honour of Haim H. Cohn* (New York: Sabra Books, 1971). Also quoted in Ishay, *The History of Human Rights*. The full biblical quotation in Leviticus 19:18 is: 'Do not seek revenge or bear a grudge against anyone among your people, but love your neighbour as yourself.' The 'stranger injunction' is from Leviticus 19:34.

102 Bishop Belo, 'The Dignity of the Individual', in *Reflections on the Universal Declaration of Human Rights: A 50th Anniversary Anthology*, ed. B. van der Heijden and B. Tahzib-Lei (The Hague: Kluwer, 1998), 59. The full quote from Genesis 5:1 is: 'On the day that God created man, He made him in the likeness of God.'

103 Khaled Abou El Fadl, 'Islam and the Challenge of Democratic Commitment', in *Does Human Rights Need God?* ed. Elizabeth M. Bucar and Barbra Barnett (Grand Rapids, MI: Eerdmans Publishing, 2005).

104 For example, John Witte and M. Christian Green, *Religion and Human Rights: An Introduction* (Oxford: Oxford University Press, 2012); George Newlands, *Christ and Human Rights* (Aldershot, UK: Ashgate, 2006); Roger Ruston, *Human Rights and the Image of God* (London: scm press, 2004); Carrie Gustafson and Peter Juviler, eds, *Religion and Human Rights: Competing Claims?* (New York: M.E. Sharpe, 1999); and Irene Bloom, J. Paul Martin and Wayne L. Proudfoot eds, *Religious Diversity and Human Rights* (New York: Columbia University Press, 1996).

105 Ruston, *Human Rights and the Image of God*, (London: scm press, 2004), 14.

106 Hossein Mehrpour, 'Human Rights in the Universal Declaration and the Religious Perspective', in van der Heijden and Tahzib-Lei, *Reflections on the Universal Declaration of Human Rights*, 191.

107 Max L. Stackhouse, 'Why Human Rights Needs God: A Christian Perspective', in Bucar and Barnett, *Does Human Rights Need God?* 25–40.

108 Ishay, *The History of Human Rights*, 17.

109 Morsink, *The Universal Declaration of Human Rights*, 295.

110 Articulated more fully in John Finnis, *Human Rights and the Common Good: Collected Essays Vol 111* (Oxford: Oxford University Press, 2011), 48.

111 John Stuart Mill, *On Liberty* (1859; London: Penguin, 1982), 72.

112 In *On Liberty*, Mill interestingly cites the 'despotic power of husbands' (p. 175) in the family as a site of legitimate state interference to prevent harm to wives and children, which was a refinement of the earlier gender-blind approach.

113 Morsink, *Inherent Human Rights*, 35. See also MacIntyre, *After Virtue*, 50.

114 Gray, *Enlightenment's Wake*, 204.

115 Alan Gerwith, *Human Rights: Essays on Justification and Applications* (Chicago: University of Chicago Press, 1982), 12. See also, Carlos Santiago Nino, *The Ethics of Human Rights* (Oxford: Clarendon, 1993), 34.

116 Klug, *Values for a Godless Age*, chapters 3 and 4.

117 Francesca Klug, 'Human Rights: Above Politics or a Creature of Politics?' *Policy and Politics Annual Lecture* 32, no 4 (October 2004): 563–72.
118 Morsink, *The Universal Declaration of Human Rights*, 281.
119 Quoted in Morsink, *The Universal Declaration of Human Rights*, 19.
120 Carl Wellman, *The Moral Dimension of Human Rights* (Oxford: Oxford University Press, 2011), 5.
121 Ibid., 55.
122 Mosink, *The Universal Declaration of Human Rights*, 283.
123 Ibid., 281.
124 Ibid., 283.
125 Morsink, *Inherent Human Rights*, 20.
126 Bikhu Parekh, *Rethinking Multiculturalism: Cultural Diversity and Political Theory* (Cambridge, MA: Harvard University Press, 2000), 134.
127 Winter and Prost, *Renee Cassin and Human Rights*, 239.
128 Morsink, *The Universal Declaration of Human Rights*, 245.
129 Louis Henkin, 'Introduction: The Human Rights Idea', in *The Age of Rights* (New York: Columbia University Press, 1990), 8.
130 Simpson, *Human Rights and the End of Empire*, 601.
131 Abdullahi A. An-Na'im, 'Islam and Human Rights: Beyond the Universality Debate', *American Society of International Law Proceedings* (2000): 95.
132 All quotes from UN Transcript, 98th and 99th meeting of the Third Committee, 9 October 1948 (see note 96).
133 Morsink, *The Universal Declaration of Human Rights*, 296.
134 All phrases are from the UDHR Preamble.
135 Anatole France, *The Red Lily* (Calman-Lévy, 1894), chapter 7. See Christopher McCrudden, ed., *Understanding Human Dignity* (Oxford: Oxford University Press, British Academy, 2013), for a detailed exposition of current debates about the meaning and implications of the idea of human dignity.
136 Quoted in Morsink, *Inherent Human Rights*, 209.
137 The 1776 American Declaration of Independence asserts that 'all men are created equal' whilst the 1789 French Declaration of Rights declares that 'men are born free and remain free and equal in rights.'
138 Quoted in Winter and Prost, *Renee Cassin and Human Rights*, 343.
139 Quoted in Bernard Schwartz, *A History of the Supreme Court* (Oxford: Oxford University Press, 1993), 119.
140 Convention on the Elimination of All Forms of Racial Discrimination (CERD, 1965), Convention on the Elimination of All Forms of Discrimination Against Women (CEDAW, 1979), Convention on the Rights of the Child (1989), Convention on the Rights of Persons with Disability (2006).
141 Quoted in Morsink, *The Universal Declaration of Human Rights*, 118.
142 Ibid., 278.
143 Ibid., 274.
144 Quoted in Winter and Prost, *Renee Cassin and Human Rights*, 252.
145 Quoted in Morsink, *The Universal Declaration of Human Rights*, 71.
146 Paine, *Rights of Man*, 114.
147 See Jeremy Waldron, ed., *Nonsense upon Stilts: Bentham, Burke and Marx on the Rights of Man* (London: Methuen, 1987), 53. Also see Klug, 'Human Rights: Philosophy, Politics or Law?'
148 See earlier, and Klug, 'Rights and Righteousness: Friends or Foe?' 1.
149 Quoted by Mary Ann Glendon, 'Introduction', in Malik, *The Challenge of Human Rights*, 2.
150 ECOSOC paper E/CN/4/SR.14, 5 February 1947, 4.
151 Ibid., 5.
152 Ibid., 6.
153 ECOSOC paper E/800, 98th meeting of the 3rd Committee of the UN General Assembly, 9 October 1948, 87.

154 Morsink, *The Universal Declaration of Human Rights*, 244.

155 Ibid., 248.

156 Alan Gerwith, *The Community of Rights* (Chicago: University of Chicago Press, 1996), 6.

157 Erica-Irene Daes, *Freedom of the Individual under the Law: A Study of the Individual's Duties to the Community and the Limitations on Human Rights and Freedoms under Article 29 of the UDHR* (United Nations, 1990), 19.

158 See, for example, Lord Steyn in *Brown v Stott* [2001] 2 WLR 817 discussed in Section II.

159 Onora O'Neill, 'Agents of Justice', in *Global Justice*, ed. Thomas Pogge (Oxford: Blackwell, 2001), 193.

160 Ibid., 191.

161 Morsink, *Inherent Human Rights*, 43.

162 Judgment of the International Military Tribunal, transcript of proceedings, 1 October 1946.

163 Quoted in Morsink, *Inherent Human Rights*, 181.

164 See, for example, Anne Phillips, 'Who Is the Human in Human Rights?' *Open Democracy*, 26 August 2014. See also Margaret Thornton, ed., *Public and Private: Feminist Legal Debate* (Oxford: Oxford University Press, 1995), and Rebecca Cook, *Human Rights of Women: National and International Perspectives* (Philadelphia, PA: University of Pennsylvania Press, 1994).

165 Andrew Clapham, 'Rights in the Private Sphere: Non-state Actors, Paramilitary Organisations, Regulating Business and Other Private Relationships', unpublished paper, LSE Certificate in International Human Rights Law and Practice, 8 December 2014. See also Clapham, *Human Rights in the Private Sphere* (Oxford: Clarendon Press, 1996), for a detailed legal analysis of the subject.

166 *Eweida and Others v United Kingdom* (2013) 57 EHRR 8.

167 Ibid.

168 *SAS v France* (2014) ECHR 695 at 147;5–7;17.

169 Francesca Klug, 'Freedom of Expression Must Include the Licence to Offend?' *The Journal of Religion and Human Rights* (2006) 1: 225–7.

170 Both ECHR, Article 10, and International Covenant on Civil and Political Rights, Article 19, refer to the 'duties' and 'responsibilities' attached to free speech.

171 Ronald Dworkin, *Taking Rights Seriously* (London: Duckworth, 1977), xi. Dworkin does qualify this position on page xv and in chapter 12 to develop a more nuanced relationship between individual and collective rights, both deriving from 'concern and respect'.

172 ECOSOC paper, 9 October 1948, 110 (see note 153).

173 Malik, *The Challenge of Human Rights*, 235.

174 Samuel Moyn, *The Last Utopia*, 122, 197. Moyn's thesis will be referenced further in Section II of this book.

175 Quoted in Morsink, *The Universal Declaration of Human Rights*, 38.

176 ECOSOC paper, 3 (see note 150).

177 Morsink, *The Universal Declaration of Human Rights*, 98.

178 Singh, *The Development of Human Rights Thought*, 4.

179 ECOSOC paper E/CN.4/SR.50, HRC 3rd Session, summary record of the 50th meeting, 27 May 1948, 10. The irony of Cassin using the term 'brotherhood' in this context seems to have been lost on him.

180 Morsink, *The Universal Declaration of Human Rights*, 327.

181 Hannah Arendt, *The Origins of Totalitarianism* (1951; New York: Harcourt, Brace and Jovanovich, 1979), 296–7.

182 Seyla Benhabib, *Dignity in Adversity: Human Rights in Troubled Times* (Cambridge: Polity, 2011), 13.

183 Ibid., 17.

184 ECOSOC paper E/800, 11 October 1948, 122 (see note 153).

185 Ibid., 24 November 1948, 655 (my emphasis; see note 153).

186 Ibid., 6 October 1948, 92 (see note 153).

187   ECOSOC paper E/CN.4/SR.8, 8th meeting of the HRC, 31 January 1947, 3.

188   Quoted in Morsink, *Inherent Human Rights*, 62.

189   Michael Freeman, 'Human Rights: Asian and the West', in *Human Rights and International Relations in the Asia-Pacific*, ed. T.H. Tang (London: Pinter, 1995), 13, 17.

190   Jack Donnelly, *Universal Human Rights in Theory and Practice* (Ithaca, NY: Cornell University Press, 2003), 86.

191   Quoted in Morsink, *Inherent Human Rights*, 63.

192   An-Na'im, 'Islam and Human Rights', 38.

193   Quoted in Morsink, *Inherent Human Rights*, 63.

194   See Douglas Hodgson, *The Protection of Individual Duty within the Human Rights System* (Farnham, UK: Ashgate, 2003), 124.

195   Freeman, 'Human Rights', 14.

196   Article 4(h) of the Constitutive Act of the AU affirms the 'right of the Union to intervene in a Member State pursuant to a decision of the Assembly in respect of grave circumstances, namely war crimes, genocide and crimes against humanity'.

197   Quoted in Winter and Prost, *Renee Cassin and Human Rights*, 165.

198   Report of the International Commission on Intervention and State Sovereignty, 'The Responsibility to Protect' (2001).

199   In December 2014 the US Senate Select Committee on Intelligence published a classified version of its *Study of the CIA's Detention and Interrogation Program*, confirming that the CIA systematically tortured detainees in secret prisons in different parts of the world. See Shami Chakrabarti, *On Liberty* (London: Penguin, 2014), for a penetrating analysis of earlier related developments.

200   Gray, *Enlightenment's Wake*, xvii.

201   See Chaloka Beyani, 'Reconstituting the Universal: Human Rights as a Regional Idea', in *The Cambridge Companion to Human Rights Law*, ed. Conor Gearty and Costas Douzinas (Cambridge: Cambridge University Press, 2012), chapter 9.

202   For a critique of this and other aspects of the ICC see Stephen Hopgood, *The Endtime of Human Rights* (Ithaca, NY: Cornell University Press, 2013), 142–3.

203   An-Na'im, 'Islam and Human Rights', 101. See also An-Na'im, 'The Interdisciplinarity of Human Rights', in Gearty and Douzinas, *The Cambridge Companion to Human Rights Law*, chapter 5.

204   Mary Robinson, speech to Amnesty International, Belfast, 6 May 2011.

205   See, for example, Nadje Al-Ali, 'Sexualised Violence in Iraq: How to Understand and Fight It', *Open Democracy*, 29 September 2014.

206   Karima Bennoune, *Your Fatwa Does Not Apply Here: Untold Stories from the Fight against Muslim Fundamentalism* (New York: Norton, 2013), 22.

207   Ibid., 316.

208   Yanaki B. Stoilvov, 'Are Human Rights Universal?' in *Human Rights in Philosophy and Practice*, ed. Burton M. Leiser and Tom D. Campbell (Aldershot, UK: Ashgate, 2001), 99.

209   John Gray, 'The Best We Can Hope for Is Tolerance', *The Spectator*, 17 February 2007.

210   Reported in *The Guardian*, 23 July 2014.

211   Of course UN mechanisms themselves are often found wanting. See 'UN Rights Chief Rebukes Security Council for Failures to Act', *Yahoo News UK*, 21 August 2014. See also Rosa Freedman, *The United National Human Rights Council: A Critique and Early Assessment* (London: Routledge, 2013).

212   Grand juries declined to prosecute the white police officers who, in separate incidents, shot eighteen-year-old Michael Brown in Ferguson, Missouri, in August 2014, and forty-three-year-old Eric Garner in Staten Island, New York, in July 2014. Amateur video footage established that Garner gasped 'I can't breathe!' while being placed in a chokehold as he was arrested for selling loose, untaxed cigarettes. In addition, twelve-year-old Tamir Rice was shot dead by a police officer on 22 November 2014 after he brandished a replica gun.

213   H.L.A. Hart, 'Are There Any Natural Rights?' *Philosophical Review*, 64, No. 2 (1955), 175–91.

214   Jospeh Raz, *The Morality of Freedom* (Oxford: Clarendon, 1988).

215 For example, in Jurgen Habermas, *Between Facts and Norms: Contributions to a Discourse Theory of Law and Democracy* (Cambridge, MA: MIT Press, 1996).

216 Morsink, *Inherent Human Rights*, 56.

217 Ibid., 119.

218 Ibid., 31.

219 Ibid., 67.

220 Isaiah Berlin, *Four Essays on Liberty* (Oxford: Oxford University Press, 1969).

221 Nussbaum, *Frontiers of Justice*, 77–8.

222 In Charles R. Beitz, *The Idea of Human Rights* (Oxford: Oxford University Press, 2009).

223 Sen, 'Elements of a Theory of Human Rights', 333.

224 Ibid., 323.

225 Conor Gearty, *Can Human Rights Survive?* Hamlyn Lectures (Cambridge: Cambridge University Press, 2006), 39.

226 Richard Rorty, *Philosophy and Social Hope* (London: Penguin, 1999), xxxii.

227 Ibid., 87.

228 Ibid., 85.

229 Beitz, *The Idea of Human Rights*, 197.

230 Ibid., 104.

231 Waldron, op cit note 147.

232 Alidair MacIntyre, *After Virtue* (South Bend, Indiana: University of Notre Dame Press, 1981), 69.

233 C. Gearty 'Human Rights: The Necessary Quest for Foundations', in *The Meanings of Rights: The Philosophy and Social Theory of Human Rights*, ed. Costas Douzinas and Conor Gearty (Cambridge: Cambridge University Press, 2014), 32, 33.

234 Ibid., 38.

235 Ibid., 30 (Gearty's emphasis).

236 Jean H. Quataert, *Advocating Dignity: Human Rights Mobilisation in Global Politics* (Philadelphia: Penn Press, 2009), 3.

237 Benhabib, *Dignity in Adversity*, 19. See also Moyn, *The Last Utopia*.

238 Mary Midgley, 'Towards an Ethic of Global Responsibility', in *Human Rights in Global Politics*, ed. Tim Dunne and Nicholas J. Wheeler (Cambridge: Cambridge University Press, 1999), 160–1.

239 Benhabib, *Dignity in Adversity*, 72. See also note 208.

240 Gearty, *Can Human Rights Survive?* 67–8.

241 Douzinas and Gearty, *The Meanings of Rights*, 1.

242 Louis Henkin, 'Religion, Religions and Human Rights', in Bucar and Barnett, *Does Human Rights Need God?* 154.

243 Seyla Benhabib, 'Another Universalism: On the Unity and Diversity of Human Rights', *Address to the Eastern Division of the American Philosophical Association*, Proceedings and Addresses of the American Philosophical Association, Vol. 81, No. 2, Nov 2007, 7–32. 12.

244 Gearty, *Can Human Rights Survive?* 42.

245 Nelson Mandela quoted in van der Heijden and Tahzib-Lei, *Reflections on the UDHR*, 256.

246 Benhabib, *Dignity in Adversity*, 74.

247 Malik, *The Challenge of Human Rights*, 25.

248 Quoted in Morsink, *The Universal Declaration of Human Rights*, 33.

249 The final estimate of civilian casualties in Operation Protective Edge, which began on 8 July and ended on 26 August 2014, according to the UN Office for the Coordination of Humanitarian Affairs (OCHA), was 2,189 Gazans killed (including 513 children), 66 Israeli soldiers and 5 Israeli civilians (including one child).

250 Navi Pillay, 'Human Rights Situation in the Occupied Palestinian Territory, Including East Jerusalem', address to an emergency meeting of the UN Human Rights Council, 23 July 2014.

251 According to the Talmudic story, when the first-century BC rabbinic sage Hillel was asked to relate the whole Torah on one foot he replied 'That which is hateful to you, do not unto another: This is the whole Torah. The rest is commentary – [and now] go study.'

SECTION I
Anthology

1

HUMAN RIGHTS

A common standard for all peoples?

Reclaiming Britishness:
Living together after 11 September and the rise of the radical rights
(Foreign Policy Centre, 2002)

The link between tall towers, diverse communities and a common language is of biblical proportions. Literally. In the Old Testament story of the Tower of Babel we learn that those who build high to boast loud risk being brought down to size and that the struggle to understand each other is made much more difficult when we speak different languages, both literally and metaphorically. We have been confronted with these issues, it seems, since the beginning of recorded history. In the year 2002 – as we grope around in the aftermath of September 11th and tensions and disturbances closer to home – we find we are still grappling with them.

September 11th

When those Gemini planes sliced through the twin towers we learnt what unites us as well as what separates us as human beings. Anger, bewilderment, empathy, shock. These are profoundly human responses which momentarily, at least, bound together nearly everyone in the UK. We walked down the street, got on a bus, went in a shop, knowing that we were all reverberating from this terrifying event.

Yet even as our common humanity was underlined by the horror we shared at the intentional mass slaughter of our fellow human beings, we knew that we could not all experience this atrocity in identical terms. Inevitably we viewed it through the prism of our own backgrounds and experiences.

If the significance of September 11th is as much about lifting the veil on changes that had already happened as about ushering in a new era, one consequence was to illuminate the extent to which multiple identities had become commonplace in the UK. Whereas once only international relations experts were wheeled out to explain events on a world scale now different sections of the British community were frequently called upon to do so.

Entire communities were held to account. Muslims up and down the country felt they had to prove they did not support the attacks and that their religion did not condone such atrocities. Many were physically or verbally harassed simply because they were Muslim (and sometimes because they were Sikh but mistaken for Muslims). Some were picked up by the police under anti-terrorist legislation, for the most part to be released or charged only with immigration offences.

Afghanis, many of whom were asylum seekers who fled the brutal Taliban regime, found themselves moved to challenge the portrayal of their country as irredeemably primitive and misogynistic. Members of the Jewish community, regardless of their political affiliations, were linked with Israel, which was in turn blamed for the whole conflagration, regardless of the many factors involved.

Above and beyond this, the rest of the world had encroached on these shores. It can hardly have escaped the notice of anyone in this country that events far away can determine our fate day to day from the state of our economy to our personal security. To that extent we are all global Britains now.

Communal conflict

It was against this backdrop, on 9 December, that the Home Secretary, David Blunkett, declared in an interview with *The Independent on Sunday* that:

> "We have norms of acceptability and those who come into our home – for that is what it is – should accept those norms just as we would have to do if we went elsewhere."[1]

At the point when most of us were starting to feel our way in this evolving global environment of plural loyalties and identities, the Home Secretary articulated a vision of the UK which revolved around 'we' whose 'home' this is and 'those' who need to "accept" our "norms." It was like an echo from a previous era.

While emphasising in the same interview that he was "in favour of diversity" and "the interplay of different cultures" Mr Blunkett was widely quoted as adding that "we won't tolerate the intolerable under the guise of cultural difference," citing "enforced marriages" and "genital mutilation" as practices that "are unacceptable in Britain."[2]

The background to these statements heralded from events prior to September 11th. During the spring and early summer of 2001 there were disturbances between different sections of the community in a number of Northern towns, notably Oldham, Bradford and Burnley. With substantial evidence of infiltration by the British National Party, longstanding tensions over the distribution of resources between Asian and white communities in these deprived urban areas, erupted into violent conflict over a period of many weeks.[3]

Among other initiatives, the Home Secretary established a Review Team, led by Ted Cantle, on local policies to promote social cohesion. It was on the eve of the publication of this report which recommended "a greater sense of citizenship based on (a few) common principles"[4] that the Home Secretary made his 'norms of acceptability' statement to *The Independent*. A few months later, in a White Paper on 'immigration asylum and citizenship,' the Government expanded the scope of its concern about 'cultural differences' to include marriages to partners from abroad (or more specifically the Asian sub-continent). There is, the paper stated:

> "a discussion to be had within those communities that continue the practice of arranged marriages as to whether more of these could be undertaken within the settled community here."[5]

Expanding on this reference, Mr Blunkett subsequently said:

> "We need to be able to encourage people to respond, particularly young women, who do actually want to be able to marry someone who speaks their language – namely English – who has been educated in the same way as they have, and has similar social attitudes."[6]

The debate on 'Britishness'

The ensuing reaction to these references in the press and broadcasting media was as polarised as the communities whose cohesion was at the centre of the debate. The *Sun*'s Littlejohn applauded the Home Secretary's "bold attempt to reign in the tyranny of multiculturalism and forge a common British identity."[7] Nick Griffin, leader of the British National Party promised to "quote David Blunkett, but only saying we've been saying these kind of things."[8] Lord Tebbit said "We should all be grateful to Mr Blunkett for stating what most of us had long believed."[9]

The Home Secretary received vocal support for some of his statements, in particular the importance he attached to learning English for participating in civic life.[10] A subsequent BBC poll found widespread approval for this proposal.[11] However Milena Buyum of the National Assembly of Racism spoke in similar terms to a number of other commentators when she said:

> "Telling established British communities whom they should or should not marry is quite abhorrent to these communities. To propose interfering in their private choice of who to marry is a big infringement of their cultural rights."[12]

The esteemed *The Independent* columnist Yasmin Alibhi-Brown lamented the implication:

> "that people of colour entering this country are coming into someone else's home and must therefore always conform, never dissent from the set norms, and always be grateful."[13]

The term 'British' she suggested:

> "has lost its old meanings and symbols. It is time to bury that version and plant a new vision which brings together all the tribes of Britain."[14]

Yet the Home Secretary, both through the White Paper and many subsequent statements, emphasised that it was not "assimilation to a prevailing monoculture"[15] which the Government was proposing.[16] On the contrary, "diversity" is endorsed as "a source of pride" which "helps to explain our cultural vitality, the strength of our economy and our strong international links."[17] According to the White Paper on citizenship, notably subtitled *Diversity in Modern Britain*:

> "Common citizenship is not about cultural uniformity, nor it is born out of some narrow and outdated view of what it means to be 'British.' The Government welcomes the richness of the cultural diversity which immigrants have brought to the UK – our society is multi-cultural and is shaped by its diverse peoples."[18]

This is as strong a statement in support of an evolving sense of 'Britishness' as you are likely to see anywhere.

So how is it that protagonists on all sides read a similar message into the Home Office's string of statements on citizenship, only differing in their reactions to it? How is it that they all understood the message to be, not the value of difference, but the requirement of conformity? For or against, what people heard, in *Evening Standard* prose, was that "immigrant communities should respect the British way of life and not engage in practices which might have been acceptable in Africa or Asia, but are not British."[19] Or in the inimitable style of a *Daily Star* leader "When in Rome, do as the Romans do."[20]

Integration into what?

The government's stated aspiration in the White Paper is "social integration."[21] To this end, it is proposed that we develop a "stronger understanding of what citizenship means" to replace the historically "weak sense of what active citizenship should entail."[22]

The components of this 'stronger citizenship' are not spelt out in full. But the proposed contours are quite clear.

First, citizenship should be 'active' in the sense of implying "full participation in British society."[23]

Second, diversity is not only accepted but positively welcomed: "We want British citizenship positively to embrace the diversity of background, culture and faiths that is one of the hallmarks of Britain in the 21st century."[24]

Third, the naturalisation process should be orientated towards learning about becoming British. To this end aspiring citizens will have to pass an English language test, swear a slightly updated oath of allegiance to the Queen which "reflects a commitment to citizenship, cohesion and community" and attend a new citizenship ceremony. A short statement about "what it means to be a British citizen" will also be issued to all new applicants.[25]

Fourth, integration is defined to mean acceptance of certain basic values:

> "The laws, rules and practices which govern our democracy uphold our commitment to the equal worth and dignity of all our citizens. It will sometimes be necessary to confront some cultural practices which conflict with these basic values-such as those which deny women the right to participate as equal citizens."[26]

Without any elaboration, the White Paper proposes that "the Human Rights Act 1998 can be viewed as a key source of values that British citizens should share." This unexpected link between the new Human Rights Act (HRA) and the search for a set of common values which could aid 'cohesion' and 'social integration,' begs more questions than answers.

First, how can a statute that confers legal rights on individuals be a source of common values? Second, is the White Paper inferring that the HRA is essentially an expression of British norms? Third, if not, then what is the source of values in the Act and do they have the potential to aid social cohesion in a diverse society?

The Human Rights Act as a statement of values

Responding to these in order, the link between the Human Rights Act and the values which define modern Britain is not immediately clear. The only time when the Act reaches public consciousness, by and large, is when the tabloid press has fun at its expense following a court judgement it does not like.[27] But the HRA is effectively our bill of rights and bills of rights, as is well known, are more than legal documents. In 18th century France and America, and more recently in Canada and South Africa, they have helped to reflect a country's national identity by affirming the principles it stands for in a simple document expressed in broad terms.

Ronald Dworkin, the renowned law professor has explained:

> "Most contemporary constitutions declare individual rights against the government in very broad and abstract ways . . . the moral reading proposes that we all – judges, lawyers, citizens – interpret and apply these abstract clauses on the understanding that they invoke moral principles about political decency and justice."[28]

Of course what sets the British route to a bill of rights apart from many others is that the HRA was passed without the kind of social upheaval or constitutional revolution that generally precedes such a development, although this gradualism is by no means exclusive to the UK.[29] Labour promised to incorporate the European Convention on Human Rights (ECHR) into UK law in its 1997 manifesto after a long campaign by radical lawyers and civil rights groups which was generally speaking lost on the rest of the population.[30]

Lord Browne-Wilkinson, the former Law Lord, has described the ECHR as a "code of morals."[31] The principles it upholds like the right not to be subject to inhuman or degrading treatment, to have one's dignity, lifestyle and privacy respected, to listen to one's conscience, to speak and protest freely and choose whether or not to marry and found a family – and not to be discriminated against in the exercise of these rights – together paint a picture of what a society based on mutual respect and tolerance should look like. Rights to life, liberty, security and a fair trial and prohibitions on forced labour, torture and inhuman punishment all point to a vision of what a just society might be.

Taken as a whole, the rights and limitations set down in the ECHR are described by the European Court of Human Rights as the "values of a democratic society"[32] which are "pluralism, tolerance and broadmindedness."[33] But in case there is any misunderstanding, ". . . democracy does not simply mean that the views of a majority must always prevail; a balance must be achieved which ensures the fair and proper treatment of minorities and avoids any abuse of a dominant position."[34]

Our bill of rights is different from all other Acts in that, expressed in very general terms, its aim is to ensure that all our laws and policies are informed by broad ethical values. Fundamental rights to dignity and respect enshrined in the HRA can be translated into practice which informs everyday life. If the values in the Act were incorporated into training programmes (much as equalities legislation has been), then we should no longer read about old ladies being tied to toilet seats in care homes or people with learning difficulties refused permission to freely associate in day centres.

In its early days, the ministers responsible for piloting the HRA through Parliament were keen to emphasise its moral content. According to former Home Secretary Jack Straw "deciding day to day legal questions on the basis of such fundamental ethical principles, set out in statute, is a new departure."[35] Or as Lord Irvine, the Lord Chancellor, put it, the HRA "will create a more explicitly moral approach to decisions and decision-making."[36]

Human rights as British values?

The Human Rights Act may be distilled from a set of ethical values but do these have a nationality? Could the Act be fairly described, to quote Michael Wills, then minister with responsibility for human rights in the Lord Chancellors Department, as "a statutory expression of historic British freedoms and rights?"[37]

It is fair to say that many Convention rights were already well recognised in the UK long before the HRA was a gleam in ministers' eyes. Indeed the origin of some of these rights, like the right to a fair trial or prohibitions on inhuman and degrading treatment, can be directly traced back to these shores.[38] Other entitlements, on the other hand, like the right to a private life and to dignity were not fully recognised in English law before the HRA came into force.

However, despite the common boast that Britain is a country which cherishes civil liberties, freedom and the rule of law, in the absence, since 1688, of any written charter or statement of rights this take on 'being British' has competed with other more enduring ones.

The symbols which have emerged down the ages as representative of the UK – in particular the monarchy, the Anglican church and the Empire[39] – do not unambiguously reflect "historic British freedoms and rights",[40] to say the least. Whilst the loss of empire, for example, is still routinely portrayed as a trauma the UK has only just recovered from, the reality is that for about a third of the population of London this loss was their liberation. Learning English and speaking a common language will not alter the different meaning attached to such emblems by various sections of the community.

The reality is that traditional British ideals of liberty and freedom have both contributed to, and developed from, evolving international human rights norms. The English common law failed to give any recognition to the principle of non-discrimination, for example, save to require inn-keepers to accept all travellers who were "in a reasonably fit condition to be received."[41] It took a series of Acts in the 1960s and 1970s to remedy this, 20 or more years after the UN's Universal Declaration of Human Rights (UDHR) established that protection from discrimination was a fundamental human right.

What is the source of human rights values?

The values expressed in the European Convention on Human Rights (ECHR), incorporated into our law through the HRA, are directly drawn from the 1948 Universal Declaration of Human Rights (UDHR). It is often said that British lawyers had a significant role in drafting the ECHR. This is true but as the preamble to the European Convention recognises, its broad principles were already established by the UDHR.

The impetus for drafting the Universal Declaration was the devastation of the second world war. The purpose was to set down a set of common norms that spoke to people of all religions and creeds, as well as none. The consequence was a document drafted by men and women from different communities around the globe (and without whom the UDHR might have looked quite different) drawing upon all major religions and philosophical viewpoints.[42] The values it upholds cannot be laid claim to by an exclusive national or social group.

The UDHR represented the start of a new phase in human rights thinking. It established the principle that all human beings are bestowed with inalienable rights from the moment of their birth. This was not as a result of their nationality or citizenship, but as a consequence of their common humanity.

Whilst it is not a legally binding treaty as such, the Universal Declaration has exerted a huge moral and legal influence around the world. The rights within it have formed the basis of all the subsequent international and regional human rights treaties. Its provisions have been cited or used so often over the years that it is generally accepted that parts of it are now 'customary international law' and hence binding on states.

The UDHR is essentially an ethical document which underlines the values of dignity, equality and community as well as liberty and justice. It sets down a minimum vision of how human beings could live with each other in peace and mutual respect. Mary Robinson, the UN High Commissioner for Human Rights and former President of Ireland presents the Declaration in these terms:

> "My vision of the Universal Declaration . . . strays beyond its legal and political significance . . . I would venture to suggest that it has become an elevating force on the events of our world because it can be seen to embody the legal, moral and philosophical beliefs held true by all peoples and because it applies to all."[43]

This has meant that, whilst the claim that the UDHR equally reflects the values of all communities in the world is hotly – and quite reasonably – contested, it has proved possible for different religious leaders to square human rights discourse with their own beliefs.[44] The renowned South African Bishop, Desmond Tutu, and Hossein Mehrpour, Professor of Law in Teheran and an Islamic scholar, are both from this tradition. Mehrpour writes:

> "apart from that aspect of religion which consists of the important duty to spiritually guide and instruct, there are no serious differences or contradictions in their social aspects and application between religious teachings and human rights."[45]

Given these influences, it is unsurprising that the post war rights vision does not begin and end with isolated individuals pitted against mighty states; individuals who, in the words of the French Declaration of Rights, should have the power "to do whatever is not injurious to others." Instead it is a vision in which the "personality" of individuals, can only effectively develop in "community" with others to whom we all owe "duties."[46] This is an approach to rights established in the very first article of the UDHR which reads almost like a commandment:

> "All human beings . . . should act towards one another in a spirit of brotherhood."

This emphasis on the social nature of human beings and their responsibilities to others and the wider community reflected the beliefs of many of the delegates. But, as importantly, it also stemmed from the task the drafters set themselves. This was not just to 'set the people free' but to find common values in which the liberties of individuals would be respected without weakening the bonds of the wider community, so essential for human development. It was a different understanding of the concept of freedom than the West had earlier embraced.

Values to aid social cohesion?

This attempt at synthesising 'communitarian' themes with a more classically liberal approach to protecting individual rights, is also reflected in the European Convention on Human Rights, and hence the HRA. Some ECHR rights are expressed in absolute terms like the right not to be subject to torture or slavery. But most of the rights are qualified or limited in some way, usually to protect the rights of others or the needs of the community as a whole. Freedom of expression, for example, "since it carries with it duties and responsibilities," may carry restrictions that are "necessary in a democratic society."[47]

Flowing from such injunctions, there is inherent in virtually the whole of the ECHR a search to find a fair balance between the protection of individual rights and the interests of the wider community.[48] But it is not a 'balance' in the sense that fundamental rights and its limitations are given equal weight. The case law developed by the European Court of Human Rights has established that the principle of 'proportionality' is pivotal to finding this balance. This concept is as central to human rights thinking as any of the substantive rights. It means that any limitation on individual rights must not only be necessary to pursue a legitimate goal, like protecting society from a public health scare, but must not go beyond what is strictly necessary to achieve that purpose. Encouraging and persuading parents to vaccinate their children against contagious diseases, yes. Imprisoning them for not doing so, no.

It is misguided to understand the Human Rights Act, therefore, purely as a legal document designed to protect individual liberties from abuse by the state, regardless of the implications for society as a collective entity. Although it is very important to be clear that human rights are not contingent on responsible behaviour, they can be legitimately limited, in a proportionate way, to protect the fundamental rights of others.

Conclusion: human rights and citizenship

Would David Blunkett have inspired the same reaction to his statements about British citizenship if he had suggested that human rights values provide the core of what can unite the diverse communities which make up the UK? If, as the Cantle report suggests, "many of the present problems" seem to owe a great deal to the failure "to communicate and agree a set of clear values that can govern behaviour"[49] is it helpful for anyone to suggest or imply that it is specifically British values that we all need to learn?

Cantle, in fact, resisted the temptation to set out what these core values might be. The White Paper, as we have seen, suggests that the 1998 Human Rights Act could provide a key source but omits to expand on what its values are. This is a shame given the common assumption that human rights is a Western creed which worships at the altar of individualism at the expense of the wider community and as such is incompatible with religious perspectives, in particular Islam.

In reality, as shown above, post-war (or 'second wave') human rights thinking was much richer than this. Among other creeds, it drew on religious Islam – as well as secular liberalism – and emphasised the needs of the wider community (as distinct from the state) as well as the rights of individuals. Its origins and authors should not be confused with what Yasmin Alibhai-Brown calls "the founding fathers of liberalism" who "believed utterly in the superiority of European societies."[50]

This does not make human rights an uncontestable set of values. Of course not. The very fact that it is not a religious faith means that its underlying principles must be open to challenge and will never be universally accepted. But the vision of human dignity, equality and community inherent in 'second wave' rights thinking is universally *applicable* and in this sense speaks to those of all faiths and creeds and those of none.

It is our bill of rights which can provide the legally enforceable 'bottom line' of unacceptable practices that many commentators seek. Practices like 'female genital mutilation' – or for that matter internet child pornography – violate universal human rights norms. That is why they should be outlawed; not because they are an 'offense' to specifically British customs.

A bit of humility, in other words, would not come amiss in the search for social cohesion. But then that was what the story the Tower of Babel tried to teach us, long before the word tower became indelibly associated with a particular date.

Notes

1 *The Independent on Sunday*, 9.12.2001.
2 *The Independent on Sunday*, 9.12.2001.
3 See John Lloyd, 'Poor Whites,' *Prospect*, June 2000. See also John Lloyd 'The End of Multiculturalism,' *New Statesman*, 27.5.2002.
4 Ted Cantle, *Community Cohesion, A Report of the Independent Review Team*, Home Office, December 2001, p10.
5 *Secure Borders, Safe Haven: integration with diversity in modern Britain*, White Paper, CM 5387, 2002, p18.
6 Quoted in *The Independent*, 8.2.2002.
7 *Sun,* 11.12.01.
8 Quoted in the *Financial Times*, 11.12.01.
9 *Mail on Sunday*, 10.2.02.
10 Notably from Jagdeesh Singh of the Sikh Community Action Network and Manzoor Moghal of the Muslim Council of Britain.
11 A Poll for BBC News published in May 2002 found that 75% of black people and 68% of Asians agreed with the Home Secretary's plans for English and citizenship classes for new citizens.

12 *The Guardian*, 8.2.02. See also letters by Faz Hakim, former race relations advisor to the PM, *The Guardian*, 12.12.01. and from Simon Woolley of Operation Black Vote et al, *The Independent*, 11.12.01.

13 *The Independent*, 10.12.01.

14 *The Independent*, 16.12.01. For a discussion of these issues see Yasmin Alibhi-Brown, *After Multiculturalism*, Foreign Policy Centre, 2000. See also Runnymede Trust, *Commission on the Future of Multi-Ethnic Britain*, 2000.

15 White Paper, op cit, p10.

16 In a landmark speech on 'Race, Equality and Community Cohesion' to the Social Market Foundation on 26.6.2002, David Blunkett remarked that 'Britain has changed significantly in the last the thirty years. We have become a diverse and tolerant society, enriched by immigration . . .'

17 Ibid.

18 White Paper, op cit, p29.

19 Leader, *Evening Standard*, 12.12.01.

20 Leader, *Daily Star*, 10.12.01.

21 White Paper, p10.

22 Ibid.

23 Ibid, p29.

24 Ibid.

25 Ibid, p34.

26 Ibid, p3.

27 Often these are judgements by the European Court of Human Rights rather than the domestic courts – for example on the respective roles of judges and Home Secretaries in determining the length of sentence of life prisoners. The press has notably been less hostile to the HRA since it has discovered that it has much to gain itself from its free expression provisions which were not explicitly set down in statute before the HRA.

28 Ronald Dworkin, 'The Moral Reading of the Constitution,' *New York Review*, 21.3.96.

29 The New Zealand Bill of Rights was introduced in 1990 in not dissimilar circumstances to the UK.

30 See Francesca Klug *Values for a Godless Age, the story of the UK's new bill of rights*, Penguin 2000 for a full description of the events leading up to the implementation of the 1998 Human Rights Act.

31 Lord Browne-Wilkinson, 'The Impact on Judicial Reasoning,' in *The Impact of the Human Rights Bill on English Law*, Basil Markesinis (ed), Clarendon, 1998, pp22–23.

32 *Kjeldsen Busk Madson and Peterson v Belgium* (1979–80) 1 EHRR 711, para 53.

33 *Handyside v UK* (1979–80) 1 EHRR 737.

34 *Young, James & Webster v UK* (1982) 4 EHRR 38, para 63.

35 Jack Straw, 'Building a Human Rights Culture,' *Address to Civil Service College Seminar*, 9 December 1999.

36 'The Development of Human Rights in Britain under an Incorporated Convention on Human Rights,' Tom Sergant Memorial Lecture, *Public Law*, summer 1998, p236.

37 Quoted in an interview with Rachel Sylvester, *Daily Telegraph*, 15.12.2001.

38 From the Magna Carta and the 1688 Bill of Rights respectively.

39 It is extraordinary how enduring these symbols are. When the Queen Mother died in April 2002, for example, commentators routinely referred to her as 'the last Empress of India' without any reflection on what that title might evoke for British citizens of Indian ancestry.

40 Michael Wills, op cit.

41 *Constantine v Imperial Hotels Ltd*, 1944. The 'basic interests' prioritised by the Common law prior to the HRA were personal liberty, due process, property rights, reputation and free expression. See F. Klug, K. Starmer & S. Weir, *The Three Pillars of Liberty, political rights and freedoms in the UK*, Routledge, 1996.

42 Including Islam, Socialism and Confucianism. However, as a result of colonialism sub-Saharan Africa, in particular, was massively underrepresented.

43 Mary Robinson, 'The Universal Declaration of Human Rights, the international keystone of human dignity,' in *Reflections on the Universal Declaration of Human Rights: A 50th Anniversary Anthology*, Kluwer, 1998.

44 See Bikhu Parekh, 'Non-ethnocentric universalism', in *Human Rights in Global Politics*, Cambridge University Press, 1999; Mahmood Monshipouri, 'The Muslim World Half a Century after the Universal Declaration of Human Rights: progress and obstacles,' *Netherlands Quarterly of Human Rights*, Vol 16 No 3, September 1998; and Michael J. Perry 'Are human rights universal? The relativist challenge and related matters,' in *Human Rights Quarterly*, 19 (1997) pp461–509.

45 Hossein Mehrpour, 'Human Rights in the Universal Declaration and the Religious Perspective,' in *Reflections on the Universal Declaration of Human Rights*, op cit.

46 UDHR, Article 29 (1) reads: 'Everyone has duties to the community in which alone the free and full development of his personality is possible.'

47 ECHR Article 10.

48 See, for example, the case of *Soering v UK* (1989) 11 EHRR 439, para 89.

49 op cit p18.

50 *The Independent*, 15.10.01.

2

THE UNIVERSAL DECLARATION OF HUMAN RIGHTS

60 years on

Public Law, April 2009, 205–17

2008 is quite a year for 60th anniversaries.[1] The National Health Service is 60 years old this year. So is Prince Charles, the World Health Organisation, the game of Scrabble and, of course, the BBC Radio 4 programme "Any Questions?". At a special birthday edition, the "Any Questions?" panellists were asked about the most significant developments of the last 60 years. Some mentioned the NHS, others the internet and globalisation. But no one uttered a word about the Universal Declaration of Human Rights and the revolution in rights consciousness it gave birth to. I found myself wondering what the drafters of that famous document would think if they were to come back today and hear that this illustrious panel had overlooked their contribution?

A cast of five ghosts assembled before me to give their verdict on the last 60 years. First up was Eleanor Roosevelt, the wife of the US president. As the first chair of the fledgling United Nations' Commission on Human Rights,[2] she drove the process that led the United Nations (UN) to adopt the Universal Declaration of Human Rights (UDHR). Her role in drafting the declaration is sometimes overstated, but it would probably never have seen the light of day without her. Eleanor clearly fitted her own description of a woman as "like a tea bag – you never know how strong she is until she gets in hot water".

Second came Chang Peng-Chun, the Chinese playwright, philosopher and diplomat who was vice-chair of the Commission. He is credited as resolving philosophical and ideological stalemates in the negotiations over drafting by quoting Confucian proverbs like "sweep the snow in front of one's own door; overlook the frost on others' roof tiles". My third apparition was Dr Charles Malik, the Lebanese academic and ethicist who, as rapporteur, played a vital role in shaping the ethical contents of the UDHR. Fourth, was René Cassin, the Jewish resistance activist and legal adviser to Charles de Gaulle, who played a major drafting role. He later went on to become president of the European Court of Human Rights. Finally, John Humphrey, the Canadian representative of the UN Secretariat who, as a legal academic, provided the first draft of the declaration. Like civil servants the world over, his contribution is often overlooked.

These five central figures were joined on the UN Human Rights Commission by representatives from 14 other nations from different regions of the world, including Australia, Belgium, Chile, Egypt, India, Iran, the Philippines, the Soviet Union and the United Kingdom.[3] The most notable exception was sub-Saharan Africa, still largely colonised by the European powers, although in enunciating a set of internationally agreed standards for all humankind, the UDHR was subsequently to provide a lever in some struggles for independence.

The aims of the drafters can be summed up as threefold:

- To enhance protection for individuals from state tyranny and abuse wherever they live in the world, and regardless of other cultural or religious differences.
- To foster peace between nations on the basis that states that treat their own citizens well were less likely to have aggressive designs on other nations.
- To promote understanding of the inherent dignity and equal worth of "all members of the human family".

How would these ghosts of drafters past assess progress on these goals over the last 60 years?

Bolstering the protection of individuals by influencing governments throughout the world

In their quest to fulfil goal number 1 – bolster the protection of individuals by influencing governments throughout the world – they would surely be gratified that whereas eight countries abstained[4] when the UDHR was adopted by 48 governments on December 10, 1948,[5] nowadays all 192 UN Member States have accepted the Declaration as a condition of UN membership. The drafters would be pleased that December 10 is still celebrated in the four corners of the globe as international human rights day. And they would surely be delighted to know that the Guinness Book of Records now describes the UDHR as the "most translated document" in the world? And whilst the declaration was never intended to be a legally binding treaty as such, most informed commentators agree that, despite all the terrible events of the last six decades, it has exerted a significant moral and legal influence across the globe. Parts of its terms are cited so often that they have become generally accepted as part of customary international law.

Even its critics would generally accept that the UDHR was a triumphant example of the optimism of the intellect *and* the will (to misquote Gramsci). Crafted to celebrate the best that humans are capable of, amidst the debris and ashes of a devastating world war, it is very difficult to imagine the nations of the world agreeing to draft such an aspirational declaration now.

It is easy to forget that until the UDHR was adopted, virtually *any* criticism – let alone interference – by one government with the treatment of the citizens of another, was considered a breach of the principle of national sovereignty. Human rights abuses were perfectly lawful if they complied with a country's domestic law. However *morally* repugnant, Nazi Germany's racial purity policies were all in accordance with the law. The influence of the UDHR has not stopped at exhortation. It has followed the biblical injunction to go forth and multiply. Its 30 articles – which gave equal weight to traditional civil and political liberties alongside path-breaking economic, social and cultural rights – have formed the backbone of about 30 subsequent international and regional treaties. Most attribute their parentage to the UDHR in their preamble. Nearly two decades after its introduction, two legally binding international covenants were adopted by the United Nations; one on civil and political rights (which Britain was very influential in drafting) to please the west and the other on economic, social and cultural rights to please the soviet dominated east (this was the Cold War after all).[6] Together with the UDHR, these were labelled the international bill of rights.

There is no equivalent to the European Court of Human Rights to enforce these treaties, but there is a mechanism for victims (whose states have ratified the relevant protocol) to complain to the UN Human Rights Committee which can name and shame states that violate their citizens' rights.[7] A new International Criminal Court, just six years old but recognised by 108 states – plus ad hoc international tribunals in Rwanda, Kosovo, the former Yugoslavia, Cambodia and East Timor – signal to dictators and torturers that they can no longer rely on the world turning away.

The UDHR has also served as the model for many domestic bills of rights around the world. This includes the United Kingdom's Human Rights Act 1998 (HRA). Although drafted to respect Britain's constitutional tradition of parliamentary sovereignty with Parliament, rather than judges, having the final say, the rights in the HRA are, of course, drawn from the European Convention on Human Rights (ECHR). It is not always appreciated that the ECHR explicitly owes its genesis to the UDHR. The civil and political rights it protects are largely drawn from the UDHR, refined and adapted by British lawyers, generally to make them more specific, or limited.

More than 80 human rights commissions, committed to promoting the values and importance of human rights – often at great risk to the lives of their staff – now operate in virtually all regions of the world. One of the newest kids on the block is our own Equality and Human Rights Commission (EHRC). Our first statutory human rights body, charged with protecting and promoting human rights and the HRA, is also celebrating the 60th anniversary in December 2008, though thankfully without putting any of us in danger; unless you include the risk of falling flat on your face when giving lectures!

Sitting on a human rights inquiry panel for the EHRC over the last few months, we have heard evidence that human rights can fortify individuals to challenge bureaucracies or participate more effectively in the decisions that affect their lives and can help public officials to design policies that are more respectful of the most vulnerable people in their care. Ghost number 1 should be pleased, for this precisely conforms to Eleanor Roosevelt's aspiration that the UDHR should spur protection,

> "in small places . . . so close and so small that they cannot be seen on any maps of the world . . . the world of the individual person; the neighbourhood he lives in; the school or college he attends . . . such are the places where every man, woman, and child seeks equal justice, equal opportunity, equal dignity without discrimination. Unless these rights have meaning there, they have little meaning anywhere."[8]

But it hardly needs saying that the UDHR's goal number 1 is far from realised in the "big places" of the world. The catalogue of human misery around the globe appears to continue unabated, mocking the call of "never again" which resounded in the ears of the drafters. In 2007 Amnesty International documented instances of torture and other cruel, inhuman or degrading treatment in 81 countries. The international bill of rights might have provided a stronger benchmark by which to judge such violations, but their transparency is aided as much by the ingenuities of satellite television and the internet, as by UN reporting mechanisms. Just in the last month we have witnessed peaceful democracy protesters in Burma sentenced to 65 years in prison, the live burial or stoning of rape victims in the border areas of Afghanistan and Pakistan, unspeakable atrocities on all sides in the Democratic Republic of Congo, and the distressing collapse of the once thriving Zimbabwe.

As I write this lecture, nearly 200 people lie dead in Mumbai, killed not by state forces but by a group of young men. Terror as a political weapon is not new, but its indiscriminate use and potential for mass casualties is escalating. It was Mary Robinson, the former UN High Commissioner for Human Rights, who was the first to describe the scale and systematic nature of the attacks on September 11, 2001 as a "crime against humanity".[9] Human rights values speak loudly to such callous disregard for human life. "By any means necessary" is no part of the human rights lexicon.

Contributing to the ending of war

Peace on earth has self-evidently not broken out. If the drafters' second goal – of contributing to the ending of war – was ever realistic, it seems a more remote possibility than ever. That said, there is some evidence that allegiance to a common standard of democracy and human rights, bolstered by the ECHR, has helped secure peace in formerly turbulent Western Europe in the last 60 years, just as Winston Churchill envisaged when he championed the Council of Europe, with human rights as its central mandate. What the UDHR drafters could *not* have predicted in 1948 was that a new kind of war would be declared at the beginning of the 21st century; on a noun – terror – not a country. A war whose first casualty was the human rights protections that it was supposedly waged to defend. A war fought in the name of democracy and liberty using some of the techniques of those who most despise democracy and liberty. There is not much more that can be said about this which has not already been said, but the greatest difficulty with this war has been that the ground rules that were carefully and delicately put together after 1945 were said no longer to apply in this new undefined battlefield.

If we think back 60 years to 1948, what a contrast! It was a year of much tension and renewed conflict around the world – between peoples, as well as between states – although only three years after the end of the Second World War. Ghandi was assassinated and the fall-out over the partition of India and Pakistan was reverberating with catastrophic results that are still continuing. The State of Israel was recognised by the United Nations and the Middle East conflict, which still rages, kicked off with all its concomitant human misery. And the descending cold war and arms race was already freezing out hopes for a peaceful future. Yet the response of global leaders to the fractured world of 1948, and the Holocaust and war which preceded it, was not that torture *could* be legitimate in certain circumstances, but that it should be *forever* banned. Not that fair trials and indefinite detention were negotiables, but that the natural justice principles of the Magna Carta needed to be revived.

Now, perhaps, we have reason to be optimistic that the war on terror, at least, might be drawing to a close. I know there are more expectations on President Elect Obama than on Santa Claus at Christmas, but his statement in October 2007 that "it's time to tell the world that America rejects torture, without exception or equivocation"[10] gives cause for hope, audaciously or otherwise. It certainly bears contrast to his predecessor. The previous year, amidst allegations that the CIA used water boarding as a permissible interrogation technique, George W. Bush queried the meaning of the phrase *"outrages* on human dignity", in the Geneva Convention.[11] It was, of course, "barbarous acts which outraged the conscience of mankind" – as the preamble to the UDHR puts it – that drove the lobbying of NGOs like the NAACP,[12] the Federal Council of Churches and the American-Jewish Committee at the end of Second World War. They were determined that the sacrifice of a generation, and the near genocide of a people, would not be in vain. An international bill of rights would become as iconic of what it means to be human, as the US bill of rights was symbolic of what it means to be American.

Global recognition of the inherent dignity and worth of all human beings

This is the backdrop by which to judge the third, and in my view most important, goal of the drafters – to gain global recognition of the inherent dignity and worth of all human beings. Why do I say *most* important? Partly because, as a non-legally binding declaration, this is the only realistic way to judge it. If the UDHR does not score well on that count, it arguably does not score at all. But also because, for the very same reason, it has not been "captured and drained of life by lawyers" (to quote Professor Conor Gearty),[13] freeing the declaration to stand as a set of broad ethical values – or in Professor Amartya Sen's terms, "ethical demands"[14] – which can inspire present and future generations worldwide. This is the mission of the UDHR. To underline common standards of decency in a diverse world, in a manner which reflects that diversity. The essential message of the UDHR is often assumed or taken for granted, with little interrogation of its precise terms. Critics and supporters alike generally presume it is fundamentally a creature of the western Enlightenment, repackaged for the mid-20th century, with pretensions – substantiated or otherwise – to universality. Yet this is to miss the distinguishing features of the declaration, reflecting the circumstances in which it was drawn up and the diverse philosophies and backgrounds of the drafters.

Notwithstanding the triumph of the defeat of fascism, the identity of Europe as the so-called "crucible of civilisation" had been deeply shaken by the events of the 1930s and 1940s which had taken root on European soil. The collapse of the Weimar Republic in Germany had exposed democracy as a weak defence against a ruthless demagogue determined to exploit its loopholes and capable of rousing citizens effectively to disenfranchise themselves. "Enlightenment values" of liberty and justice had been reviled and betrayed by Hitler's Germany and Stalin's Russia alike, apparently two ends of a political spectrum, uniting in their disdain of individual rights and freedoms. The dream of Soviet style communism as liberation, which had ignited a generation, was looking tarnished at best and preposterous at worst. But it was the specific nature of the persecution and suffering which gave birth to the UDHR that demonstrated, if any demonstration were needed, that tyranny cannot be conquered by restraints on governments alone.

This is all the more the case when majorities turn on minorities, as the Holocaust had so amply demonstrated, with its industrial methods of extermination to which so many private businesses and public officials had contributed. Across Europe Jews, Gypsies, homosexuals, disabled people, trade unionists and political opponents had been dehumanised and massacred in their millions, with the active collaboration or passive acquiescence of thousands of their fellow citizens.

The UDHR is generally understood as a restatement of the fundamental rights which are necessary to protect individuals against such tyranny; deservedly so. It is also beyond argument that many of the basic assumptions of the "natural rights movement" which had heralded the French and American revolutions were reproduced in the UDHR, most notably this statement in the preamble: "it is essential, if man is not to be compelled to have recourse, as a last resort, to rebellion against tyranny and oppression, that human rights should be protected by the rule of law."

But ghost number 4, René Cassin, was keen to establish that the UDHR was *more* than an "offshoot of the eighteenth century tree of rights".[15] There were three distinctive features to the UDHR, each of which bears some exploration.

First, the preamble was not just addressed to states, or to the citizens of particular countries, as in the idiom of the French and American bills of rights. For the first time this was a document aimed at *all* "the peoples" of the world, not just to protect them from abuse of power by others, but to encourage them to take responsibility for justice and peace *themselves* and to "strive by teaching and education to promote respect for rights and freedoms" (as the preamble puts it).[16] The drafters of the UDHR concluded that freedom from unnecessary restraint was not a sufficient ideal on which to stake the future of the world. Freedom had to be capable of being realised, not just formally granted.

The experiences they had just lived through led them to conclude that international peace and prosperity were *unachievable* unless every man, woman and child has a stake in their own future, an opportunity to flourish and an entitlement to be treated with equal respect and dignity. But to achieve this vision, people needed to be active participants, not passive recipients of a benign order. "All human beings . . . should act towards one another in a spirit of brotherhood" the first article thunders. If this sounds like an Old Testament injunction, it is because it was intended to. According to René Cassin, it was inspired by the biblical imperative to "love thy neighbour as thyself".[17] This attempt to persuade people of the equal worth of every individual through moral exhortation, rather than legal compulsion, was emphasised by Cassin who described the declaration as "the first document about *moral* value adopted by an assembly of the human community".[18]

The second departure from a classical enlightenment frame addressed head-on critics as diverse as Edmund Burke, Jeremy Bentham and Karl Marx who dismissed the idea of "inalienable rights" not just as "nonsense upon stilts",[19] but as fostering a society of isolated individuals, pursuing their selfish wants and needs. The drafters devoted considerable time to discussing the social nature of human beings and the responsibilities they owe to each other and the wider community, on whose flourishing individual rights depend. You could be forgiven for thinking you have stumbled on a debate between Jack Straw, David Cameron, the Archbishop of Canterbury and Shami Chakrabarti if you immerse yourself too deeply, as I have, in the range of passionately held views expressed six decades ago in the UN Human Rights Commission on the interrelationship between rights and responsibilities. The drafters disdained the idea that they were creating a new philosophy. Humphreys (our ghost number 5), in the way of all good civil servants, especially eschewed this as a project. Yet a fusion of liberal and socialist principles, with deeply held tenants from the Abrahamic faiths combined with Confucian philosophy, produced an alchemy best summed up by ghost number 2, P.C. Chang, when he said,

> "the aim of the United Nations was not to ensure the selfish gains of the individual but to try and increase man's *moral* stature. It was necessary to proclaim the duties of the individual, for it was a consciousness of his duties which enabled man to reach a high moral standard."[20]

But before some of our political leaders get too excited, the drafters explicitly ruled out producing a catalogue of individual duties or constructing a framework in which individuals forfeited their rights if they failed in their responsibilities. Instead they affirmed, in art.29,[21] the interrelatedness of human beings, and the consequential duties individuals owe to the *community* – a term carefully chosen instead of state – without which none of us could hope to flourish or develop our full personality. This was the context in which proportionate limitations on individual rights were given legitimacy (also in art.29) to "respect the rights of others and . . . the general welfare in a democratic society". Translated, this means human rights are there to protect us from threats to our safety by other people, and not just states. This affirmation of the social aspect of human beings was part of a deeper exploration of what it is to be human; the third and, to my mind, most interesting distinguishing feature of the UDHR. The different convictions and ideologies which the delegates brought to the drafting process created tensions throughout; often creatively, sometimes less so. It is estimated that Member States voted more than 1,400 times on practically every word and clause of the text. But they never agreed on a formal definition of human rights. According to the Soviet delegate, there was a tacit understanding they would not do so. In contrast to their Enlightenment forebears, they also refrained from declaring the *source* of human rights, whether in God or nature.[22] But drawing on traditions of faith, as much as eastern and western philosophy, they developed a *framework* in the first article from which the justification of all the subsequent rights was deemed to flow. This framework is usually described as affirming the essential dignity of every human being; both as a fundamental value and the framing of a right to respectful and dignified treatment. This owed as much to the biblical belief that human beings are created in the image of God as it did to Kantian notions of intrinsic worth.

The underlying premise of the UDHR is that human beings are an end in themselves; and never a means. They are of value simply because they are human and their fundamental rights – or what philosopher Martha Nussbaum terms their central capabilities[23] – flow from our collective wisdom of the ages; our experience of what is necessary for humans to flourish. There was no reference to "human dignity" in the "Enlightenment" bills of rights, whilst it is expressed five times in the declaration (twice in the preamble and most prominently in art.1). This impacted on the declaration in three ways.

First, it provided a justification for the path-breaking catalogue of social, economic and cultural rights in the UDHR, to further "an existence worthy of human dignity" as the text said.[24] An individual who is free to starve is not free at all, and is certainly not dignified.[25]

Secondly, the reference to dignity fleshed out what is meant by equality. Dignity tells us that equal treatment does not take us very far if we are all treated equally badly. The UDHR contains the first modern anti-discrimination clause but equality was to mean more than non-discrimination and *less* than equality of outcome. To experience a life of dignity is to have your individual needs appreciated and differences catered for. True equality can only be achieved when differences are respected, and even celebrated. This is the root to the various charters that have flowed from the UDHR on race, gender, children and most recently disability, all of which address the dignity of difference.

Thirdly, the importance attached to dignity means that no individual should fall so far that they are denied all rights, but only those rights that are necessary to protect others and the common good. It is this approach that gets human rights into hot water, of course, with people who believe that those who commit crimes or anti-social behaviour are undeserving of any human rights. In this sense the UDHR has more in common with Christian notions of redemption, than secular ideas of retribution. But the more I study the debates on the UDHR, the more I conclude that the concept of dignity is *not* a sufficient way to understand the justification for the human rights it proclaims.[26] The references to dignity in the declaration are linked to another important insight. Human beings, art. 1 declares, are endowed with "reason and conscience" which is both why – and how – we should all treat each other well.

Our essential nature as human beings is rooted in two elements, it is proposed: our ability to think and reason in the classical Enlightenment mould, but also our capacity to feel and care; our conscience. It is the fact that we are capable of moral choices that distinguishes us as humans and makes us able to treat others with respect; and be deserving of respect ourselves. This insight into the human condition is what makes the whole enterprise of the declaration worthwhile. If we could not feel empathy for others, the project to create a fairer and more just world would have been doomed from the outset.

There are many testimonies to the capacity of the UDHR to inspire and inform (and thus fulfil the drafters' third and most important goal). Nelson Mandela has written movingly about the impact of its adoption in South Africa, where apartheid was formally introduced in the same year:

> "for all the opponents of this pernicious regime, the simple and noble words of the Universal Declaration were a sudden ray of hope at one of our darkest moments. During the many years that followed, this document . . . served as a shining beacon and an inspiration to many millions of South Africans."[27]

But if our ghosts of drafters past were to judge the success of the UDHR, and in particular their third goal of enhancing all our understanding of human rights, by the quality of the current debate on human rights in the United Kingdom, they would probably wish to haunt us for the rest of their days. In summary this debate appears to boil down to three propositions:

- That human rights encourage selfishness and what we need are more responsibilities, not rights.
- That bad people get too many rights and should forfeit them.
- That British liberties are in our DNA, whereas human rights are either something foreigners lack or something they have imposed on us.

This is a lecture about the UDHR and these charges are for another day. I have already touched upon points one and two in my exploration of the ethical framework of the UDHR and the treaties it begat. But some political leaders are now playing with human rights like a kitten with a ball of wool. Whilst human rights should be as open to challenge as any other idea, myths and misinformation are scattered about like confetti. Our ghost number 3, Dr Malik, was prescient when he predicted that the historical significance of the UDHR will be determined by whether,

> "a sufficient number of morally and politically powerful countries will so identify themselves with its doctrine, *in all sincerity and truth*, as to use it as a potent weapon in the ideological warfare which is the mark of the contemporary scene".[28]

This observation is as true now as it was then. The responsibility on us all to speak with "sincerity and truth", as Dr Malik put it, is considerable, as we are forced in this era to defend our democratic values and way of life from those who would undermine them, more clearly and resolutely than at any period in my lifetime.

Relevance for British bill of rights debate

So here is a slice of sincerity and truth to conclude with, in answer to the specific charge that human rights are somehow foreign, whether derived from the UDHR, the ECHR or the HRA – all of which, I hope I have demonstrated, are intimately related to each other.

When Eleanor Roosevelt proclaimed the UDHR she announced her hope that it "become the international Magna Carta of all men everywhere".[29] The influence of the British tradition of liberty is reflected throughout the UDHR and the whole world understands that. Indeed it was Britain which invented the idea of a Bill of Rights in 1689. But as ground-breaking and enduring as these early documents and the rights within them were, the Magna Carta also disparaged women and Jews and the 1689 Bill of Rights discriminated against Catholics. There is no right to free expression, association, privacy or family life and no anti-discrimination protection in these older charters; nor would you expect there to be. It was Winston Churchill – the British conservative, war-time hero – who, after the war, called for a new charter of rights for the whole of Europe, based on the British tradition of liberty but enriched by the passage of time, and what we have learnt from our own history and what we share with others. In his opening speech to the Congress of Europe in May 1948, Churchill proclaimed that the new Europe,

> "must be a positive force, deriving its strength from our sense of common spiritual values. It is a dynamic expression of democratic faith based upon moral conceptions and inspired by a sense of mission. In the centre of our movement stands the idea of a Charter of Human Rights, guarded by freedom and sustained by law."[30]

The ECHR is as British as custard. The ECHR, which forms the backbone of the HRA, was not only drafted by British lawyers, it was crafted only because of Winston Churchill and his vision for all our futures. There is nothing foreign or alien about it. It is just the next stage in the evolution of thinking about fundamental rights that Britain has contributed to every step of the way. It was the British Foreign Office delegate to the United Nations, Ernest Davies, who, when the UDHR was adopted, spoke of the "UK's sense of pride" at having been part of the drafting process, proclaiming, *proudly,* not ashamedly, that the,

> "declaration is not merely a statement of western thought or the common view of a country of homogenous background and outlook, . . . it is an expression of world opinion of what in our day and age the rights of man should be".

As we look around our shrinking world from the vantage point of six decades later, do we not, more than ever, need a set of principles that unite rather than divide? If we are to live in a global capital market, do we not also need the security of "a common standard of achievement for all peoples and all nations", as the UDHR puts it; the first experiment in globalisation? As we take pride in and benefit from our own diverse society are we not right to base our sense of who we are and what we stand for on principles which *everyone* can own, no matter what their heritage or family background? Although the universal applicability of the declaration is inevitably questioned by some dictators, and those who only see western values reflected in its terms,[31] most modern democracies seem relaxed – or even proud – to trace the links between their *own* bills of rights or written constitutions and the UDHR.

The 1982 Canadian Charter of Rights has become emblematic of Canadian democracy. It is an excellent charter. It is based mainly on the United Nations' International Covenant on Civil and Political Rights, the second leg of the international bill of rights, drafted with significant input from the United Kingdom, and with sections reflecting Canada's distinctive *modern* national identity. Should we go on to adopt another bill of rights we should similarly take pride in fusing any civil liberties we uniquely associate with this island with the values that already have global recognition through the UDHR, many of which are reflected – word for word – in the HRA. It is neither rational nor honest to conjure a bill of rights based on "British liberties" that is somehow an entirely different species to the HRA, whilst we stay signed up to the ECHR in order to secure our place in Europe. It is not possible to better Ken Clark's description of such a proposal as "xenophobic and legal nonsense".[32]

Speaking at last year's anniversary, Barack Obama emphasised the alchemy of the UDHR, which makes its broad values relevant for our times, but not alien or foreign. Describing the principles encompassed in the declaration, he remarked that,

> "the declaration also wove together a remarkable variety of political, religious and cultural perspectives and traditions. The US and the UK championed civil liberties. The French . . . helped devise the structure of the declaration.

India added the prohibition on discrimination. China stressed the importance of family and . . . that every right carried with it companion duties."

He concluded "today should be a day of celebration, a day when we hail the universality of these core principles, which are both beacons to guide us and the foundations for building a more just and stable world".[33]

Notes

1 This is the text of a lecture delivered at Chatham House, London, on December 8, 2008.
2 The Commission on Human Rights, a standing body of the UN, was constituted to undertake the work of preparing what was initially conceived as an International Bill of Rights. The membership of the Commission was designed to be broadly representative of the then membership of the UN with representatives of the following countries serving: Australia, Belgium, Byelorussian Soviet Socialist Republic, Chile, China, Egypt, France, India, Iran, Lebanon, Panama, Philippines Republic, UK, US, USSR, Uruguay and Yugoslavia.
3 The full list of 18 nations represented on the first UN HRC were: Byelorussia, China, Lebanon, Panama, UK, Uruguay, Egypt, France, India, Iran, Ukraine, Soviet Union, Australia, Belgium, Chile, Philippines, US, Yugoslavia. In 1948, after two years, Byelorussia and Panama were replaced by Denmark and Guatemala.
4 The eight abstainers consisted of all the Soviet bloc states, South Africa, and Saudi Arabia.
5 The following countries voted in favour of the Declaration: Afghanistan, Argentina, Australia, Belgium, Bolivia, Brazil, Burma, Canada, Chile, China, Colombia, Costa Rica, Cuba, Denmark, the Dominican Republic, Ecuador, Egypt, El Salvador, Ethiopia, France, Greece, Guatemala, Haiti, Iceland, India, Iran, Iraq, Lebanon, Liberia, Luxembourg, Mexico, Netherlands, New Zealand, Nicaragua, Norway, Pakistan, Panama, Paraguay, Peru, Philippines, Thailand, Sweden, Syria, Turkey, UK, US, Uruguay, Venezuela.
6 International Covenant on Civil and Political Rights (ICCPR), and the International Covenant on Economic, Social and Cultural Rights (ICESCR), both adopted on December 16, 1966 and ratified 10 years later.
7 In relation to the ICCPR. A similar mechanism for the ICESCR is in the process of being adopted by the UN.
8 Eleanor Roosevelt, "The Great Question", address to the UN Commission on Human Rights, New York, March 27, 1958.
9 Mary Robinson, "Five years on from 9/11 – Time to Re-Assert the Rule of Law", Justice International Rule of Law Lecture, London, March 20, 2006.
10 Barack Obama statement, "Torture and secrecy betray core American values", October 4, 2007, available at *http://www.barackobama.com/2007/10/04/obama torture and secrecy betr. php* [Accessed February 22, 2009].
11 President G.W. Bush, Press Conference, Washington, September 15, 2006. Bush is misquoting the Third Geneva Convention (the Geneva Convention Relative to the Treatment of Prisoners of War), August 1949, Pt 1, art.3 which speaks of "outrages on personal dignity", not "outrages on human dignity" as Bush says. This is among the acts that are and shall remain prohibited at any time and in any place whatsoever with respect to persons presently taking no active part in hostilities, including prisoners of war.
12 National Association for the Advancement of Colored People.
13 C. Gearty, "Doing Human Rights: social justice in a post-socialist age", lecture delivered at the launch of the Las Casas Institute, Blackfriars Hall, Oxford, November 25, 2008, available at *http://www.bfriars.ox.ac.uk/casas resources.php* [Accessed February 22, 2008].

14 A. Sen, "Elements of a Theory of Human Rights" (2004) 32 *Philosophy and Public Affairs* 319.

15 Johannes Morsink, *The UDHR, origins, drafting and intent* (University of Pennsylvania Press, 1999), p.245.

16 Preamble, last para.

17 "Leviticus XIX, From the Ten Commandments to the Rights of Man", René Cassin, speech in France, 1969. Published in Shlomo Shoham (ed.), *Of Law and Man* (Sabra Books, 1971).

18 Morsink, *The UDHR* (1999), p.33.

19 Jeremy Waldron (ed.), *Nonsense Upon Stilts – Bentham, Burke and Marx on the Rights of Man* (Methuen, 1987).

20 Ninety-fifth meeting of the Third Committee of the UN General Assembly, October 6, 1948, E/800 p.87.

21 art.29: "(1) Everyone has duties to the community in which alone the free and full development of his personality is possible. (2) In the exercise of his rights and freedoms, everyone shall be subject only to such limitations as are determined by law solely for the purpose of securing due recognition and respect for the rights and freedoms of others and of meeting the just requirements of morality, public order and the general welfare in a democratic society. (3) These rights and freedoms may in no case be exercised contrary to the purposes and principles of the United Nations."

22 See M. Glen Johnson and Janusz Simonides, *The Universal Declaration of Human Rights, a history of its creation and implementation,* 1948–1998 (Unesco, 1998), pp.42–48.

23 Martha Nussbaum, "Capabilities as Fundamental Entitlements: Sen and Social Justice", LSE Public Lecture, March 13, 2002.

24 art.23(3).

25 art.22.

26 Francesca Klug, *Values for a Godless Age, the story of the UK's new Bill of Rights* (Penguin, 2000).

27 See Klug, *Values for a Godless Age* (2000), p.110.

28 Third Session of the General Assembly, December 9–10, 1948.

29 Eleanor Roosevelt, Address to the United Nations General Assembly on the Adoption of the Universal Declaration of Human Rights, December 1948, published by the Department of State in *Human Rights and Genocide: Selected Statements; United Nations Resolution Declaration and Conventions* (1949).

30 Winston S. Churchill, Complete Speeches, 1897–1963 (R.R. James (ed.), 1974), pp.7635–7639.

31 On June 30, 2000, members of the Organization of the Islamic Conference officially resolved to support the Cairo Declaration on Human Rights in Islam, an alternative document that says people have "freedom and right to a dignified life in accordance with the Islamic Shari'ah".

32 Rachel Sylvester, "Has Cameron thought it through or is he just thinking aloud?", *Daily Telegraph,* June 27, 2006.

33 Statement by Senator Barack Obama on International Human Rights Day, December 10, 2007.

3

HUMAN RIGHTS

Philosophy, politics or law?

Unpublished lecture, LSE Centre for the Study of Human Rights, Certificate in international Human Rights law and practice 7 October 2013, LSE (edited and abridged)

1. Introduction

It is undoubtedly now far more widely accepted than it was a generation ago that human beings have certain fundamental rights purely as a result of their common humanity, rather than their citizenship status or any other external characteristic. Notwithstanding the commonplace observation that human rights standards are honoured more in their breach than in their observance, how do we account for their continuing expansion? Is the idea of human rights best understood through the prism of philosophy, politics or law?

2. Human rights as philosophy

It sometimes seems that everything to do with human rights is contentious – even their historical origins. If we trace the history of the idea of human rights we come against different conceptions of what human rights are.

> Under one conception, human rights are conceived as a code of ethics with origins that can arguably be traced to all the main religions, confounding a common [mis]conception of human rights as uncompromisingly secular. The focus on the dignity of every human being in the 1948 UDHR has been presented by some human rights theorists and practitioners as a secular formulation of the biblical notion that all human beings are created in the image of God.[1]

René Cassin, one of the prime authors of the UDHR, maintained that the proclamation in Article 1 that all human beings "should act towards one another in a spirit of brotherhood," corresponds to the biblical injunction to "love they neighbour as thyself" and "love the stranger as you love yourself." [Leviticus 19; repeated in Mark 12]. "We must not lose sight of fundamentals," Cassin wrote, in noting that "the concept of human rights comes from the bible."[2]

Going back even earlier, the Babylonian Hammurabi Code represents what is generally recognised as the oldest surviving collection of moral principles. These influenced later ethical religious tests. For example, slaying an innocent individual is like killing the whole world, according to the Quran.

Under a slightly different conception of human rights, they are characterised as an absolute set of universal values or truths from which flows a notion of the common good which, as rational beings, we can all discover. From this perspective, their origins can arguably be traced to the ancient Greek philosophers Plato and Aristotle and their followers. Plato argued that a universal standard of moral justice exists that transcends immediate circumstances.[3] Socrates maintained that people have a general comprehension of what constitutes the good. They refuted the claim that goodness is simply relative to the customs of each society, just as modern proponents of fundamental human rights maintain their absolute standards in the face of cultural norms that do not comply with them.

Most early philosophical theories of natural law focused on universal responsibilities and duties rather than rights. The *Christian* idea of natural law was deeply influenced by the ancient Stoics but with a new twist. Medieval Christian philosophers like Saint Thomas Aquinas redefined the belief in natural law as *divinely* willed and progressed the notion of a duality of human existence wherein everyone was subject to both the authority of law *and* the authority of God. Through this divine legitimacy he was able to argue the then [and maybe now] radical doctrine that if 'man-made' laws were not just, people had a right to disobey them. Aquinas built on the thinking of the early Christian theologian Saint Augustine (353–340) to develop the Catholic doctrine of a just war [which by implication meant there were unjust wars].

The transformation of natural *law* into a case for natural *rights* is generally traced to 17th century Europe and in particular to the ideas of the Dutch jurist Hugo Grotius. He argued that natural law existed independently of political authority and stood above all governments serving as a measure against which the laws and justice of regimes could be measured. This provided all humans with certain 'natural rights' of protection and just and equal treatment regardless of status.[4]

Influenced by Grotius, and writing at the dawn of the Enlightenment that he was to fundamentally influence, the English political philosopher John Locke sought to clarify the relationship between natural law, natural rights and duties. In his *Second*

Treatise of Government [1690] he maintained that every individual, as children of God, possessed certain 'natural rights' in a state of nature prior to the existence of organised societies. Prefiguring modern human rights discourse, he stressed that individuals are everywhere born in a state of "perfect equality" with "a title to perfect treatment and uncontrolled enjoyment of all the rights and privileges of the law of nature equally with any other man or number of men in the world."

On one reading, the UN's 1948 Universal Declaration of Human Rights (UDHR) is an updated and modernised reiteration of the Western Enlightenment's theory of natural rights. The preamble is pure Locke when it declares "whereas it is essential, if man is not to be compelled to have recourse, as a last resort, to rebellion against tyranny and oppression, that human rights should be protected by the rule of law." But there is a notable distinction in the *justification* given for "faith in human rights." The dignity and worth of every individual, underlined in the very first line of the preamble to the UDHR, can be understood as the drafters' response to the 'natural rights' debate.

In the UDHR the concept of dignity replaced the idea of God or nature as the putative foundation or justification of 'inalienable rights.' This reflected the transition from 'natural rights' to 'human rights,' a term which did not come into common usage until after World War II. Whilst the 1776 American Declaration of Independence declared "these truths to be self-evident, that all men are created equal and that they are endowed by their *creator* with certain inalienable rights," and whilst the preamble to the 1789 French Declaration of the Rights of Man and Citizen referred to "the presence" and "the auspices of the supreme being," any reference to the divine was expunged from the UDHR.

Under the UDHR, no longer was a higher being or pre-existing state of nature cited as a source of inalienable rights but rights were to be understood as the birth right of *all* human beings, without distinction, because of their common humanity. And what was signified as the hallmark of our common humanity? Not just dignity, but in the words of the very first article of the UDHR, our endowment with "reason and conscience" on the basis of which we should "act towards each other in a spirit of brotherhood." In other words, whether you believe in God or not, human rights reflect what the drafters appear to view as the very essence of what it is to be human; and the essence of humanity, distinguishing us from animals, is our capacity to reason and to empathise, according to the drafters of the UDHR.

The expunging of God or nature from the UDHR meant that the dignity and the essential nature of the human person was relied on to justify human rights instead. If human rights can be claimed by everyone in every culture it stands to reason, the argument goes, that they must somehow be grounded in features that all people necessarily share.[5] John Rawls, the renowned American legal theorist, conceived of human rights as a class of especially urgent rights that stem from shared principles and norms in a liberal society. He claimed that unlike so-called natural rights, human rights must be justified by some form of "public reason" that is above the fray of everyday arguments about right and wrong.[6]

A further variant in this search for a justification of human rights can be found in the theory of "basic human capabilities," as advanced by American law and ethics professor Martha Nussbaum and the renowned Indian economist and Nobel Prize winner, Amartya Sen. They developed the so-called 'capability approach' in different ways. Nussbaum defines a human right as "an especially urgent and morally justified claim that a person has by virtue of being human." Her list of "central human capabilities" seeks to identify the types of claims necessary for a "free and dignified human being, a maker of choices."[7] These include life, bodily health and integrity, thought, emotions, reason, respect, play and control over one's environment.

Sen views human rights as specifically "ethical demands" rather than simply legal constructs. To qualify as human rights, demands have to have special importance and *social* significance. Sen would argue that the freedom to achieve tranquillity, for example, would most likely not pass the threshold of social significance to qualify as a human right. But "poverty as well as tyranny, poor economic opportunities as well as systematic social deprivation . . ." are all factors in the achievement of human rights.

Sen's "open public reasoning" approach attempts to answer critics who condemn both the idea and ideal of a set of universal human rights to which all should aspire, as a form of cultural imperialism. This kind of critique goes back to the dawn of international human rights. Responding to the universalism of the UDHR as it was being drafted, the American Anthropological Association executive board, for example, issued a statement that a justifiable conception of "world-wide standards of freedom and justice" should be based on "the right of men to live in terms of their *own* traditions."

Sen attempted to develop a theory of human rights which leaves room for further debate and internal variations.[8] In his book *Development As Freedom* Sen expounds on what he describes as "the ability of different people from different cultures to share many common values and to agree on some common commitments."[9] In other words, according to Sen, for human rights to survive as a universal ideal in a diverse world they must be open to public scrutiny and criticism. Sen maintains that freedom-orientated perspectives were also present in ancient Asian thought, for example, countering the argument that so called Asian values are inherently incompatible with Enlightenment-driven human rights.

The American philosopher Charles Beitz characterises this kind of approach as a form of "agreement theory."[10] The fact or prospect of intercultural agreements on human rights is treated as both a criterion for identifying them and a means of justifying them. In other words, the fact that human rights values can be identified to some degree in the moral codes of most of the world's religions or belief systems becomes the source of their authority. Human rights should be "reachable" from each world view by a "sound deliberative route," as Beitz puts it. Confining human rights to the contents of possible intercultural agreements – although skirting over gender, sexual and equality rights seen as difficult to achieve consensus on – has seemed to some scholars and human rights activists as the best defence against relativist objections.[11]

There is also a pragmatic perspective to this approach. The Islamic scholar Abdullahi An-Na'im argues that "unless people accept these rights as binding upon themselves from their own cultural, religious and/or philosophical point of view, they will neither voluntarily comply in practice, nor require their government" to do so.[12]

3. Human rights sceptics

Criticisms of the idea of human rights are not confined to cultural relativists. The late 18th century British philosopher and reformer Jeremy Bentham set the tone for a long line of human rights sceptics in his book *Anarchical Fallacies* when he famously remarked "in proportion to the want of happiness resulting from the want of rights, a reason exists for wishing there were such things as rights. But reasons for wishing there were such things as rights are not rights . . . natural rights is simple nonsense" and "natural and imprescriptible rights" [a quote from the French Declaration of Rights] "nonsense upon stilts."[13]

In common with most of the British legal theorists of his day, and since (at least until recently), Bentham was a legal positivist – the only rights that could be said to exist were dependent on their recognition in law. If there is no law governing a right you don't have one! From a legal positivist perspective, for rights to have any substance they have to depend on the obligations of others to fulfil them who in turn need to be under some kind of sanction if they are not fulfilled (which is a long way of saying there is no right without a remedy). To maintain that men had an unbounded right to liberty was rubbish, Bentham argued (no-one other than the great feminist theorist Mary Wollstonecraft was then suggesting that women did) and to argue that men had an unbounded right to both equality and property was self-contradictory. In practice such rights would be limited by law, so rights which were asserted against executive and legislative powers were in reality *defined* by them.

Bentham was also a utilitarian. So-called Utilitarians are probably the most robust and longstanding critics of human rights and their criticisms echo to this day. From a utilitarian perspective, what is right is that which produces the best outcome for most individuals – commonly known as 'the greatest happiness of the greatest number' principle. As a legal positivist and a utilitarian, Bentham epitomises the mainstream of the British approach to law and social policy, which is arguably still dominant. The traditional human rights approach so far discussed posits: a) that there are certain fundamental rights or entitlements that all human beings can lay claim to whether or not they are recognised by national (or even international) laws and b) that it is the few not the many who frequently most need their fundamental rights protected by the enforcement of standards which apply to all, regardless of citizenship or status and regardless of majoritarian-determined policies. Equal protection of fundamental rights for every individual is given precedence over the happiness of the majority, in other words. But Bentham's critique of natural rights theories was not just empirical i.e. based on fact, but normative, i.e. based on how he thought the world *ought* to be. Whether they existed or not, he argued that broad statements of rights were anyway wrong and even dangerous. Declarations of individual rights burst the cords that bind 'selfish passions' when the cohesion of society depends on their restraint, he maintained. This view was strongly influenced by his take on the French Revolution which he initially supported but came to strongly oppose.[14]

He might have been surprised, some half a century later, to find he was echoed in this view of rights by arguably the world's strongest *advocate* of revolution, Karl Marx. Although not entirely hostile to the French Revolution's proclamation of citizens' rights, Marx, along with his collaborator Frederick Engels, took the view that the idea of a morality not based on class relations was a great deception. "None of the so-called rights of man . . . go beyond egoistic man" he wrote ". . . that is an individual withdrawn into himself, into the confines of his private interests and private caprice, and separated from the community." Rights encourage individuals in "their egoistic selves,"[15] Marx insisted.

A more modern critique of human rights which is conceptual, rather than either empirical or normative, is driven by what is known as an 'anti-foundationalist approach.' In other words, it is not so much the idea or ideal of rights that is criticised as the argument that there is some objective foundation to them beyond choices or claims made by particular groups and individuals at a specific time and place. British communitarian philosopher, Alasdair MacIntyre, famously wrote in 1982 that "[t]he truth is plain: there are no such rights, [i.e., human rights, natural rights, rights of man,] and belief in them is one with belief in witches and in unicorns."[16]

For the late American philosopher Richard Rorty "human rights foundationalism is outmoded." The quest for human rights defenders is *not* to establish the 'truth' of human rights, according to Rorty.[17] The challenge is 'doing human rights' which for Rorty involves "increasing our ability to see the similarities between ourselves and people very unlike us as outweighing the differences." This is what he calls "sentimental education."[18] In other words, human rights cultures are *made, not discovered*. They are dependent on the human capacity to empathise – to discover that which you have in common is greater than that which separates us from our fellow human beings. Rorty's scepticism about the value of human rights *theory* does not translate into scepticism about the *practical* value of human rights.

4. Human rights as politics

The quest for an objective justification for human rights – whether in God, or nature or the essence of humanity – will undoubtedly continue. But even if this is, as anti-foundationalists maintain, a fruitless task, the *reality*, as Beitz suggests, is that human beings have claimed, and will continue to claim, that there are fundamental human rights to which everyone is entitled by virtue of being human, whether they can be 'objectively validated' or not.

Such claims have now been codified and recognised, if not by all peoples everywhere, at least by global institutions and international treaties (not to mention domestic bills of rights). If this system has accumulated a measure of moral authority, however much it is also disputed or opposed, then arguably the study of human rights involves an understanding of the *political* factors which have led to this acceptance, as well as the *legal* principles that it reflects.

We have established that the assertion of fundamental and enduring ethical values based on notions of human dignity, natural laws or natural rights has a long pedigree, and a far wider and richer ancestry than western thought. But if we trace the history of the *political struggle* for human rights (rather than the origins of the *idea*) the focus changes to particular parts of the globe in specific eras.

In the English context, it is arguably reasonable to begin with the battles which led to the 1215 Magna Carta and the struggles in the English Civil War that culminated in the 1689 Bill of Rights. These are widely recognised as the antecedents of modern human rights.

Whilst the Magna Carta was primarily a series of concessions extracted by medieval barons rebelling against King John, one section confirmed people's rights under the common (or judges') law. The right to a fair trial and to jury trial in particular, is sometimes traced back to this medieval English document. It wasn't all sweetness and light. There is some unpleasant medieval anti-Semitic stereotyping within it [indeed two generations later all Jews were expelled from England in 1290 which puts into context some of the more exaggerated claims that the Magna Carta ushered in the dawn of universal human rights!]. But it *is* fair to attribute the Magna Carta with establishing the *principle* of the rule of law in England (however frequently it was breached then and since, particularly in Ireland, Scotland and Wales and subsequent colonies, not least through the slave trade). The idea that 'none was so high that they were above the law,' was truly novel in the era of the divine right of kings. Reflecting its enduring *symbolic* significance over 700 years later, one of the UDHR's prime drafters, Eleanor Roosevelt, expressed her wish to the UN General Assembly on 10 December 1948 that the Declaration "may well become the international Magna Carta of all men everywhere."

Whilst the 1689 Bill of Rights passed in the wake of the English civil war was the first to bear that name, it is probably the only bill of rights in history aimed *primarily* at establishing the rights of Parliamentarians vis a vis the Monarch, rather than proclaiming the rights of the people vis a vis those who make the laws. Its significance, besides its name, lies in its influence on the UK's current, largely unwritten constitutional settlement and explains why we talk of 'parliamentary sovereignty' rather than 'people's sovereignty.' However it was also ahead of its time in ushering in rights to bail and not to be inflicted with 'cruel or unusual punishment,' both of which found their way into modern international human rights treaties.

Tom Paine, the 18th century English radical and pamphleteer who was exiled from Britain for his radicalism but went on to play a leading role in both the French and American Revolutions, not only gave voice to the natural rights theories of John Locke but extolled what we would now called social and economic rights. In *Rights of Man Part Two*, published in 1791, his chapter on *Ways and Means* came as close to proposing a welfare state funded through progressive taxation on landed property as anything that emerged for another 150 years.[19]

All typologies are largely subjective but I would suggest that understanding the evolution of human rights as *waves*, helps to conceptualise their dynamic essence. As we have seen, the first wave of rights as a popular political movement can be traced to the period known as the European Enlightenment. Ideas like the 'natural rights of man' gave intellectual coherence to a generalised discontent with despotic rulers and church leaders. Together with the suppression of religious and intellectual freedom in parts of Europe and the new world, these factors helped to fuel the French and American uprisings at the end of the eighteenth century.

Whilst liberty, autonomy and justice were not the only values driving these revolutions they were certainly the predominant ones. Although lip service was paid to equality, in reality women were largely excluded and black slaves were shockingly declared to be three fifths of a man in the original American constitution.

The second wave of rights developed in a very different context. It was a direct response to the horrors of the Second World War, and subsequently the Soviet gulag. This was the era when the international human rights movement as we now know it was born.

The United Nations Charter was signed on 26 June 1945. In the face of opposition from two (otherwise ideologically opposed) Allied powers – the Soviet Union and the UK – lobbying by a combination of largely Latin American states and a range of prominent NGOs (including the civil rights supporting NAACP and the American-Jewish committee) led to the inclusion of several references to human rights in the UN Charter. These committed the member states of the fledgling body to "cooperate" to promote respect "for human rights and for fundamental freedoms." Although States were perceived to be the main *transgressors* of human rights, they were also tasked with being the principal *enforcers* of their own human rights responsibilities, whilst new UN mechanisms were to supervise the enactment of this responsibility. The stresses and contradictions of this approach were apparent from the beginning.

Significantly, the UN's authority to promote, let alone protect, human rights was qualified – if not contradicted – by another provision of the Charter denying it authority to "intervene in matters which are essentially within the domestic jurisdiction of any state" (A.2(7)). This recognition of each state's national sovereignty is primarily what brought the UK and USSR on board.

Thus a new ethical approach to international relations was overlaid on a traditional model of state sovereignty providing the basis for the enduring tension between the universal pretensions of human rights, and the UN's mission to protect the independence of sovereign states. The decolonisation process which began around the same time only contributed to this tension as newly independent states understandably guarded their independence from *interference* by – what is still widely seen as – a Western-driven agenda of human rights. This political and legal quagmire has played out ever since and is behind the on-going debate about whether, and if so how and in what circumstances, the UN and its constituent states have a "responsibility to protect" human rights from gross violations by sovereign states. From Bosnia to Rwanda, Kosovo to Libya and now Syria this tension has not been resolved.

Meanwhile the references to human rights in the UN Charter also disappointed many rights advocates by not including a *legally enforceable* international bill of rights within its terms. This proposal was *opposed* by most of the major colonial powers and America which was racked by racial inequalities and legal discrimination. There was obvious nervousness on their part about integrating a bill of rights within the fabric of the UN Charter. Instead a Commission on Human Rights was established, chaired by Eleanor Roosevelt, the wife of the by now late President. It met for two years and the result was the 1948 Universal Declaration of Human Rights (UDHR) which was adopted with the support of 48 countries and 8 abstentions, including the USSR, Saudi Arabia and South Africa. The UDHR has spawned or inspired all subsequent regional and international human rights treaties, including the European Convention (ECHR) and many national bills of rights around the globe.

The UDHR represented the start of a new phase in human rights thinking by ushering in the idea that rights are *universal* and should apply to all people everywhere (although many states that adopted the UDHR, including the colonial powers, resisted this in practice and still do). The experience of Nazi Germany had turned the former Enlightenment-era assumption on its head, that democracy would in itself be a guarantor of fundamental rights and that citizenship status would suffice. The Nazis had, of course, initially used the mandate of democratic legitimacy to disenfranchise German citizens and remove all rights from sections of the population in an era where there were no agreed international norms, let alone enforcement mechanisms, to hold them to account.

Although not a legally binding treaty as such (the Declaration is as it says on the tin – a *declaration*), the UDHR has exerted a huge moral and legal influence around the world. Its provisions have been cited or used so often over the years that it is generally accepted that parts of it are now 'customary international law' and hence binding on states. Whilst, like the bills of rights of the Enlightenment, the UDHR still sought to protect individual freedoms and liberty, this was in a new context. It was not only states that were implicated in the persecution and genocide which had disfigured the world. The inhumanity that individuals had shown to their fellow human beings, under orders or otherwise, conveyed to the drafters of the UDHR that a neutral concept like 'freedom' was an insufficient basis on which to build the peaceful and tolerant world they sought to achieve.

In essence, the transition from the first to the second wave of rights is represented by a shift from a preoccupation with the rights and liberties of individual citizens within particular nation states to a preoccupation with creating a better world for everyone. Both waves were aimed at protecting individuals from tyranny but the vision of how to achieve that goal had shifted. In the earlier era the main target was to set people free; in the later period it was to create a sense of moral purpose for all humankind by underlining the values of dignity, equality and community (on which, more later).

The third wave of rights signals the *globalisation* of rights and their take up by civil society throughout the world. It marks a return to grass roots human rights movements driving the agenda forward as we have witnessed most recently in the (so-called) Arab spring, summer and autumn. In *Values for a Godless Age*, I suggest that this wave took off from 1989 with the (so-called) Velvet Revolutions of Eastern Europe which signalled the end of the Cold War that had frozen, and arguably disfigured, the evolution of human rights into a zero sum game between the two superpowers. The respective championing of civil and political rights (by Western powers and their sponsors) and social and economic rights (by the Soviets and their satellites) had pitted both sets of rights against each other as part of an ideological war between states and their spheres of influence. The Velvet Revolution reclaimed rights as a dynamic force, with demands for freedom and dignity claimed by millions of disempowered human beings. This set off a chain reaction, I suggest, where human rights language to some degree displaced Socialism and nationalism as the motor of liberation and change. The historian Samuel Moyn, in his book *The Last Utopia*, develops an alternative thesis. He suggests that it was in the post-colonial 1970s when human rights took off amongst global civil society, in response to the failed utopias of Marxist regimes and new national movements.[20] Whether the decisive decade is the 1970s or the 1990s, the argument remains that the human rights ideal has become a driver of many political movements around the world in an era of failed utopias.

5. Human rights as law

There is a paradox about the exponential growth in human rights law. The more that human rights norms are reflected in international and domestic law, the more that its defenders can rely on legal positivism to justify them; yet, as we have seen, human rights partly developed in response to a legal positivism which maintained there were no rights outside the law.

Even accepting the centrality of law to any understanding of human rights, international human rights treaties are not comparable to most technical, domestic legislation but are based on a framework of ethical values. As we have seen, a contextual reading of the UDHR and other post-war human rights Instruments would suggest that the principles they embody are not just the Enlightenment ideas of liberty, autonomy and justice but also a positive conception of equality alongside communitarian concepts like dignity, and community.[21] But how are each of these values interpreted in a human rights law context?

First dignity. The emphasis on the concept of dignity in the UDHR had two, very different, consequences. First, from this I think we can trace the origins of the so-called 'teleological' approach – adopted by courts such as the European Court of Human Rights (ECtHR) – to interpret human rights law in a *purposive* way to enhance fundamental values and principles. This is a world away from the British legal positivist tradition we've discussed which focuses on the plain meaning of words.

The other, quite separate implication of the second wave concept of dignity concerns the role of the state. If the dignity of human beings is to be respected then it follows that the state has to do more than refrain from interfering or oppressing. It has to ensure that the basic requisites of human dignity are provided for. *This*, as much as the direct importation of the value of equality is a major route into socalled second generation social and economic rights which are fused with civil and political in the UDHR. The concept of inherent dignity illuminates the obvious point that the freedom to choose your own path in life is pretty hollow if in reality you have few choices. What does it mean to have a right to life, for example, unless you have the wherewithal to live and survive in economic terms or a right to a private life if you have no home?

This has led, perhaps inevitably, to the growing jurisprudence of recent years that states have '*positive obligations*' to secure individual rights in certain circumstances even when this requires interfering between two *private* parties; for example, to protect the victims of hate crime by members of far right groups or phone hacking by tabloid journalists. Tyranny and fear are not solely perpetrated by nation states, particularly in a globalised world where private trans-national companies can wield enormous power, employing their own security apparatus and intelligence gathering personnel.

The second defining value in post-war or 2nd wave human rights Instruments is equality. Equality before the law – meaning all laws should apply to everyone equally – is different to the law acting to *promote* and *protect* equality. Modern antidiscrimination law can be traced to the UDHR which in turn altered the way human rights defenders viewed the principle of liberty. Once people are told they cannot be free to choose who to let their house to or who to hire and fire if their choice is based on racial or sexual discrimination etc, then freedom takes on a new and more complex meaning.

Perhaps the most surprising feature of second wave rights is the incorporation of concepts like community and responsibilities. One obvious lesson drawn from the descent into barbarism that had contaminated virtually the whole of

Europe in the Second World War, was that the same individuals who require protection from tyranny can also contribute to it. Although it is generally states who are the bearers of responsibilities under international law, the 1946 Nuremberg Tribunal, established to try war criminals, developed a doctrine of individual responsibility.

The view that the UDHR should include the responsibilities as well as the rights of the individual was widespread amongst the drafters from the outset. French representative, René Cassin, one of the Declaration's prime authors, was keen not to present the UDHR as a mere imitation of eighteenth century rights.

> *"All human beings . . . should act towards one another in a spirit of brotherhood"* commands Article 1.
>
> Article 29 (first clause) states simply that: *"Everyone had duties to the community in which alone the free and full development of his personality is possible."*

The wording of this article expresses two intertwined ideas. First, that individuals have responsibilities as well as rights. But second – and often missed – that individuals do not exist in the world as isolated beings but live in societies, or more specifically communities, to which they must act responsibly if they are to develop their true humanity.[22]

The second clause in the same Article 29, which sets out general grounds for qualifying individual rights – like protecting the rights and freedoms of others or to maintain public order – is found in some form in most of the binding treaties which flow from the Declaration, including the ECHR. Such qualifying clauses simultaneously set limits on how far governments can go in restricting rights whilst establishing the acceptable boundaries of individuals' rights. This in turn provides a guide as to where the exercise of rights might hurt others, for example by inciting racial hatred through freedom of speech or infringing privacy through intrusive photos. In this sense the obligations of individuals to others and to the broader society in which they live are indirectly, but clearly, established. The qualifications on rights set the legitimate terms within which a right can be exercised.

By the time that members of the Council of Europe came to draft the European Convention on Human Rights (ECHR) a year or two after the UDHR, the spectre of Communism was as much in the minds of the delegates as the horrors of fascism. With some nifty drafting by a former Conservative Lord Chancellor, Sir David Maxwell-Fyfe, and other British lawyers, the list of qualifications and limitations on rights increased. The late Lord Chief Justice, Lord Bingham, once remarked that there is "inherent in the whole of the Convention . . . a search for balance between the rights of the individual and the wider rights of the society . . . neither enjoying an absolute right to prevail over each other."[23] In this sense, this is quite a different approach to the North American individualistic conception of rights which has been famously characterised by the renowned American law theorist Ronald Dworkin as "trumps" over other claims.[24]

Not all the rights in the ECHR are qualified or limited (for example, freedom of conscience, freedom from torture and from slavery can fairly be described as absolute rights). Nor can rights just be limited at the whim of the state either. To adopt the phrase in the ECHR, restrictions must be "prescribed by law" and "necessary in a democratic society." To determine when an interference with a qualified right is *necessary* or *legitimate,* the ECtHR has developed four tests: legality, necessity, proportionality and non-discrimination.

In brief, legality means you must be able to know in advance what the law is that limits or qualifies your rights so that you can regulate your behaviour accordingly. Necessity means that limitations on rights must meet a 'pressing social need' (e.g. to curtail protest on public safety grounds). Proportionality means that even where there is a legitimate ground for limiting rights as set out in the Convention, such restrictions must not go beyond what is strictly necessary in a democratic society to achieve that purpose and a less restrictive, but equally effective, alternative should be used when available. Nor must such limitations on rights unnecessarily discriminate against protected classes of people in the way they are applied. Overall this doctrine of necessity and proportionality is probably the most significant principle of interpretation developed by the ECtHR. Translated into ordinary language it means, don't use a sledgehammer to crack a nut![25]

Conclusion

We began by asking whether human rights are best conceived of as philosophy, law or politics. I said I wouldn't answer that and I won't. But if I was forced, under torture or otherwise, to respond to my own question it would be this:

Human rights are a set of ethical values capable of legal expression that derive from human struggles and the lessons human beings have learnt about how to make life liveable.

In other words, the law reflects the values which in turn are human made. Try as we might we will not find an objective justification for them which is immune from intellectual and political challenge.

Notes

1 For example, Hossein Mehrpour in "Human Rights in the Universal Declaration and the Religious Perspective," *Reflections on the Universal Declaration of Human Rights,* Kluwer 1998.
2 René Cassin, 1972. See Micheline Ishay, *The History of Human Rights: From Ancient Times to the Globalization,* University of California Press, 2004, p19.
3 *The Evolution of International Human Rights,* Paul Gordon Lauren, Pennsylvania Press, 2003, p12.
4 *On the Law of War and Peace,* 1625.
5 Charles R Beitz, *The Idea of Human Rights,* OUP, 2009, p59.
6 Professor John Tasioulas, "Towards a Philosophy of Human Rights," Inaugural Lecture, UCL, January 2012.

7 Martha Nussbaum, "Human Rights Theory: Capabilities and Human Right," *Fordham Law Review*, 66 (1997) pp 292 & 296.
8 Amartya Sen, "Elements of a Theory of Human Rights," *Philosophy and Public Affairs*, Vol 32, No 4, p322.
9 Oxford Paperbacks, 2001.
10 Charles R Beitz, op cit, p79.
11 Ibid, p84.
12 Abdullahi An-Na'im, "Universality of Human Rights: An Islamic Perspective," *Japan and International Law: past, present and future*, N Ando (ed), Kluwer Law International, 1999 p315.
13 See Jeremy Waldron (ed) *"Nonsense upon Stilts," Bentham, Burke and Marx on the Rights of Man*, Methuen, 1987, p53.
14 See John Dinwiddy, *Bentham*, OUP, 1989, pp77–8.
15 Karl Marx, *On the Jewish Question*, 1843.
16 Alisdair MacIntyre, *After Virtue*, University of Notre Dame Press, 1981, p69.
17 Richard Rorty, "Human Rights, Rationality and Sentimentality," in *On Human Rights: the Oxford Amnesty Lectures*, Susan Hurley and Stephen Shute (eds), Basic Books, 1993, p116.
18 Ibid, p129.
19 Tom Paine, *Rights of Man*, Penguin Classics, 1984.
20 Samuel Moyn, *The Last Utopia, human rights in history*, Belknap Press, 2010.
21 See Johannes Morsink, *The Universal Declaration of Human Rights*, Penn Press, 1999 and *Inherent Human Rights, philosophical roots of the Universal Declaration*, Penn, 2009.
22 Erica-Irene Daes, *Freedom of the Individual under Law: a study of the Individual's Duties to the Community and the Limitations on Human Rights and Freedoms under Article 29 of the UDHR*, UN, 1990, p19.
23 *Leeds City Council v Price and others* [2006] UKHL 40, para 181.
24 Ronald Dworkin, *Rights as Trumps*, J Waldron, *Theories of Rights*, OUP, 1984, pp153–67.
25 See Keir Starmer, European Human Rights Law, Legal Action Group, 1999.

4

RIGHTS AND RIGHTEOUSNESS

Friends or foe?*

Strategic visions for human rights: Essays in honour of Professor Kevin Boyle,
Geoff Gilbert et al. (eds) (Routledge, 2011)

Two years after the second world war a little known, but remarkable, symposium of philosophers and writers was published by UNESCO. Giants in their field, including Harold Laski, Aldous Huxley and Mahatma Gandhi, contributed their reflections on the meaning and nature of rights and, and their inter-relationship with duties, to a Committee of Experts in Paris.[1] The following year their deliberations fed directly into the drafting of the founding document of the modern international human rights movement, the Universal Declaration of Human Rights.

Six decades later many of the same issues are still the subject of fraught debate in the UK and beyond; the relationship between rights and duties, legitimate limitations on individual rights, the role of culture and religion in the articulation of rights and whether human rights are necessarily secular. Looking back at the historical development of rights, this chapter considers the relationship, if any, between religious values and human rights.

Rights and righteousness

Before I worked for Professor Kevin Boyle as a Research Fellow at Essex University in the early 1990s, I had little exposure to the values that drove the development of international human rights law. Until then I had understood human rights to be a set of legal entitlements by the individual against the state. Kevin Boyle's scholarship revolutionised my understanding of international human rights as a set of ethical values which shaped the law. His insights into faith-based values, and their influence on human rights discourse, were a revelation to me.

To mark the sixtieth anniversary of the UNESCO symposium, Kevin and I were invited to Belfast to address a conference, organised by the Northern Ireland Human Rights Commission and the Irish School of Ecumenics, on the theme of 'Rights and Righteousness'. This intriguing pathway into discussing religious values and human rights led me to research the etymology of both terms to explore whether they shared a common ancestry. The English Oxford Dictionary defines righteous as "just, upright, virtuous, law abiding." The word 'right' has many definitions, with "just and fair treatment" amongst them. This suggested that there was enough common ground between the two to explore whether, in the modern world, rights (or specifically *human* rights) and righteousness can be seen understood as inter-related ideas with common roots, or alternatively potential antagonists – staring at each other across a gulf of incomprehension and mistrust.

According to *Proverbs* "he who is steadfast in righteousness (defined as uprightness and right standing with god) attains to life". Psalms tells us that "the righteous shall inherit the land, and dwell therein for ever" and Matthew proclaims "blessed are they who hunger and thirst for righteousness, for they will be satisfied".[2] If the 19th century evangelist and writer Dr Herbert Lockyer is correct, the root meaning and essential idea of the term "*righteousness*" is that of "rightness, or being right or just in all things."

Rights, on the other hand, have an altogether different connotation in public discourse. The legal theorist, William Edmundson, in his 2004 *An Introduction to Rights,* describes human rights as rooted in the recognition of "extraordinary, special basic interests" which "sets them apart from . . . even moral rights, generally".[3] Michael Freeman, in his introductory textbook, defines human rights as "just claims or entitlements that derive from moral *and/or legal* rules".[4]

Rights as selfish interests?

The association between human rights and individual interests, or technical legal rules – and by extension individualism and selfishness – has a long and varied pedigree.

Former Archbishop of York, Lord Habgood, spoke for many ecclesiasts when he argued in a lecture at Westminster Abbey in the same year the UK Human Rights Act (HRA) was introduced that:

> "the indiscriminate use of the concept of rights can undermine morality at its very core by focusing attention on what the world owes us, rather than on the network of mutual obligations and shared assumptions which compose the fabric of a healthy society."[5]

Lord Jakobovits, the late Chief Rabbi, made a similar point when he argued:

> ". . . could it be that the greatest moral failure of our time is the stress on our rights, on what we can claim from others – human rights, women's rights, workers' rights, gay rights and so on – and not on our duties, on what we owe to others? In our common tradition, the catalogue of fundamentals on which our civilisation is based is not a bill of rights, but a set of ten commandments, not claims but debts".[6]

The former pope, John Paul II, lamented that human rights are being reduced to simple "self-centred demands". He said in 2004 "over the last 40 or so years . . . while political attention . . . has focused on individual rights, in the public domain there has been a growing reluctance to acknowledge that all men and women receive their essential and common dignity from god and with it the capacity to move towards truth and goodness . . . detached from this vision" he continued "rights are at times reduced to self-centred demands". [7]

Cambridge philosophy professor Onora O'Neill, who has described human rights as the "idol of our age", warned in her 2002 Reith lecture that "it was dangerous to be looking at rights without looking at obligations".[8] And the current Chief Rabbi, Jonathan Sacks, has likewise called for a new politics which would *"think more expansively about the citizen as a bearer of duties, sharing responsibility for the civic order and not merely as bearer of rights . . . and the pursuit of claims-as-rights."*[9]

All these commentators might be surprised to learn that they share their exception to a framework of rights devoid of duties with Karl Marx and Friedrich Engels. Marx's 'Statutes of Organization of the International Federation of Labour' stated that "The Federation recognizes that there shall be no rights without duties and no duties without rights".[10] Engels complained that *"instead of 'everyone shall have equal rights,' we would suggest 'everyone shall have equal rights and duties.'"*[11]

It is no exaggeration to say that the rights/responsibilities nexus has become a central feature of modern political discourse. But whilst the portrayal of a society plagued by rights inflation and devoid of responsibilities or mutual obligations (the antithesis of righteousness perhaps) will resonate with many people, this is, I would suggest, largely based on a misconception of the history and nature of *human* rights; it is as profound a caricature as describing religion as 'the opiate of the masses.'

Human rights as secular?

Virtually every serious modern scholar of human rights traces the roots of the idea that every human life is of equal worth and dignity to the biblical notion that human beings are created in the image of god or the divine; an idea replicated in most of the world's major religions. It follows that every human being has inalienable value which is why no human being should ever be instrumentalised or treated as a means to an end; the foundational idea of human rights.

But many of the early 'natural rights' theorists of the European Enlightenment went further than expounding this ancient doctrine in new terms. They saw God or the creator as the literal *source* – and explicit *justification* – of the idea of 'natural rights.'

The words of the *American Declaration of Independence* have echoed down the generations but its reference to a higher authority is often overlooked:

> "We hold these truths to be self-evident, that all men are created equal; that they are endowed by their *creator* with certain inalienable rights; that among these are life, liberty and the pursuit of happiness".

The revolutionaries of the Enlightenment may have been in revolt against the apparent divine right of kings and the established church to control their minds as well as arbitrarily curtail their freedoms, but it was to their 'maker' that many of them turned for legitimation of their cause.

For all his championing of individual rights, Jean-Jacques Rousseau, for example, maintained that religious belief was a necessary foundation of virtue. "It is not enough, believe me," he wrote "that virtue should be basis of your conduct, if you do not establish this basis itself on an unshakable foundation."[12] Although their emphasis was on the God-given rights individuals were supposedly born with (well white, European, Christian men anyway), the moral obligations individuals supposedly owed to each other, was not entirely absent from the world view of the early rights theorists.

Tom Paine, the famous 18th century English radical wrote that when the 1789 French Declaration of Rights was debated in the National Assembly there was a call for a Declaration of Duties to accompany it. His response:

> "a declaration of rights is, by reciprocity, a declaration of duties also. Whatever is my right as a man, is also the right of another; and it becomes my duty to guarantee as well as possess." [13]

The American academic theologian, Michael Westmoreland, whose wife is a Baptist minister, traces the idea of "human rights" as a source of political struggle to the divinely inspired Levellers who emerged during the English civil war. "Human rights are a Christian heritage" Westmoreland argues "and yet, today" he says "this concept of basic justice for everyone" is regarded as "secular thinking" by the Christian community itself.[14]

This portrayal of human rights as essentially secular — in the sense of being sceptical or opposed to religious belief — is not uncommon amongst human rights activists either. It is sometimes warn as a badge of pride. This label can be adopted as an attempt to capture the universal features of human rights; a means of signalling that they are not the property of any particular belief or creed. But the term *secular* does not sufficiently convey the nature and historical evolution of human rights.

The separation between church and state in France and America (and, for that matter, in modern Turkey) have driven this association between human rights and secularism. But this is to confuse a constitutional arrangement in a few countries with the values which drive an idea of global force. All over the world religion has, of course, been a prime force behind campaigns for human rights, often explicitly so.

The role of the American and English Protestant churches in anti-slavery campaigns is well known. There have also been links of equal significance between Hinduism and the embracing of human rights in post-colonial India, Catholicism and liberation struggles in South America, Islam and modern day protests against human rights atrocities in Palestine and Sudan and between Buddhism and the ongoing struggles in Tibet and Burma. The Israeli-based peace movement, Rabbis for Human Rights, speaks for itself.

Some years ago I wrote a book with the worst judged title in history, *Values for a Godless Age*, to coincide with the introduction of the HRA.[15] A snappy title, which helps to sell books, but one I would not use again. Less than a year after it was published the events of 9/11 crashed onto our world and God was back as a driver of passions and disputes across the globe.

The point of my title was *not* to portray human rights as essentially a *secular* idea, as some people understandably thought. On the contrary, my intention was to suggest that the way to understand human rights is not, primarily, as *legal* entitlements for individuals, but as ethical values for a diverse society; values which stem from some of the same insights that have guided the great religions.

I am far from alone in this view. The Islamic scholar and Iranian law professor Hossein Mehrpour has declared that "apart from that aspect of religion which consists of the important duty to spiritually guide and instruct, there are no serious differences or contradictions . . . between religious teachings and human rights."[16]

René Cassin, one of the prime drafters of the 1948 Universal Declaration of Human Rights (UDHR), was more specific still. He maintained that the "first article in the UDHR that all human beings 'should act towards one another in a spirit of brotherhood,' corresponds to the injunctions familiar to the Abrahamic religions that we should 'love thy neighbour as thyself' and 'love the stranger for you were strangers once'". "We must not lose sight of fundamentals," Cassin wrote, in noting that "the concept of human rights comes from the bible."[17]

Human rights as ethical values?

The ethical ambitions of the UDHR were widely shared amongst its drafters. H. Santa Cruz, the Chilean delegate, expressed his hope that "the International Bill of Human Rights should not just be a Bill but rather a true spiritual guide for humanity enumerating the rights of man which must be respected everywhere."[18] When the Declaration was finally adopted by the UN in 1948, Cassin said "something new has entered the world . . . the first document about *moral* value adopted by an assembly of the human community".[19] This conception of human rights as rooted in an ethical vision for humanity, stands in stark contrast to their portrayal as steeped in selfishness and individualism.

The link between human rights and ethical values – or, put another way, the link between human rights and the right way to behave, or righteousness – is easier to understand if we trace the evolution of the idea of human rights over time. The influence of the UNESCO symposium on the drafting of the UDHR is stark. An extract from the 1947 papers amply demonstrates the convergence of the common themes of individual dignity and mutual respect:

> "faith in freedom and democracy is founded on faith in the inherent dignity
> of men and women . . . these rights are claims which all men and women
> may legitimately make, in their search, not only to fulfil themselves at their
> best, but to be . . . capable . . . of becoming in the highest sense citizens of the

various communities to which they belong and of the world community, and in those communities of seeking to respect the rights of others, just as they are resolute to protect their own."[20]

Both the UNESCO publication, and the drafting of the UDHR the following year, were driven by a set of cataclysmic events which were, of course, very different to those which preceded the first wave of rights Charters in late 18th century Europe and America; although it is the latter, more distant, era which is probably more rooted in the modern public consciousness.

The UDHR (like its Enlightenment counterparts) was aimed at protecting individual freedoms and liberty from arbitrary power and state tyranny. But the context was new. Present in the minds of the drafters were the immediate horrors of the Second World War, the death camps and the persecution and dehumanisation of non-Aryans which led thousands of fellow citizens to 'walk on the other side'. If the main target of the 'first wave' Enlightenment era was to set people free, in the post-war period it was to create a sense of *moral purpose* for all humankind. In the words of Mary Robinson, the former UN High Commissioner for Human Rights and former President of the Republic of Ireland, the UDHR was "an elevating force on the events of our world".[21]

Since this time, the drafters of international human rights treaties (including the European Convention on Human Rights) have sought to establish a framework of ethical values driven not just by the *ideals* of liberty, autonomy and justice but also by normative *values* like dignity, equality and mutuality. One obvious lesson drawn from the descent into barbarism that had given impetus to the development of an International Bill of Rights, the collective name given to the UDHR and the two binding treaties which flowed from it,[22] was that the same individuals who require protection from tyranny can also contribute to it. Creating mechanisms to prevent states from abusing the rights of their citizens was crucial, but plainly not enough to guarantee liberty. The thinking was that individuals *themselves* needed to be inculcated with a sense of *moral purpose* if there was 'never again' to be a genocide like the one unleashed by the Nazis.

Rights and duties

The question was, how to achieve this sense of 'moral purpose'? Jacques Maritain, one of the contributors to the UNESCO papers, maintained that rights and duties are correlative:

> ". . . a declaration of rights should normally be rounded off by a declaration of man's obligations and responsibilities towards the communities of which he is a part, notably the family group, the civil society and the international community".[23]

For similar reasons, the Latin American states, in particular, were in favour of including a list of duties in the UDHR. The Chinese delegate, Dr Peng-chun

Chang, was also supportive because "The aim of the United Nations was not to ensure the selfish gains of the individual but to try and increase man's moral stature. It was necessary to proclaim the duties of the individual for it was a consciousness of his duties which enabled man to reach a high moral standard."[24]

There was considerable debate amongst the UN delegates about who owed rights and obligations to whom. Was it just the state which owed obligations to individuals who are the sole bearers of rights or do individuals have duties to the state? In the end they agreed to a framework rooted in mutual obligations based on what individuals owe each other and the community in which they live (as distinct from what they owe the state).

This approach is directly reflected in Article 29 of the UDHR which states simply that "Everyone has duties to the community in which alone the free and full development of his personality is possible." The wording of this Article expresses two intertwined ideas. First, that if human rights protection is to be effective, this involves an appreciation that all individuals have responsibilities to each other, as well as rights that must be protected by the state, as Tom Paine remarked 150 years earlier.

Second – and this was to some degree a departure from the earlier 'natural rights' framework – that individuals do not exist in the world as isolated beings but live in societies, or more specifically communities, on which they depend. In this sense the sometimes false dichotomy between individual and collective rights can miss the point. Human beings don't usually flourish in dysfunctional communities so there is little purpose in granting individuals' rights if the cost is the demise of the community in which they live. But all communities are not the same, of course, and the responsibilities individuals owe will differ, depending on the context.

The word 'alone' in Article 29 is significant here. It was added to Article 29 at the suggestion of the Australian delegate, Alan Watt, and was supported by the UK delegate because it "stressed the essential fact that the individual could attain the full development of his personality only within the framework of society."[25] According to Professor Johannes Morsink, the word 'alone' "may well be the most important single word in the entire document for it helps answer the charge that the rights set forth in the Declaration create egotistic individuals who are not closely tied to their respective communities".[26]

So important was the content of Article 29 to the UDHR that it was originally drafted as the first Article of the Declaration. Cassin had placed the 'responsibilities Article' first because he thought it "essential" before defining the concrete rights, such as the right to life, to define "values which were higher than life itself".[27] Others supported this proposed sequence to emphasise to the reader from the outset that the rights and freedoms in the Declaration were to be enjoyed within the framework of a functioning society.[28]

The communitarian themes of Article 29[29] – there is no more accurate word for them – partly reflected the political, philosophical and religious backgrounds of the drafters of the UDHR which, in addition to liberalism, social democracy and socialism, included Islam, Judaism, Christianity and Confucianism.[30] But the reflections on responsibilities, as well as rights, mainly stemmed from the same mission which influenced so much of the contents of the Declaration. This was not just to set the people free but to find common values in which the liberties of individuals would be respected without weakening the bonds so necessary for human flourishing. It was a different understanding of the concept of freedom. In other words, the earlier 'natural rights charters' were not simply being replicated in a global bill of rights. For René Cassin, the UDHR was not "a mere offshoot of the eighteenth century tree of rights".[31]

There is no better illustration of this evolution in the human rights framework than in the contrast between the First Amendment of the American Constitution, which declares that "congress shall make no laws prohibiting fee speech", and the responsibilities-driven right to free expression in Article 10 of the European Convention on Human Rights (ECHR). The latter explicitly recognises that the exercise of free expression "carries with it duties and responsibilities" by individuals, as well as states, so that the right to free speech can be legitimately limited to protect the rights and reputation of others and various other social goods, like public safety or the prevention of crime.[32]

Addressing tensions and conflicts between rights

At the root of the mischaracterisation of human rights as essentially individualistic or egoistic lies the failure to appreciate that the post-war human rights framework was partly designed to address tensions and conflicts *between* rights – and between individuals and groups – that are inevitable in diverse societies and in the global community. This is the practical purpose – the utility – of human rights, which has been achieved with varying degrees of success.

Protecting individual freedoms from an overweening state is only one element of the post-war vision of rights, therefore. For as well as potential violators, states are given the prime role as *protectors* of human rights in international law – referees, if you like, between competing needs and interests. Human rights values are intended to provide a framework through which to umpire differences. Case law from the European Court of Human Rights (ECtHR), and our own domestic courts applying the Human Rights Act (HRA), provide countless examples of how this framework of competing values can play out in practice.

When Mark Anthony Norwood, a BNP member, placed a poster in the window of his house which depicted the New York twin towers in flames with the phrases "Islam out of Britain" and "protect British people" emblazoned on the poster, he was convicted of a "religiously aggravated" offence under the Public Order Act.[33] The ECtHR found that he could not claim his right to free speech had been violated because his anti-Islam images were a public attack on all Muslims.[34] The ECHR (Article 17) explicitly prohibits individuals from using human rights as a pretext to violate the rights of others.

But in this case the attack was against a religious (or some would say ethnic) *group* rather than a religious *belief.* Attacks on ideas or beliefs raise more complex issues. The ECtHR has often emphasised that freedom of expression is a fundamental right that applies not only to ideas that are inoffensive but also to those which "offend, shock or disturb", and that pluralism demands tolerance of views critical of religious beliefs.[35] But the state also has a responsibility to protect the right to freedom of conscience and religion which can exist in tension with free speech.

The ECtHR refused to interfere when the Austrian state seized copies of a film by the Otto Preminger Institute which satirised Jesus as a mental defective attracted to the Virgin Mary.[36] The Court affirmed that even the devout must tolerate and accept the denial by others of their religious beliefs, but the *manner* in which religious beliefs and doctrines are opposed by private individuals can become the responsibility of the state if it inhibits freedom of worship or belief. The Court declared that governments have a duty, in extreme cases, to prevent portrayals of religious objects that are so provocative as to be a malicious violation of the spirit of tolerance which lies at the heart of the ECHR. A controversial decision to many, including me, as it clearly involved a considerable incursion into free speech. But it is possible to elaborate on the *principles* this judgment articulated without supporting censorship or bans (outside the context of incitement to violence or hatred).

Human rights values, such as those just described, potentially provided a way through the morass that surrounded the so-called 'cartoon controversy' that engulfed Europe and the Middle East in 2005/6. The European editors who published the Danish cartoons that suggested an association between Islam and terrorism, explicitly sought to make a stand against self-censorship in the name of what they saw as a threat to the supreme Enlightenment value of free speech. They maintained that freedom of expression *must* include the licence to offend – licence in the sense of complete freedom rather than just legal permission.

But the human rights framework suggests that self-restraint can be necessary to prevent the demonisation or denigration of minorities in certain contexts, whilst maintaining a free and uncensored press. The right to free expression is the *only* right in the ECHR and the ICCPR[37] which explicitly refers to *individual* responsibilities. As the Nazi Holocaust, the Rwandan genocide and the Bosnian massacres demonstrated, we now *know* that free speech, the cornerstone of a democratic society, can also be used to deny, or even obliterate, the rights of others in certain circumstances. They may not have known that in the Europe of the Enlightenment but we cannot shun this knowledge today. The post-war human right to free expression encompasses the *totality* of this perception.

Exercising the right to free expression in 'a spirit of brotherhood', in the words of Article 1 of the UDHR, sometimes involves refraining from speaking – or indeed drawing – when it is not the state or other sources of power that are being attacked but vulnerable individuals whose core identity is at stake.

Any serious debate about religious belief or doctrine should expect to be protected by the ECHR. But serious debate was entirely absent from these graphics which caused fear and outrage, not just to those they lampooned. The principles of tolerance and dignity that define plural societies can also provide the basis for necessary and proportionate limitations on free expression.

The exercise of religious freedom does not begin and end with belief of course. Although international human rights law provides *absolute* protection of the right to religious (and non religious) thought and conscience, the *manifestation* of belief can be limited to the extent that is necessary (but not more than that) to protect the fundamental rights of others, and in some circumstances, the common good. This is the doctrine of proportionality which lies at the heart of the post war human rights framework and the ECHR in particular. Whilst there are some values, like freedom from torture and slavery, which are absolute, most rights are limited or qualified in line with the communitarian approach established by the 'responsibilities Article' of the UDHR.

After a bitterly contested case in the domestic courts, Shambo, an ill fated holy bull who lived in a Welsh Hindu temple and tested positive for the bacterium that causes bovine TB, was slaughtered under the authority of the Welsh Assembly. The Court of Appeal ruled that Shambo's slaughter was potentially a grave and serious breach of the Hindu community's manifestation of religious expression, but it was a *necessary* limitation on religious freedom to protect public health, making the slaughter regrettable but proportionate.[38] It is possible to agree or disagree with this decision, of course. But the point is that in plural societies with diverse beliefs and creeds it is essential to have a transparent framework of consistent principles – rooted in a search for what is just and fair – to address different, and sometimes directly conflicting, perspectives.

The sometimes tortuous debate over the degree to which it is 'just and fair' for religious bodies to opt out of laws prohibiting discrimination, underlines the difficulty of applying such a framework in practice. There was equal controversy over *exempting* religious organisations from complying with sexual orientation regulations to avoid conflicting with the "strongly held religious convictions" of (a significant number of) their members,[39] as there was over *requiring* publicly funded bodies, like Catholic adoption agencies, to comply with them.[40] Righteousness in action requires practical solutions to difficult dilemmas. A human rights framework is an attempt to root such solutions in 'the right thing to do' rather than simply what the majority want, or what is easier or cheaper to achieve.

Conclusion

What is the justification for such a framework – who is to say a human rights approach is of more value than any other? It is absolutely true that, in contrast to the early 'natural rights' theorists, modern human rights charters do not rely on a creator, or God, to justify the ethical value system human rights proclaim. The concept of dignity has replaced the idea of 'God' or 'nature' as the foundation of 'inalienable rights'. The essential dignity of all humanity is sufficient to warrant equal treatment, the argument goes, regardless of whether you believe that human dignity stems from a higher being or not.

But this emphasis on dignity rather than the divine does not mean that human rights are fundamentally individualistic *or* necessarily secular in orientation. The idea of human rights is rooted in a belief that there is sufficient common ground between all humanity – between men and women of *all* religions and beliefs and none – to establish a set of bottom-line values rooted in respect for the equal worth of everyone.

Human rights are not the same as religious belief of course. There is no truth to promote beyond the inherent dignity of all human beings, no doctrine beyond fair and equal treatment. Human rights are very much rooted in the here and now rather than the afterlife. The purpose is not to *compete* with the spiritual values and *private* convictions heralded by the world religions. It is to seek agreement on what values we can share so that we can live together in peace – and mostly in harmony – in a diverse world where people of many creeds and philosophical beliefs share the same political and geographical spaces.

The very first Article of the UDHR recognises that we humans are more than material beings with definable needs and rights, natural or otherwise. It proclaims that human beings "are endowed with reason and *conscience* and should act towards one another in a spirit of brotherhood". Our essential nature as human beings is rooted in two elements, it is proposed. Our ability to think and reason in the classical Enlightenment mould, but also our capacity to care, to feel empathy – 'to suffer with,' in the Ancient Greek conceptualisation of the term.

This insight into the human condition underlines the whole enterprise of the UDHR. If human beings were only capable of rational thought but couldn't feel empathy for others the project to create a fairer and more just world would have been doomed from the outset – or even more doomed than it has proven to be.

Where a human rights and a religious or spiritual framework seemingly overlap the most, therefore, is where they require us to stay in touch with our conscience. The strongest confluence is where they drive us to be aware of more than we can see with our eyes – whether this concerns deporting or 'rendering' people to places where they will be tortured out of sight or fundamental questions about end of life decisions that take place in the twilight. It is this search of our conscience that I understand to be at the root of the quest for righteousness, as well as human rights. It is arguably why, as the dictionary suggests, there may well be common roots to both terms.

Notes

* This paper is based on Francesca Klug's keynote speech to the 'Rights and Righteousness: Religious pluralism and human rights' conference, in Belfast, 1–2 November 2007, organised by the Northern Ireland Human Rights Commission and the Irish School of Ecumenics. Her speech has subsequently been published by the Irish School of Ecumenics.

1 *Human rights: comments and interpretations*, A Symposium edited by UNESCO, with an introduction by Jacques Maritain, Columbia University Press, 1949.
2 http://nccbuscc.org/nab/bible/matthew/#foot7.

3 William Edmundson, *An Introduction to Rights*, Cambridge University Press, 2004.

4 Michael Freeman, *Human Rights*, Polity Press, 2002, p6.

5 Lord Habgood, The Sydney Bailey Memorial Lecture, Westminster Abbey, London, April 1998.

6 Debate on 'society's moral and spiritual well-being', House of Lords *Hansard*, vol.573, col.1717, 5 July 1996.

7 Address of John Paul II to the Bishops of the Church in Colorado, Wyoming, Utah, Arizona, New Mexico and Western Texas on their "Ad Limina" visit, 4 June 2004.

8 Onora O'Neill, A Question of Trust: The BBC Reith Lectures 2002, Cambridge University Press, 2002.

9 Jonathan Sacks, *The Politics of Hope*, Jonathan Cape, 1997, p233.

10 Quoted in I. Szabo and others, *Socialist Concept of Human Rights*, Budapest: Akademiai Kiado, 1966, pp52–61.

11 Quoted in Erica-Irene Daes, "Freedom of the Individual Under Law," UN, 1990, p40.

12 Julie ou La Nouvelle Heloise (1761).

13 Thomas Paine, *Rights of Man*, [1791], Penguin, 1984, p114.

14 See http://blog01.kintera.com/christianalliance/archives/2006/12/international_h.html.

15 *Values for a Godless Age: The Story of the United Kingdom's New Bill of Rights*, Penguin, 2000.

16 Hossein Mehrpour, "Human Rights in the Universal Declaration and the Religious Perspective," in *Reflections on the UDHR*, Kluwer, 1998.

17 René Cassin, 1972. See Micheline Ishay, *The History of Human Rights: From Ancient Times to the Globalization*, University of California Press, 2004, p19.

18 E/CN.4/AC.1/SR.2/p3, 13 June 1947.

19 Quoted in Johannes Morsink, *The Universal Declaration of Human Rights: Origins, Drafting and Intent*, University of Pennsylvania Press, 1999, p33.

20 See n.1, p260.

21 'A Declaration of Human Rights: A Living Document', address at the Symposium on Human Rights in the Asia-Pacific Region, Tokyo, 1998.

22 The 1966 International Covenants on Civil and Political Rights and Economic, Social and Cultural Rights.

23 Above, n.1, p76.

24 Ninety-Fifth meeting of Third Committee, 6 October 1948, E/800, p87.

25 Hundred and Fifty-Fourth meeting of Third Committee, 24 November 1948, E/800, p660.

26 Above, n.19, p248.

27 E/CN.4/AC.2/SR.2/p6, 5 December 1947.

28 E/CN.4/SR.77/p2–3, 28 June 1948.

29 The pinpointing of community as a central political idea can be traced to a group of thinkers known as communitarians. For decades a debate raged in the US between academic communitarians like Michael Sandel and liberal philosophers like John Rawls. The communitarians quarrelled with the idea that states should provide a neutral framework of rights and freedoms within which individuals can pursue their private ideals. For communitarians, good government involves recognising and conserving the networks that individuals belong to. Rights entail a responsibility to participate in these networks and to care about the moral tone of society as a whole. See, for example, Michael Sandel, *Liberalism and the Limits of Justice*, Cambridge University Press, 1982; Charles Taylor, *The Ethics of Authenticity*, Harvard University Press, 1991.

30 Johannes Morsink, above n.19, chapters 1, 2 and 8.

31 Ibid, p245.

32 A similar reference to duties and responsibilities is found in the right to freedom of expression in the International Covenant on Civil and Political Rights (ICCPR) which gave legal enforcement to the civil and political rights of the UDHR.

33 *Norwood v DPP* [2003] EWHC 1564 (Admin).

34 *Norwood v UK* (2005) 40 EHRR SE11.

35 *Handyside v UK* (1976) 1 EHRR 737.

36 *Otto-Preminger Institute v Austria* (1994) 19 EHRR 34.
37 See n.32.
38 *R (Suryananda) v Welsh Ministers* [2007] EWCA Civ 893.
39 Equality Act (Sexual Orientation) Regulations 2007.
40 *Catholic Care (Diocese of Leeds) v The Charity Commission for England and Wales*, Charity Tribunal decision, 1 June 2009.

5

HUMAN RIGHTS

Above politics or a creature of politics?

Policy and Politics Annual Lecture 32, no 4 (October 2004): 563–72

For the last forty years or more, this country has appeared to be in the grip of one kind of national panic or another. In the 1960s and 1970s it was a *moral* panic that took hold of 'middle England'. Self-styled hippies and lefties were charged by an older generation with threatening the fabric of society. In the 1980s it was threats to national security that appeared to strike fear in the heart of the nation, from IRA terrorists to the spectre of a Soviet nuclear attack. As the 1990s progressed we were back to a moral panic again. The view that contemporary society was characterised by 'too many rights and not enough responsibilities' was shared by politicians, priests and political commentators alike.

And then September 11 happened and the thousands of trees which were sacrificed to lament the 'me-too culture' of the previous decade obtained a reprieve. The nation's focus was once again on national securty. With the so-called 'war against terrorism' still raging – surely the first war in history with no discernible beginning and therefore potentially no end – this is where the nation's attention still rests.

This is not to suggest that every national crisis is a figment of people's collective imagination. There is plenty of evidence to support the Prime Minister, Tony Blair, in his assertion that Al Qaida and allied groups are motivated to kill as many civilians as they can for goals that cannot be met through "negotiable political demands" (Blair, 2004). (Although whether they have the *capacity* to do so is far less clear.) But the point is, in a world in which terrifying and tangible risks and dangers are mingled with perceived and exaggerated ones, it is understandable that many of us reach out for something (or someone) enduring to steady us.

From the earliest time, human beings have sought touchstones to protect them from the unpredictable. For many people, now and in the past, God or religious values provide an element of consistency and comfort in a world that is both forever changing and forever racked by fears. But for those of us who have never been certain that we can rely on the supernatural to guide us – and even for many of us who do not harbour such doubts – human rights provide an attractive refuge from the vicissitudes of our world.

It was this take on human rights that I sought to capture with the title of my book, *Values for a godless age*, that I wrote three years ago on the introduction of the 1998 Human Rights Act (HRA). I suppose that title will go down as one of the worst predictions of the future ever. Post September 11 the world feels anything but godless and those human rights values whose time had come – or so I argued at the time – are actually facing greater challenges than ever. The point of the title of my book was to suggest that there is a degree to which belief in human rights is coming to substitute for religious belief. The title was a kind of plea not to turn human rights into a talisman against uncertain times but to recognise the dynamism that has catapulted this idea from the margins to the mainstream. A momentum which, in my view, flows from the ultimately contingent nature of human rights as values 'for the people, by the people and of the people'.

When governments toss aside hard-won rights and freedoms, as the British government can fairly be accused of doing at the moment, it is very difficult to argue that such a seductive idea as the legal certainty of human rights standards should be passed over for a more contingent world view. For just as laws which allegedly protect national security or moral certainty provide a bulwark against disorder and chaos for many governments and their supporters, so human rights laws which are said to obtain their authority from outside the democratic political process can equally provide some reassurance in uncertain times.

This, I believe, is what the learned Judge Sir John Laws was driving at when he wrote that inalienable rights are:

> " . . . values which no democratic politician could honestly contest; values which, therefore, may be described as *apolitical* since they stand altogether *above* the rancorous but vital dissensions of party politicians."
>
> *(Laws, 1995: 93; my emphasis)*

It is also what I understand the former Secretary General of Amnesty International, Pierre Sane, to have meant when he said:

> "A true democracy has to be founded on a consensus about the duty of all to respect, protect and fulfil all fundamental rights and existential needs. *A consensus which places human rights above politics and above class divisions.*"
>
> *(Sane, 2000; my emphasis)*

It is worth pausing to try to unpack what is being suggested here. Is what is being proposed that human rights *should* be above politics for instrumental purposes? In other words, that a functioning democracy is so reliant on there being laws which protect individual freedoms and promote political participation that human rights law, although a product of the democratic process itself and therefore ultimately subject to change, should receive some degree of special protection? Should human rights be constitutionally protected so that politicians cannot bend fundamental rights to respond to the popular will? Or is what is being suggested that human rights values are so fundamental and enduring that by their *nature* they cannot be, nor should be, subject to democratic or popular engagement?

The first proposition has long been the subject of dispute. The issue of whether we should go the American way, and have a Supreme Court that could overturn legislation which breaches fundamental rights, drove the debate on whether the UK should have its own bill of rights on and off for twenty years.

The model adopted in the Human Rights Act (HRA) does not allow the courts to overturn Acts of Parliament but to 'declare' that legislation is breached instead. It is then for Parliament (or more realistically the government) to determine how to proceed. (For a full explanation of this model, see Wadham et al, 2003.) The rationale for this approach – very crudely put – was to try to *reconcile* the need for mechanisms to stop the government of the day from overturning fundamental rights without judicial scrutiny, with the democratic principle that political decisions should ultimately rest in the hands of elected politicians rather than unelected judges. It was a deliberate attempt to maintain political engagement with fundamental rights whilst preventing ministerial meddling with those rights at will.

The contrary argument is that human rights can only be protected if human rights law is "above the reach of statute and state" (Lester, 2001: 694). Translated into policy, this argument holds that the courts must be constitutionally empowered to strike down laws which breach fundamental rights.

The American experience, however – from the post-war McCarthy era to the *Patriot Act*[1] and allied anti-terrorist legislation of the current day – does not bear out the hypothesis that making the courts the ultimate arbiter of human rights or civil liberties law *necessarily* makes either inviolable. There are a number of reasons why the American Supreme Court, with all its powers, has failed to act to protect fundamental rights and freedoms when they are most at risk – whether now or four decades ago. One factor that is difficult to dismiss is that judges themselves are influenced by the perceived or real crises of their era.[2]

Lord Scarman famously called for a bill of rights in 1974 to protect the law from the "will of Parliament" when fear "is stalking the land" (Scarman, 1974). Current developments appear to bear out his point. What this perspective overlooks, however, is that it may be precisely when judges are most required to fend off the excesses of the executive that they may *themselves* be most susceptible to arguments that national security or public order trump other concerns. But whatever the merits or otherwise of this argument about the constitution, this is distinguishable from the common proposition that the *nature* of fundamental rights is such that they themselves are essentially "above politics" (see Laws, 1995). This is a claim often made, quite casually, by human rights lawyers and advocates.

The search for a special justification for rights which takes them outside the realm of ordinary dispute and disagreement can be traced back to the birth of the modern rights movement in the late 17th century and the 'natural law' theories of Thomas Hobbes and John Locke. Locke (1689) claimed to have "proved" that "man" was "born . . . with a title to perfect freedom". The exercise of power by rulers was legitimate only as long as citizens' 'natural rights' to property and liberty etc were respected. Tom Paine, the eighteenth-century British radical, who set Locke's ideas alight in his best-selling pamphlet *Rights of man* (Paine, [1791] 1984) went on to influence the American revolution with these ideas, having been present at the French.

The direct lineage between Locke's writings, Paine's popularisation of them and the preamble to the American Declaration of Independence is as self-evident as the rights that are proclaimed:

> "We hold these truths to be *self-evident*, that all men are created equal, that they are endowed by their *Creator* with certain *inalienable* Rights; to secure [these] rights, governments are instituted among men, deriving their just powers from the consent of the governed. . . . "
>
> *(Preamble, American Declaration*
> *of Independence; my emphasis)*

Supporters of 'natural rights' maintained that the rights which fuelled upheavals across two continents were not primarily political aspirations seeking legal expression, but a product of 'nature', if not 'god'. This insistence inspired the utilitarian philosopher Jeremy Bentham to famously remark that natural rights were "simple nonsense" and "natural and imprescriptible rights" were "nonsense upon stilts" (quoted in Bowring, 1843: 501). Rights not created by specific laws or by governments were illusory, according to Bentham. To say that 'men' had an unbounded right to liberty was rubbish, he maintained, and to say they had a right to both property and equality was self-contradictory.

The debate between 'foundationalists' and 'non-foundationalists' over whether or not there are '*essential*' features that justify human rights and take them outside political discourse into the realms of the supernatural, resurfaced as recently as 1948 during the drafting process of the Universal Declaration of Human Rights (UDHR) (see Freeman, 1994). An attempt was made by some of the drafters to tie human rights to 'nature' in the preamble of the UDHR and bring 'god' into the text. In the end this was specifically rejected. No longer was a higher being or pre-existing state of nature cited as the source of fundamental rights as in the American Declaration of Independence. According to the UDHR, rights accrue to all human beings, without distinction, because of their essential *dignity*.

However, the search to find an objective 'foundation' for human rights continues. Constructionists like John Rawls and Ronald Dworkin are taken to task by communitarians like Michael Sandel or Alasdair MacIntyre over their quest to construct an *objective justification* of human rights from basic principles (see Nino, 1991). Denuded of *celestial* support for the 'special' place for human rights, it has become necessary for 'foundationalists' or their successors, to rely on so-called 'objective principles' of justice or dignity.[3] The classification of rights as 'objective', and 'external' to political engagements leaves largely unexplained the important question of *how* or *why* rights have taken the pre-eminent place they have as a motor for change at particular points in history, or as a means of expressing individual and collective *aspirations* as well as legal entitlements.

The evolution of what constitutes fundamental rights over time – from the right to bear arms to the right of transgender people to have their birth certificates altered – and the influence of different beliefs and cultures on the way they have evolved, is almost entirely lost by an attempt to cast them outside the realm of politics. I want to try to offer an alternative narrative to one which places rights outside the political realm. One which traces the now commonplace acceptance of some aspirations as so important that they can be classified as rights, and given legal protection, to the grubby world of political conflict and struggle.

The idea of rights did not – of course – emerge fully clothed out of the minds of the great philosophers to be handed over to judges and legal theorists for interpretation. Their evolution has been shaped by people who chose to act together to claim rights in different circumstances and with varying goals in mind. Although the changing conception of rights over time is commonly described in terms of 'three generations of rights', in my view the dynamism involved in the evolution of rights is more aptly captured by the phrase 'three waves of rights'.[4] Implicit in the term 'wave' is the recognition that there have been distinct periods when the idea of rights has come to prominence, and others where its influence has waned. The 'first wave of rights' burst on the scene in the period known as 'the Enlightenment'. Ideas like the 'natural rights of man' gave intellectual coherence to a generalised discontent with despotic rulers and church leaders. Together with the suppression of religious and intellectual freedom in parts of Europe and the New World, these ideas helped to fuel the French and American uprisings at the end of the 18th century and eventually inspired widespread democratic reform across Western Europe.

Although the philosophical basis of the movement for 'inalienable rights' has roots which go back much further, it was only in the Enlightenment that the idea became sufficiently popular to bring about widespread change. While liberty, autonomy and justice were not the only values driving the first wave of rights, they were certainly the predominant ones. Phrases from this time – like "the natural, inalienable and sacred rights of man"[5] and "men are born and remain free and equal in rights" (drawn from the 1789 French Declaration of the Rights of Man and Citizen) – have echoed down the generations.

Every bill of rights and international or regional human rights treaty that has been drafted in the ensuing years owes something to these original texts. The basic idea that all human beings without distinction are endowed from the moment of their birth with inalienable rights and are entitled to justice and equality before the law remains the founding principle of what we now call human rights. Such ideas have been evoked to challenge authority for 200 years. Principles like 'liberty' and 'equality,' for example, were widely appealed to during the 19th-century anti-slavery struggles in Europe and America. Particularly in the United States, these values went on to fuel a 'rights consciousness' which in turn helped to shape the civil rights and women's movements of the last century.[6] It is very hard indeed to see them as 'above politics' in any sense.

The 'second wave of rights' developed in a very different context but hardly one that could be described as apolitical either. It was a direct response to the horrors of the Second World War, and subsequently the Gulag. This was the era when the international human rights movement, as we now know it, was born. Whilst the UN's 1948 UDHR still sought to protect individual freedoms and liberty, this was in a new context. It was not only states that were implicated in the persecution and genocide which had disfigured the world. The inhumanity that individuals had shown to their fellow human beings, under orders or otherwise, conveyed to the drafters of the UDHR that a neutral concept like 'freedom' was an insufficient basis on which to build the peaceful and tolerant world they sought to achieve. In essence, the transition from the first to second wave of rights is represented by a shift from a preoccupation with the rights and liberties of individual citizens within particular nation states, to a preoccupation with creating a better world for everyone. Both waves were aimed at protecting individuals from tyranny but the vision of how to achieve that goal had shifted. In the earlier era the main target was to set people free; in the later period it was to create a sense of moral purpose for all humankind.

The drafters of the plethora of international human rights treaties which the UDHR has spawned,[7] have sought to establish a framework of ethical values driven not just by the Enlightenment ideals of liberty, autonomy and justice but also by the three defining values of modern human rights treaties: dignity, equality and community. The entry of these new values into human rights discourse in turn reflected the preoccupations not only of the drafters of the UDHR, but of the changed world they were seeking to improve. The UDHR is peppered with the term dignity. It appears to denote a recognition that human beings have more complex needs than to be free from restraint, which was uppermost in the minds of the 'first wavers'. To quote from the Universal Declaration, all human beings, endowed with "reason" and "conscience", and have a "personality" whose "free and full development" are essential elements of human dignity.

In a sense the adoption of the term *dignity* can be understood as the UN delegates' 'answer' to the 'natural rights' debate. The concept of dignity replaced the idea of 'god' or 'nature' as the foundation of 'inalienable rights'. This completed the transition from 'natural rights' to 'human rights'; a term which did not come into common usage until this time. The drafters of the UDHR drew from the ethical principles of *all* the major religions as well as from socialist, liberal and other secular thinking. The concept of inherent dignity illuminated the obvious point that the freedom to choose your own path in life is pretty hollow if in reality you have few choices.

If the dignity of human beings is to be respected then it follows that the state has to do more than refrain from interfering or oppressing. It has to ensure that the basic requisites of human dignity are provided for. *This* was the route into so-called second-generation economic, social and cultural rights which are fused with civil and political in the UDHR.[8] It is also the route to the interpretation of the European Court of Human Rights that states have 'positive obligations' to protect individuals from the abuse of rights by others, widening the protection of fundamental rights instruments to encompass the prevention and investigation of crime, and indeed terrorism.[9]

Turning to what I have identified as the second major value distinguishing second- from first-wave rights, equality, an obvious objection is that this was a major facet of the first wave as well – wasn't the French revolutionaries' rallying cry "liberty, equality and fraternity"? But when the drafters of the American and French charters spoke of everyone having equal rights, they did not mean it in the way we understand it now. By equality they meant equality before the law (that is, that no one is *above* the law, not that states should outlaw discrimination).

By minorities the proponents of first-wave rights usually meant numerical minorities (often religious dissenters but also property owners and even slave traders). Women were initially largely excluded. Of course to obtain equal human rights you have to be counted as human in the first place. In the original American constitution, slaves were shockingly enumerated in the constitution as three fifths of a man. Freedom from discrimination – and racial discrimination in particular – is the unspoken first amendment guarantee of the UDHR. It has the same pre-eminence as free speech in the American Bill of Rights, by implication if not by law. This is not surprising. The Nazi Holocaust against the Jews, gypsies, homosexuals, disabled people and other minorities influenced every aspect of the deliberations of the drafters of the UDHR, leading to a new emphasis on the value of equality. This was no longer to mean only formal equality but a requirement that states take actions to route out racial hatred and discrimination of all kinds, including between private individuals.

This approach was to change the way human rights defenders viewed the principle of liberty. Once people are told they cannot be free to choose who to let their house to or who to hire and fire if their choice is based on racial or sexual discrimination, for example, then freedom takes on a new and more complex meaning. But perhaps the most striking feature of secondwave rights is the incorporation of concepts like community and responsibilities. One obvious lesson drawn from the descent into barbarism that had contaminated virtually the whole of Europe in the Second World War, was that the same individuals who require protection from tyranny can also contribute to it.

Creating mechanisms to prevent states from abusing the rights of their citizens was plainly not enough to guarantee liberty. Individuals themselves needed to be inculcated with a sense of moral purpose if there was 'never again' to be a 'holocaust' like the one unleashed by the Nazis.

The view that the UDHR should include the responsibilities as well as the rights of the individual was widespread amongst the drafters from the outset. French representative, René Cassin, one of the Declaration's prime authors, was keen not to present the UDHR as "a mere offshoot of the eighteenth century tree of rights" (Morsink, 1999: 245).

> "All human beings . . . should act towards one another in a spirit of brotherhood", commands Article 1.

Article 29 (first clause) states simply that:

> "Everyone had duties to the community in which alone the free and full development of his [sic] personality is possible."

The wording of this Article expresses two intertwined ideas. First that individuals have responsibilities as well as rights. But second – and often missed – that individuals do not exist in the world as isolated beings but live in societies, or more specifically communities, to which they must act responsibly if they are to develop their true humanity. UN Special Rapporteur on discrimination and minorities, Erica-Irene Daes, maintains that the word 'community' was also chosen to emphasise that individuals have duties, not to the state whose legitimacy (in human rights thinking) depends on it upholding the rights in the UDHR, but to the group in which they live (Daes, 1990).

These communitarian themes – despite the overturns, there is probably no better word to describe them – partly reflected the political, philosophical and religious backgrounds of the drafters of the UDHR, which included Islam and Confucianism. But they mainly stemmed from the same precipitating factors that influenced so much of the contents of the UDHR. In other words, the emphasis on the social nature of human beings and their responsibilities to others and the wider community flowed from the task the delegates set themselves as they surveyed the devastation that beset the world at the end of the Second World War. This was not just to set the people free but to find common values in which the liberties of individuals would be respected without weakening the bonds so necessary for human development. It was a different understanding of the concept of freedom.

The main difficulty with the second wave of rights, however, was the developing context of the Cold War in which it took root. The rights that had been developed by state delegates, standard setters and jurists postwar became frozen in a battle between two world views, for which neither was human rights a central concern. Both used and abused the idea to a wider end. The capitalist West declared the Soviet East, its satellites and proxy states to be major human rights abusers – using 'rights' and 'freedom' as interchangeable terms. The Soviet East accused the West of ignoring the centrality of economic, social and cultural rights without which, they argued, formal rights to liberty and free speech were of little consequence.

When the Berlin Wall tumbled down in 1989, this stand-off ended. Human rights discourse was liberated from this stifling polarity. Coinciding as it did with the combination of factors we now describe as globalisation, human rights could be said from this time to have entered a third wave in the evolution of rights discourse.

Whilst there was still the same recognition of the values of dignity, equality and community as in the second wave (and liberty, autonomy and justice as in the first) there was – and is – a growing emphasis on participation or mutuality.

Increasingly, through the use of new technology and as a consequence of the powerful effect of viewing atrocities as they happen from the living-room chair, more and more people worldwide have started relating to the great debates about fundamental rights. This product of globalisation has begun to wrest control from the well-intentioned international standard setters and jurists who have monopolised the endeavour to define what constitutes human rights since the Second World War.

In legal terms the net of liability is spreading ever wider under international human rights law. Corporations, charities and even private individuals in some circumstances are increasingly held responsible for upholding the rights of others (even if, under international law, this is indirectly through their governments). More definitively than at the dawn of the second wave, it is now established that states are not the only, or always the main, abusers of power.[10] As significantly, there is a new emphasis on seeking to uphold fundamental human rights through trade agreements, education and persuasion as well as through litigation (see Klug, 2000, chapter 5).

In essence, the third wave does not so much involve a change in the characterisation of rights as an evolution in the place of rights within society. The enrichment of human rights thinking through the engagement of civil society has never been more marked. The quest to separate human rights from political currents and political discourse had never seemed more futile. We are all potential rights upholders and rights abusers now and we all have the opportunity to engage in the debate about the nature of fundamental rights.

The central terrain of rights struggles has increasingly moved from the North to the South. Some of the most innovative rights thinking in modern times reflects this change as human rights activists, lawyers and thinkers from South Africa, Zimbabwe, East Timor, Burma, Palestine and India dominate many of the current debates on the nature and defining values of human rights.

But just as this third wave of rights – with its emphasis on mutuality and participation – has taken hold, we are faced with the daunting question of how to maintain its momentum within the new international context which has operated since 11 September 2001. One of the significant characteristics of the third wave was the growing recognition by states and inter-state bodies that international human rights standards and values could act as a benchmark in global affairs (see Clapham, 1999).

Set free from the polarities of the Cold War, it had began to be common for international or inter-state bodies like the UN or EU to use human rights indicators to evaluate and challenge (if not always successfully) the actions of the powerful in the North and West as well as in the South and East.[11]

But since the President of the US declared war on terror (not on a state but on a noun), human rights standards are once again at the mercy of the whim – not so much of the great powers – but of the one great power and its cohorts. Western, liberal regimes that quite persuasively cite gross human rights violations as grounds for justifying wars and military interventions, proceed to ignore, or unilaterally reinterpret, international human rights treaties when they allegedly obstruct the successful execution of such wars.[12]

It is ironic to note that some of the key factors that spurred on the first wave of rights in the 17th and 18th centuries are apparent again in these first years of the new millennium (see, for example, Ignatieff, 2004). Specifically:

(i) Western governments routinely cite security threats as grounds for suspending rights that had been fought for and won in the Enlightenment period, such as open trials or 'the presumption of innocence'.

(ii) The rule of law has effectively been suspended altogether with regard to the 'new enemy' (currently known as 'illegal combatants') in a manner reminiscent of the pre–Geneva Conventions era.

(iii) The fusion of religious and political ideologies in the East and the West has led to a revival of concepts like 'evil' and 'collective sin' to justify extra-judicial killings of members of a suspect group.

In the midst of these confusing and sometimes frightening times we are now living in, when we feel there is so little we can control, it is tempting to once again reach for an external force to steady us. It is inviting to search for a modern incarnation of the 'natural rights' theories developed in an earlier time of massive instability and powerlessness.

Measures like the Human Rights Act which seek to place human rights outside the *immediate* reach of populist politicians and headline-chasing ministers can provide some protection against abuse of executive power. The proposed new Commission for Equality and Human Rights, provides an opportunity for extra-judicial strategies for enhancing awareness of, and compliance with, human rights values and standards (DTI, 2004). But if such statutes and strategies seek to place human rights outside the reach of political discourse altogether – on the basis that they are a species apart – there is a risk of them ossifying into a code of technical laws, devised by external forces whose origins are no longer clear.

As I have tried to illustrate in this lecture, the idea of human rights derived from people struggling to address abuses of power. The evolution in rights thinking which has taken place over the last two centuries is itself powerful evidence that it is possible to hold on to the fundamental principles behind this idea, whilst allowing it to grow and develop with changing circumstances. Those who maintain that human rights can only survive insulated from politics, need to take account of their 'political origins'. They need to weigh in the balance the proposition that any institutionalised measures to protect human rights must not stifle the dynamism that has kept this enduring idea alive through three waves of rights.

Notes

1 Full title: *Uniting and Strengthening America by Providing Appropriate Tools Required to Intercept and Obstruct Terrorism, USA Patriot Act, 2001.*
2 This thesis is examined by Epp (1998).
3 Most famously by Rawls (1972).
4 I develop this argument further in Klug (2000).
5 The precise terms used depend on the translation. Tom Paine, for example, writing in 1791, used 'imprescriptible' rather than sacred.
6 See, for example, Epp (1998: 32). Interestingly, there has never been a Socialist movement in America on the scale of Europe.
7 For example, the International Covenants on Civil and Political and Economic, Social and Cultural Rights (1976) and the UN Convention on the Rights of the Child (1989).
8 For example, Article 23.3 states:" Everyone who works has the right to just and favourable remuneration ensuring for himself and his family *an existence worth of human dignity . . .*" (my emphasis).
9 For a full discussion of the European Court's doctrine of 'positive obligations' on states in relation to crime, see Klug (2004).

10 There is, for example, a growing awareness of the human rights abuses of care or domi-cilliary workers to elderly and disabled people in relation to whom the standards in the Human Rights Act apply. See Audit Commission (2003).

11 See, for example, *Human rights: Quarterly review of the Office Of the United Nationals High Commission for Human Rights*, 1999–2000.

12 Most notably, of course, in the context of the wars in Iraq and Afghanistan. See Hersch. (2004).

References

Audit Commission (2003) *Human rights: Improving the delivery of public services*, London: Audit Commission.

Blair, T. (2004) 'The threat of global terrorism', Speech, 5 March.

Bowring, J. (ed) (1843) *The works of Jeremy Bentham*, vol 11 (1838–43), Edinburgh: William Tait.

Clapham, A. (1999) 'Globalisation and the rule of law', in Adama Dieng (ed) *Globalisation, human rights and the rule of law*, London: International Commission of Jurists.

Daes, E.-I. (1990) *Freedom of the individual under law: A study of the individual's duties to the community, and the limitations on human rights and freedoms under Article 19 of the UDHR*, UN: 17.

DTI (Department of Trade and Industry) in association with the Department for Constitutional Affairs, Department for Education and Skills, Department for Work and Pensions and Home Office (2004), *Fairness for all: A new Commission for Equality and Human Rights*, White Paper, Cmnd 6185, London: DTI.

Epp, C.R. (1998) *The rights revolution: Lawyers activists and Supreme Courts in comparative perspective*, Chicago, IL: University of Chicago Press.

Freeman, M. (1994) 'The philosophical foundations of human rights', *Human Rights Quarterly*, vol 16.

Hersch, S. (2004) 'The grey zone: annals of national security', *The New Yorker*, 18 May.

Ignatieff, M. (2004) 'Lesser evils', *New York Times Magazine*, 20 May.

Klug, F. (2000) *Values for a godless age: The story of the UK's first bill of rights*, Penguin.

Klug, F. (2004) 'Human rights and victims', in Ed Cape (ed) *Reconcilable rights? Analysing the tension between victims and defendants*, London: Legal Action Group.

Laws, Sir John (1995) 'Law and democracy', *Public Law*: 93.

Lester, A. (2001) 'Developing constitutional principles of public law', *Public Law*, Winter: 694.

Locke, J. (1689) 'Of political or civil society', in *The second treatise on government*.

Morsink, J. (1999) *The Universal Declaration of Human Rights, origins, drafting and intent*, Pennsylvania, PA: University of Pennsylvania Press.

Nino, C.S. (1991) *The ethics of human rights*, Oxford: Clarendon Press.

Paine, T. ([1791] 1984) *Rights of man*, Harmondsworth: Penguin.

Rawls, J. (1972) *A theory of justice*, Oxford: Clarendon Press.

Sane, P. (2000) 'Human rights and democracy: the challenge of impunity', Speech on Secretary General's mission to Chile, October.

Scarman, Lord (1974) 'English Law, the new dimension', Hamlyn Lecture.

Wadham, J., Mountfield, H. and Edmundson, E. (2003) *Blackstone's guide to the Human Rights Act, 1998*, Oxford: Oxford University Press.

6

FREEDOM OF EXPRESSION MUST INCLUDE THE LICENCE TO OFFEND?

Religion and Human Rights 1 (2006): 225–7

Guest Editorial

An address originally made at:
Intelligence Squared and the London Jewish Cultural Centre public debate
Royal Geographical Society, London, 7 June 2006
Speaking against the motion[1]

There should be no *legal* bans and no state censorship of free expression on the grounds of hurt feelings. Plays like *Beshti*, books like *Midnight's Children*, satires like *Jerry Springer's Opera*, wonderful films like *The Life of Brian*, these all offend people of various faiths, deeply and passionately in many cases. To ban them on the grounds that they may cause offense would be to deny the *essence* of free speech which, as the European Court of Human Rights is wont to say, "constitutes one of the essential foundations of a democratic society, applicable not only to information or ideas that are favourably received . . . but also to those that offend, shock or disturb." However, formal permission is only one aspect of the dictionary definition of license. The other is liberty of action, or complete freedom, especially when *excessive*.

Reflect for a moment on the following distinction. The statement that freedom of expression *must exclude* unwarranted censorship and bans and therefore *can* include the licence to offend, is *not* the same as the proposition that freedom of expression *must* include the licence to offend. But it is only the latter statement we are debating here. Let us look at each proposition in turn. But first a word about free expression – the idea which is *central* to this debate.

Our right to freedom of expression is set down in the 1948 Universal Declaration of Human Rights – and the many treaties it spawned – whose values and principles provide the bedrock of virtually every written constitution or bill of rights in the democratic world and beyond, including the Human Rights Act (the exception is the earlier American Bill of Rights). This right to free expression is not unfettered. In fact quite the contrary. It can legitimately be limited, in a proportionate way, where necessary to protect people from libel or incitement to murder, amongst other grounds. Under the UN Bill of Rights there is actually a *duty* on states to *limit* free speech by outlawing incitement to national, racial or religious hatred.

But *offence*, in and of itself, is *not* one of the legitimate reasons for *the state* to limit free speech. Freedom of expression, in other words, clearly *can* include a licence to offend. But *must* it? That is the question we are debating. Must we, *in all circumstances*, offend if the alternative is to shut up, to temper what we say and how we say it, to self-censor if you like?

The editors of the Danish newspaper *Jyllands Posten* clearly took the view that free expression *must* include a licence to offend. Their point was *not* to defy the *authorities* in the idiom of the great Enlightenment heroes. They had no doubt of their *legal* right to publish a cartoon of the prophet Mohammed with a missile in his turban. The only people they were bent on defying were the Muslim community, a large number of whom, in the context of the world-wide war on terror, were indeed likely be 'offended' – if that is the right word – by a set of cartoons published in a national newspaper, many of which unmistakably associated Islam with indiscriminate violence and terror. Anyone who tells you that the core of this issue was a benign portrayal of the prophet Mohammed published in violation of the tenets of Islam, has either not seen the cartoons or is ignoring acres of comment that the nub of the offence was the association of Islam, and therefore Muslims, with terror.

So why were they published? They were published in the name of free expression and with the knowledge that the cartoons were likely to cause offence and distress. The original Danish publishers, and even more so their counterparts across Europe, went further and argued that it was their *moral duty* to speak out to protect free expression in Europe from the scourge, as they saw it, not of *state censorship* but of *self-censorship.*

Like the proposors of this motion, these editors maintained that freedom of expression *must* include the licence to offend – license in the sense of complete freedom rather than just legal permission. That is their opinion, and I would, of course, defend to the death their right to express it [to paraphrase Voltaire]. I do not so much hate what they say, but dispute its validity. For simply put, just because you have a legal right to publish does not make it *right* to do so.

The Universal Declaration of Human Rights is not primarily a legal document at all. It is a declaration of values, addressed as much to the people of the world as to their governments, drafted after the Second World War, in the wake of "barbarous acts which have outraged the conscience of mankind" to quote the preamble; acts carried out by citizens as well as states. The very first Article reminds us all "to act towards one another in a spirit of brotherhood". No-one is entitled to quote the exercise of one right as grounds for destroying the rights of others. All the rights interact with each other; in exercising free speech we also have to respect the equal dignity and worth of our fellow human beings, especially those already marginalized.

The only right – yes, the *only* right – which explicitly refers to individual responsibilities in the European Convention on Human Rights and UN Bill of Rights is free expression. Why? Because the experience of the Second World War and the Holocaust demonstrated that sticks and stones may break my bones but words can soften up whole populations to collude in genocide. Not necessarily by direct incitement to hatred, which is notoriously difficult to prove, but by the drip, drip effect of dehumanisation and negative associations. A phenomenon we tragically witnessed again in Rwanda, decades later.

We now *know* that free speech, the cornerstone of a democratic society, can also be used to deny, or even obliterate, the rights of others in certain circumstances. They may not have known that in the Europe of the Enlightenment but we can't shun this knowledge today. The post-war human right to free expression encompasses the *totality* of this perception. To exercise our right to free expression in a spirit of brotherhood, in other words, sometimes involves refraining from speaking – or indeed drawing – when the people you are defying or denigrating are clearly more vulnerable than yourself, and it is them or their core identity you are attacking, rather than a philosophical or religious belief.

The cartoon controversy illustrates the thin line between offence, denigration, and incitement. We need to distinguish between offence based on difference of opinion and offence based on denigration. If we do not want to be plagued by laws banning free speech, we must develop the wisdom – and yes ethical sensibility – to make these distinctions *ourselves*. As the European Court of Human Rights is apt to remind us when defending Holocaust denial legislation in the lands where the genocide took place, in exercising such judgement *context is everything*.

To conclude, why are we even having this conversation at this time? The unspoken backdrop is the claim that we need to hold our ground in the light of a growing clash of civilisations. Yes we are living in testing times and I don't disagree that we need to be able to clearly articulate the defining values of liberal democracies. But we are suffering more from a confusion of principles than a clash of cultures.

We likely all agree that free expression is a cherished principle of our society, hard won and easily lost. But does it follow that we therefore stand for the denigration of the vulnerable or the ridicule of the marginalized in the name of free speech? Is that what we want to say we stand for when we defend our values from those who would question their worth? As Aristotle reminds us: "Where we are free to act, we are also free not to act."

Freedom of expression must include a *legal right* to offend. But not, in all circumstances, the complete *licence, to do so.*

Note

1   Also speaking against the motion were David Cesarani and Tariq Ramadan. Speaking for the motion were Lisa Appignanesi, Alain Finkielkraut and Kenan Malik.

When universal human rights hit home

Introduction

'A farcical institution run by a lot of cranks' was the *Daily Express*'s estimation of the Council of Europe (CoE) in 1953, after the UK became the first country to ratify the European Convention on Human Rights (ECHR).[1] The newspaper's wholly negative view of this 'Strasbourg folly', and the human rights court which interprets it, has barely budged in sixty years. This was its position before a single case had been heard and it remains its position now. Like some other British tabloids, the *Express* cheered from its front page when the Conservative Party announced on 3 October 2014 that if it is returned to power in 2015 it will withdraw from the ECHR unless certain conditions are met.[2] In its policy paper, 'Protecting Human Rights in the UK', an unprecedented ultimatum was issued to the Council of Europe to accept a completely new relationship with one of its member states, in breach of its own treaty. Unless there is agreement that the judgments of the European Court of Human Rights (ECtHR) will be converted into purely 'advisory' opinions, the UK will achieve the dubious honour of being the first state to voluntarily leave the ECHR.[3]

The architects of the ECHR would surely be aghast if they knew that in little more than six decades an edifice built to last already seems to be crumbling. Few would put money on this post-war regional human rights apparatus surviving in any recognizable form if one of its founders and most prominent members were to exit. It is not difficult to imagine that states such as Russia or Ukraine, which are far more prone to be found in breach of the ECHR than the UK, would soon follow suit.

The disputed parentage of the European Convention on Human Rights

The Council of Europe's Web site lists six men, all leading statesmen, as its 'founding fathers'. This includes two from Britain: former Conservative Prime Minister Winston Churchill and former Labour Foreign Secretary Ernest Bevin. Although

Churchill's role as a leading champion of the Council of Europe and ECHR is often proclaimed, it cannot be said that the identity of the other founders is well imprinted on the popular consciousness.

The obscure parentage of the ECHR is one of many factors which throughout the years has blurred its identity. Rarely a week passes without a journalist or politician wrongly attributing its genesis to the European Union (EU), when it is in fact a creature of the older and larger Council of Europe (CoE). If the original leitmotif of what is now called the EU was to create a 'common market' amongst a small group of European states, from the time the CoE was established in 1949 its mission was to promote 'human rights, democracy and the rule of law' across war-shattered Europe. Whilst the EU now comprises twenty-eight countries in what is described on its Web site as 'an ever closer economic union', the much looser structure of the CoE encompasses the whole of the continent except Belarus. The ECHR is intended as a common standard for 820 million human beings residing in forty-seven member states.

Tracing the origins of the CoE and its best-known progeny, the ECHR, is not as straightforward a task as delving into the birth of the United Nations (UN) and its famous offspring, the Universal Declaration of Human Rights (UDHR). This is largely because the context within which the ECHR was drafted was becoming more complex and murky even as negotiations on it proceeded.

It would have been inconceivable for the ECHR to have been drafted in pre-war Europe, but by the time the CoE was established in 1949 some of the immediate post-war idealism that drove the adoption of the UDHR the previous year (outlined in Section I) was already wearing thin, and new factors were coming into play. The Cold War was underway and was competing for attention with the Second World War about what should be the primary focus of the new body: lessons learnt from the persecution and bloodshed just passed or ideological warfare against the perceived new threat ahead? The CoE was swiftly becoming an anti-Communist alliance against the Soviet Union and its satellites, beginning a long process of co-opting human rights rhetoric into the service of fighting the Cold War. Post-war reconstruction was monopolizing the resources of most of the continent and discontent and rebellion were bubbling away in the empires of the colonial powers. All of these factors provided an immediate challenge to the human rights and democratic values the CoE claimed to champion.

Yet the ECHR did not just reflect these new European realities either. Before the Second World War there was almost no serious appetite for the international protection of human rights. But previously unimaginable atrocities that had just been uncovered at the heart of so-called democratic Europe drove a newfound belief in the importance of insulating democracies from the degradation they were evidently capable of. Europe had just torn itself apart for the second time in thirty years. At an elite level at least, some of the motivation for drafting the ECHR reflected an idealistic belief that it was possible to create a lasting peace that was ethical and just as well as tranquil. This vision was not confined to Europe of course. It is highly doubtful whether the ECHR would ever have been drafted, and certainly not in the form it took, had not the UDHR made its debut a couple of years before. There was some open plagiarism involved in the text, which no one hid. This is emphatically acknowledged in the Preamble to the ECHR, which begins with 'Considering the Universal Declaration of Human Rights proclaimed by the General Assembly of the United Nations on 10th December 1948', and continues: 'Considering that this Declaration aims at securing the universal and effective recognition and observance of the Rights therein declared'. It concludes with:

> Being resolved, as the governments of European countries which are like-minded and have a common heritage of political traditions, ideals, freedom and the rule of law, to take the first steps for the *collective enforcement of certain of the rights stated in the Universal Declaration.*[4]

This unambiguous assertion in the Preamble, that the ECHR represented 'the first steps' in the 'collective enforcement' of aspects of the UDHR, gained even more significance after the 1969 Vienna Convention on the Law of Treaties came into force in January 1980. This determined that the preamble to any international treaty is an integral part of the instrument itself and therefore relevant to its interpretation. The ECHR's pedigree clearly owes as much, if not more, to international human rights law as to any specifically *European* legal framework.

Britain might claim Winston Churchill as the founding father of the European Convention, but hidden from view is the founding mother, Eleanor Roosevelt. It was the UN Commission on Human Rights she chaired – comprised of multi-national, multi-ethnic and multi-religious UN delegates who drafted the iconic UDHR – which indirectly provided the core of many of the articles in the ECHR. This 'Disputed Parentage of the European Convention on Human Rights' is the subject of an unpublished lecture on its origins reproduced here as the first anthology piece in this section. It seeks to puncture the myth that the ECHR is the product of a separate species called 'European law'. By tracing the Convention's birth and ancestry to the evolution of regional human rights treaties around the world that derived from the UDHR, the lecture argues that 'the ECHR is a regional manifestation of a global phenomenon.'[5]

The significance of the disputed – or more accurately dual – parentage of the ECHR lies in our need to understand precisely what is at stake should the UK withdraw from this treaty. As the European Court of Human Rights Judge Robert Spano has observed, the adoption of the ECHR signified that 'all the Contracting Parties agree that, in principle, the protection of human rights is not an issue that is purely a matter of domestic concern.'[6] This commitment to making the safeguarding of the fundamental rights of human beings *anywhere* the business of us all *everywhere* was, as we saw in Section I, at the core of the mission of the UDHR and all the treaties that have evolved from it.

The momentum behind adopting a human rights charter in Europe was largely led by what became known as the European Movement, a higher powered NGO established in 1948 to encourage greater European co-operation across the war-ravaged continent. From the outset there was consensus that the treaty would be based on the UDHR. This was highly significant for a number of reasons.

First, as emphasized in Section I, the 1948 Declaration was the first charter of its kind in the history of the world to declare that *all* human beings are *equally* worthy of respect and dignity, wherever they were born, and that it was the business of the international community to secure this birthright when national governments fail to do so.

Second, the UDHR represented a significant variation on the values of the Enlightenment, which had until then been widely viewed as the hallmark of 'European civilisation'. By agreeing to base the first ever European-wide treaty on this recent product of the UN, rather than on a re-working of the French Declaration of the Rights of Man and Citizen, for example, the 'founding fathers' were acknowledging that, as UDHR drafter René Cassin put it, 'something new had come into the world.'[7] They were implicitly embracing the emphasis on dignity, equality and community that characterizes the UDHR and distinguishes it from the 'Enlightenment values' which drove earlier charters.[8] They were accepting the terms of a Declaration drafted by delegates from around the globe who brought new insights and experiences to our understanding of what it means to be a human being with certain basic entitlements. This did not go unremarked by the chief authors of the Universal Declaration. Writing in 1951, the year after the ECHR was adopted, Dr Charles Malik, the Lebanese delegate to the UDHR drafting committee, commented: 'A pact on human rights deeply influenced by the Declaration was signed last year in Rome by the nations of Western Europe.'[9]

Even the UK government was aware that it was adopting a treaty based on the UDHR. A minute of a Cabinet discussion noted the UN's influence on the draft Convention:

> In discussion some concern was expressed about the possible implications of accepting the Convention; and the point was made that this was an instance of duplication between the Council of Europe and the United Nations.[10]

Third, as explained in Section I, the UDHR was drafted as the first leg of an international bill of rights, but it was already clear that the two other legs, which were intended to turn the lofty aspirations of the Declaration into enforceable rights, were still a long way from fruition. The superpowers quickly displayed cold feet at the very notion of such an instrument, and the international community was beginning to turn its attention to the demands for freedom from colonial rule which were growing in strength around the globe. By pushing for a European treaty with a court to enforce its standards the champions of the ECHR were fast-forwarding history and ensuring that the iconic UDHR did not fade from significance before its standards could be seen to bite. When the legally enforceable International Covenants referenced in Section I were finally drafted in 1966, and came into force a decade later, the status of the UN Human Rights Committee established to enforce them was no match for the ECtHR.

The mixed marriage of universalism and the common law

The legal historian Brian Simpson, who has written a forensic account of the negotiations which led to the ECHR, relates how by January 1949 the initiative for drafting the text had passed to the British section of the European Movement, and in particular to Sir David Maxwell Fyfe, a former member of Churchill's wartime government and the British Deputy Chief Prosecutor at the Nuremberg Trials.[11] He, in turn, hired a British lawyer, John Harcourt Barrington, to help him push the project forward and was also assisted by two professors, Arthur Goodhart from Oxford and Hersch Lauterpacht from Cambridge. Lauterpacht, as noted in Section I, was very influential in devising many aspects of the post-war international human rights architecture.

The plan was to produce both a concise statement 'based mainly upon the Universal Declaration of Human Rights' and 'measures for the implementation or enforcement of those fundamental rights'.[12] In his autobiography Maxwell Fyfe explained how he became drawn in to drafting the text and his motive for doing so:

> One day in 1947 Winston called me across the smoking room of the House of Commons and asked me if I would join the committee of the United Europe Movement, of which he was chairman. I had always been anxious to do something positive after the part I had played in destroying Nazi ideology, and I accepted with enthusiasm. I wanted to do something about human rights.[13]

Maxwell Fyfe's involvement in the process of drafting the ECHR was key. In certain ways in his very person he also provided a living link between the Convention and the UDHR. Just as the Universal Declaration reflected the insights and experiences of men and women who had just witnessed, and in some cases had been personally devastated by, the events of the Second World War so the text of the European Convention was moulded by a man who had been indelibly affected by the same epoch-defining events. Still fresh from interrogating Goering, Hess and Ribbentrop, Maxwell Fyfe, in unpublished letters to his wife, Sylvia, related how he:

> went to a pre-view of the Russian film in Auschwitz concentration camp. When one sees children of Mo's age and younger in this horrible place and the clothes of infants who were killed, it is worth a year of our lives to help to register for ever, and with practical result the reasoned horror of humanity.[14]

Having been exposed as a lawyer and a human being to the ultimate brutalities of a political ideology driven by genocidal racism and extreme nationalism, Maxwell Fyfe expressed an appreciation of the ideals of 'universalism' in terms reminiscent of the key drafters of the UDHR (discussed in Section I). In summing up at the

Nuremberg trial, he cited Rupert Brooke's famous War Sonnet V, *The Soldier*, to impart his worldview:

> It might be presumptuous of lawyers who did not claim to be more than the cement of society to speculate or even dream of what we wish to see in place of the Nazi spirit, but I give you the faith of a lawyer, some things are surely universal: tolerance, decency, kindliness . . . When such qualities have been given the chance to flourish in the ground that you have cleared, a great step will have been taken. It will be a step towards the universal recognition that: 'sights and sounds, dreams happy as her day, And laughter learnt of friends, and gentleness, And hearts at peace' are not the prerogative of any one country. They are the inalienable heritage of mankind.[15]

The European Movement went on to publish a draft text of the Convention with significant input from both Maxwell Fyfe and Barrington. An introduction to this early draft maintained that since the UDHR had already been adopted by the UN as a common standard for all nations,[16] there was no need for a separate European Charter as such. What was urgent, instead, was a judicial mechanism of enforcement which was to be the main purpose of the treaty.

The debate that ensued centred on whether the new Convention should simply guarantee all the rights in the UDHR un-amended or whether something more precise was required. Some of the advocates for a European charter were concerned that if the articles were expressed in very general terms – sourced from the non-enforceable Universal Declaration – this might 'render them unsusceptible to legal enforcement.'[17]

The Foreign Office, which took the lead in the ECHR drafting process on behalf of the UK government, was particularly vexed by the broad nature of the proposed text, but not because it was keen to see rights enforced by a European court. On the contrary, it was implacably opposed to such a proposal. The UK was initially only prepared to submit to *political* supervision by the CoE. There was far more resistance to judicial enforcement at a pan-European level then there had been by the British delegates to the UN, who had favoured moving much more swiftly to a legally binding treaty than many other state representatives involved in drafting the UDHR. A crucial difference was that there was never a serious proposal to establish the equivalent of the European Court of Human Rights at the United Nations.

Similarly, despite the UK's involvement in drafting the UDHR, which was significant rather than substantial, common law lawyers and civil servants were worried about the undue influence of European civil lawyers on the tenor of the proposed text. The British influence was focused on making the draft tighter and more precise, with specific limitations and qualifications tied to many of the articles, in contrast to the single, broad limitation clause in the UDHR.

British uneasiness about proposals to reproduce unadulterated articles from the Universal Declaration was as much about legal culture as anything more substantive. In contrast to countries with written constitutions, such as the one the Allies had just bestowed upon defeated Germany, Britain's system of parliamentary sovereignty forbade judges from determining whether legislation breached 'a higher law' such as a bill of rights. Common law lawyers, steeped in the traditions of 'black letter law' based on applying legal precedents to 'material facts' on a case-by-case basis, or 'literal interpretations' of statutes,[18] were uncomfortable with *any* broadly expressed declarations of rights which they barely considered to be law at all. These had been rejected by the British establishment as alien and foreign since the French Revolution, notwithstanding England's own legacy of the Magna Carta and boast of producing the first-ever enactment to carry the name Bill of Rights in 1689. The nineteenth-century English legal theorist A. V. Dicey famously advocated the superiority of the common law over bills of rights and written constitutions for protecting basic liberties in his *Introduction to the Study of the Law of the Constitution*:

> Where the right to individual freedom is a result deduced from the principles of the constitution, the idea readily occurs that the right is capable of being suspended or taken away. Where, on the other hand, individual freedom is part of the constitution because it is inherent in the ordinary law of the land, the right is one which can hardly be destroyed.[19]

The article of faith that freedom is inherent in the English system of law cut across all political parties. It not only drove the UK's response to the drafting of the ECHR, but galvanized opposition to the creation of a court which would be empowered to determine whether UK law conformed to broad international human rights standards. This explains the vehemence with which the Labour Lord Chancellor of the day, W. A. Jowitt, declared that:

> It was intolerable that the code of common law and statute law which had been built up in this country over many years should be made subject to review by an international Court.[20]

Jowitt was not prepared 'to encourage our European friends to jeopardise our whole system of law which we have laboriously built up over the centuries, in favour of some half-baked scheme to be administered by some unknown court'.[21] This is not a view that died in 1953 when Jowitt's government ratified the ECHR. It is instantly recognizable to anyone attuned to the current debate on the future of the UK's adherence to the ECHR. The inherent superiority of the common law has no more eloquent a champion today than the Conservative MEP Daniel Hannan, a prominent Eurosceptic in the European Parliament. In his immodestly titled book, *How We Invented Freedom,* Hannan echoes Dicey precisely in asserting that there is an important

> difference between the Anglosphere conception of civil liberties – that is inherited rights won by our ancestors . . . and passed down in the form of an inheritance and the European notion that rights are bestowed by governments.[22]

The relevant Cabinet Papers reveal that the post-war Labour government as a whole was clearly worried about the ECHR encroaching on UK law. Part of this reflected a priori concerns that its socialist programme would be hedged in by a treaty based on individual rights; a not altogether unreasonable fear given that this potential outcome was a source of Conservative *support* for the same measure. According to one Minute, the Cabinet 'expressed a violent, if ill-defined, dislike of the Convention'.[23] But Ministers' reservations about the text did not primarily revolve around concerns to defend the British concept of liberty from the allegedly more restrictive Continental approach. On the contrary, it was the potential impact that a legally enforceable, universally applicable human rights treaty could have on demands for *more* freedom from the UK's restive colonies which most alarmed British ministers. This, even more than legal culture and worries about anti-Labour bias, accounted for the government's initial aversion to the proposed Convention.

The role of the Empire on British nervousness

The Colonial Office, in particular, regretted that the ECHR had ever been conceived of. There was no appetite for rights and freedoms to be exported to Britain's imperial possessions at the very time that demands for independence were mounting. As *The Daily Express* characteristically warned:

> Certainly this ridiculous Declaration will give encouragement to all those who make a sport of besmirching Britain's Colonial Administration. Any malcontent or trouble-maker from the Colonies can now go trotting off to air his grievances at Strasbourg.[24]

The fear that the UK would no longer remain wholly unaccountable for its actions in the colonies was not unfounded. The very first interstate complaints under the ECHR were taken against the UK by Greece in 1956 and 1957 regarding allegations of severe human rights abuses, including torture, by the British authorities in suppressing insurrections in Cyprus.[25] Conservative MP Sir Ian Gilmour later suggested in a letter to the former Home Secretary R. A. Butler that the extension of the ECHR to the Empire must have occurred 'in a fit of perhaps excessive enthusiasm'.[26] He could not have been more wrong. The Colonial Office was anything but enthusiastic but became resigned when the penny dropped that the zeitgeist of the times meant that the momentum for a pan-European human rights treaty was unstoppable. The reservations of the Labour government did not extend to wishing to isolate the UK. Even ruling out the ECHR's application to the many territories the UK still controlled was a hopeless cause, given the ECHR's intentionally universal philosophy. The government's way through these competing pressures was to put its efforts into making *optional* the extra-territorial application of the Convention to the colonies on a piecemeal basis, with a state being explicitly allowed to 'extend [it] to all or any of the territories for whose international relations it is responsible'.[27]

This 'territories clause' was adopted, but not without considerable debate. Belgium, which still ruled over the Congo (now Zaire) had originally suggested a rider to the 'territories clause' to the effect that the ECHR should be applied with 'due regard . . . to local conditions'. After being defeated on this, Belgium surprisingly proposed deleting the clause entirely for 'the moral reason' that it 'would transform the European Declaration of Human Rights into a Declaration of European Human Rights. This would be to deny the same rights to other men.'[28] For those who viewed the ECHR at least partly as a regional manifestation of the new universal human rights ethic developed through the UN (discussed extensively in Section I), it would have been unthinkable for its writ not to run in the colonies governed by European powers. These were the very territories which were fast becoming major sites for new human rights struggles. To exclude them would have exposed the idea of universal human rights to infinite mockery and cynicism. Yet in reality gross human rights abuses were routine in the colonies, Britain's amongst them. Charges of hypocrisy were levelled at the British government at the press conference held in late 1953 to announce the extra-territorial extension of the ECHR to 42 British dependencies. A journalist from the *Daily Worker* asked:

> Whether under the Article about the right to trial all persons arrested without charge or trial in Malaya, Kenya and British Guiana would now be either promptly released or brought to trial?[29]

In reply the Colonial Office spokesman pointed to Article 15, the 'derogation clause'. This was also inserted at the insistence of the British government because of unrest in the colonies and Northern Ireland, meaning nations could opt-out of the Convention during 'war or public emergency threatening the life of the nation'. The 'territories clause' had a loophole.

A text that Britain supports

The negotiations which produced the final text of the ECHR took place during a relatively short period, from August 1949 to September 1950. But it wasn't all plain sailing. The frustrations about some of the processes are expressed in Maxwell Fyfe's unpublished letters to his wife:

> The Committee of Ministers have left out Human Rights so we must try and get the Assembly to put it back. . . . We spent nearly two hours drafting subjects including Human Rights. If the Council of Foreign Ministers do not take it after the Assembly has approved – as I believe they will – we are going to have a magnificent row about the rights of the Assembly as well as the rights of Man.[30]

The CoE's Committee on Legal and Administrative Questions, chaired by Maxwell Fyfe, took the European Movement's original text as its starting point. The

Teitgen report (named after its rapporteur) proposed that the articles of the new Convention should be primarily drawn from the principal civil and political rights in the UDHR, including, at that stage, its broad limitation clause (Article 29 (2)). In the final version, in line with the British insistence on tighter drafting, limitations and qualifications were introduced into individual articles, including the reference to responsibilities associated with free speech in Article 10. At the behest of the Conservative delegates, and despite Labour and European socialist opposition, virtually all the economic, social and cultural rights in the UDHR were omitted, other than the right to form and join a trade union. The protection of personal property and the right to education, with 'public-interest' qualifications, were eventually included in a Protocol not signed until 1952, two years after the rest of the text.[31]

The principle that 'each country shall have a very wide freedom of action', provided the member states respected the basic tenets of the Convention, was strongly underlined in the Teitgen report. As Simpson remarks, this approach subsequently found 'echoes in the developed European law of human rights which has adopted . . . the doctrine of the margin of appreciation',[32] discussed further on.

The greatest disagreement remained regarding the means of legal enforcement, which had been the original motive for drafting a European human rights treaty. The majority on the Teitgen Committee supported the European Movement's position in favour of legal protection at the European level. It was proposed to establish a European Commission of Human Rights that individuals could directly petition which would investigate the facts, filter out manifestly unfounded cases and try to resolve through conciliation those that proceeded, but with the option of referring cases to be heard at a new human rights court. This was explicitly not to be a supreme court of appeal from domestic courts on the American model, but a European court of last resort with national states determining how to comply with its judgments, if a violation was found.

The Committee of Ministers (CoM), the 'political arm' of the CoE, was to be given a supervisory role, but it would clearly have no guns or tanks to enforce its writ; the ultimate sanction being suspension.[33] The final shape of the enforcement mechanisms largely followed this scheme (as explained further in my anthology lecture on the origins of the ECHR). Alternative proposals to leave protection of the rights in the Convention entirely in the hands of elected governments, acting under the weight of public opinion, were rejected. For most of the states, although not the UK, a 'democratic majoritarian approach' failed to recognize the brutal truth to which the continent of Europe had just been exposed; maintaining closed systems of national sovereignty with no external checks can leave unpopular or vulnerable minorities utterly defenceless.

Towards the end of the negotiations on the ECHR, Bevin, the British Foreign Secretary, moved an amendment to make the proposal for individual petition to the Strasbourg authorities optional and, spearheaded by Sweden, such a compromise was agreed.[34] This remained the status quo until a new Protocol in 1998[35] abolished the Commission and ushered in a single full-time Court, of which it is no longer possible for any state that has ratified the ECHR to opt out.[36]

Simpson comments that 'though armed with the belief that it was in England that individual liberty had been invented, the Foreign Office was not able to dominate the European negotiations completely.'[37] The final shape of the ECHR was presented as a compromise between the British team's proposals and the European Movement's, and between common and civil-law lawyers. However, Foreign Office papers confirm what the travaux preparatoires bear out; the UK had secured all the most *significant* changes it sought:

> The final text contains all amendments which we had proposed and had received no other objectionable additions. Taken all in all it seems very much more satisfactory than we had at one time reason to fear it might be.[38]

Britain did not grant its citizens the right to petition the Strasbourg authorities until Harold Wilson's Labour government announced the decision to accept this optional provision in 1966, initially for a period of three years. It is not a coincidence that by then the British Empire was unravelling fast so that objections from a dwindling Colonial Office had faded. It was also an era of such outward-looking optimism that a Foreign Office memorandum in 1965 recommended that the 'optional clauses should now be recognised' not just for the UK but 'for those of our dependent territories to which the Convention has been extended'. In a markedly contrasting tone to that which had characterized civil service memos fifteen years earlier, it affirmed that:

> It is an object of United Kingdom policy that the rights of individuals everywhere should be protected. The European Human Rights Convention is the only international agreement yet in existence solely and specifically providing for the protection of human rights. It serves as a model for similar efforts elsewhere. . . . It is therefore in our interest to strengthen its authority.[39]

Ultimately, in spite of all reservations – some cultural, some legal and most self-interested – the UK did not block the introduction of the world's first-ever legally enforceable supranational human rights Convention. On the contrary, the Council of Europe was an institution which both Bevin and Churchill, representing opposing parties, were largely responsible for creating. Britain would have lost all credibility if it were seen to be obstructing the CoE's major stated purpose: the enhancement of 'human rights, democracy and the rule of law'. Churchill, in particular, had been clear from the outset that: 'A European assembly forbidden to discuss human rights would indeed have been a ludicrous proposition to put to the world.'[40]

Nor was the UK's most revered war leader naive about the implications of the 'closer political unity' he was proposing, even if he wasn't always entirely consistent about it, acknowledging that 'it is said, with truth, that this involves some sacrifice or merger of national sovereignty.'[41] Churchill gave his blessing to the establishment of a European human rights court which 'would depend for the enforcement of their judgments on the individual decisions of the States now banded together in the

Council of Europe'.[42] This was the model adopted, with implementation of court judgments still the responsibility of each government. When the CoE expanded rapidly in the 1990s after the fall of the Berlin Wall, as related in my anthology lecture on the origins of the ECHR, Churchill's initial ambition, which must have seemed fanciful at the time, appeared to have materialized:

> We must try . . . to make the Council of Europe . . . into a really effective League . . . the Council, when created, must eventually embrace the whole of Europe and all the main branches of the European family must some day be partners in it.[43]

Bevin also proclaimed his strong personal support for the project over time: 'The formulation of this Convention is a positive achievement by the Council of Europe of the first importance and I hope it will be possible for a signature to take place' imminently, he declared in a telegram on 27 October 1950. Eight days later, on 4 November, thirteen states, including the UK, signed up to the European Convention on Human Rights and Fundamental Freedoms (to give it its full title) in the Great Hall of the Palazzo Barberini in Rome. On 8 March 1951 the UK became the very first member of the Council of Europe to ratify the ECHR, which finally came into force on 3 September 1953.[44]

For all its bluster and prevarications, Britain had been at the forefront of every step of this journey to the world's first legally enforceable treaty based on the universal principles in the UDHR: from the establishment of the Council of Europe to the draft of the ECHR and finally as an initial signatory and the first to ratify. Should the UK withdraw under a future Conservative government it would be in the lead once again – only this time regarding the ECHR's almost certain demise. This is a subject to which I will return at the end of this section. First, how did the UK – the common law country which abhorred bills of rights – come to introduce the Human Rights Act, nearly fifty years after signing the ECHR?

On the road to the Human Rights Act

Margaret Thatcher was the first party leader of modern times to entertain the idea of introducing a UK bill of rights. Her 1979 election manifesto committed the Conservatives to holding all-party 'discussions' on 'a possible bill of rights'. This seemed to come quite literally from 'left field', given the visceral Tory hostility to bills of rights and any measures which might impact on the sovereignty of Parliament. Yet this is not quite true. Three years earlier the Society of Conservative Lawyers was amongst the first to argue in their report 'Another Bill of Rights?' that 'the ECHR should be given statutory force as overriding domestic law.' Similar proposals were backed by Lord Hailsham (formerly Quintin Hogg) who was twice Conservative Lord Chancellor and who famously coined the term 'elective dictatorship' to describe the UK's system of parliamentary sovereignty – at least when Labour was in power. Under this system there are few obstacles to governments with a reasonable majority legislating at will, with little kickback from Parliament. With the executive drawn from elected MPs whose promotion is dependent on patronage and loyalty, parliamentary sovereignty can be a misnomer for government sovereignty in all but name. Hailsham's frustration with Jim Callaghan's government led him to advocate an 'armoury of weapons against elective dictatorship' in which 'a Bill of Rights, embodying and entrenching the European Convention, might well have a valuable, even if subordinate, part to play.'[45]

According to historian Samual Moyn, the timing of these remarks and commitments was absolutely on the button. They reflected a global phenomenon in which human rights began to enjoy a 'startling spike in cultural prestige' in the 1970s 'after decades of irrelevance'.[46] Amnesty International was awarded the Nobel Peace Prize in 1977 and human rights certainly gained new credibility in the US when Jimmy Carter became president in the same year. This was an era, Moyn argues, when 'for the first time, in large numbers, people started to use the language of human rights to express and act on their hopes for a better world.'[47] Regardless of the dispute about whether human rights 'had been forged in a moment of post-Holocaust wisdom',[48] discussed in Section I, Moyn is surely right that it was only later that human rights broke through substantially 'on the terrain of idealism' for 'ordinary people'.[49]

But when attention started to turn towards introducing a bill of rights in the UK based on the text of the ECHR, it was not Moyn's 'ordinary people' who were in the vanguard, but a small elite focused on relatively parochial concerns. Initially it was often Conservative politicians and lawyers who supported incorporating the ECHR into UK law as a domestic bill of rights, partly based on a somewhat fanciful notion, stretching back to the Tory 'founding fathers' of the ECHR, that a bill of rights would stop the Labour Party from introducing measures which the Tories perceived as inimical to freedom. This mostly concerned taxation and nationalization, although it was becoming clear that there was precious little case law to back up this assumption.[50] Just as powerfully, support for a bill of rights based on the ECHR amongst Conservatives supporters reflected the view that the Convention was heir to the Magna Carta and 1689 Bill of Rights, which the UK should therefore enthusiastically embrace. When the House of Lords set up a select committee in 1978 to inquire whether to introduce a bill of rights, it was the three Conservative members, and only one Labour, who supported its introduction. The Committee unanimously agreed that 'if there were to be a bill of rights it should be a bill based on the European Convention.'

Once in power, the Thatcher government buried without trace its former commitment to hold all party 'discussions' on constitutional reform. 'Elective dictatorships' do not seem so bad when you are doing the dictating – from the backbenches, the perspective can be different. In a letter to the *Times* in March 1981, former Tory Cabinet Minister Geoffrey Rippon reminded his leader what she preferred to forget and urged the government to act on its manifesto commitment 'to discuss a possible bill of rights with all parties'. Similar to most other protagonists, he urged support for a 'bill of rights which is intended to render the provisions of the ECHR enforceable' in UK law. When Conservative MP Edward Gardner introduced a 'human rights bill to incorporate in British law the ECHR' in 1987, he garnered the support of several senior Conservative colleagues, including Leon Brittan, Rippon, Terence Higgins and Norman St John-Stevas. Other prominent Tories who expressed support for incorporating the ECHR into UK law in the context of a debate about a UK bill of rights included former Home Affairs Committee Chair Sir Ivan Lawrence and former Attorney General Sir Michael Havers.[51]

The Labour Party, at almost all levels, was for a long time much more cautious about going down this road. Some feared what the Tories had hoped, that public-school-educated judges, armed with the ECHR operating as a domestic bill of rights, might stymie a Labour government's programme. Those concerns had been expressed by ministers in the post-war Labour government, but where this might have been the case the ECHR text was carefully worded to avoid it.[52]

The first formal Labour Party document to propose incorporation of the ECHR into UK law was a 1976 discussion paper, 'A Charter of Human Rights'. This emerged from a committee chaired by Shirley Williams MP, but the party's National Executive Committee would not allow it to be discussed. Most supporters of a bill of rights in the Labour Party, like Williams and former Home Secretary Roy Jenkins, left to join the Social Democratic Party (SDP) in 1981. The Home Office, meanwhile, published its own discussion document on incorporation in 1976 but came to no conclusions.

There was, meanwhile, a quite different trigger for the nascent interest in human rights, and the ECHR in particular, which started to develop in 1970s Britain beyond Westminster. It was kicked off by the introduction of the Commonwealth Immigrants Act in 1968 by Wilson's Labour government, the same government which had granted the right of individual petition to the European Court of Human Rights just two years earlier. Passing through all its parliamentary stages in only three days amidst a tabloid frenzy, the Act prevented British Asians expelled from east Africa from entering Britain at the very time they needed the protection of their UK citizenship. Here was a Labour government using its parliamentary majority, albeit with significant (although not unanimous) all-party support, to ride roughshod over the rights of a minority. Their most basic citizenship rights were being sacrificed to appease a populist groundswell of anti-immigrant sentiment, only to see it explode further a month later when Enoch Powell made his infamous 'rivers of blood' speech.

These effectively stateless men, women and children were unable to receive any recourse in the domestic courts. They had to take a long and expensive journey to Strasbourg for that. In 1981 the expelled east-African Asians were finally vindicated by the then European Commission of Human Rights, bringing a wider awareness of the ECHR, at least to activists and campaigners, than previously. Shamefully for Britain, the Commission found that the UK government had breached Article 3, which prohibits not just torture but 'inhuman or degrading treatment or punishment'. It ruled that the practice of refusing to allow British passport holders expelled from Uganda and Kenya to live in the country they were citizens of, thereby singling out 'a group of persons for differential treatment on the basis of race', could constitute 'a special form of affront to human dignity'.[53] British parliamentary sovereignty offered these UK citizens virtually no protection at all.[54] The ECHR, in contrast, provided something nearly 800 years of 'English common law liberties' failed to do. It recognized the fundamental human rights of 'everyone' – the most important word in the ECHR – no matter how unpopular or marginalized.

The 1970s was also the era when the Northern Ireland so-called Troubles (a British understatement if ever there was one) spilled onto the streets of mainland Britain as never before. Shortly after the 1974 Guilford pub bombings came the Birmingham pub bombings, in which 21 people died and 184 were injured. Just a few days later the UK government introduced the Prevention of Terrorism Act (PTA). It took four days to pass through both houses of Parliament, virtually without amendment and with little dissent. Labour Home Secretary Jenkins admitted that his Act was a 'draconian measure unprecedented in peacetime' but that it was meant to be temporary. Instead, in one form or another, this 'emergency measure' was renewed annually until it was replaced with a 'permanent' Terrorism Act in 2000.

Amongst other provisions, the 1974 Act allowed suspects to be held up to seven days without charge (admittedly a mere shadow of the 'pick a number and double it' approach – from forty-two to ninety days – that the Labour government unsuccessfully tried to impose after the 2005 London bombings[55]). Under media-generated pressure to obtain convictions, large numbers of UK citizens and residents of Irish origin or descent were detained throughout the Troubles, creating a suspect community in an atmosphere not dissimilar to that which many Muslims experience today. Of those convicted, a number turned out to be miscarriages of justice which generated long campaigns for their release.[56] A wave of anti-Irish sentiment resulted in bomb threats and physical attacks on this minority community. The inadequacy of relying on the much vaunted British system of parliamentary sovereignty to protect minority communities in times of stress was once again exposed, although in the many debates on the renewal of the PTA during this period only the Labour MP Gerald Bermingham emphasized the need to have 'laws which comply with the European Convention on Human Rights'.[57] The ECHR might have provided more protection (as it has in the post-9/11 cases[58]) had the government not 'derogated' from the relevant article.[59] A shield the British state had insisted on when the ECHR was drafted came to its rescue.

But the loophole had a loophole; under the ECHR even during a 'public emergency' states are not permitted to torture detainees. This enabled the European Commission to uphold a complaint by the Irish government that five interrogation techniques (wall standing; hooding; white noise; deprivation of sleep, and of food and drink) used against terror suspects interned without trial in 1971 amounted to torture. The ECtHR subsequently downgraded the violation to 'inhuman and degrading treatment' but in a late twist, just as the Conservatives are threatening to withdraw from the ECHR, the Irish government has requested the Court to reopen the case and revise its judgment upwards to 'torture'.[60]

Cases such as this resulted in what gradually became a greater awareness of the ECHR. Amongst lawyers in particular, who had grown sceptical of the capacity of the common law to protect minorities in troubled times, this sometimes converted into support for a domestic bill of rights. The renowned judge Lord Scarman chose to devote one of his 1974 Hamlyn Lectures to this theme, warning that in the absence of a bill of rights:

> When times are normal and fear not stalking the land, English law sturdily protects the freedom of the individual and respects human personality. But when times are abnormally alive with fear and prejudice, the common law is at a disadvantage: it cannot resist the will, however frightened and prejudiced it may be, of Parliament.[61]

If there was one political party which consistently held the torch for constitutional reform in this period it was the Liberals (and its successors the SDP and Liberals Democrats). Its MPs sought to expose what they saw as the unaccountability of governments under Britain's un-codified constitution, arguing that the common law, with its focus on negative freedoms rather than positive rights, could not provide citizens with the protections on offer in almost all other democracies. With this reasoning, the Liberal peer Lord Wade was tireless in introducing bills to incorporate the ECHR into UK law. He was followed by Robert Maclennan MP and Anthony Lester QC, who probably did more than any other single figure to garner support for such a reform.

It wasn't the rational or impassioned arguments of QCs and MPs, but eighteen years of Conservative rule that was to turn the tide within the senior echelons of the Labour Party in favour of constitutional reform, including a bill of rights. Now Labour was out of power, it was its turn to conclude that parliamentary sovereignty equalled executive sovereignty in all but name. For most of the twentieth century, elections themselves had delivered a measure of accountability by resulting in alternative governments with reasonably differentiated political programmes. Now the Labour Party found itself unable to mount virtually *any* successful challenge to the legislation of three seemingly impregnable Conservative governments. It left the reputation of the legislature as a bulwark against an arbitrary or unjust executive pretty much in tatters.

If this wasn't widely understood, the successful pressure group Charter 88 was established in 1988 by Anthony Barnett and Stuart Weir to ensure that it was. From the poll tax to the *Spycatcher* book ban,[62] Charter 88 and its supporters tried to expose what they saw as the failure of Britain's political system – and first-past-the-post electoral system – to provide mechanisms for challenging the executive outside of general elections or riots on the streets.[63] On the basis of three elections won on a minority of the popular vote, the Conservative government demonstrated that it could enact virtually any measures it chose with the courts entirely powerless to review lawfully passed Acts of Parliament. When lobbyists from pressure groups such as Liberty and Charter 88 attempted to engage Conservative ministers on their 1979 manifesto commitment to 'discussions' on a bill of rights, the customary response was an identikit to this 1989 letter from Margaret Thatcher to Baroness Ewart-Biggs:

> The Government considers that our present constitutional arrangements continue to serve us well and that the citizen in this country enjoys the greatest

degree of liberty that is compatible with the rights of others and the vital interests of the state.[64]

Why a bill of rights?

I joined Liberty as director of their research arm, the Civil Liberties Trust, in the same year this letter was written. The view of the world from the perspective of this NGO could not have been more different to that presented in Thatcher's letter. The National Council for Civil Liberties (NCCL) had been set up in 1934 to defend the 'hunger marchers' from infiltration by undercover police who incited the demonstrators to violence, resulting in a brutal police response.[65] Similar to the Levellers and Chartists before them, Liberty's founders were motivated to defend what they saw as 'ancient English liberties', presumed to stem from the Magna Carta. Luminaries such as H. G. Wells, A. A. Milne, Vera Brittain, Clement Attlee and Ron Kidd formed the NCCL (now Liberty) to protect not only the right to peaceful dissent but also 'the whole spirit of British freedom'.[66]

Yet in 1989 there was considerable anguish at the ease with which cherished rights and freedoms, seen as emblematic of British democracy for generations, were being extinguished with no constitutional means of challenging their demise. For all the Prime Minister's insistence that these 'constitutional arrangements continue to serve us well', the announcement that the 'right to silence', well established in common law since the seventeenth century, would be abolished and that offences such as common assault could no longer be tried by a jury, demonstrated how expendable so-called traditional English liberties were.[67] Myth and reality had never seemed so far apart in modern times.

Some lawyers and civil libertarians began to look enviously at the rest of Europe and the US with their bills of rights that allowed judges to strike down unconstitutional legislation. Whereas the common law was no match in the face of the government's determination to ban *Spycatcher* – leading Lord Bridge in a dissenting judgment to comment that 'free speech is the first casualty of a totalitarian regime'[68] – the Americans had their First Amendment.[69] There were American states which had even rid themselves of their poll taxes as unconstitutional, whereas in the UK it took riotous demonstrations and a Conservative Party coup against their leader, the Prime Minister Margaret Thatcher, to achieve much the same end.

There was another factor in play here. Moyn's analysis that human rights were 'born' as a 'moral utopia when political utopias died',[70] only begins to bite in the UK in the early 1990s, not two decades earlier as he suggests. It is only then that the growing distrust of 'more maximal plans for transformation – especially revolutions' became a factor in some social movements starting to 'use the language of human rights'.[71] It was after the Berlin Wall came down in 1989, and human rights were no longer the plaything of the world's two superpowers, that the appeal of human rights broadened to encompass a wider cohort than international NGOs such as Amnesty International and Human Rights Watch.[72] Whilst this was – and still is – a minority perspective, in this new era of 'failed utopias' the transformative potential of human rights struck a chord. It was not that most of the new generation of human rights defenders had themselves necessarily been caught up in the false dawns of the previous era, but as domestic politics gradually became more technocratic from the 1990s, and discourse on human rights was no longer frozen by the icy blasts of the Cold War, some activists and NGOs began to consider the capacity of human rights values to 'define the good life',[73] beyond domestic or international laws to protect civil liberties. Even Liberty only started to describe itself as a human rights organization in this period.

No one marched on Whitehall demanding a bill of rights based on universal values, of course, but the developing language of human rights came to capture one of the mini zeitgeists of the time. This was observed by Baroness Helena Kennedy, QC, the highly respected human rights lawyer, in the forward to my book, *Values for a Godless Age*, published to coincide with the introduction of the HRA in 2000:

> Human rights is becoming the language of diplomacy and peace-keeping and the sea change is being felt not only internationally but in our domestic jurisdictions.[74]

All these factors provided the broad context in which thousands of Charter 88 signatories called for a raft of reforms, including a bill of rights. In return the government kept repeating how free everyone was.[75] The Labour-supporting think tank the Institute of Public Policy Research (IPPR) established a committee of experts to draft a prototype British bill of rights, led by Anthony Lester QC, that would allow the courts to overturn Acts of Parliament as part of a written constitution.[76] The Scottish Council for Civil Liberties and the Committee for the Administration of Justice produced their own proposals for a judicially entrenched bill of rights for Scotland and Northern Ireland, respectively.[77]

By this time momentum was building in favour of introducing a bill of rights through incorporating the ECHR into UK law amongst the senior judiciary. Lawyers schooled in the English common law, whose predecessors quivered at the Convention's broad and purposive language a generation previously, were now openly lamenting that they were constitutionally barred from importing ECHR norms into UK law. Whilst there was some pressure to incorporate 'through the back door', due to the recent practice of a new generation of judges beginning to import Strasbourg jurisprudence into their judgments where they could, this was a stunted endeavour.[78] In research for a Democratic Audit project with Keir Starmer and Stuart Weir, based at Essex University, we found that up until 1995 there were only 172 cases where domestic judges had cited the ECHR at all.[79] A correlation was drawn between the UK being one of a very few countries in the Council of Europe not to have incorporated the ECHR into domestic law in some form, and reaching the top of the league of adverse judgments before the ECtHR, although the total number was still very small.[80]

Whilst there was no more judicial appetite than there was political appetite to empower the courts to overturn statutes on the American model, other than amongst a few constitutionally enthusiastic individuals, the frustration of some judges with working within the confines of the common law had been building up for years. As LSE human rights law professor Conor Gearty recently observed, the ECtHR 'rescued the English common law from itself'.[81]

The reliance of domestic judges on the ECtHR to fill the gaps in the common law was exposed as early as 1979. In a defining case on whether it was lawful for the state to tap the phone of antiques dealer James Malone, Judge Robert Megarry VC declared that 'if the tapping of telephones by the Post Office at the request of the police can be carried out without any breach of the law, it does not require any statutory or common law power to justify it: it can lawfully be done simply because there is nothing to make it unlawful.'[82] Why? Because under the English common-law system, that which is not forbidden is allowed, even when it is the Secretary of State tapping our phones. There was no way around this, Megarry concluded: 'I see the greatest difficulty in the common law framing the safeguards required' but 'the Convention is plainly not of itself law in this country, however much it may fall to be considered as indicating what the law of this country *should be* or should be construed as being.'[83]

It took another five years before the case found its way to the European Court of Human Rights, which declared that the then total absence of regulation of state surveillance in the UK was a breach of Article 8, the right to privacy under the ECHR.[84] As a result, the Conservative government reluctantly passed the Interception of Communications Act 1985, regulating mail and phone interceptions for the first time.

The absence of any privacy protection in domestic UK law beyond this limited measure came to a head again in 1990. Gordon Kaye, the star of the television series *'Allo 'Allo*, received an unwelcome visit from a journalist and photographer from the now defunct *Sunday Sport* in his hospital room whilst recovering from a serious car crash. When his photo and story were published without his permission Kaye discovered that he had no remedy through the domestic courts. In being forced to find against him, the esteemed Judge Thomas Bingham, who later became Lord Chief Justice, lamented 'yet again, the failure of both the common law of England and statute to protect in an effective way the personal privacy of individual citizens'.[85]

Lord Bingham, a trailblazer throughout his career, gave further vent to his frustrations about the limits of the common law in the case of *Smith* in 1996 on the then blanket ban on gay men and lesbians serving in the armed forces. Anyone who was 'found out' would be subject to dismissal. An open-and-shut human rights case by the standards of today, but under the judge-made principles for judicial review the ban could only be overturned if deemed illegal – which in the absence of a bill of rights it clearly wasn't – or beyond the range of responses open to a so-called reasonable decision maker. Bingham commented that 'the threshold of irrationality is a high one' and he felt he could not make it stick in this case.[86] Instead he strongly signalled his regret that he could not ask whether the 'ban on gays in the military', as the case became known, was 'proportionate'. As a result 'it may be necessary for the appellants . . . to incur the expense and endure the delay of pursuing their claim in Strasbourg.'[87] To the further embarrassment of domestic judges, when the ECtHR did subsequently hear the case they not only overturned the ban but also subtly damned the British constitutional system for effectively excluding any consideration of the human rights of the sacked personnel.[88]

Jonathan Cooper, junior council in *Smith* and now director of The Human Dignity Trust, has movingly described how, as 'a young, gay man growing up in a Britain where sexual identity was almost invisible and voiceless' his 'journey towards an understanding of the limits of the English legal system, and its inability to create a rights framework fit for the 21st century', was forged through this case. Even though – eventually – the European Court of Human Rights vindicated the applicants and provided them with a remedy,[89] 'the human price paid by them as they were buffeted through the English courts should never be underestimated.'[90] Cases such as this demonstrated that the common law had been unable to keep up with modern times to provide protection in situations that were unimaginable a generation earlier. As Cooper saw it:

> It was evident that those cornerstones of the UK system of government: parliamentary sovereignty, Scottish law, the common law and the rule of law, couldn't guarantee respect for human rights.[91]

Towards a democratic bill of rights?

Positioned against the judges, lawyers and civil rights groups who were now in favour of incorporating the ECHR into UK law were those, particularly on the left of the political spectrum, who feared that a bill of rights would actually increase Britain's democratic deficit. They were concerned that it would merely transfer legislative power from a nominally accountable, elected executive to a fully unaccountable, public-school-educated judiciary who were incapable of comprehending the diverse society they lived in, but very capable of undermining the programme of a radical government.[92] Scholars such as Professors Conor Gearty and Keith Ewing from King's College law school argued that controversial policy decisions should be determined by elected representatives without fear that they will be subsequently overturned by judges. Ewing's case was that the 'effect of a Bill of Rights or an incorporated European Convention' would be 'to empower the judges to unsettle decisions made . . . by the people's representatives and thereby frustrate the democratic process'.[93] This was probably the predominant view within Liberty itself, as well as 'the left', at the time. It echoed the opinion on 'the right' that a bill of rights would unacceptably fetter parliamentary sovereignty, but the drivers of their mutual concerns were generally quite different.

What they shared in common was unease about the nature of bills of rights which are composed of broadly expressed values and standards that are intended to influence all other laws and policies. When they are judicially entrenched, meaning courts have the power to interpret not only how the values in this 'higher law' should be applied but also which legislation should be struck down for being incompatible with it, there is an understandable critique that judges effectively morph from law interpreters to law makers.

There were many illustrations of supreme courts overturning progressive legislation, such as controls on election campaign finance in the US[94] and tobacco advertising restrictions in Canada, which had introduced a Charter of Rights in 1982.[95] Up to a point, I was sympathetic to the approach of New Zealand's 1990 Bill of Rights, which was by then just in force and starting to produce case law. An initial proposal to allow the courts to strike down legislation had been rejected on consultation. Geoffrey Palmer, the former New Zealand Minister of Justice who originally championed a judicially entrenched bill of rights, conceded in a White Paper that 'in a great many cases where controversial issues arise . . . there is no "right" [human rights] answer.'[96] The implication of his remark was that in a democracy elected representatives, not judges, should have the final say on controversial policy issues. As persuasive as this argument was, the weakness in the New Zealand model was that it prevented the courts from reviewing primary legislation altogether, not just from overturning it. A measure which replicated this approach here would have failed to address the powerlessness people felt in the face of a government that was barely held to account when overturning historic or minority rights; the issue that had spurred calls for a bill of rights in the first place.

It was with all these considerations in mind that we approached drafting a bill of rights for public consultation at Liberty. In a document published in 1991, labelled *A People's Charter* after the Chartists' document of the same name, Liberty's two legal officers, John Wadham and Madeleine Colvin, and myself wrote a draft bill of rights based on an amalgam of compatible provisions in the ECHR, other international human rights treaties, the common law and the Magna Carta.[97] It would have seemed inexplicable then to confine a proposed bill of rights to a narrow range of so-called English liberties. As the then director Andrew Puddephatt explained in the foreword:

> In line with international human rights philosophy, most of the rights enshrined in the Bill apply to everyone in this country and not just citizens, with particular emphasis placed on the need to ensure the protection of minorities whose rights are most vulnerable to attack.

The report was produced 'with an eye both to the validity of the growing demand for a bill of rights and to the concerns of those who fear it would undermine democracy or give further scope to the state to restrict our rights'.[98] With a nod to what we saw as the legitimate unease about 'the democratic deficit' in judicially entrenched bills of rights, the executive, legislature and judiciary were each apportioned a role in its enforcement, but Parliament would have the 'final say'. Central to this model was the proposal for a new joint committee of both Houses of Parliament, foreshadowing the Joint Committee on Human Rights (JCHR) established in January 2001. Rather optimistically, we gave it a central role in enforcing the *People's Charter* through an extraordinarily labyrinthine set of proposals which I shudder to look at now. Unsurprisingly, no one took the over-complex, and ultimately unworkable, proposals in *A People's Charter* too seriously. This gave us the chance to work on the model some more, which we called a 'democratically entrenched' bill of rights.[99]

Following discussions with the office of the then Labour leader Neil Kinnock, Labour's 1992 manifesto made reference to introducing a 'democratically enforced bill of rights'. A little earlier we had managed to convince the Leader's aides, but not his deputy Roy Hattersley, that contrary to the then legal orthodoxy, it would be possible to introduce a bill of rights *without* fatally compromising the British system of parliamentary sovereignty which Labour guarded as jealously as the Tories. Derry Irvine QC, who later became Lord Chancellor, took a particular interest in these proposals.

Labour lost that election. When John Smith took over as leader he committed the Labour Party to support a UK bill of rights as part of a package of proposals that reflected his long-term interest in constitutional reform. His rationale was almost identical to that of Lord Hailsham sixteen years earlier. The purpose was to 'restore democracy to our people – for what we have in this country at the moment is not real democracy; it is elective dictatorship'.[100] In a watershed speech on constitutional reform to Charter 88, Smith clarified that 'the quickest and simplest way' of introducing 'a substantial package of human rights' would be to pass a Human Rights Act 'incorporating into British law the European Convention on Human Rights'.[101] The 1993 Labour Conference then proceeded to adopt a statement, introduced by the new shadow Home Secretary Tony Blair, supporting an all-party commission to 'draft our own Bill of Rights', following the incorporation of the ECHR into UK law.[102]

Before this conference, as Director of the Civil Liberties Trust, I had been dispatched to meet Blair who had been given the brief to develop Smith's proposals for constitutional reform. The first thing he told me was that he had previously written in opposition to bills of rights but was willing to look at a model which didn't overturn parliamentary sovereignty.

The only aspect of Smith's proposals that seemed settled was that a 'first stage' bill of rights would be based on the ECHR. All-party acceptance of this treaty that the UK had played a major role in drafting, and had been bound by since 1953, made this a much less daunting prospect for a would-be Labour government that had many higher priorities than trying to achieve agreement on a new draft. Proposals from the IPPR or Liberty for additional rights, including from the common law, were to wait for another day, which already seemed like it may never come.

In an unpublished briefing to Blair following Smith's speech, I commented that 'if the wider community are not given the opportunity to be involved in the process of agreeing' what values should underlie a bill of rights then it is 'unlikely to have the empowering and democratising impact' shadow ministers had said they hoped it would.[103] But suggestions that it was important to consult widely on as fundamental a measure as a bill of rights were dismissed as an issue for the 'second stage'. It was unnecessary for this 'first stage', as there was already widespread consensus that the

ECHR provided a 'basic floor' of rights and freedoms for everyone in the UK. Even so, it seemed short-sighted not to engage the general public in this crucial constitutional change. Liberty subsequently organized a three-day convention to consult on proposals for a UK bill of rights, attended by more than 3,000 people and NGOs, including Age Concern, Stonewall and a range of race, refugee, mental health, disability and gender-equality groups. The reach of such an exercise was obviously very small and the government-in-waiting developed no plans to extend it.[104] The Labour Party subsequently published *Bringing Rights Home*, a 'discussion document' on incorporation, but it cannot be said that a vast number of people were involved in that 'discussion'.[105]

After Smith's untimely death in 1994 Labour's commitment to constitutional reform was recognized as one of his strongest legacies. It would not have been easy for Labour's new leader, Tony Blair, to turn his back on it, and the party was anyway looking for proposals to demonstrate that it still boasted a radical edge whilst it shed bucket loads of policies associated with 'old Labour'. Blair pledged to introduce a 'Bill of Rights' as part of a package of 'democratic renewal' in his 1994 campaign literature for party leader. Like his predecessor, the new shadow Home Secretary Jack Straw was given the brief to develop this proposal, initially committing Labour to a 'two-stage process'. The incorporation of the ECHR into UK law would be followed by 'the establishment of our own British Bill of Rights'.[106]

Representatives from a consortium of groups, including Liberty, Justice, the IPPR and the Constitution Unit based at University College London, met regularly at Liberty's offices to discuss different models of 'incorporation'. The Human Rights Incorporation Project, where I was appointed a Senior Research Fellow in 1996, was established by Professor Robert Blackburn at King's College London law school to input into this process. In that capacity I was asked to advise Straw directly.

The challenge we faced was to work up an approach for incorporating the ECHR into UK law which would hold the government to account whilst *crucially* leaving Parliament with the last word on what the law should be.[107] Unless this could be satisfactorily resolved, partly by learning from the impact of bills of rights elsewhere, Straw made it clear that there could be no certainty that the policy would be implemented in government. Many of the issues we explored are set out in the second anthology piece, 'A Bill of Rights for the United Kingdom: A Comparative Summary', which was originally presented as a paper for a conference at University College, London, on a UK bill of rights.[108]

In his memoirs, Straw describes how we endeavoured to 'find a path which reconciled the benefits of incorporation with the imperative of parliamentary sovereignty'.[109] This search culminated in a paper produced by the Human Rights Incorporation Project on 'The Power of Declaration', which recommended that 'where the courts cannot interpret' statutes 'to conform with the Convention it is proposed that they be given a specific power of declaration . . . that, in their view an Act of Parliament (or section of it) breaches the Convention.'[110] The description of this approach that both Straw and shadow Lord Chancellor Derry Irvine generally favoured at the time was 'the British model of incorporation'.[111]

Mixed messages

As the 1997 election dawned, it was increasingly obvious that shadow cabinet members with a constitutional reform brief lost any appetite they might once have vaguely held for an unspecified 'second stage' bill of rights. A commitment to consult on supplementary rights 'to reflect the particular circumstances of Northern Ireland' which 'taken together with the ECHR' would 'constitute a Bill of Rights for Northern Ireland', was later included in the 1998 Good Friday agreement.[112] But Blair's 1997 election manifesto only committed Labour to 'incorporate the European Convention on Human Rights into UK law', although it emphasized that 'the incorporation of the European Convention will establish a floor, not a ceiling, for human rights.'

The confused and confusing purposes of the HRA are explored in 'The Human Rights Act: Origins and Intentions', the third anthology piece reproduced here.[113] Once the Blair government had won its landslide victory, the pressure from some Home Office civil servants and Downing Street advisors to tone down the intended impact of the proposed HRA, or better still not to introduce it at all, was apparent. It was no longer presented as a British bill of rights *based* on the European Convention but more like an elaborate European directive; the logical next stage for complying with an international treaty which the government was *already* bound by. For audiences fearful that a bill of rights was too radical a proposition and that it necessarily implied judicial dominance, the term was now mainly expunged from the New Labour lexicon. Although incorporation of the ECHR into UK law had only been proposed in the first place as a consequence of demands for a UK bill of rights, including by senior members of all the main political parties, this context was quickly buried.

The public presentation of the HRA by the government generally became one of incorporation of the Convention in order 'to enable people to enforce their Convention rights against the state in the British courts . . . In other words to bring the rights home'.[114] This would avoid the long and expensive journey to Strasbourg to claim remedies for rights the government was already bound to protect. The accompanying narrative insisted that this was no more than a common-sense measure to complete the process that had begun in 1950 with the signing of the ECHR. For anyone who didn't much like anything with the title *Europe* in it, which after eighteen years of Eurosceptic government was not uncommon, this was hardly a convincing selling point. But for a while it did placate fears that that the HRA would usher in significant change.

Yet there was a simultaneous counter narrative, depending on the audience and the minister, which was far more expansive than this, as 'The Human Rights Act: Origins and Intentions', records.[115] In line with this more expansive discourse, and because the 'bill of rights debate' provided the original impetus for the HRA, the measure was drafted to be much more than an incorporated treaty.[116] As the 'second stage commitment' receded, so there was a greater impetus to draft the HRA in the form of a bill of rights. Although 'triangulation' was already becoming a leitmotif of the Blair regime, this was still the early, optimistic phase of the New Labour government. In practice, then, 'incorporation' was not to be a mere technical measure – such as that of many European 'monist' regimes which automatically incorporate into domestic law any treaty they ratify – but a carefully calibrated Act of Parliament of some constitutional significance, as ministers were sometimes keen to claim.[117]

The genuine interest in and commitment to 'incorporation' by certain key ministers at this stage – notably Straw, Irvine, Home Office ministers Mike O'Brien and Gareth Williams and the new Attorney General Paul Boateng[118] – meant that at the first Cabinet held directly after the May election it was agreed to introduce a Human Rights Bill in the next session of Parliament. Straw has written about the significance of the 'level of thought and scrutiny given to the proposal whilst Labour was in opposition' for the speed with which the new government was able to proceed. 'In my long experience of policy development in opposition I can think of few measures to match the care invested in the proposals for incorporation' he wrote on the tenth anniversary of the Act.[119]

When I was first shown a copy of the well-drafted Human Rights Bill (HRB) on the eve of its publication, my initial reaction was relief that the square had been circled regarding parliamentary sovereignty without blunting the Bill's cutting edge. In Straw's words: 'Worries that unelected judges might end up with the power to strike down primary legislation had been at the heart of much of the earlier scepticism about incorporation.'[120] This had been addressed by section 4 of the HRA which, as we had proposed,[121] allows the higher Courts to 'declare' that an Act of Parliament breaches the rights in the HRA, but not to overturn it. It is then for Parliament – or more realistically the government working through Parliament – to decide whether, and if so how, to respond. If they so wish, ministers do not have to respond at all. The doctrine of parliamentary sovereignty was not to be overturned by the Bill, in other words, but nor would a parliamentary majority on its own be sufficient vindication of legislation and policy which breached internationally recognized human rights norms. With the HRA in place the government could not have acted with such impunity in stripping east African Asians of their UK citizenship without being held accountable before the domestic courts and, it was perhaps naively hoped, before the court of public opinion.

There were two aspects to the careful drafting of the HRB, however, that surprised me. First, that the ECHR was reproduced wholesale[122] as a Schedule to the Act. It immediately struck me that this could muddy the waters. My expectation was that the rights in the ECHR would be included in the text of the Act, not labelled as 'Convention rights' but as the basis of what would now become a domestic bill of rights. Most of the rights in the Canadian Charter of Rights are based on the International Covenant of Civil and Political Rights, but this is nowhere labelled in the text. I had expected a similar approach to be taken in the HRA. Second, I was unprepared for a specific duty on our courts to 'take into account' the case law of the Strasbourg authorities, including the ECtHR, when interpreting the Act (section 2). From my many conversations with ministers, their advisors and civil servants, I had expected the Bill to be silent about which sources of authority our courts would use to interpret the rights in the Bill, in keeping with what was heralded as a specifically 'British model'.

Yet in every other respect the Bill had lived up to expectations. The executive, legislature and judiciary would all have a role in protecting human rights. Ministers would be required to declare to Parliament whether bills they introduce are compatible with human rights and it would be for MPs to take that statement into account when debating a measure or proposing amendments. The actions and decisions of the government could now be reviewed for their impact on human rights and not just how 'rational' they are. Whilst Parliament would retain the last word, as described earlier, the courts would be constitutionally empowered to *review* Acts of Parliament for the first time (section 4). Individuals, not just citizens, would be able to claim remedies for breaches of their rights (section 8) and legislation was required to be interpreted compatibly with the rights in the Bill 'so far as it is possible to do so' (section 3).

Most creatively, it was to be unlawful for public authorities, including the courts, 'to act in a way which is incompatible with a Convention right' (section 6(1)). This signalled that there was expected to be a culture shift towards greater understanding of, and respect for, human rights in the public sector to avoid litigation and empower men and women to 'negotiate' rather than have to necessarily 'enforce' their claims under the HRA. As a further sign of the ethical human rights framework the HRA was incorporating, a successful amendment was tabled by Labour backbencher Kevin McNamara which inserted Articles 1 and 2 of Protocol 6 of the ECHR into the Bill, abolishing the death penalty during peacetime. This was a major development. Until that time periodic attempts to reintroduce capital punishment would be floated. It was clear that the HRA was a bill of rights in all but name, based on the rights in the ECHR.[123] What it clearly was *not* was the incorporation of the ECHR and its case law, lock stock and barrel.

Amendments tabled by the Conservative front bench, but rejected by the government during the passage of the Bill, were aimed at tying the domestic courts to Strasbourg jurisprudence.[124] This was a pivotal issue, even at this early stage, and one I will return to further on. Irvine and Straw, the co-sponsors of the Bill, made clear that the intention was for the domestic courts only 'to take account' of Strasbourg jurisprudence, but to be free to develop their own case law. The Tory amendment, Irvine said, would risk 'putting the courts in some kind of straitjacket where flexibility is what is required . . . our courts must be free to try to give a lead to Europe as well as to be led'.[125]

Had the Tories' amendment succeeded this would have undeniably turned the measure into the literal incorporation of the ECHR, going beyond the Bill's own long title which only refers to the Act giving 'further effect' to ECHR rights.[126] The HRA would not have been a bill of rights *based* on the rights in the ECHR but a vehicle for the importation of the case law of the ECtHR, which would have been effectively turned into a supreme court for the UK, precisely what the founders of the Council of Europe determined it would *not* be. Given current Tory aversion to this very proposition, the Conservative amendment might seem extraordinary, but the motive, as Conservative MP Edward Leigh explained at the time, was that 'we are in danger of not simply incorporating the convention in our law but going much further. What we are creating is an entirely new bill of rights.'[127] He was right. Straw described the HRA as 'the first Bill of Rights this country has seen for three centuries'.[128] Clearly the HRA is *not* a bill of rights in the classical American sense, with a Supreme Court that can strike down laws. But that does not prevent it from performing the function of a bill of rights, defined as a 'higher law' to which other law and policy should conform where possible. Academic commentators have variously labelled it a 'dialogue model', engaging the courts, government and Parliament in human rights protection or 'new commonwealth constitutionalism', since it comprises both constitutional and democratic features.[129]

The HRA received 'royal assent' in November 1998 but did not come into force until 2 October 2000. Although the Conservatives opposed the Bill at second reading in the Commons, by its final stage the shadow Attorney General Sir Nicholas Lyell, who led for the Tories, wished it well. A number of senior Conservatives actively supported it, then and now. They included Dominic Grieve, later Attorney General, and the then shadow Lord Chancellor the late Lord Kingsland, who confirmed that the Tories 'will not be voting against the Bill on Second Reading' in the Lords. He even warmly congratulated his opposite number, Lord Irvine, on 'furnishing us in his Bill with so many ingenious solutions to what seemed to be a range of intractable problems' and joined him 'in congratulating the parliamentary draftsmen', – Sir Edward Caldwell, amongst them – for 'a masterly exhibition of their art'.[130]

Straw, in turn, has acknowledged the debt the measure owed to the 'senior backbench Conservative MP Lord Gardiner'.[131] The Liberal Democrats strongly supported the Act and the input of Lib Dem peer Lord Lester is well established. The label 'Labour's Human Rights Act' might now suit the Conservative Party's purpose, but as this overview has shown, the HRA's long gestation from its original conception in the 1970s involved many parents and stepparents on the way, from all the main political parties and none.

Support for the Act in this final stage had partly been sustained by Home Office negotiations with those lobbies most opposed to it. An amendment to exempt the armed forces failed but the churches and press successfully lobbied for clauses which they were sufficiently mollified would provide them with special protections.[132] The press was particularly worried that the 'right to respect for private and family life' would open the door to the kind of accountability from which the Press Complaints Commission had generally shielded it.

Meanwhile, outside Parliament there was little knowledge of what the HRA was, even amongst the fairly small number who had heard of it. Was the HRA a UK bill of rights of great constitutional and cultural significance or was it the technical-sounding 'incorporation of the Convention' which introduced no new rights and barely changed the status quo? No one was very clear, maybe not even the government itself. What was obvious, even at this early stage, was that these conflicting messages would cause confusion:

> People don't know what [the HRA] is. It remains the subject of a dialogue between lawyers, politicians and occasionally (at the moment) the media with everyone else shut out. It would be as if devolution were referred to only as the Scotland Act. It's a bill of rights and we need to acknowledge that in the land of the Magna Carta the people finally have their own bill of rights, like the people of virtually every other democracy in the world.[133]

Principles and values

It would be unfair to say that the government took no steps to prepare for the introduction of the HRA, even if most of the population was kept in the dark about it. In the two years between the passing of the HRA and its coming into force the Judicial Studies Board, a government quango, spent £4.5 million training judges in preparation for the new more 'purposive' approach to legal interpretation of statutes that any bill of rights requires. The Home Secretary set up a Human Rights Task Force in January 1999 to which I was appointed, along with representatives from several NGOs and professional and public bodies. Its remit was to advise on implementation outside the law courts. The new Human Rights Minister, Mike O'Brien, became chair and it was also attended (and sometimes chaired) by the late Lord Gareth Williams, who was a champion of the Act. Ministers and civil servants from the Lord Chancellor's Department and Cabinet Office were also usually present. Monthly meetings were used to explore the implications of the Act for Whitehall with officials across departments. Having advised on aspects of the 'democratic' model that was adopted, I was also appointed for a short time as an independent consultant to the Home Office on other aspects of implementation. It was clear to me that at this early stage that both ministers and civil servants took seriously their responsibility to ensure a smooth introduction of the HRA.

The attendees of a Civil Service College seminar in 1999 might have been surprised to hear the Home Secretary signal that terms such as 'ethical' and 'moral' would be entering the legal and political lexicon to an unprecedented degree through the HRA. In Straw's words:

> By and large our legal culture is about finding the true meaning of the law . . . Moral norms and ethical principles don't normally come into it . . . Deciding day-to-day legal questions on the basis of such fundamental ethical principles [in the HRA] is a new departure.[134]

Although the introduction of a bill of rights based on the ECHR was a significant constitutional change, for me personally the injection of ethical human rights values into public life was even more significant. These are analysed in some detail in 'The Human Rights Act: Basic Principles and Values' (the fourth anthology piece in this section).[135] It is not that these principles were necessarily absent before, of course, but the intention was that they would become far more transparent and consistently applied.

The Law Lord Nicolas Browne-Wilkinson suggested something similar when he wrote about the intended consequence of the HRA:

> In large part the Convention is a code of the moral principles which underlie the common law [but] there has hitherto been no attempt to formulate those judicial moral views in a code of any kind . . . As these moral questions come before the courts in Convention cases the courts will be required to give moral answers to the moral questions.[136]

Lord Rogers, former Scottish Lord Advocate and Law Lord, likewise reflected in a landmark case that 'Convention rights are to be seen as an expression of fundamental *principles* rather than a set of mere rules.'[137] My hope was that the ethical standards given expression in the Universal Declaration of Human Rights, which in turn formed the basis of the text of the ECHR, would now explicitly enter our law and policy, not as a blueprint but as a framework for debate and decision making.[138] In an early key case which confirmed that Scotland's drunk-driving laws were compatible with the HRA, Lord Steyn quoted Article 29 of the UDHR to emphasize the communitarian element of modern human rights laws:

> The fundamental rights of individuals are of supreme importance but those rights are not unlimited: we live in communities of individuals who also have rights. The direct lineage of this ancient idea is clear: the European Convention (1950) is the descendant of the Universal Declaration of Human Rights (1948) which in article 29 expressly recognised the duties of everyone to the community and the limitations on rights in order to secure and protect respect for the rights of others.[139]

At their most enthusiastic, the ministers who sponsored the HRA initially emphasized their ambition for the Act as the source of a new culture of respect for human rights. In evidence before the Joint Committee on Human Rights (JCHR) in 2001, Irvine expansively expounded on this phrase:

> What I mean, and I am sure what others mean when they talk of a culture of respect for human rights, is to create a society in which our public institutions are habitually, automatically responsive to human rights considerations in relation to every procedure they follow, in relation to every practice they follow, in relation to every decision they take, in relation to every piece of legislation they sponsor.[140]

I was personally sometimes a little uneasy with the messianic undertones of the phrase 'human rights culture' when left unexplained, but the JCHR usefully clarified its institutional and ethical underpinnings in a 2003 report on the case for establishing a Human Rights Commission. The Select Committee emphasized the overlooked potential of the HRA outside the courtroom and the capacity for human rights values to build 'a sense of social obligation'. The grounds for this assertion lay in ECHR jurisprudence which requires 'a fair balance' between 'individual rights and the needs of a democratic society and the wider public interest'.[141]

In the early, relatively optimistic days of the HRA some public authorities and inspectorates took seriously the obligation on public authorities not to act incompatibly with the HRA; the prisons and mental health inspectorates, the Association of Chief Police Officers (ACPO), the Northern Ireland Policing Board,[142] the Parole Board and the Audit Commission (AC) amongst them. A 2003 AC report lamented that 58 per cent of the public bodies it surveyed had not adopted a human rights strategy. I was surprised at the 42 per cent that had.[143]

The British Institute of Human Rights (BIHR) undertook extensive consultancy and training in human rights values in the health, social care and voluntary and community sectors with verifiable results.[144] I once attended a BIHR training session for Southwark social workers. Having been one myself in a previous incarnation, I understood why they would find the HRA framework helpful for decisions which require a balance between individual rights and the public interest. 'The Human Rights Act: Basic Principles and Values' was initially presented as a paper to local government officers at the Harrogate Management Centre as part of their introduction to the Act.

Some senior figures were outspoken in their view that the HRA could be a useful tool for public officials required to make difficult ethical judgments in their everyday work. In 2009 Sir Hugh Orde, the outgoing Chief Constable of the Northern Ireland Police Service and incoming President of ACPO, called for human rights to be put at the heart of British policing:

> There is a myth that human rights prevents good policing . . . Human rights are a set of principles . . . we operate against . . . It makes sense to see if your policies comply with human rights and that there's no conflict. . . . And we haven't been stopped doing the policing we need to do by human rights. It has helped us . . . Focusing on human rights provides a welcome antidote to the performance culture of the last few years that has pushed us into chasing numbers rather than really delivering the style of service that people want. A human rights emphasis will make us shape our services around what people have a right to expect in terms of protection, reassurance and the defence of civil liberties.[145]

Sensible cases clarifying earlier case law on the responsibilities of public authorities under the HRA confirmed that it did not require anything approximating the 'human rights madness' the tabloids liked to conjure. The House of Lords ruled that the Act does not require public authorities to be overly formalistic: 'a construction of the Human Rights Act which requires ordinary citizens in local government to produce formulaic incantations would make it ridiculous' and 'what matters in any case is the practical outcome'.[146]

A Human Rights Commission to promote and protect human rights, including explaining the common-sense principles in such case law, was established in Northern Ireland as early as 1999, and subsequently in Scotland. Compliance with the ECHR is embedded in their respective devolution statutes, as it is in Wales.[147] The absence of a Human Rights Commission for the rest of the UK in the early days of the HRA meant that there was no public body to provide similar guidance to the public sector in England and Wales, beyond the introductory material from the Home Office. When the Equality and Human Rights Commission (EHRC) was finally established in 2006, it was as an amalgamation of the three national existing equality bodies combined with new areas of responsibilities.[148] Within such a broad mandate, human rights promotion and protection were underresourced. In 2008 the EHRC established an evidence-based Inquiry into human rights practices chaired by Baroness Nuala O'Loan, on which I sat as lead commissioner.[149] We took evidence from 2,855 people who expressed varying degrees of understanding of human rights and different views on their application in the public sector.

The Inquiry's findings, perhaps disappointingly from the EHRC's perspective, did not bear out David Cameron's assertion that 'this whole health and safety, human rights act culture, has infected every part of our life.'[150] Instead, the Inquiry report concluded that 'where public sector providers had adopted a "human rights approach" to service delivery . . . they reported improved services . . . and heightened staff morale.'[151] Providing evidence to this effect, the then Parliamentary and Health Services Ombudsman Ann Abraham referred to the change of perspective on human rights amongst public-sector workers, as the HRA had bedded down:

> I detect a sea change . . . with definite shift away from seeing human rights as being just about civil liberties, crime, national security to a much more inclusive approach that recognises the small places where human rights play a part in ordinary life.[152]

This description would have pleased Eleanor Roosevelt, without whom there would arguably never have been a Human Rights Act in the UK. It parallels her insistence that human rights should begin in 'small places', which she asserted when addressing the UN in 1958, a decade after the UDHR was adopted:

> Where after all do universal human rights begin? In small places, close to home – so close and so small that they cannot be seen on any map of the world. Yet they are the world of the individual person: The neighbourhood he lives in; the school or college he attends; the factory, farm or office where he works. Such are the places where every man, woman, and child seeks equal justice, equal opportunity, equal dignity without discrimination. Unless these rights have meaning there, they have little meaning anywhere. Without

concerted citizen action to uphold them close to home, we shall look in vain for progress in the larger world.[153]

Disability-rights campaigner and cross-bench peer Jane Campbell made a similar plea when she argued for 'stretch[ing] the meaning of "bringing rights home" a little' to include 'bringing rights *into* the home'. Emphasizing the transformative potential of human rights for disabled people who frequently experience inhuman treatment in their private as well as public lives, she argued:

> By actively changing the narrative that describes the role of human rights in our society, I hope we can reassert their unique and crucial role in helping all people, whatever their age or disability, to enjoy 'being valued human beings'.[154]

This vision is important for another reason. Before the HRA, human rights in the UK had largely been seen as something foreigners lack or only lawyers assert. As Abraham suggested, within the UK they had generally been assumed to be synonymous with civil liberties. The broader vision of human rights championed by Roosevelt and enshrined in the UDHR, which recognizes that dignity is as essential to well-being as liberty and that humans need functioning communities to flourish, was almost entirely unappreciated. Yet, as Cameron has made clear, this cultural 'infection' is also in his sights.[155] Speaking after the 2011 London riots, which the Prime Minister implicitly partly blamed on the HRA, he asserted with no hard evidence to back up his statement that:

> The truth is, the interpretation of human rights legislation has exerted a chilling effect on public sector organisations, leading them to act in ways that fly in the face of common sense, offend our sense of right and wrong, and undermine responsibility.[156]

Dominic Raab MP, a trenchant critic of the HRA, sees Strasbourg jurisprudence as the route to what Cameron has described as the 'twisting and misrepresenting of human rights'.[157] In his book, *The Assault on Liberty*, Raab berates domestic judges for 'trying to divine and decipher the murky case law emanating from Strasbourg' instead of giving effect to (undefined) 'British rights'.[158]

Gearty has made a persuasive case that it is quite misleading to characterize the principles the HRA asserts as an alien implant on the common law, as Raab implies – a particularly ironic accusation by Raab, given the common law's Norman origins. The 'respect for parliamentary sovereignty shown by the Act is not foreign' either to the British or Convention systems of rights, Gearty asserts, whilst:

> respect for civil liberties, legality and human dignity. . . . serve to fit the Human Rights Act and the European Convention much more comfortably within the British constitutional tradition than the bald words and large claims in these instruments, viewed in isolation, would suggest.[159]

Assuming Gearty is right, this goes a long way to explaining why, by and large, most judges and senior lawyers have not struggled to apply the HRA as intended. In 2010, when the Act had already been in force for a decade, the former Lord Chief Justice Tom Bingham asserted that to his knowledge there has not been 'any judicial complaint that the Act requires judges to decide questions unsuitable for judicial decision'.[160] The current President of the Supreme Court Lord Neuberger has recently contrasted the current era with 'the dark ages, the period before 1951, when the UK simply did not recognise human rights other than through the common law' which 'was in many ways the origin and promoter of individual rights [but] it developed such rights in a somewhat haphazard and leisurely way'. He concluded:

> I think that the introduction of the Convention into UK law has been a breath of fresh air for the judiciary, the legal profession and legal academics. I think it has made us more questioning about our accepted ideas and assumptions.[161]

Critiques and controversies

Neuberger might be right that the HRA has been 'a breath of fresh air for the judiciary', but very early into its life it was deluged by a torrent of cold air. Tabloid hostility to the Act greeted its birth and preceded any cases, but it was the reaction of political leaders, ranging from discomfort to hostility, which was to set the tone. To my mind a third, more controversial, factor has led to the current impasse on the HRA's future, which could inelegantly be described as 'legalism'. It is the fusion of these three factors that has proved so combustible.

Parental neglect and political wrangles

Even before the HRA was implemented there was reason to believe that Downing Street was having cold feet about it coming into force. Liberty let it be known that it would consider legal action if the enactment was further delayed. The Home Office and Lord Chancellors Department (LCD) made plans for a launch event in London on 2 October 2000, which they optimistically dubbed 'human rights day', and a competition for school students, which continued for several years afterwards, brought coaches of young people to the capital from around the country. It was already clear that outside those two sponsoring departments there was little interest in, let alone enthusiasm for, the HRA. Initial proposals from the Human Rights Task Force to herald the introduction with explanatory leaflets for every household, on the perhaps naive basis that every resident was entitled to know about their new bill of rights, were replaced by plans for publications aimed at informing public authorities of their responsibilities under the Act. Most people found out about the HRA from the press, and it was the tabloids who shouted the loudest about it.

Generally speaking, governments demonstrate commitment to, if not pride in, the legislation they spawn. This early parental neglect did not give the HRA an auspicious start. Nevertheless, after thirty years of debate about whether to incorporate the ECHR as a UK bill of rights, Lord Bingham described its introduction as 'one of the outstanding achievements, if not *the* outstanding achievement, of the first Blair Government'.[162] Early cases were largely uncontroversial. Writing before he became a judge, Rabinder Singh QC described the HRA as 'a success story from a legal perspective'.[163]

It is arguable that if the world had not shifted on its axis after 9/11 – less than a year after the HRA came into force – it might well have bedded down by now to become an accepted part of the legal and constitutional landscape of the UK. Instead, the national and international preoccupation with domestic and global security – memorably termed 'the war on terror', by US President George W. Bush[164] – meant that the HRA was tested in the most challenging of circumstances. If the 9/11 atrocity had occurred a little earlier, it is unimaginable that the HRA would ever have been introduced.

Shami Chakrabarti, the charismatic director of Liberty who wrote the foreword for this book, explores the dynamics of this period with great clarity in *On Liberty*.[165] She sums up the 'three trends', as she sees it, which swiftly emerged 'from the political and legislative response to the horror of 9/11' as:

> The death of privacy, the denigration of due process (access to fair legal trials) and the deliberate and determined discrimination against 'others,' Muslims and foreign nationals in particular, with especially harsh treatment that won't do for the majority population . . . All three represent a kind of attack on the 'presumption of innocence'.[166]

From the government's point of view, the HRA became a thorn in its side in circumstances where the executive was prepared to detain suspects without trial[167] or, when that was declared incompatible with the HRA, to introduce a kind of house arrest called 'control orders', which the courts proceeded to modify.[168] For those for whom there were no other laws they could rely on, the HRA provided some measure of protection, regardless of citizenship, especially once the Prime Minister announced that 'the rules of the game are changing'[169] a month after the 7/7 London tube and bus bombings in which fifty-two people were killed. In contrast to the east African Asians of the late 1960s or the Irish detainees of the 1980s, Muslim terror suspects at least had recourse to the domestic courts.

Senior ministers spent the years following 9/11 regularly sniping at the HRA, hinting at amending it, in particular for impeding their freedom to deport terror suspects to countries where they faced a real risk of torture. The UK courts had been refusing to do this before the HRA was enacted following a 1996 case which the UK lost at the ECtHR involving the deportation of a Sikh separatist leader who had unsuccessfully sought asylum in the UK.[170] Sometimes ministers openly disparaged the Act; other times they privately briefed against it to friendly journalists.

After 7/7 Blair announced that 'should legal obstacles arise, we will legislate further, including, if necessary, amending the Human Rights Act, in respect of the interpretation of the ECHR.'[171] The following December, Home Secretary Charles Clarke confirmed that this was still under active consideration,[172] but a review carried out by the Department of Constitutional Affairs, under the auspices of the Lord Chancellor Charlie Falconer, concluded that the HRA was working as intended.[173] Human Rights Minister Cathy Ashton planned a promotional campaign to explain the HRA, which had failed to materialize when the Act came into effect in 2000, but this was once again blocked by Downing Street.

When Cameron announced in a series of speeches and articles in 2006 that 'it is time to replace the Human Rights Act with a British Bill of Rights that will enable ministers to act within the law to protect our society,'[174] the ground had already been laid for him by the Labour government which introduced the Act. Compared with the iconic struggles that had led to bills of rights around the world, and to the international human rights treaties that forged the HRA, Cameron's stated reasons for replacing the HRA with a British Bill of Rights were honest but unusual: 'It is hampering the fight against crime and terrorism. And it has helped to create a culture of rights without responsibilities.'[175]

Cameron's determination from the outset to repeal the HRA, for the specific purpose of detaching the UK from the ECHR, has been a long and personal crusade for him. He proposed as early as 2005, when he was still shadow Education Secretary, that 'we must will the means to the end that we desire and amend the Human Rights Act or, if necessary, leave – perhaps temporarily – the ECHR.'[176]

When Gordon Brown became Prime Minister in July 2007 he took a different tack, promising consultation on a 'British Bill of Rights and Responsibilities' and floating the possibility of a written constitution by 'the 800th anniversary of the signing of the Magna Carta in Runnymede in 1215'.[177] In a Green Paper published by the Ministry of Justice shortly after Brown took office, repeal of the HRA was *explicitly* ruled out and a 'Bill of Rights and Duties' which built on the HRA was ruled in.[178]

I was part of a small group approached to work with Brown's advisors on these proposals, and was subsequently appointed to the small Ministry of Justice Bill of Rights and Responsibilities Reference Group, chaired by human rights minister Michael Wills.[179] The project had no real shared objectives. Straw was Lord Chancellor and Justice Secretary by this time and his emphasis was on inserting responsibilities into the HRA, telling *Daily Mail* readers that he understood their apparent concerns that it was perceived as a 'a villains' charter' due to interpretations by the courts.[180] Wills was keen to engage citizens around the country in a statement of common values, and he held an extensive consultation exercise for that purpose. He was genuinely committed to a bill of rights which built on the HRA to safeguard basic entitlements to education, health and housing from future governments which might too easily remove them, but it was obvious that there was no appetite within the Cabinet for any extension of rights. Some civil servants and ministers saw Brown's support for a 'British Bill of Rights and Responsibilities' as an opportunity to curtail the HRA, or weaken its enforcement mechanisms, but this was courageously blocked by Wills and the project eventually stalled.

The 2010 Conservative Party manifesto commitment to repeal the HRA was expected, but Cameron was prevented from acting on it by the Coalition Agreement with the Liberal Democrats who had pledged to defend the Act at the same election. Given that it was the Liberal Democrats who had been the loudest cheerleaders for incorporating the ECHR into UK law in the form of a bill of rights, this was one manifesto commitment they could not renege on. Instead, the new coalition government established a Commission on a Bill of Rights, composed almost entirely of lawyers, which published its report in December 2012.[181]

The push to establish this body came almost entirely from the Conservative Party. In return, the Commission's terms of reference were strongly shaped by the Liberal Democrats, in particular the requirement that any bill of rights 'incorporates and builds on all our obligations under the European Convention on Human Rights (ECHR)'.[182] Comprised of eight political appointees divided broadly along coalition party lines, with retired civil servant Sir Leigh Lewis in the Chair, the Commission was widely viewed as long-grass territory during its twenty-one months of deliberation.[183]

The Commission resulted in a stalemate, and was almost immediately buried in the thicket from which it had emerged. A minority report by Baroness Kennedy and Philippe Sands QC recommended retaining the HRA, partly influenced by the large majority opposed to scrapping it amongst respondents to the Commission's consultation paper and the complete lack of appetite for repeal in Northern Ireland, Scotland and Wales. Much of the hostility to the HRA has never found the same echo in the devolved territories. Far from being frowned upon, the opportunities for cultural change the HRA offers have generally been embraced by the relevant authorities.[184] Under the devolution settlements, the Scottish Parliament and the Northern Ireland and Welsh Assemblies do not have the power to pass laws which are incompatible with 'Convention rights', and measures which are deemed incompatible can be struck down by the courts, much like subordinate legislation elsewhere. Parliamentary sovereignty effectively means Westminster sovereignty, which no longer commands equal support throughout the UK. If the HRA were repealed this would almost certainly require amendments to the devolution statutes and may need the consent of the devolved institutions.[185] Responding to the Tories' proposals for a British Bill of Rights, the Scottish Community Safety and Legal Affairs minister, Roseanna Cunningham, called on all parties at Holyrood to back the HRA, attacking 'escalating and irresponsible anti-Europe, anti-human rights rhetoric from prominent members of the UK Government'.[186] In Northern Ireland, meanwhile, there are still efforts to secure a Northern Ireland Bill of Rights which builds on the ECHR in line with the Good Friday Agreement, which does not allow for withdrawal.

The majority on the Bill of Rights Commission took the view that 'on balance, there is a strong argument in favour of a UK Bill of Rights',[187] but their reasons for doing so varied. For some commissioners the purpose of a new Bill of Rights would be to increase 'ownership' by labelling the rights British and defining them more clearly. For others a new bill would provide an opportunity to weaken the HRA's enforcement mechanisms, link rights to responsibilities or, more controversially, introduce three tiers of rights holders. Two commissioners, Jonathan Fisher QC and Lord Faulks, went outside the terms of reference to assert that 'the cause of human rights . . . would be better served by withdrawal from the Convention' altogether.[188] In their minority report, Kennedy and Sands presciently rejected the 'majority' conclusions which they suggested 'will be used to support efforts to decouple the United Kingdom from the European Convention'.[189] When the Conservative Party published its report, Protecting Human Rights in the UK, in October 2014, it proposed, as the dissident commissioners had predicted, that 'in the event that' a future Tory government was 'unable to reach agreement' with the Council of Europe that the judgments of the European Court of Human Rights would be purely 'advisory' and no longer automatically binding on the government, 'the UK would be left with no alternative but to withdraw from the European Convention on Human Rights at the point at which our Bill comes into effect.'[190] With these words, the predicted link between the Tory-proposed 'British Bill of Rights' and withdrawal from the ECHR was officially confirmed.

Myths and monsters

Senior politicians from both main political parties have insisted to me at times that their criticisms of the HRA are more in sorrow than in anger, but as elected politicians they have to respect democratic opinion as reflected in the popular press. This always reminds me of the Jewish joke about the boy who kills both his parents and then, as an orphan, throws himself on the mercy of the courts. It is invariably political leaders themselves who have either initiated or parroted most of the fanciful stories in the media,[191] either openly or through off-the-record briefings.

Both of the main political parties have been at it. In 2007 the then Labour Home Secretary John Reid called for a 'major overhaul of the Human Rights Act', citing people's fury 'when we were refused permission to deport the killer of Phillip Lawrence', the head teacher who was tragically murdered outside his school. This line was repeatedly peddled in the tabloid press but the UK court's decision was primarily taken under European Union laws on freedom of movement and had little to do with the HRA. Addressing the Police Federation in the same year, Cameron, then Leader of the Opposition, parroted most of the prominent HRA myths in one speech:

> Look at the effects of the Human Rights Act . . . Over the last few years we've seen a series of disgraceful incidents. Prisoners given access to pornography. Burglars given Kentucky Fried Chicken. One Chief Constable prevented from publishing wanted posters for murderers on the run, on the grounds that to do so would infringe their human rights. No wonder the public thinks that the authorities are on the side of the criminals.[192]

None of these events were true or were precipitated by the HRA. The reference to prisoners accessing pornography is an allusion to the serial killer Dennis Nilsen, whose case was thrown out at the first hurdle. Yet this fabrication still sits on the *Mail's* and *Sun's* Web sites as an illustration of 'madness' under the HRA. The 'fiddler on the roof' story is equally fanciful.[193] The police, as they themselves insisted, were simply responding to a burglar's demands for food as part of their negotiating strategy.[194] Nor was there any evidence of the 'disgraceful incidents' Cameron cited of police forces banning wanted posters of murderers on the run. In October 2009 the Derbyshire police force even had to take the extraordinary step of issuing an official statement denying assertions by senior Tory politicians at their party conference that they had ever 'refused to release photographs on the grounds of the human rights of the offenders'.[195]

Perhaps the most well-known HRA legend was initiated by Home Secretary Theresa May at the 2011 Tory Party Conference. Insisting that 'I am not making this up,' she then proceeded to do just that when she asserted that an 'illegal immigrant . . . cannot be deported because . . . he had a pet cat. This is why I remain of the view that the Human Rights Act needs to go.'[196] This case was all over the tabloids,[197] but the cat was merely cited as one of a number of factors providing evidence of a long-term relationship between the man in question and his gay partner. Because they had lived together as partners for four years, he was allowed to remain in line with Home Office policy at the time. Any other factors, including ownership of the cat, were deemed immaterial by the Senior Immigration Judge, rejecting the Home Office's challenge of the decision, nearly three years before the Home Secretary's speech.[198]

The 'monstering' of the Human Rights Act by sections of the media has been amply recorded.[199] Even before the Act came into force in October 2000 the press warned that school uniforms would be abolished, sex in school showers would become rampant, the prison doors would be flung open and virtually no one would ever again be convicted of a crime. When none of these predictions materialized the tone changed from humorous to hostile. The *Sun* and *Daily Express* are both apt to refer to the 'Hated Human Rights Act' whilst the *Daily Mail* regularly calls it a 'charter for criminals and parasites'. Attempts to elicit corrections by the human rights lawyer and blogger Adam Wagner for the most flagrant mis-reporting has only recently resulted in small, half-hearted retractions. The reliably inaccurate reporting on the HRA and ECHR by most of the tabloids and Tory-supporting press led Lord Justice Leveson to observe in his 2012 landmark report on newspaper ethics that:

> It is one thing for a newspaper to take the view that . . . the asylum and/or human rights system should be reformed . . . it is another thing to misreport stories either wilfully or recklessly as to their truth or accuracy.[200]

What Leveson understandably does not explore is motive, and here it would be naive to omit that press hostility towards the HRA is not just a consequence of following the lead of friendly politicians or even the lure of selling papers on the back of 'shock horror' stories that another foreign suspect/criminal/asylum seeker has been allowed to stay in the UK because of their human rights. As I discuss in 'The Press, Privacy and the Practical Values of the Human Rights Act', the fifth piece in this anthology, much of the press believes it has a direct interest in the repeal of the HRA.[201]

Whilst *The Guardian* newspaper had campaigned for a bill of rights based on the incorporation of the ECHR for many years, hostility towards the HRA amongst most of the tabloids, in particular, was instantaneous and preceded it coming into force. Tabloids had been used to operating in a climate where there were no effective privacy laws, as discussed earlier. Lord Wakeham, then chair of the Press Complaints Commission, introduced an amendment to the Human Rights Bill in the House of Lords to exclude the media altogether from its reach. When this failed he negotiated with Straw the special recognition of free expression inserted into the HRA as section 12, explained earlier.

Since the *Sunday Times* won its famous contempt of court case at the ECtHR in 1979, after the UK Attorney General prevented it from exposing the inadequacy of compensation for Thalidomide victims, it has been clear that freedom of the press is given special recognition in the ECHR,[202] over and above free speech more generally.[203] Most of the protections of journalists' sources,[204] access to closed courts,[205] qualified privilege in libel cases[206] and removal of 'anonymity orders' in terrorist cases[207] have come directly from successful HRA cases taken by journalists and media outlets in the UK courts or at the ECtHR. It is equally true that the evolving common law right to privacy, developed to comply with the HRA, has been used to curtail some of the exposures of celebrities whose wealth allowed them access to justice to an extent denied many others. But it is not true that people outside the public eye have failed to benefit from the privacy protections that were simply non-existent before the HRA.[208] There was a point in time when the courts appeared to be too ready to issue pre-publication privacy injunctions for the rich and famous, but the weight of public opinion against this seems to have reduced them.[209] At any rate the impact of such injunctions pales into insignificance compared to the successful free-speech bans of the pre-HRA age.[210]

'The Press, Privacy and the Practical Values of the Human Rights Act' was written for the law-reform NGO Justice shortly after the full extent of the phone-hacking scandal at the Murdoch-owned *News of the World* came to light, resulting in the Prime Minister establishing the Leveson Inquiry in July 2011. When Wagner asked on his *UK Human Rights Blog* in the same month 'Was it human rights wot won the phone hacking scandal?' he was referring to the regulation of interceptions of communications, including mobile phones, which – step by step – had been introduced entirely because of ECHR case law, as discussed in my Justice article. Without such measures phone hacking would have remained lawful. Whilst the 2000 Regulation of Investigatory Powers Act 2000 (RIPA) is now widely recognized as outdated and open to serious abuse, including the accessing of phone logs of reporters by the police, its regulatory provisions were an advance on the 'silence of the law' which preceded it. The irony of the HRA-hating *Sun*, citing human rights in its legal action against the Metropolitan Police after it was revealed that RIPA was used to access its political editor's telephone records, has not gone unremarked.[211]

What to make, then, of the recent commitment by Culture Secretary Sajid Javid to enhance press freedom should the Conservatives win the next election? Speaking at a Society of Editors' Conference in November 2014, he promised that his party's proposed 'British Bill of Rights will include specific protections for journalists and a free press'.[212] It is obviously open to the government to legislate *now* to prevent the abuse of RIPA the Culture Secretary condemned in the same speech; but in fact an amendment to this effect was recently rejected by the Home Office and the issue has been kicked into the long grass of an Interception of Communications Commissioner Inquiry.[213]

Free-press protections are already demonstrably enshrined in the HRA. At the same Society of Editor's Conference Sir Alan Moses, the chair of the new Independent Press Standards Organisation (IPSO) which replaced the PCC, advised his audience: 'I would not, if I were you, be too ready to quit the safeguards the Strasbourg court has traditionally and continually offered the press.'[214]

Whilst it is always possible to strengthen such safeguards, Javid made clear that it is the right to privacy that the Conservatives have in their sights:

> Article Eight, protecting the right to privacy, was created to fend off the threat of secret police conducting arbitrary searches for totalitarian regimes. But in 2014 it is little more than an excuse for well-paid lawyers to hide the shady pasts of wealthy businessmen and the sexual indiscretions of sporting celebrities.[215]

In one fell swoop the removal or curtailment of the privacy protections that were such a significant driver of the introduction of the HRA could both please the bulk of the celebrity-pursuing press and reduce obstacles to the expansion of state surveillance which the Conservatives are so keen to pursue.[216] From the government's point of view, Article 8, which protects the right to privacy as well as family life, is a particular bug bear. It is being cited, along with Article 10's free-speech protections, by Liberty, Amnesty International, Privacy International and some overseas human rights groups in their applications to the Investigatory Powers Tribunal (IPT). They are complaining that their private communications may have been monitored under the Government Communication Headquarters (GCHQ)'s electronic surveillance programme Tempora, or through its participation in the American National Security Agency's equivalent programme, PRISM, as revealed by former CIA agent Edward Snowden in June 2013.[217]

Those sections of the press that seemed unperturbed by the government's attempts to suppress Snowden's revelations on state surveillance assiduously covered by *The Guardian*,[218] whilst claiming to oppose any state interference in the press, fail to see how they can appear to be parroting the government's own agenda. This prompted former *The Guardian* editor Peter Preston to comment:

> But the question for those stentorian voices that fancy a cosy British bill of appropriate rights remains. If politicians can't be trusted to keep their

chartered hands off a 'free, fair, unruly press' . . . how can they be trusted to construct its new legal foundations? Javid makes a fulsome pitch as he throws existing definitions of privacy in the bin. But he also shows just how easily principle and experience can bite the political dust.[219]

The dead hand of the law?

The common interest between much of the press and government ministers (of whatever party) in attacking the HRA goes a long way to understanding its vulnerability, but it is not enough to fully explain it. Nor is this an adequate account of how, only sixty years after it was ratified, withdrawal from the ECHR has apparently become respectable. Those of us who believe in the enduring importance of human rights as they were developed in the wake of the Second World War have, if we are honest, struggled to articulate the purpose and value of human rights legislation in the land of the Magna Carta.

Polling data suggest that human rights are nowhere near as unpopular as the popular press would suggest. A recent YouGov poll, for example, revealed that despite the relentless negative reporting of the past fourteen years, there is no majority for withdrawing from the ECHR, with national support for remaining inside the system actually increasing between 2013 and 2014. Nearly 60 per cent of the population believe 'there are some rights that all people have, simply because they are human,' although there are significant disparities between the Liberal Democrat and Labour parties, whose supporters are overwhelmingly in favour of this view, and the Conservative Party and the UK Independence Party (UKIP), where only 50 per cent and 41 percent agree with this statement, respectively.[220]

Yet earlier Ipsos Mori poll data for the EHRC found that despite the fact that nearly two-thirds of people surveyed *dis*agreed with the statement that 'human rights are meaningless to me in everyday life,' 66 per cent stated that they knew nothing or not much about the Human Rights Act itself.[221] Additionally, as many as 82 per cent agreed (or tended to agree) that there should be a 'set of human rights for how public services treat people'.[222] A number of submissions from public authorities and individuals to the EHRC Human Rights Inquiry referred to earlier suggested a negative feedback loop between hostile perceptions of the HRA churned out by sections of the media and some politicians and the effective implementation of the Act by public authorities. This in turn impacted on the degree to which the public was aware of it or could be supported by it.[223]

Other evidence suggested that press and political negativity were not the only factors which explained the lack of awareness and understanding of the HRA. A further problem is that it was perceived as complex and as a matter for lawyers only, despite the fact that the schedule of rights in the Act is relatively simple and short, compared to most legislation. A senior Ministry of Justice Official stated: 'Part of the problem with the HRA is it had got stuck on lawyers' desks'.[224]

This is evidence of what Professor Gearty calls 'the crisis of legalism'[225] and is the third factor, interacting with government and press hostility, that drives the critiques and controversies which have dogged the HRA in its relatively short life. There is an obvious paradox here. Without the cutting edge of the law a measure such as the Human Rights Act would have little impact, but the inevitable effect of judicial interpretations of the broad values in the HRA is to create winners and losers, supporters and opponents on a case-by-case basis. This, in turn, can cloud understanding of the ethical basis of a judgment which may appear random and opaque.

As Gearty reminds us, this is an inevitable consequence of all bills of rights:

> Like all similar modern rights instruments, the Human Rights Act leaves to the courts the job of resolving the ambiguities within, the breadth of exceptions to, and the clash of priorities between, the various rights drawn from the European Convention.[226]

But once the courts and other administrative processes become involved, not only might the ethical basis of human rights become obscure to many people but their radial edge can also become blunted, as Finnish international lawyer and scholar Martti Koskenniemi suggests:

> While the rhetoric of human rights has historically had a positive and liberating effect on societies, once rights become institutionalised as a central part of political and administrative culture they lose their transformative effect and are petrified into a legalistic paradigm.[227]

Whilst the law is the necessary means by which standards are set and abuses remedied, the very process of transforming a norm into a legal entitlement can remove the human agency necessary for an ethical framework such as human rights to be understood and applied by human beings in their everyday interactions with each other. Professor Emile Hafner-Burton, author of *Making Human Rights a Reality*, highlights this paradoxical nature of human rights law.

> On the one hand international law plays the central role in defining human rights and the universal norms of international law are profoundly appealing. On the other hand, much of the effort that actually advances those norms lies somewhere outside the universal legal system . . . and hinges on the adoption of strategies, many of which include a turn away from global legalism.[228]

As a result of its legal manifestation human rights can become as remote from the human beings they are meant to protect and liberate as the state or corporate forces they need protection from. This conundrum is brilliantly captured by the Sudanese human rights scholar Adullahi An-Na'im who writes: 'any enforcement of a norm is a negation of its human rights quality, yet the lack of voluntary compliance is what constitutes a violation of the right.'[229]

He goes on to assert that:

> The essential doctrine of human rights can only be realised by entrusting the effort to the human agency of the subjects of those rights and shifting action to the essentially *political nature of the struggle.* National and international legal strategies can only follow political action, never lead or replace it.[230]

Gearty seeks to find a way through this impasse:

> How can we hold on to a law of human rights which does useful civilising work but at the same time does not succumb to the temptation to lord it over politics?[231]

For Gearty the answer lies in the HRA itself:

> Here we have a set of clear human rights, with duties imposed on courts and public authorities to make sure that these rights are properly protected and enforced.[232]

However because courts are not permitted to strike down statutes, and the Act itself is not insulated by special parliamentary majorities but can be amended or repealed like any other legislation, Gearty argues that these legal duties do not have to overwhelm the necessarily political edge to human rights.

> [The HRA] deliberately undermines its own authority, inviting the political back in to control the legal just at the moment when the supremacy of the legal discourse seems assured.[233]

So why has this not worked to bolster the HRA from the battering it has received? My own view is that allowing space for political dialogue and disagreement, which is a feature of the HRA as Gearty suggests, is necessary but not sufficient. An additional task is to convey the *ethic* of universal human rights; a major challenge in a discourse dominated by whichever legal cases attract the greatest publicity at any given time. This has to involve sometimes disagreeing with judgments that do not appear to sit well with this ethic. In a context where judges, both domestic and at Strasbourg, are under constant attack for not being 'elected' or 'accountable' – which is arguably the whole point of the judiciary – when and how to criticize the courts can pose serious dilemmas for human rights defenders. Liberty's critique of the ECtHR decision to uphold the so-called *burqa* ban in France, discussed in Section I, is a good example of how effective an independent evaluation of a legal case can be in clarifying the autonomous nature of human rights values which stand above, not below, case law.[234]

Not long after the HRA came into force a small gathering of human rights NGOs and academics discussed the practical and theoretical dilemmas of promoting human rights in a mature democracy. In an unpublished lecture, 'Issues in Communicating Human Rights' (the last in the anthology), I tried to subject my own narrow assumptions to self-criticism. In the fourteen years since this was written it is interesting to reflect how some of what was then still controversial amongst more libertarian NGOs has now become mainstream human rights practice. It was then still necessary to comment that human rights are about not just protecting individuals from abuses by the state but also *requiring* the state to protect children, and potential victims, from abuse by other individuals. What is still just as challenging is the task of conveying what is essentially an ethical framework generally dressed in legal clothes:

> Reflected in the UDHR is the realisation that for a human rights culture to sustain itself, laws to protect individuals from tyrannical states, whilst essential, are not enough. What was needed, the drafters decided, was to establish a set of universal values based largely on the common ethical principles of the world's major religions and belief systems, suffused – so far as it was possible – with the old enlightenment ideals of free speech, freedom of religion etc. Only if these values were widely accepted and understood would the peoples of the world hold their rulers sufficiently in check to guarantee human rights. Judges and courts could not be expected to do it alone.[235]

The eminent legal theorist Ronald Dworkin long ago articulated the more traditional human rights view that it is in the courts, rather than the political sphere, where 'the most fundamental issues of political morality will finally be set out and debated as issues of principle . . . a transformation that cannot succeed, in any case not fully, within the legislature itself'.[236]

There is no doubt that the courts do have the capacity to articulate issues of principle, removed from the sometimes brutal populist pressures facing politicians. This can sound shocking to democrats, and a frequent question is: Who are 'unelected' judges to determine issues of policy in a democratic society? Following Dworkin, the law and philosophy scholar John Finnis records the familiar distinction between courts, which are characterized as 'the forum of principle' and legislatures which 'though not unconcerned with principle, are the forum of policy'.[237] The former are generally focused on the rights and obligations of the parties before them, whereas the latter are concerned with utilitarian considerations of 'the greatest good for the greatest number',[238] or perhaps more realistically, with 'what will keep me in office'. On this account, both are necessary if a democracy is truly for *everyone* – the most important word in the ECHR – but the role of the courts in bolstering democratic principles is far from clear to many people. Courts provide protections for individuals and groups who cannot expect to find shelter under the umbrella of institutions dedicated to majority rule. Yet despite the acknowledged major trust deficit in elected politicians, there is currently a simultaneous crisis of confidence in court judgments which do not appear to reflect common perceptions or values.

Unless human rights defenders are prepared to clearly and consistently articulate their conception of the 'common good', Finnis implies, on what basis should anyone be persuaded by a 'pragmatic argument' that rights to free speech or privacy, for example, are 'rights declared in the European Convention and other standard bills of rights' and therefore should be respected as the court dictates?[239] Was it ever realistic that decades after post-war human rights treaties were drafted, with the memory of their original purpose and context starting to fade, their survival could rely on a repetition of the mantra that we have 'international human rights obligations' and therefore judicial interpretations of them should be followed without question? Courts make decisions on the cases brought before them. They cannot possibly be expected to take on the burden of articulating the human rights ethic in a consistent and coherent manner. If this articulation is to come from anywhere, it has to come from human rights defenders and supporters, as the UDHR conceives, presented as the basis of debate and discussion, not missionary-like certainty. Unless the basic principles that underline human rights treaties are conveyed by those who support them, is hard to conceive how 'human rights' will 'survive'.[240]

Back to the future?

When the Conservatives published their policy document, *Protecting Human Rights in the UK*[241] on 3 October 2014 (hereafter called the policy document) the question of whether the post-war human rights framework *will* survive in the UK beyond the next election shifted overnight from a question of academic speculation to practical implementation. With UKIP – the potential coalition partners to the Conservatives in the event of a widely Predicted hung parliament – strongly committed to withdrawal from the ECHR, the exit door is firmly in sight. As the respected legal commentator Joshua Rozenberg put it: 'Tory plans for European human rights convention will take UK back 50 years.'[242] A former world beckons where a 'sovereign' UK would no longer be bound into the human rights framework that was established after the Second World War.

Churchill, Maxwell Fyfe and Bevin would all be incredulous that it only took more than sixty years before we are on the edge of destroying what they believed was an edifice built to last. The Council of Europe, which they were so instrumental in establishing, commented the day after the Tories' plans were published that: 'We take note of these proposals by the Conservative Party. As they stand, the proposals are not consistent with' the ECHR. Their statement highlighted Article 46, which requires all state signatories to 'undertake to abide by the judgment of the Court in any case to which they are party'.[243] The authors of the Tory policy would have known it is inconsistent with remaining signed up to the ECHR and that it 'undermines entirely the principles that underpin international law' as former Attorney General Dominic Grieve put it.[244]

Of course, there is an alternative to the UK withdrawing from the ECHR. The whole structure could unravel. In truth the ECHR architecture is not much sturdier than a straw dwelling, and it would only take one lone wolf to blow the house down or at least shake its foundations.

The CoM have no tanks or guns to enforce the ECtHR judgments which they are mandated to supervise. If they had, then there would not have been a nine-year standoff with successive UK governments regarding whether they will end the almost blanket ban on allowing convicted prisoners to vote.[245] It is for individual states to determine how they should comply with the Strasbourg court's judgments, just as the architects of the ECHR envisaged. An all-party parliamentary Committee, established in 2013 to recommend to Parliament how to proceed, proposed that prisoners serving sentences of twelve months or less should be given the vote. It noted that the enfranchisement of a few thousand prisoners is far outweighed by the significance of 'a refusal to implement the Court's judgment, which is binding under international law'.[246] This Committee's recommendation would have amply complied with the relevant ECtHR case, but the stalemate continues.

Damages awarded against states that do not provide 'just satisfaction' for applicants who win their case and powers of suspension and expulsion are all the CoM has in its armoury. Should they agree that a judgment of the ECtHR could become purely 'advisory' for the UK, 'and only be binding in UK law if Parliament agrees' according to 'a new Parliamentary procedure',[247] how could the CoM possibly prevent other states following suit?

Former Justice Secretary Ken Clarke, who like Grieve was sacked from the Tory cabinet in July 2014 to make way for these proposals which they had both hitherto blocked,[248] observed that Russia would also 'welcome the idea that the Duma could set [ECtHR judgments] aside, but so far they wouldn't have been able to win that concession'.[249]

The Secretary General of the Council of Europe, commenting on recent signs of progress in Azerbaijan following adverse ECtHR rulings, was uncharacteristically forthright on the impact of the Tory proposals:

> When politicians in established democracies such as the UK threaten to leave the ECHR for essentially domestic reasons, this is likely to have negative repercussions on the respect of fundamental freedoms in Europe's younger democracies. Conservative party proposals to render the binding decisions of the Strasbourg court merely advisory, if enacted, will be welcomed by regimes less committed to human rights than the UK.[250]

There are already signs of the 'domino effect' working outside Europe. Foreign Office officials must have realized that if Cameron were to deliver his 'muscular liberalism' speech again he would be laughed out of court – the Strasbourg court to be precise.[251] They didn't have long to wait. Less than two weeks after the Tory policy was published, Kenya's President Uhuru Kenyatta, the first serving head of state to appear before the International Criminal Court before charges against him were dropped in December 2014 for lack of admissible evidence,[252] cited the Tory's human rights stance in a speech to the Kenyan national assembly:

> The push to defend sovereignty is not unique to Kenya or Africa. Very recently, the Prime Minister of the United Kingdom committed to reasserting the sovereign primacy of his Parliament over the decision of the European Human Rights Court. He has even threatened to quit that court.[253]

When Lord Faulks, former Bill of Rights Commissioner and now junior minister to Justice Secretary Chris Grayling, who led on the Tory policy paper, was asked whether he was concerned about the signal withdrawal would give to other countries, he responded: 'I am not particularly concerned about the effect on Putin or Belarus that any decision may or may not make.'[254]

Would he still take this view listening to the bereaved families of the 2004 Beslan massacre[255] who visited Strasbourg for a public hearing of their case against the Russian authorities? Describing the precipice the entire post-war human rights settlement is balancing on as a consequence of Britain's threat to pull out, Ella Kasayeva, who lost many family members in the massacre, predicted that if the UK were to withdraw:

> It would be an excuse for our government to say 'we don't want it either.' Putin would point at the UK straight away. It would be a catastrophe. [The UK] has to understand; we all live in the same world and we all have an impact on one another.[256]

Nearly half of all adverse ECtHR judgments in 2013 were against Russia, Turkey, Romania and Ukraine. Only 1 per cent, eight adverse judgments in all, concerned the UK. In 2012 there were ten such cases. The vast majority of applications to the Court against the UK (97 per cent) are declared 'inadmissible' and never heard.[257] Since the HRA has come into force the direction of travel has been a reduction in applications to the court: there were just 395 in the first seven months of 2014. With such figures in mind, Joshua Rozenberg commented:

> Depriving people of their rights does seem to be something of an overreaction to one or two adverse rulings from the human rights court. Surely it would be simpler just to allow a few more prisoners the vote?[258]

Perhaps this is too rational a question to capture the drivers of this potential demolition of the post-war human rights settlement. *The Guardian* commentator Jonathan Freedland put it down to 'crude politics' with the Tories desperate 'to blunt UKIP's bayonets' before the general election plus a deeper set of emotions:

> Anger about excessive powers supposedly wielded by Strasbourg judges . . . is not really about institutional arrangements. It is instead the outlet of a much

more visceral rage, the furious sense that the word is not as it should be – and that someone faraway must be to blame.[259]

Perhaps this sentiment was best captured by Jacob Rees-Mogg, Conservative MP for North East Somerset, speaking in Parliament two years before the Conservatives finally declared their hand on the ECHR:

> Does the Lord Chancellor recall that in the reign of Henry VIII it was made high treason to take an appeal outside this kingdom? Has not the time come for this Parliament once more to legislate to prohibit appeals to foreign courts and to prohibit the judgments of foreign courts leading our judiciary?[260]

Inflation or interpretation?

Grieve's evaluation of the Tory proposals for a 'British Bill of rights' was that it contained legal 'howlers' and was 'not properly thought through'.[261] A number of 'factual inaccuracies and misinterpretations of ECHR judgments' were also highlighted in the legal 'opinion' of the proposals by Tim Owen QC and Alex Bailin QC.[262] But in terms of broad and deliverable policy objectives, the direction of travel seems clear.

For some years a number of lawyers and campaigners held out hope that a new bill of rights would include additional entitlements, such as jury trials or children's rights, which are missing from the HRA. Free-speech campaigners believed it might introduce a comparable protection to the American First Amendment on free expression. A common view was that given the government's continued adherence to the ECHR – withdrawal being unthinkable – the domestic judges would continue to interpret this new measure in conformity with the Convention, whatever its precise terms, as otherwise disgruntled petitioners would still seek remedies at the Strasbourg court. Moreover, as this new bill would be redefined as 'British' this would make it more popular (disregarding how this might be received amongst many communities in Northern Ireland, Scotland and Wales).[263]

Yet if Cameron were to achieve his dual ambition to both 'abolish the Human Rights Act' because 'it is hampering the fight against crime and terrorism and it has helped to create a culture of rights without responsibilities' and introduce a Bill of Rights 'so that Britain's laws can no longer be decided by unaccountable judges',[264] this new measure would clearly have to be very different from the HRA. If a 'British Bill of Rights' were to simultaneously end the hostile headlines about the so-called 'wrong' people getting rights, as Cameron has effectively promised, and 'ensure that decisions are made in this *Parliament* rather than in the courts',[265] then the interpretative powers of domestic judges would need to be severely curtailed and the Strasbourg court removed from the picture. That is the circle which the Tories have sought to square with their proposals.

The Conservatives' policy document is explicit: the proposed British Bill of Rights 'will not introduce new basic rights.' There will not only be no inflation of rights but even their interpretation 'would benefit from a more precise definition'.

The purpose is not to expand or even 'bed down' the HRA but 'to tackle the misuse of the rights contained in the Convention'. The new Bill will 'limit the use of human rights to the most serious cases' instead. Beyond broad-brush statements that 'serious cases' involve 'criminal law and the liberty of an individual, the right to property and similar serious matters', no definition of these 'serious cases' is provided.[266] It is interesting that 'property rights' are perceived as sufficiently weighty to be included. Stanley Johnson – father of London Mayor Boris Johnson – who has reportedly called for a 'popular uprising' in London's Primrose Hill against the proposed HS2 train line citing the right to protection of property under the HRA, would presumably be gratified that his case is still deemed 'serious'.[267] But ironically, those who are neither criminal defendants, suspects or prisoners appear most likely to lose out under this new 'British Bill of Rights and Responsibilities'.

The purpose of this new criteria for cases to proceed appears to be to counter the 'mission creep' of the ECtHR 'living instrument' doctrine,[268] which was first developed in a 1978 UK case concerning judicial corporal punishment – the use of the birch on a fifteen-year-old boy – in the Isle of Man.[269] The ECtHR rejected the UK government's argument that this could not be considered 'degrading punishment' because it 'did not outrage public opinion in the island', the utilitarian measure of what is 'right' which human rights law has developed to temper. Instead the Court argued that 'the Convention is a living instrument which . . . must be interpreted in the light of present-day conditions,'[270] a principle which ECtHR Judge Robert Spano maintains itself reflects 'the original intention of the founders of the Convention'.[271]

Former President of the ECtHR Sir Nicolas Bratza spoke the 'common sense'[272] which the Conservative policy document says it aims to restore to human rights when he wrote: 'It hardly needs to be said that many aspects of contemporary human activity, which by any definition fall within the intended sphere of protection of the Convention, would certainly not have been envisaged by the drafters in 1950' from changes to 'the nuclear family' to 'developments in the field of bioethics and communication'.[273]

With the justification that the ECHR is intended to guarantee rights which are 'practical and effective' not 'theoretical or illusory', over the decades homosexuality has been decriminalized in Northern Ireland;[274] transgender people,[275] travellers[276] and disabled people[277] have all moved the boundaries of the original text by taking cases; and even environmental damage has been recognized as compromising human rights in some circumstances.[278] None of these groups and issues were in the minds of the original drafters, if for no better reason than that times have changed. Every one of these cases might have been knocked out as 'trivial' according to the markers in the Tory policy document.

The policy document implies that this 'problem' cannot be solved just by making ECtHR judgments 'advisory' because 'the living instrument' doctrine has infected UK law since the introduction of the HRA, resulting in far more domestic cases in which ECHR rights are claimed than in Strasbourg. It is perfectly true that our courts have employed this approach when 'taking into account' Strasbourg case law, but to suggest this is new would be to completely ignore that the common law has long developed a similar approach. As Lord Nicholls put it: 'For centuries judges have been charged with the responsibility of keeping this law abreast of current social conditions and expectations.'[279]

If this had not been the case, as remarked in the 'Introduction', the due-process provisions in the Magna Carta would still only extend to the landed aristocracy and the 800th anniversary celebrations might have been a very muted affair.

The people who the Conservatives appear to have in their sights by repealing the HRA, it seems, are not just 'the undeserving' and 'unpopular' – who keep the tabloid newspapers in business – but men, women and children from all walks of life who have received help through the Act. Legal-aid cuts have meant that these 'everyday cases' are being squeezed anyway, although sometimes a negotiated settlement supported by human rights NGOs such as Liberty or BIHR provide the change, or simple acknowledgement, people are seeking.

Under this new 'British Bill of Rights' how many of the following issues or HRA cases would be 'struck out' as unworthy of the label 'the most serious'?

- The failure of the Metropolitan Police Service to effectively investigate more than 105 rapes and sexual assaults perpetrated between 2002 and 2008, which our courts ruled constituted a breach of the HRA.[280]
- The police restraint of a severely autistic and epileptic teenager at a swimming pool who was forced by police officers to lie on the floor in handcuffs and leg restraints and was subsequently detained in the back cage of a police car for about forty minutes, in breach of the HRA.[281]
- The refusal of the Metropolitan Police to investigate a report of threats and violence against an employee, whose passport and wages had been withheld in breach of the prohibition on slavery and forced labour.[282]
- The surveillance by Poole Borough Council of a mother and her children to determine whether they lived within a school catchment area, using powers under RIPA, which was ruled unlawful and a breach of their right to respect for private life under the HRA.[283]
- The requirement that before a local authority residential care home is closed, the effect of the closure on the residents' emotional and physical health must be included in any consultation.[284]
- The elimination of the discriminatory effect of the Rent Act 1977, which prevented the survivor of a gay or lesbian couple from inheriting a statutory tenancy when their partner died.[285]
- The interpretation of legislation to permit a woman to become a parent through the stored sperm of her late husband[286] and the naming of a deceased father on a birth certificate.[287]
- The recognition of trade unions with collective bargaining rights in compliance with the right to freedom of assembly and association.[288]
- The duty to hold effective investigations into deaths at the hand of the state which has not only been applied when people die in custody – such as Zahid

Mubarak, who was forced to share a cell with a racist cell mate in Feltham Young Offenders Institution[289] – but has contributed to the re-opening of the Hillsborough inquest.

Insanity or humanity?

None of these apparently less-serious examples could conceivably be described as evidence of 'the human rights madness' that the tabloids and some senior politicians regularly mention, but then again you would struggle to find much media coverage of everyday life stories like these, despite their increase in volume.[290] Those cases which are routinely described as 'insane' are often the *least* trivial ones, in fact, involving detention, fair trials and torture. Aspects of these are also in the Conservatives' sights.

The policy document asserts that 'there is nothing wrong with the original' ECHR and that its text will be inserted into the new Bill. But the beating heart of 'that original document' is universalism and that is precisely what the proposals seek to restrain. As discussed in the 'Introduction', it was the evolving universal reach of the Magna Carta, within the UK at least, which eventually saved the Great Charter from great irrelevance. Now, as then, it is not so much the rights themselves that are at issue as who has access to them and in what circumstances. The Conservatives propose several changes to the scope and interpretation of ECHR rights, beyond excluding all but 'the most serious cases', leading Cambridge law academic Dr Mark Elliot to comment:

> It follows that the Bill of Rights would not give effect to the Convention rights as curated by the ECtHR and understood across the Council of Europe; rather it would give effect, in some instances, to bastardised versions of those rights . . . it is disingenuous to claim that the Bill of Rights would include all of the Convention rights.[291]

The press release accompanying the policy document singles out 'travellers claiming the right to family life to breach planning laws' as one group whose rights the proposed Bill is aimed at limiting, rather than extending.[292]

Another sector the policy paper specifically targets is 'British armed forces overseas'. The plan is to 'limit the reach of human rights cases to the UK' so as to rule out 'persistent human rights claims that undermine' soldiers' 'ability to do their job and keep us safe'.[293] The question of keeping the armed forces themselves 'safe' seems to be of less concern. There are proposals to eliminate the kind of claims that have led to an inquest to establish how a British soldier serving in Iraq died from hyperthermia in a UK military base.[294] The capacity to take proceedings to establish whether the Ministry of Defence (MoD) should be held liable for 'negligence' for failing to provide better equipment following the death or injury of soldiers killed on patrol, or through 'friendly fire' – but not in battle – could also be eliminated.[295] It is difficult to see how such cases adversely affect armed conflicts given that the doctrine of 'combat immunity', which excludes liability for deaths on the battle-field, has recently been reaffirmed.[296]

The question of the territorial application of the ECHR, a source, as we saw, of considerable friction in colonial Britain when the ECHR was being drafted, is back on the agenda. The signpost to the exit door of the ECHR becomes illuminated by such proposals. For as long as the UK is subject to the Convention, it is not possible to completely exclude countries such as Iraq and Afghanistan from its reach in situations where the state has exercised 'authority and control' over individuals, such as those whom the army detained en masse. The Grand Chamber of the ECtHR has been unambiguous on this. It held that British soldiers engaged in security operations in Basrah exercised sufficient 'authority and control' over the Iraqis who were killed to bring them within the jurisdiction of the UK.[297] It seems that it is extremely 'serious' cases such as these which the policy document proposes to 'strike out' as much as those described as 'trivial'.[298] This makes sense from the government's – *any* government's – point of view.

Other means have already been used to close down allegations of ill treatment of detainees in Iraq and Afghanistan. The five interrogation techniques which were meant to have been banned in the 1970s following the *Ireland v UK* case described earlier, were in use again; the knowledge of the ban having apparently been 'lost'. Six months before twenty-six-year-old Iraqi civilian Baha Mousa was detained, tortured and beaten to death by British soldiers, as established by the Gage Inquiry in 2011,[299] Lieutenant Colonel Mercer, the former chief legal adviser in Iraq following the 2003 invasion, advised that a judge be sent to Iraq to supervise the handling of prisoners. The response of the MoD was to ignore Mercer's request and brief against him, effectively ending his army career.[300]

Extraordinarily, given its pre-eminence in both international and common law rights protections, the prohibition on torture is also hedged about in the policy document. At issue is not the right itself but *who* can lay claim to it and in what circumstance. In virtually every situation in which the UK, as a modern democracy, is likely to be implicated in such a discredited practice, current prohibitions will be weakened. If our troops engage in torture abroad they would be beyond 'the reach' of this new British bill of rights, as we have seen. If our courts wished to stop governments from exporting torture by deporting people to countries where there is any 'real risk' that is what they will face – they would no longer be able to apply this test established by the ECtHR.[301] A new less-exacting threshold would be introduced which is not spelt out. Whether the domestic courts would be prepared to ignore the standards laid down in UN treaties prohibiting torture, which the government is presumably not intending to withdraw from alongside the ECHR, is highly questionable.[302]

Having raised expectations so high, the Conservatives would obviously be anxious to avoid the acres of headlines that greeted a case such as that of Abu Qatada, which would now be laid at the door of their new Bill of Rights. Qatada was arrested and detained indefinitely by Home Secretary David Blunkett in 2002 and began a long legal battle against deportation to Jordan to stand trial on terrorism charges. This was eventually blocked directly by the ECtHR in 2012 because of a strong probability that his trial would be based on evidence obtained by torture, rather than because he faced the risk personally.[303] This judgment attracted particular ire, presumably on the basis that it is acceptable to facilitate a trial relying on evidence procured from torture provided the defendant is not British and had been deported to another country where the trial will take place. When the Home Secretary skilfully negotiated a change to Jordon's constitution prohibiting evidence obtained from torture, this resulted not just in Qatada's deportation in July 2013 but also his eventual acquittal without the tainted evidence. The change to Jordanian law is of lasting effect, but this example of the universality of the ECHR achieving global results was not presented this way by any of the main party leaders.

The government has already introduced legislation to severely curtail deportations that the courts deem breach Article 8, the right to family life, but the plan is to further 'clarify' this right.[304] There is a debate to be had, of course, about whether foreign criminals who have served their sentence should or should not automatically be deported when they leave prison, however long and deep their association with the UK. Successive governments have repeatedly made clear that the former is their intention and on this basis some tribunal decisions not to deport can seem arbitrary, particularly following heinous crimes such as murder or rape. But the frequent tabloid tale that the HRA has effectively ended such deportations is pure fiction. In 2012 only 151 foreign nationals offenders (FNOs as they are officially called) successfully appealed their deportation on Article 8 grounds, out of thousands that were deported, but this was presented as reason enough to mount frenzied campaigns to overturn 'human rights madness'.

Mostly, where deportations are stopped, it is for reasons that have nothing to do with the HRA, often because of Home Office error. Paul Houston, the father of Amy Houston who was tragically killed by an Iraqi hit-and-run driver in 2003, has honourably made this very point, criticizing the way official incompetence has been shielded by using his daughter's death to call for the repeal of the HRA. He movingly wrote in *The Guardian*:

> My daughter's case has been used as an example of all that is wrong with the Human Rights Act. I want to be clear: I support human rights. We have no need for a new bill of rights because the Human Rights Act already contains all the protection we need. I support the right to asylum and rights of victims. I support the right to family life that, as the courts know, is always balanced against other rights.[305]

In cases where deportations have been halted to protect family unity it is nearly always the rights of other family members that are pivotal, not the person taking the case, especially when they are FNOs. A simple word for this approach is not insanity but humanity. Lord Brown made this plain when he asserted that a person's Article 8 rights have 'to be looked at by reference to the family unit as a whole and the impact of removal upon each member'.[306] Usually it is children who are at the centre of such decisions, where, as Lady Hale, the only female judge in the Supreme Court, put it:

> The overarching issue . . . is the weight to be given to the best interests of children who are affected by the decision to remove or deport one or both of their parents from this country.[307]

Further fiddling with the text of the ECHR is signalled by a commitment to 'clarify the Convention rights to reflect a proper balance between rights and responsibilities'.[308] Recognizing that qualifications and limitations are in fact built into virtually every Article,[309] the document also warns that 'our new Bill will clarify these limitations on individual rights in certain circumstances.'[310] As with Jack Straw's earlier proposals along these lines, it is unclear whether this is intended to be an amplification of the 'balance' between individual and community rights that is at the heart of the ECHR,[311] or an insertion of a different philosophy in which so-called 'bad people' forfeit rights altogether, far beyond what is necessary to protect others or the common good. Who amongst us has not sometimes thought: Why should someone who has taken a life or abused a child and so forth be able to claim human rights at all? But the approach developed through human rights treaties is not to strike out whole categories of *people* but categories of *behaviour* so that an individual's rights are limited to the extent that is necessary to protect the rights of others and the common good.[312]

The received wisdom, according to the tabloids at least, is that 'responsibilities' need reasserting because the HRA is little more than a 'villain's charter' protecting suspects and criminals. Obliquely responding to the Conservatives' proposals to repeal the HRA a few days after they were published, Lord Neuberger tried to defend it by asserting that human rights have been 'very beneficial' to court rulings and that it was 'particularly important' that the rights of criminals who were incarcerated as a danger to society were 'not ignored'.[313]

This is an instantly recognizable human rights paradigm from the President of the Supreme Court, articulated in a principled fashion. But many might be surprised to learn from former Director of Public Prosecutions, Keir Starmer, that it is the *victims* of crime who have been the overwhelming beneficiaries of the HRA, and that 'there has been no fundamental shift in defendant's rights and most of the HRA challenges brought by defendants in our courts have failed.'[314] What he has to say, based on direct experience, is so counter-intuitive to the ingrained assumptions about the impact of human rights legislation, that it is worth quoting him at length:

> The HRA has heralded a new approach to victims' rights. Before the HRA, individuals in the UK did not have the right to an effective investigation into serious allegations of criminal wrong doing. Even where the police clearly and obviously failed to protect victims or to investigate properly, the common law offered nothing. The 'positive obligation' to protect life and limb found in the HRA changed all that. Often after many years of struggling to be heard,

victims now have a right to have serious allegations taken seriously and to be protected and supported by the police whether they have died in the hands of the state or have been abused by other individuals.

Those who have benefited most from the HRA are not murderers and rapists but 'child victims of trafficking, women subjected to sexual violence, prisoners who have died in custody and those with vulnerabilities that inhibit reporting of abuse'.[315]

Perhaps there is no starker example of the contrast between perception and reality than the role the HRA played in securing an inquest into the circumstances which led to the tragic death of Naomi Bryant, who was killed in 2005 by convicted sex offender Anthony Rice, wrongly released on parole as a result of mismanagement. This is one of several incidents in which, in a spate of media hysteria, the HRA was blamed for a young woman's murder when in fact, with Liberty's support, it was only as a result of the HRA that her mother, Verna, was able to find out about the catalogue of errors which led to her daughter's killing.[316]

This role of the HRA as a 'victims' charter' is not very surprising if the post-war human rights framework is better understood.[317] It is more than twenty years since it was held that the state has a 'positive obligation' under the ECHR to provide adequate protection for a woman facing sustained sexual harassment from her ex-partner.[318] It is nearly thirty years since the ECtHR established a 'positive obligation' on states to ensure that the powerful cannot abuse the powerless 'even in the sphere of the relations of individuals between themselves',[319] a principle which so enrages libertarian critics of human rights.[320] Despite areas of overlap, Raab is quite right to distinguish this human rights framework from the more libertarian one he supports:

> Whereas fundamental liberties were developed in Britain to stop the government interfering with the freedom of the individual, many of these novel rights have the reverse effect – increasing both the state's responsibility for what happens to the citizen and the citizen's dependence on the state. The consequence has been to inflate, rather than restrain, the role of the state in our lives.[321]

The common law developed on the principle that what is not forbidden is allowed and that for individuals to be free there have to be considerable limits on state power. Human rights values and standards evolved out of this framework to establish the parameters of a 'good society' in which accountability and protections are required *wherever* power is grossly abused, increasingly in the private as well as the public sphere. This might involve obligations on the state to take actions to protect one individual from another, whether that person be a discriminatory boss or an abusive partner, as Starmer amplified.[322] It is this approach that is now potentially at risk from the plan to repeal the HRA and disconnect from the ECHR. It helps to explain why even some committed civil libertarians such as Raab,[323] who are dedicated to weakening the state where possible to enhance individual freedom, are part of the campaign for repeal.

Alive or dead?

It is the fault line between these perspectives which goes some way to explaining why we are facing the juxtaposition of being on the brink of scrapping the HRA whilst simultaneously experiencing the largest nationwide celebration of the Magna Carta the UK has ever known.[324] The 700th anniversary was mired by the First World War. In June 2015 the government plans to more than make up for this. Of course there is plenty to celebrate. The Magna Carta continues to inspire campaigns to limit unaccountable state power across the political spectrum. The late socialist MP Tony Benn memorably referred to the parliamentary debate on forty-two days[325] as 'the day Magna Carta was repealed'.[326] I imagine a time-travelling Eleanor Roosevelt would be moved to say something similar should the UK ever withdraw from the ECHR.

There are other reasons for this juxtaposition between celebration and repeal that have nothing to do with philosophy. It is not very challenging to nostalgically support a medieval document that in legal terms is effectively dead. Only three clauses are still in force, all of which have been surpassed by subsequent legislation and none of which impact on the freedom of the state to legislate at will. The HRA, by contrast, is very much alive. If it was as legally ineffective as its 800-year-old ancestor, I suspect the government might have managed the odd birthday party for it as well.

The commentary in the Conservative's Bill of Rights policy document on questions of legal enforcement is where it is at its most confused. The Labour Party, similar to the Liberal Democrats and Greens, immediately opposed the document's proposals, if in a fairly muted way. Shadow Justice Secretary Sadiq Khan, leading the Labour attack, declared on the day the report was released: 'the HRA *is* a British Bill of Rights' so 'if what they're promising is different to what we already have, the British people deserve to know' how.[327]

One way in which it is different is that it is unclear whether what is being suggested as a replacement for the HRA is in any meaningful sense a bill of rights at all. Charting the scheme step by step, it is proposed that 'the European Court of Human Rights is no longer binding over the UK Supreme Court.' That is simple to achieve, as it never has been. The ECtHR has never wielded sovereignty over any domestic courts. As we saw, the 'founding fathers' were very careful to avoid this. Only rulings in which the UK is a party impact directly on this country, and then the treaty obligation is with the state, not the courts. Parliament can pass any legislation it likes, but the one thing it does not have the power to do is *decide* to make ECtHR rulings advisory. The only way this can be achieved, given that the Council of Europe has already made it clear that there is no possibility of 'negotiating' to overturn the very purpose of the ECHR, is for the UK to withdraw. This is the logical conclusion of the paper's analysis because no new bill of rights could relieve the UK state of this treaty obligation. The HRA could be repealed tomorrow and the obligation to end the blanket ban on prisoners' voting, for example – in line with virtually every other country in Europe[328] – would persist.

Lord Irvine, the co-parent of the HRA, has been very clear that there was no confusion about this when the Act was conceived:

> Treaty obligations only bind the State as an actor in public international law. They are not directly incorporated in, or enforceable under, our domestic legal system . . . If the UK does not comply with its obligations then the consequences which may follow are a matter of international relations, and inter-State diplomacy . . . Any implementation action is consequently a matter for political decision within the CoE and is not of a judicial character.[329]

There has been a raft of criticisms levelled at the ECtHR, which struggled to adapt to the rapid increase of cases after the membership of the CoE expanded once the Berlin Wall came down. These have begun to be addressed quite successfully, including a significant reduction in waiting lists.[330] Former Justice Secretary Ken Clarke used the coincidence of the UK's turn to chair the Committee of Ministers falling under his watch to implement reform, resulting in the 2012 Brighton Declaration.[331] This resulted in a new Protocol to the ECHR which has inserted into the Preamble the principle of 'subsidiarity'; the inelegant term for asserting that states have 'the primary responsibility' for securing ECHR rights, a principle which we saw was present from the outset. Also referenced is the Court-driven 'margin of appreciation' doctrine, which is the operational tool for implementing that principle.[332] This doctrine is fundamental to how the ECHR is applied. The ECtHR frequently takes the view that 'national authorities', which can include parliaments as well as domestic courts, governments and decision makers, are 'in a better position than the international judge to give an opinion'.[333] In practice this can apply to a considerable number of issues and cases.

But none of this has made the slightest difference to an agenda based on reasserting 'national sovereignty' against a 'foreign court' and allergic to any treaty with the word *European* in it. There is no reform or argument that can satisfy this position other than withdrawal.

This still leaves the question of the constitutional status of the 'British Bill of Rights and Responsibilities' it is proposed will take the weight of 'protecting human rights in the UK'[334] once the HRA is repealed. The policy document promises a 'break' in 'the formal link between British courts and the European Court of Human Rights'.[335] There *is* no such formal link beyond the reference in HRA (section 2) for courts to 'take into account' Strasbourg jurisprudence. This was the provision that, as we saw, the Conservatives tried to amend to bind the domestic courts to 'follow' ECtHR case law instead.[336] They failed, but this is nevertheless how section 2 has effectively been interpreted by some judges.[337] Much recent criticism by the senior judiciary has been aimed at this interpretation but reported as if they are seeking the repeal of the HRA itself.[338] Even the sternest critic, Lord Hoffman, made clear that 'I have no difficulty about the text of the European Convention or its adoption as part of the United Kingdom law in the Human Rights Act 1998.'[339] Given that the margin of appreciation doctrine means that the ECtHR frequently defers to the domestic courts anyway, the prospect of our courts in turn deferring to Strasbourg conjures up the theatre of the absurd.

Chivvied by the senior judiciary,[340] recently UK courts have more frequently developed their own independent interpretations of the HRA, which has sometimes involved disagreeing with Strasbourg case law, whilst still 'taking [it] into account'.[341] Of course this does not necessarily mean they will always adopt constructions that the government of the day would prefer.[342] But increasingly they have been treating the HRA more like the domestic bill of rights it was intended to be; incorporating ECHR rights but not its case law. Lord Irvine put it like this in his first public comment on the intent behind this interpretative clause:

> It is plain that Parliament intended that the interpretative exercise was a task for the domestic Courts, and that they are not bound by Strasbourg's views . . . Section 2 of the HRA means that it is our Judges' duty to decide the cases for themselves and explain clearly to the litigants, Parliament and the wider public why they are doing so. This, no more and certainly no less, is their Constitutional duty.[343]

Lord Justice Laws posed the question in his November 2013 Hamlyn Lecture: if the courts are in fact free under the HRA to develop their own case law, 'what remains'? His answer: 'A distinctive human rights jurisprudence of our own'.[344]

It seems quite extraordinary, then, to use parliamentary time to repeal one 'British Bill of Rights' in order to introduce another on the false charge that 'Labour's Human Rights Act undermines the role of UK courts in deciding on human rights issues in this country,' when it demonstrably doesn't. For the avoidance of doubt, section 2 could be rephrased or amended, but this hardly calls for the complete overturning of the HRA. The twin charge that the Act 'undermines the sovereignty of Parliament' is still more misleading given that the whole purpose of the 'declaration of incompatibility model', described in detail earlier, was to leave the last word with Parliament – which it does.[345]

This deception has been played out before, helping to build the case for repeal with what Gearty has called 'this fantasy of judicial supremacism in human rights law'.[346] Following a Declaration of Incompatibility in 2010, issued because sex offenders have no opportunity to appeal against their lifelong inclusion on the sex offenders' register,[347] the Prime Minister told the House of Commons: 'It's about time we started making sure decisions are made in this parliament rather than in the courts.'[348] Given that there was no obligation on the government to respond to the ruling at all, let alone change the law, it is disappointing, but not surprising, that the opposition did not accuse the Prime Minister of seriously misleading Parliament.

So when the authors of the policy document say the 'new British Bill of Rights and Responsibilities' will 'ensure that *Parliament* is the ultimate source of legal authority',[349] they choose their words advisedly. The standard provision typical of most bills of rights which requires courts to interpret measures compatibly with human rights where 'possible' (section 3) will be repealed because it 'undermines

Parliamentary sovereignty in practice';[350] the courts will be instructed which cases are not 'serious' enough to take; and they will be told how to interpret a host of terms in the new Bill from 'torture' to 'family life' to 'responsibilities'. Even the judicial application of the 'doctrine of proportionality', applied since the HRA to evaluate competing rights and interests, is given notice.[351] The former Attorney General, in a powerful speech in December 2014, lamented 'the failure of ambition represented' in the policy document 'and the narrowness of its moral and political vision'.[352] For me, personally, to conclude, as the document does, that the consequence of these proposals will be to make 'the Supreme Court . . . supreme in the interpretation of the law' makes me want to grab for my George Orwell.

The HRA has been frequently criticized by civil libertarians for not having been able to prevent the introduction of liberty-limiting legislation under this government and the previous, but that would be incompatible with a measure which ultimately *does* protect parliamentary sovereignty.[353] A Bill of Rights which grants even more authority to governments to hedge about with judicial interpretations, consistent with other attempts by this government to stymie judicial review,[354] is on most reckonings barely a bill of rights at all. The failed cases on privacy which drove the introduction of the HRA, and the ban on gay people serving in the military, would probably have served no better under these proposals.[355]

Margaret Thatcher was the first party leader in modern times to commit to consulting on a bill of rights. It never happened. Now her biographer, Charles Moore, has reviewed the Tory plan to repeal the HRA approvingly. But on the proposal to replace it with a British Bill of Rights he 'wonder[s] if that is such a brilliant idea . . . Would it not be better' he asks 'to use the Strasbourg Convention as an advisory manual and leave it at that?'[356]

Conclusion: human rights – endgame or lit flame?

When I concluded the first section of this book in July 2014 bombs were dropping on Gaza, killing many innocent human beings who could find nowhere safe to shelter. I could not record my understanding of the human rights ethic as it has evolved since the Second World War without reflecting on this atrocity taking place as I wrote. The fighting has ended for now but the fundamental issues of principle it raised remain.

On a different dimension, I am similarly aware that by 'homing in' on proposals to repeal the Human Rights Act and withdraw from the ECHR, I risk the possibility that these may have changed by the time this book is published, if not thereafter. But the significance of the UK Prime Minister sanctioning his party's intention to either neuter or quit the ECHR, should they be in power after the general election in May 2015, is not one that can be glossed over in a book such as this either.

I started this book with the reflection that if time-travelling medieval English barons were to land in modern Britain, they would be pretty chuffed with the scale of the June 2015 celebrations planned for the 800th anniversary of the Magna Carta. I think it is safe to say that if René Cassin, French resistance member and one of the prime drafters of the UDHR, were to appear back on Earth right now he would feel very short changed in comparison. When he was awarded the Nobel Peace Prize, two decades after the UDHR was adopted, Cassin affirmed that the ECHR, along with the European Social Charter,[357] 'aims at the effective application of the Universal Declaration'. His assessment, even then, was that 'it works'. But he presciently warned with regard to the future of human rights:

> There must be no question of permitting any diminution of the universality of the Declaration. There are fundamental liberties and rights common to all human beings, without possible discrimination. It is the most oppressed, the weakest of these individuals who would be threatened by any attempts to fragmentize the effective scope of the Declaration.[358]

When Cassin spoke these words he had reason to be cautiously confident that his warning would be heeded. European empires were unravelling and the momentum behind the civil-rights movement in the United States and elsewhere was unstoppable. But Apartheid was set to worsen before it was overthrown, and the Cold War was raging with devastating consequences in Vietnam and other countries scarred by the East–West split. By the time I drafted the final anthology piece on 'Issues in Communicating Human Rights' in 2001, the ice had melted and I was able to write with sunny optimism:

> After a century of failed utopias . . . this is a uniquely propitious time to be having such debates, not just in the UK but in the wider world. There is an openness to fresh ideas most of us have not seen in our lifetime . . . The tightly drawn ideological battles which drowned out most of the subtleties of the human rights project since its inception no longer dominate the world. Human rights arguments seem fresh and appealing in many quarters where once they sounded weak and stale.

It was possible to dare to hope that a human rights approach might square the circle between the quest for individual freedom on the one hand and the search for a more just society on the other, where humans would have obligations to each other as well as valid demands from the state. No longer did these alternative worldviews have to slug it out for victory. But a decade later human rights had rapidly descended from an idea whose time had come to an ideal routinely deprecated both domestically and internationally.

In the wake of 9/11, the rehabilitation of detention without trial and arguments in the West regarding the permissible parameters of torture, together with ethnically or religiously driven nationalisms reasserting themselves all over the globe, have made this a notably *less* propitious time even for the *idea* of human rights to flourish. This toxic combination has increased cynicism about the double standards of the West whilst stiffening the resolve of ideological opponents to human rights, from the Chinese state to extremist 'jihadist' groups whom researchers estimate killed 5,000 people, the majority of whom were Muslim civilians, in November 2014 alone.[359] Within affluent democracies, most governments tend to treat human rights norms as a burden rather than a defining characteristic of their states. Harvard professor Jacqueline Bhabha remarks in her landmark study of child migration:

> The claim to protective intervention or fiscally backed social engagement is ever-diminishing now that concerns over the Holocaust and the brutalities of the Cold War have given way to apprehension about terrorists and welfare scroungers.[360]

For Professor Stephen Hopgood this is no surprise. He maintains that 'international human rights are not in reality embedded to anything like the degree required for us to speak of them as global norms' and that 'the only effective international law is based on the reciprocal interests of states.'[361] This international relations scholar will not be the last to predict that the hubris and hypocrisies which litter international mechanisms and power structures leave 'human rights' in terminal 'decline'.[362] But similar to the death of Mark Twain, the 'endtimes of human rights'[363] have been greatly exaggerated. In reality, people all over the globe are using the language of human rights, and sometimes its legal structures, to stake a claim for a better world. A recent survey carried out by YouGov for the British Council of the eighty greatest landmarks in the past eighty years canvassing 10,000 adults from different parts of the world, placed the UDHR fourth, beaten only by the technological advances of the Internet, penicillin and personal home computers.[364] Such responses give a dollop of credence to the aspirations of the Chair of the Nobel Peace Committee who, when awarding Cassin the prize in 1968, expressed her 'belief' that the UDHR 'marked the beginning of a new era' even 'a *revolutionizing* evolution'. She said:

> To the millions of people who live today in the darkness of oppression, this document was unknown. But *a small light was lit* and the moral commandments contained in the Declaration, like those written on the tablets of Moses, will in the years to come lay a forceful role in reforming the conscience of man and his understanding of what is right and wrong.[365]

There is stronger evidence than a British Council survey that despite many reasons for the ethic of human rights to wither away, it stubbornly persists. Numerous examples are discussed in the first section of this book. Here is another. Kamal Elgizouli, Secretary General of the Sudanese Writers' Union, counters charges that human rights are a stooge of Western imperialism by discrediting such allegations as a cloak for state impunity. He makes the case for his president, who was issued with an arrest warrant in 2005 regarding alleged war crimes in Darfur, to be finally brought to trial at the International Criminal Court. Asserting the proposition that was supposedly settled at the end of the Second World War, he writes: 'Sovereignty has ceased to become the absolute right of the state to decide the affairs of its people as in the past.'[366]

It is this fundamental principle, increasingly championed by people all over the world, that the British Prime Minister, and those who support him, threaten in daring the Council of Europe to either immobilize the ECHR enforcement mechanisms or watch them unravel like a knitting pattern. The argument that liberty-loving Britain has an exceptional claim to immunity from human rights accountability is to revive suspicions that post-war human rights standards really *are* just a cover for the West to judge the rest. It is not Cassandra-like to predict that if the UK walks away from the ECtHR the credibility of the entire post-war human rights edifice will be severely shaken, possibly terminally so. It has not had 800 years to bed down. It is less than seventy years old.

In the land of the Magna Carta this anti-universal human rights rhetoric brooks relatively few opponents and a potentially growing number of supporters. Mostly it meets indifference. Blunted by the paradox of legalism, for too many people human rights are understood as the last court case they heard of, usually through the megaphone of the tabloid press. The ethic of human rights is drowned out in the cacophony that ensues. Yet every day this ethic is expressed in cases that are constantly lampooned, as Lady Hale eloquently demonstrated:

> It is a purpose of all human rights instruments to secure the essential rights of members of minority groups, even when they are unpopular with the majority. Democracy values everyone equally even if the majority does not.[367]

There are broader currents which are pulling the UK away from the human rights tide. In a country disfigured by remorseless 'austerity' and distorting disparities in wealth and power, combined with a sense of powerlessness in the face of global forces beyond our control, the tendency to turn away from the foreigner, the immigrant, 'the other' is reasserting itself. Swollen by the rise of the most inward looking of the political parties, UKIP, this resurgence of a primary allegiance to 'the nation' challenges the avowal of our common humanity which is the beating heart of human rights.

Professor Costas Douzinas reminds us that 'humanity' is a 'modern' idea.[368] It should not be confused with a disdain for national identity. Nor is it anti-statist. Human rights standards and norms *rely* on nation states to implement them. Some of the worst human rights atrocities occur in failed states. Around the world, from Mexico to Nigeria, campaigners demand *more* state protection in the name of human rights. Yet when the chips are down, if national preoccupations overwhelm our sense of a common humanity, then human rights count for nothing unless they helps us find the language to speak out when atrocities occur to other 'members of the human family' that the UDHR affirmed. They serve little purpose unless we are spurred to take action when our fellow human beings beseech us for assistance which we are capable of delivering.

The human rights activist and writer Veena Vasista comments that 'the roots of many injustices lie in the act of constraining other people's humanity, rendering it invisible, or denying it completely.'[369] This aptly describes how many of us viewed the Home Office's recent support for the significant scaling down of the EU search-and-rescue operations in the Mediterranean on the grounds that it provided a 'pull factor' for immigrants. More than 3,000 people have died this year trying to cross these shores, many children amongst them. But the existing Italian-led operations which are to be extinguished have so far reportedly saved the lives of approximately 150,000 people, desperate to find sanctuary from the terror and conflicts most have fled from.[370] This EU decision was cited by Jordanian officials when favourably comparing their own country's record in providing sanctuary to one million Syrians in a conflict which the UN estimates has so far taken more than 200,000 lives and created more than three million registered refugees.[371] Although the UK is the second biggest contributor of financial aid to the war-torn country, the latest figures show that only one hundred Syrians have been given shelter in the UK under the 'vulnerable person relocation scheme'.[372]

Whilst it cannot halt this growing fortress around Europe, the ECtHR has provided financial compensation for a group of twenty-four Somali and Eritrean nationals who were intercepted in their vessels by the Italian military and returned to Libya in May 2009. Fourteen of the applicants were subsequently granted refugee status by the UN. Although they never reached the European mainland, the Court concluded this had been a case of 'the collective expulsion of aliens'[373] from Europe – a protection that had been inserted into the ECHR as a direct consequence of the mass deportation of Jews by the Nazis and their allies.[374] The repeated mantra from ECHR critics that the problem is that the text is no longer interpreted as originally intended – whilst simultaneously insisting that the circumstances of the era when it was drafted do not apply today – was exposed as the flimsy excuse that it is.

Cassin insisted that: 'Our declaration represents the most vigorous, the most essential protest of humanity against the atrocities and the oppression which millions of human beings suffered through the centuries.'[375] The tools the UDHR drafters declared we need to wage this 'protest of humanity' are resources virtually every one of us has in our possession. They are 'reason and conscience', and through these we can know how to 'act towards one another in a spirit of brotherhood'.[376]

This appeal to 'conscience', and not just 'reason', relates to what the late American philosopher Richard Rorty called 'doing human rights'.[377] He coined the term 'sentimental education', which he described as 'increasing our ability to see the similarities between ourselves and people very unlike us as outweighing the differences'.[378] In other words, human rights are *made, and remade, not discovered*. They are dependent on the human capacity to empathise; on the ability to identify with others. The zeitgeist of our time pulls in a different direction, illuminating why we need 'reason' as well as 'conscience'. The human rights standards and structures so painstakingly crafted in the wake of the man-made[379] catastrophes that preceded them were never designed for utopia. They were built in the certain knowledge that consciences *will* fail and hence legal safeguards will always be necessary; that we human beings need constant concrete reminders of our common humanity and protections against those who will abuse their powers.

I am completing this book on 10 December 2014, sixty-six years to the day since the UDHR was adopted in Paris. This year 'human rights day' has coincided with official acknowledgement that the American CIA systematically tortured detainees in secret prisons around the globe, as well as at Guantanamo Bay, during its self-styled 'war on terror'.[380] According to the Senate Select Committee on Intelligence, this torture programme produced no original or reliable intelligence at all. There are those who might argue that this exposure of double standards, not to mention double dealings, in 'the land of liberty' heralds the certain death of human rights. For me it is quite the contrary. This confirmation amplifies the clear sightedness of human rights defenders around the globe, including the Council of Europe, who in the thirteen years since 9/11 have doggedly used the values and standards bequeathed by the UDHR to shine a spotlight on the dark places where such abuses take place. Without their persistence, it is far from certain that there would have been the impetus to unearth this shame at the heart of American democracy. It is the ethic of human rights which helps keep democracies 'clean'.

This gives me renewed hope that whilst Acts may be repealed and treaties dis-membered, if new generations grasp the ethical purpose of human rights protec-tions these edifices will be built anew. Europe and the West have long since ceased to be at the centre of the new perspectives on human rights. Memories of atrocities and the wisdom, as well as anguish, they can bring are not confined to any part of the globe. The ethic of human rights shows no sign of extinguishing. It will con-tinue to offer hope and inspiration to millions of people around the world. The human rights revolution, which the Nobel Peace Prize Chair dreamed of in 1968, lives on.

Notes

1 'Strasbourg Folly', *Daily Express*, 27 October 1953.
2 'Human Rights Madness to End', *Daily Express*, 3 October 2014.
3 Conservative Party, 'Protecting Human Rights in the UK: The Conservatives' Proposals for Changing Britain's Human Rights Laws', 3 October 2014.
4 Excerpts from the Preamble to the 'European Convention for the Protection of Human Rights and Fundamental Freedoms', Rome, 4 November 1950 (my emphasis).
5 F. Klug, 'The Disputed Parentage of the European Convention on Human Rights: Ori-gins and Controversies', unpublished lecture for MSc in human rights, LSE Centre for the Study of Human Rights, 2013.
6 Robert Spano, 'Universality or Diversity of Human Rights?' *Human Rights Law Review* 14, no. 3 (2014): 487–502.
7 Quoted in Johannes Morsink, *The Universal Declaration of Human Rights: Origin, Drafting and Intent* (Philadelphia, PA: University of Pennsylvania Press, 1999), 33.
8 The distinction between 'Enlightenment values' and those which drove the drafting of the UDHR, and the factors which shaped them, are analysed in detail in Section I of this book.
9 Charles Malik, *The Challenge of Human Rights and the Universal Declaration*, ed. Habib C. Malik (Oxford: Centre for Lebanese Studies, 2000), 208.

10 Quoted in Geoff Marston, 'The United Kingdom's Part in the Preparation of the ECHR 1950', *International and Comparative Law Quarterly* 42, no. 4 (1993): 796–826, 820.

11 Sir David Maxwell Fyfe, later known as Lord Kilmuir, subsequently became Home Secretary and Lord Chancellor in Winston Churchill's post-war government.

12 A. W. Brian Simpson, *Human Rights and the End of Empire: Britain and the Genesis of the European Convention* (Oxford: Oxford University Press, 2001), 650.

13 *Political Adventure: The Memoirs of the Earl of Kilmuir* (London: Weidenfeld & Nicholson, 1964), 174.

14 Unpublished letter to Sylvia Maxwell-Fyfe, 13 January 1946, reproduced with kind permission of Tom Blackmore, grandson of Sir David Maxwell Fyfe.

15 Proceedings of the Trial of the Major War Criminals Before the International Military Tribunal, Vol. 22, 29 August 1946.

16 See the Preamble of the UDHR.

17 Quoted in Simpson, *Human Rights and the End of Empire,* 658.

18 See, for example, Geoffrey Samuel, *A Short Introduction to the Common Law* (Cheltenham: Edward Elgar, 2013).

19 A. V. Dicey, *Introduction to the Study of the Law of the Constitution* (London: Macmillan, 1885), 197.

20 Quoted in Simpson, *Human Rights and the End of Empire,* 728.

21 Letter from W. A. Jowitt to Hugh Dalton, 3 August 1950.

22 Daniel Hannan, *How We Invented Freedom and Why It Matters* (London: Head Zeus, 2013), 359.

23 Minutes of 11 September 1950, FO 372/88755/US17311/88.

24 'Strasbourg Folly', *Daily Express,* 27 October 1953.

25 *Greece v. United-Kingdom (I)*, 176/56 07.05.1956; *Greece v. United-Kingdom (II)*, 299/57 17.07.1957.

26 Letter, 1964. FO 371/178983/WUC1734/17.

27 Then Article 62(1); now Article 56(1).

28 Quoted in Simpson, *Human Rights and the End of Empire,* 738. See also C. Heyns, 'African Human Rights Law and the European Convention', *South African Journal of Human Rights* 2 (1995): 252, at 254 for an analysis of the contradiction between ECHR negotiations and what was happening on the ground in Africa.

29 Quoted in Kirsten Sellers, *The Rise and Rise of Human Rights* (Stroud, UK: Sutton, 2002), 86.

30 Unpublished letter, 20 August 1949. See also note 14.

31 Protocol 1, which also includes the 'right to free elections'. The protection of property has been interpreted to apply to welfare benefits in specific circumstances.

32 Simpson, *Human Rights and the End of Empire,* 676.

33 The Committee of Ministers has the statutory role under the European Convention on Human Rights to supervise the implementation of judgments of the European Court of Human Rights.

34 Then Article 23; now Article 34, but no longer optional.

35 Protocol 11.

36 This and other aspects of the developing ECHR architecture are described in my anthology lecture on the origins of the ECHR, 'The Disputed Parentage of the European Convention on Human Rights' (see note 5).

37 Simpson, *Human Rights and the End of Empire,* 649.

38 FO 371/88755 /US 17311/81/.

39 FO 371/184367/WUC1745/16.

40 Simpson, *Human Rights and the End of Empire,* 670.

41 Winston S. Churchill, *His Complete Speeches, 1897–1963* (8 vols.), ed. R. R. James (London: Chelsea House Publishers, 1974), 7635–9.

42 Quoted in Simpson, *Human Rights and the End of Empire,* 670.

43 Ibid., 228.

44 By then Denmark, Germany, Greece, Iceland, Ireland, Luxembourg, Norway, the Saar and Sweden had also ratified. France didn't ratify until 1974.

45 Lord Hailsham, *The Dilemma of Democracy: Diagnosis and Prescription* (London: Collins, 1978), 174. He first coined the phrase 'elective dictatorship' in his Richard Dimbleby lecture in 1976.

46 Samuel Moyn, *The Last Utiopia: Human Rights in History* (Cambridge, MA: Belknap, 2010), 122.

47 Ibid., 120.

48 Ibid., 214.

49 Ibid., 122.

50 In *Young, James and Webster v UK* (1981) 4 EHRR 38, dismissal for failure to join a trade union – otherwise known as 'the closed shop' – which was permitted under Labour's 1974 Trade Union and Labour Relations Act, was held to violate the ECHR when refusal was based on a deeply held conviction. But subsequent ECtHR jurisprudence has affirmed that the right to take industrial action can be protected by Article 11, which declares that 'everyone has the right to form and join trade unions.' See, for example, *RMT v UK* (2014) ECHR 336. See also *R v Central Arbitration Committee* [2014] EWHC 65 (Admin).

51 For a more detailed examination of party political support for incorporation of the ECHR see F. Klug, 'Party Pieces', in *Common Sense: Reflections on the Human Rights Act* (London: Liberty, 2010), and Jesse Norman and Peter Oborne, *Churchill's Legacy: The Conservative Case for the Human Rights Act* (London: Liberty, 2009).

52 For example, in Protocol 1: 'No one shall be deprived of his possessions *except in the public interest* and subject to the conditions provided by law and by the general principles of international law.' These 'provisions shall not, however, in any way impair the right of a State to enforce such laws as it deems necessary to control the use of property in accordance with the general interest or *to secure the payment of taxes or other contribution or penalties*' (my emphasis).

53 *East African Asians v UK* (1981) 3 EHRR 76 at para 207. See Anthony Lester, 'Thirty Years On: The East African Case Revisited', *Public Law* [2002] PL Spring Pages, 52–72.

54 The government, by way of concession, created a special voucher scheme to allow entry to an annual quota of British Asians from east Africa as refugees rather than as British subjects exercising their right of residence.

55 For a full account of this saga see Shami Chakrabarti, *On Liberty* (London: Penguin, 2014), chapter 3. Were it not for Liberty's successful campaigning, the Blair or Brown governments may well have succeeded.

56 The best known amongst them were the Guilford 4, Birmingham 6 and Maguire 7. After a long campaign they were eventually released when their convictions were declared 'unsafe and unsatisfactory', having each served between fifteen and sixteen years in prison.

57 Quoted in David Kinley, *The European Convention on Human Rights: Compliance without Incorporation* (Aldershot, UK: Dartmouth, 1993), 55.

58 For example *A and Others v UK* (2009) 49 EHRR 29, where the Grand Chamber confirmed the House of Lords judgment in *A v Secretary of State for the Home Department* [2004] UKHL 56 (the Belmarsh case) that the indefinite detention of foreign terror suspects who could not be deported was a breach of Article 14 together with Article 5.1 on the grounds that the UK derogation was disproportionate in that it discriminated unjustifiably between nationals and non-nationals. See also *Gillan and Quinton v UK* (2010) 50 EHRR 45 where the ECtHR ruled that the UK's stop-and-search powers, without reasonable suspicion under the Terrorism Act 2000, were a violation of Article 8, the right to privacy.

59 Article 5, the right to liberty and security. The seven-day detention provision and subsequent derogation (under Article 15) were challenged respectively in *Brogan and Others v UK* (1989) 11 EHRR 117 and *Brannigan and McBride v UK* (1994) 17 EHRR 539, but the ECtHR upheld the UK derogation, in contrast to its 2009 judgment (*A and Others v UK* (2009)).

60 'Ireland to Clash with the UK at Human Rights Court over Hooded Men Judgment', *The Guardian*, 2 December 2014. The original case was *Ireland v UK* [1978] ECHR 1.

61 Lord Scarman, 'English Law: The New Dimension', in *Hamlyn Lectures*, 26th series (London: Stevens Publication, 1974).

62 *Spycatcher: The Candid Autobiography of a Senior Intelligence Officer* (Australia: Heinemann, 1987), written by Peter Wright, former MI5 officer, was initially banned in England as was the reporting of it, which the ECtHR declared a breach of Article 10 in 1991. The poll-tax riots took place in 1990 and were accredited with being the main reason for the tax's abolition.

63 See Peter Thornton, *Decade of Decline: Civil Liberties in the Thatcher Years* (London: Liberty, 1989), for a summary of the measures which impacted on civil liberties in the 1980s.

64 Letter from Margaret Thatcher to Baroness Ewart-Biggs, 26 May 1989.

65 See Janet Clark, *The National Council for Civil Liberties and the Policing of Interwar Politics: At Liberty to Protest* (Manchester: Manchester University Press, 2012).

66 Letter, *The Guardian*, Sunday, 23 February 2014.

67 The Criminal Justice Act 1988 removed a number of offences triable by jury, affecting an estimated 10,000 defendants a year. In October 1988 the Home Secretary announced the abolition of the 'right to silence' (without adverse inferences being drawn by the prosecution) in criminal trials in Northern Ireland. This was subsequently extended to England and Wales by the 1994 Criminal Justice and Public Order Act.

68 *A-G v Guardian Newspapers* [1987] 1 WLR 1248 at 1287.

69 The First Amendment to the American Constitution states: 'Congress shall make no law respecting an establishment of religion, or prohibiting the free exercise thereof; or abridging the freedom of speech, or of the press.'

70 Moyn, *The Last Utiopia*, 214.

71 Ibid., 121.

72 Founded in 1961 and 1978, respectively.

73 Moyn, *The Last Utiopia*, 214.

74 H. Kennedy, 'Foreword', in F. Klug, *Values for a Godless Age: The Story of the United Kingdom's New Bill of Rights* (London: Penguin, 2000), xi. The description 'human rights lawyer' was itself new at this time.

75 As in the letter from Margaret Thatcher to Baroness Ewart-Biggs, 26 May 1989.

76 Anthony Lester et al., *A British Bill of Rights* (London: IPPR, 1991).

77 Scottish Council for Civil Liberties, *A Charter of Rights for Scotland* (1991); Committee for the Administration of Justice, *Making Rights Count* (1990).

78 For an analysis of this claim that judges were effectively incorporating the ECHR into their judgments without an Act of Parliament, see F. Klug and K. Starmer, 'Incorporation through the Back Door?' *Public Law* (Summer 1997), 223–33. See also Murray Hunt, *Using Human Rights Law in English Courts* (Oxford: Hart Publishing, 1997).

79 The research used a Lexis search to evaluate all reported cases cited in the higher courts from 1972 to 1995. See F. Klug, K. Starmer and S. Weir, *The Three Pillars of Liberty: Political Rights and Freedoms in the UK* (London: Routledge, 1996), 136.

80 There were thirty-five UK cases which gave rise to at least one violation at the ECtHR between 1959 and 1995. This pole league table position does not take account of population variation between states and was before the membership of a large contingent of Eastern European countries when the CoE was half the current size.

81 Conor Gearty, 'On Fantasy Island: British Politics, English Judges and the European Convention on Human Right', 36th Corbishley Lecture, London School of Economics, 6 November 2014.

82 *Malone v Commissioner for the Metropolitan Police (No. 2)* [1979] 2 All ER 620, 638.

83 Ibid., 648 and 638, respectively (my emphasis).

84 *Malone v UK* (1984) 7 EHRR 14.

85 *Kaye v Robertson and Another* [1991] FSR 62 at 70.

86 Under the doctrine of so-called Wednesbury reasonableness. *R v Ministry of Defence ex p. Smith* [1996] 1 All ER 257 at 266.

87 Ibid., 267.

88 *Smith and Grady v UK* (1999) 29 EHRR 493 at 138.

89 Ibid.; *Lustig-Prean & Beckett v UK* (2000) 29 ECHR 548.

90 Jonathan Cooper, 'Reflections on the Human Rights Act 1998', in *Law Reform 2015: A Manifesto for Change,* ed. Stephen Hockman, 111, 114 (London: Profile Books, 2014).

91 Jonathan Cooper, 'The Human Rights Act and Preserving the Union', *Huffington Post,* 22 September 2014. www.huffingtonpost.co.uk/jonathan-cooper/human-rights-act.

92 See, for example, Keith Ewing and Conor Gearty, 'Rocky Foundations for Labour's New Rights', *European Human Rights Law Review* 2 (1997): 146–51. A new generation of judges schooled on human rights principles have subsequently dispelled much of this argument, even for some of its erstwhile proponents.

93 Keith Ewing, 'Judicial Review and the Role of Human Rights and Labour Law', in *Human Rights and Labour Law: Essays for Paul O'Higgins,* K.D. Ewing, C.A. Gearty and B.A. Hepple, (eds) (London: Mansell, 1994), 156.

94 In *Buckley v Valeo* 424 U.S.1 (1976) the Supreme Court ruled that campaign finance laws breached the absolute prohibition on free-speech limitations in the First Amendment of the US Constitution. This was further affirmed in *Citizens United v Federal Election Commission* 558 U.S. 310 (2010) and *McCutcheon v Federal Election Commission* 572 U.S. (2014).

95 *RJR Macdonald Inc. v Canada* [1995] 3 SCR 199.

96 'A Bill of Rights for New Zealand', White Paper, 1985. www.justice.govt.nz/new-zealand-bill-of-rights.

97 F. Klug, *A People's Charter, Liberty's Bill of Rights: A Consultation Document* (London: Liberty, 1991).

98 Andrew Puddephatt, 'Foreword', in F. Klug et al., *A People's Charter, Liberty's Bill of Rights.*

99 See Francesca Klug and John Wadham, 'The "Democratic" Entrenchment of a Bill of Rights: Liberty's Proposals', *Public Law* (Winter 1993). For a review of the purposes and procedures of the JCHR see 'The Klug Report' in *The Committee's Future Working Practices,* Joint Committee on Human Rights, 23rd Report of Session 2005–2006, HL Paper 239, HC 1575.

100 John Smith, 'A New Way Forward' speech, Bournemouth, 7 February 1993.

101 *A Citizen's Democracy,* Charter 88, March 1993.

102 *A New Agenda for Democracy: Labour's Proposals for Constitutional Reform,* NEC, 1993.

103 Unpublished briefing paper for Shadow Home Secretary Tony Blair (1993) retained at the LSE Centre for the Study of Human Rights, along with other unpublished papers cited further on.

104 This, and other steps on the road to the introduction of the HRA, are described in more detail in Klug, *Values for a Godless Age,* 158–63.

105 Labour Party, *Bringing Rights Home: Labour's Plan to Incorporate the European Convention on Human Rights into UK Law* (1996).

106 Jack Straw, speech, Community Links, November 1995.

107 F. Klug, 'Briefing on Incorporation of the European Convention on Human Rights into UK Law: The "British Model"', unpublished paper, Human Rights Incorporation Project (HRIP), King's College Law School, London 1997, retained at the LSE Centre for the Study of Human Rights along with other unpublished HRIP papers.

108 F. Klug, A 'Bill of Rights for the United Kingdom: A Comparative Summary', *European Human Rights Law Review* 5 (1997): 501–7.

109 Jack Straw, *Last Man Standing: Memoirs of a Political Survivor* (London: Macmillan, 2012), 273.

110 F. Klug and R. Singh, 'The British Model of Incorporation: The Power of Declaration', unpublished paper, Human Rights Incorporation Project, King's College Law School, London, 1997.

111 Ibid., and see also note 107.

112 The Belfast (Good Friday) Agreement of 1998 (GFA),was not only a peace agreement between the Unionists and Republicans of Northern Ireland but also a bilateral treaty

between the UK and the Republic of Ireland. Its provisions were enacted by the UK Parliament in the Northern Ireland Act 1998.

113 F. Klug, 'The Human Rights Act: Origins and Intentions', in *Confronting the Human Rights Act: Contemporary Themes and Perspectives*, Nicolas Kang-Riou, Jo Milner and Suryia Nayak (eds) (London: Routledge, 2012).

114 'Rights Brought Home: The Human Rights Bill', White Paper, Cmnd 3782, paras 1.18 and 19.

115 Klug, 'The Human Rights Act'.

116 The HRA excludes Articles 1 and 13 of the substantive rights in the ECHR and includes two additional provisions, sections 12 and 13, drafted as amendments when the Human Rights Bill was being debated in Parliament, concerning freedom of expression and freedom of religion, respectively. These effectively reinforce the relevant articles in the ECHR (10 and 9, respectively). For a legal exposition of the scheme of the HRA see John Wadham, Helen Mountfield, Anna Edmundson and Caoilfhionn Gallagher (eds), *Blackstone's Guide to the Human Rights Act*, 4th ed. (Oxford: Oxford University Press, 2007). See also Keir Starmer, *European Human Rights Law: The HRA 1998 and the ECHR* (London: Legal Action Group, 1999).

117 Under the UK's 'dualist constitution', international treaties such as the ECHR are entered into by the executive, and unless a specific Act is passed to incorporate them into domestic law, such as the HRA, it is the government which is *directly* bound by them, not the courts.

118 Boateng co-drafted Labour's discussion paper on the HRA with Straw in December 2006. See note 105.

119 Jack Straw, 'The Human Rights Act: Ten Years On', *European Human Rights Law Review Special Issue*, 6, ed. F. Klug and J. Gordon (2010): 578.

120 Ibid.

121 See notes 107 and 110. The basic scheme of the HRA is set out in very simple terms in Klug, 'The Human Rights Act'.

122 Minus Articles 1 and 13. See note 116.

123 As reflected in the subtitle I chose for my book on the Act, *Values for a Godless Age: The Story of the United Kingdom New Bill of Rights*, see note 74.

124 This is explained in more detail in Klug, 'The Human Rights Act'.

125 *Hansard*, HL Vol 583 (18 November 1997) col. 514–15.

126 The long title of the HRA is 'An Act to give further effect to rights and freedoms guaranteed under the European Convention on Human Rights'.

127 *Hansard,* HC 313 (3 June 1998) 398.

128 Speech, IPPR, 13 January 2000.

129 See Danny Nicol, 'The Human Rights Act and the Politicians', *Legal Studies* 24, no. 3 (2004): 451–79; Janet Hiebert, 'Parliamentary Bills of Rights: An Alternative Model?' *Modern Law Review* 69, no. 7 (2006): 13–14; Stephen Gardbaum, 'How Successful and Distinctive Is the Human Rights Act? An Expatriate Comparatist's Assessment', *Modern Law Review* 74, no. 2 (2011): 195–215. See also F. Klug, 'The Human Rights Act: A Third Way or Third Wave Bill of Right?' *European Human Rights Law Review* 4 (2001): 361–72.

130 *Hansard*, HoL, vol 582 (3 November 1997) col. 1234.

131 Straw, 'The Human Rights Act', *European Human Rights Law Review Special Issue*, 576.

132 See note 116.

133 F. Klug, 'Presenting the Human Rights Act', unpublished briefing paper to the Home Office, May 2000.

134 Jack Straw, 'Building a Human Rights Culture', address to Civil Service College Seminar, 9 December 1999.

135 F. Klug, 'The Human Rights Act: Basic Principles and Values', *Journal of Local Government Law* 2 (2001): 41–7. See also Aileen Kavanagh, 'Reasoning about Proportionality under the Human Rights Act 1998: Outcomes, Substance and Process', *Law Quarterly Review* 130 (2014): 235.

136 Lord Browne-Wilkinson, 'The Impact on Judicial Reasoning', in *The Impact of the Human Rights Bill on English Law*, B. Markesinis (ed) (Oxford: Clarendon, 1998), 21–3.

137 *Wilson v First Country Trust Ltd (no 2)* [2003] UKHL 40, para 181.

138 As discussed extensively in Section I, this ethical framework is built not just on the principles of liberty, justice and fairness, long perceived as the hallmarks of the common law, but also the values of dignity, equality and community analysed extensively in Section I.

139 *Brown v Stott (Procurator Fiscal, Dunfermline) and another* [2001] 2 All ER 97, 118.

140 Evidence to the JCHR, 19 March 2001, JCHR HL 66-ii HC 332-ii.

141 JCHR, *The Case for a Human Rights Commission*, 6th report of session 2002–2003, 11–12.

142 The Northern Ireland Policing Board appointed barristers Keir Starmer and Jane Gordon as human rights advisors in 2003.

143 Audit Commission, *Human Rights: Improving Public Service Delivery* (London, 2003).

144 See, for example, British Institute of Human Rights, *The Difference it Makes: Putting Human Rights at the Heart of Health and Social Care* (London, 2013). See also Jenny Watson and Mitchell Woolf, *Human Rights Act Toolkit* (London: Legal Action Group, 2008), and Frances Butler, *Human Rights: Who Needs Them? Using Human Rights in the Voluntary Sector* (London: IPPR, 2004).

145 'New ACPO Chief Wants Human Rights to Be Put at Core of Policing', *The Guardian*, 21 June 2009. Quoted in Jane Gordon, 'A Developing Human Rights Culture in the UK? Case Studies of Policing', 609–20, *European Human Rights Law Review Special Issue*, ed. F. Klug and J. Gordon (2010).

146 *Belfast City Council v Miss Behavin' Ltd (Northern Ireland)* [2007] UKHL 19; *Begum, R (on the application of) v Governors of Denbigh High School* [2006] UKHL 15.

147 Northern Ireland Act 1988, Scotland Act 1988, Government of Wales Act 1988, respectively.

148 The Commission for Racial Equality, the Disability Rights Commission and the Equal Opportunities Commission. The new areas of responsibility were age, religion and belief and sexual orientation as well as human rights. See Sarah Spencer, 'Equality and Human Rights Commission: A Decade in the Making', *Political Quarterly* 79, no. 1 (2008): 6–16. Spencer's proposals at the IPPR for merging the former commissions were very influential in this development.

149 'Human Rights Inquiry: Report of the Equality and Human Rights Commission' (2009). The other Inquiry members were EHRC Commissioners Bert Massey and Neil Wooding.

150 David Cameron, Leader of the Opposition, Conservative Party conference speech, 1 October 2008.

151 'Human Rights Inquiry: Report of the Equality and Human Rights Commission' (2009), Executive Summary, 20. For a more recent appraisal, see 'EHRC Guidance on 'Human Rights in Action: Case Studies from Regulators, Inspectorates and Ombudsmen' (2014).

152 'Human Rights Inquiry: Report of the Equality and Human Rights Commission' (2009), 15.

153 Eleanor Roosevelt at the presentation of 'In Your Hands: A Guide for Community Action for the Tenth Anniversary of the Universal Declaration of Human Rights', 27 March 1958, United Nations, New York.

154 Baroness Jane Campbell, 'Bringing Rights "into" the Home', speech to the Legal Action Group Community Care Conference, 16 October 2009.

155 Cameron, Conservative Party conference speech, 1 October 2008.

156 David Cameron, speech given at Oxford, 15 August 2011.

157 Ibid.

158 Dominic Raab, *The Assault on Liberty: What Went Wrong with Rights* (London: Fourth Estate, 2009), 223.

159 Conor Gearty, *Principles of Human Rights Adjudication* (Oxford: Oxford University Press, 2004), 25.

160 Lord Bingham, 'The Human Rights Act: A View from the Bench', *European Human Rights Law Review Special Issue*, ed. F. Klug and J. Gordon (2010): 568–75. Lord Bingham sadly passed away before his piece was published and the special issue is dedicated to him.

161 Lord Neuberger, 'The Role of Judges in Human Rights Jurisprudence: A Comparison of the Australian and UK Experience', speech given at a Conference at the Supreme Court of Victoria, Melbourne, 8 August 2014.

162 Bingham, 'The Human Rights Act', *European Human Rights Law Review Special Issue*, 574.

163 Rabinder Singh QC, 'The Human Rights Act and the Courts: A Practitioner's Perspective', *European Human Rights Law Review Special Issue*, ed. F. Klug and J. Gordon (2010): 589.

164 The term was first used by George W. Bush on 20 September 2001.

165 Chakrabarti, *On Liberty,* in particular chapters 3 and 5.

166 Ibid., 3. See also F. Klug, 'New Labour and the Distribution of Power', in *Reassessing New Labour,* ed. Patrick Diamond and Michael Kenny (Oxford: Wiley-Blackwell with Political Quarterly, 2011).

167 *A v Secretary of State for the Home Department* [2004] UKHL 56, see also note 58.

168 *Secretary of State for the Home Department v JJ* [2007] UK HL 45; *Secretary of State for the Home Department v AP* [2010] UKSC 24.

169 Tony Blair, statement on anti-terror measures, 5 August 2005. www.theguardian.com/politics/2005.

170 *Chahal v The United Kingdom* (1996) 23 EHRR 413.

171 Blair, statement on anti-terror measures, 5 August 2005.

172 Written Ministerial statement, 15 December 2005.

173 Joint Committee on Human Rights, *The Human Rights Act: The DCA and Home Office Reviews* (HC 2005–06, 1694).

174 David Cameron, 'We Need a Minister for Terror', *Sunday Times,* 12 November 2006.

175 David Cameron, 'Balancing Freedom and Security – A Modern British Bill of Rights', speech to the Centre for Policy Studies, London, 26 June 2006.

176 David Cameron, speech to the Foreign Policy Centre, August 2005.

177 Gordon Brown, 'Towards a New Politics', speech to the Institute of Public Policy Research, 2 February 2010.

178 'The Governance of Britain', Green Paper, CM 7170, July 2007.

179 The other members were Keir Starmer QC, before he became the DPP, and Lord Lester, who Gordon Brown had appointed as an unpaid advisor on constitutional affairs. In March 2009 the Ministry of Justice produced a Green Paper, 'Rights and Responsibilities: Developing Our Constitutional Framework', CM 7577, spearheaded by Michael Wills MP.

180 Interview with Jack Straw, Lord Chancellor, *Daily Mail,* 8 December 2008.

181 Commission on a Bill of Rights, *A UK Bill of Rights? The Choice before Us, Volume 1* (2012) 459–68. The following section draws liberally from Francesca Klug and Amy Williams, 'The Choice Before Us? The Report of the Commission on a Bill of Rights', *Public Law* (July 2013).

182 Main terms of reference: 'The Commission will investigate the creation of a UK Bill of Rights that incorporates and builds on all our obligations under the European Convention on Human Rights, ensures that these rights continue to be enshrined in UK law, and protects and extends our liberties. It will examine the operation and implementation of these obligations, and consider ways to promote a better understanding of the true scope of these obligations and liberties.'

183 Commission members: Anthony Speaight QC, Lord Faulks QC (replacing Dr Michael Pinto Duschinsky), Jonathan Fisher QC and Martin Howe QC appointed by the Prime Minister; Professor Sir David Edward QC, Baroness Kennedy QC, Lord Lester QC; Professor Philippe Sands QC, appointed by the Deputy Prime Minister.

184 See, for example, Scottish Human Rights Commission, Scotland's National Action Plan for Human Rights (2013), www.scottishhumanrights.com/actionplan/snap.

185 See Qudsi Rasheed, *Devolution and Human Rights* (London: Justice, 2010).

186 Reported in the *Scottish Sunday Herald*, 12 November 2014.

187 Commission on a Bill of Rights, *A UK Bill of Rights?*, para 78.

188 Ibid., 188, 189. See also Francesca Klug and Amy Williams, 'The UK's 1998 Human Rights Act: Clarity and Confusion', in *Ireland and the European Convention on Human Rights: 60 Years and Beyond*, ed. Suzanne Egan et al. (London: Bloomsbury, 2014).

189 Commission on a Bill of Rights, *A UK Bill of Rights?*, para 32.

190 Conservative Party, 'Protecting Human Rights in the UK', 8.

191 For a discussion of this link see Adam Wagner, 'The Monstering of Human Rights', 7, paper presented to Liverpool University Conference on Human Rights in the UK Media, 19 September 2014, *UK Human Rights Blog*.

192 David Cameron, speech to the Police Federation, Blackpool, 17 May 2007.

193 'How a Suspected Car Thief . . . Was Granted His Human Right to a KFC Bargain Bucket and a 2-litre Bottle of Pepsi,' *Daily Mail*, 7 June 2006.

194 'Human Rights Fact and Fiction', briefing paper, Ministry of Justice, 2008.

195 This is Derbyshire.co.uk, 8 October 2009. Major police forces in England and Wales have pictures of those most wanted in their area on their Web sites.

196 Speech to the Conservative Party Conference, Manchester, 4 October 2011. Exceptionally, following the speech, the Royal Courts of Justice issued a statement confirming that the pet cat was immaterial to the decision.

197 For example, the *Telegraph*, 17 October 2009; the *Sun*, 9 February 2011; the *Daily Mail*, 17 June 2011.

198 Judge Gleeson, Asylum and Immigration Tribunal, Appeal No: IA/14578/2008, issued 10 December 2008.

199 See note 191.

200 Lord Justice Leveson, *Report into the Culture, Practice and Ethics of the Press*, Vol 11, November 2012 at 8.48–9.

201 F. Klug, 'The Press, Privacy and the Practical Values of the Human Rights Act', *Justice Journal*, December 2011: 81–87.

202 *The Sunday Times v United Kingdom* (1980) 2 EHRR 245.

203 See, for example, the principles established in *Handyside v. UK* (1976) 1 EHRR 737.

204 *Goodwin v UK* (1996) 22 EHRR 123; *Financial Times LTD v Interbrew* SA [2002] EWCA Civ 274; *Mersey Care NHS Trust v Ackroyd* [2007] EWCA Civ 101; *Malik v Manchester Crown Court and Chief Constable of Greater Manchester et al* [2008] EWHC 1362 Admin.

205 *A v Independent News and Media and others* [2010] EWCA Civ 343.

206 *Reynolds v Times Newspaper* (2001) 2 AC 127; *Jameel v Wall Street Journal Europe* [2006] UKHL 44.

207 *Guardian News and Media Ltd and others v Ahmed and others* [2010] UKSC 1.

208 See Klug, 'The Press, Privacy and the Practical Values of the Human Rights Act'.

209 Ibid.

210 For example, the 1985–1987 *Spycatcher* book ban; the 1986–1987 Zircon BBC documentary affair; and the 1988–1994 IRA broadcasting ban.

211 Loulla-Mae Eleftheriou-Smith, 'Last Week the Sun Wanted to Abolish the Human Rights Act – This Week They Want to Use it to Protect Their Journalists', *The Independent*, 6 October 2014.

212 Sajid Javid, speech at the Society of Editors Conference, Southampton, 11 November 2014.

213 Letter from Home Office Minister Lord Bates to Lord Strasburger, 3 November 2014.

214 Quoted in *The Observer*, 16 November 2014.

215 Javid, speech at the Society of Editors Conference, 11 November 2014.

216 See, for example, Elspeth Guild, 'What Does Mass Surveillance Do to Human Rights?' *Open Democracy*, 12 May 2014.

217 In December 2014 the IPT rejected claims that the HRA had been breached through the lack of a clear legal framework, within RIPA or otherwise, to sanction GCHQ's collection and storage of vast amounts of untargeted communications. The NGOs that took the case are now applying to the ECtHR. The IPT has yet to hear the legal challenge concerning the interception of the communications of the human rights groups themselves.

218 Ben Emerson, 'It's Outrageous to Accuse the Guardian of Aiding Terrorism by Publishing Snowden's Revelations', *The Guardian,* 2 December 2013.

219 Peter Preston, 'Press Freedom Is a Human Right Too – Ask Strasbourg', *The Observer,* 16 November 2014.

220 YouGov Poll on human rights attitudes, 22 July 2014. it.com/uk/174416-uk-human rights-poll/

221 A further 4 per cent had not heard of the HRA at all.

222 Ipsos Mori, *Public Perceptions of Human Rights* (EHRC, 2009). See note 151.

223 'Human Rights Inquiry: Report of the Equality and Human Rights Commission', 106.

224 Edward Adams, in 'Human Rights Inquiry: Report of the Equality and Human Rights Commission', 104.

225 Conor Gearty, 'Can Human Rights Survive?' in *Hamlyn Lectures* (Cambridge: Cambridge University Press, 2006), chapter 3.

226 Gearty, *Principles of Human Rights Adjudication,* 21.

227 Quoted in Philip Alston, ed., *The EU and Human Rights* (Oxford: Oxford University Press, 1999), 99.

228 Emile Hafner-Burton, 'Beyond the Law: Towards More Effective Strategies for Protecting Human Rights', *Open Democracy,* 6 May 2014.

229 Abdullahi An-Na'im, 'Human Rights and Its Inherent Liberal Relativism', *Open Democracy,* 25 August 2014.

230 Ibid.

231 Gearty, 'Can Human Rights Survive?' 92.

232 Ibid., 93.

233 Ibid., 95.

234 *SAS v France* [2014] ECHR 695.

235 Francesca Klug, 'Issues in Communicating Human Rights', unpublished lecture, 2001.

236 R. Dworkin, *A Matter of Principle* (Cambridge, MA: Harvard University Press, 1985), 287.

237 John Finnis, *Human Rights and Common Good: Collected Essays, Volume III* (Oxford: Oxford University Press, 2011), 29.

238 These distinctions are discussed in Section I. See F. Klug, 'Human Rights, Philosophy, Politics or Law?' unpublished lecture, Centre for the Study of Human Rights, LSE, Certificate in International Human Rights Law and Practice, October 2013.

239 Finnis, *Human Rights and Common Good,* 39.

240 Conor Gearty titled his 2005 Hamlyn Lectures 'Can Human Rights Survive?', see note 225.

241 Conservative Party, 'Protecting Human Rights in the UK'.

242 Joshua Rozenberg, 'Tory Plans for European Human Rights Convention Will Take UK Back 50 Years', *The Guardian,* 3 October 2014.

243 Quoted in 'Tories Risk Isolation over Threat to Ignore Rights Court', Owen Bowcott, Nick Watt and Henry McDonald (eds), *The Guardian,* 4 October 2014.

244 Dominic Grieve, 'Human Rights Act: Why the Conservatives Are Wrong', *Prospect Magazine,* October 2014.

245 *Hirst v UK (No 2)* [2005] ECHR 681.

246 'Report of the Joint Committee on the Draft Voting Eligibility (Prisoners) Bill', Session 2013–2014.

247 Conservative Party, 'Protecting Human Rights in the UK', 6.

248 'Tory Minister Dominic Grieve "Was Sacked after Taking Stand on ECHR"', Michael Savage and Richard Ford (eds), *The Times,* 21 July 2014.

249 Ken Clarke, *World at One,* 3 October 2014. When David Cameron first proposed, as leader of the Conservative Party, to replace the HRA with a 'British bill of rights' in 2006, Ken Clarke famously described this as 'xenophobic and legal nonsense', *Daily Mail,* 28 June 2006.

250 Thorbjorn Jagland, 'Azerbaijan's Human Rights Are on a Knife Edge: The UK Must Not Walk Away', *Guardian Comment Is Free,* 3 November 2014. https://www.theguardian.com/UK/commentisfree.

251 David Cameron's 'muscular liberalism' speech was given in Munich in the first year after he was elected, 5 February 2011. It is discussed in Section I.

252 Kenyatta was accused of unleashing a wave of post-election violence in 2007–2008, claiming 1,300 lives.

253 Ian Dunt, 'Kenyan Leader Cites Cameron's Human Rights Attack', politics.co.uk (blog), 22 October 2014; Adam Wagner, *UK Human Rights Blog*, 24 October 2014. www.ukhumanrightsblog.com.

254 'We Should Leave the Convention if We Can't Negotiate', *The Times*, 28 August 2014.

255 A three-day siege of a school seized by Chechen separatists resulted in 331 people losing their lives, including 179 children. The families have accused the Russian authorities of failing to prevent the massacre despite detailed intelligence warnings.

256 Quoted by Dr Alice Donald, 'UK Must Not Only Think of Itself', *UK Human Rights Blog*, 24 October 2014.

257 For a thorough analysis of the ECtHR see Alice Donald, Jane Gordon and Philip Leach, *The UK and the European Court of Human Rights* (London: Human Rights and Social Justice Research Institute, 2012). See note 242.

258 Rozenberg, *The Guardian*, 3 October 2014.

259 Jonathan Freedland, 'Scrapping Human Rights Law Is an Act of Displaced Fury', *The Guardian*, 4 October 2014.

260 Jacob Rees-Mogg MP, Question to Lord Chancellor, House of Commons, 13 November 2012.

261 *Sky News* transcript, 3 October 2014.

262 Tim Owen QC and Alex Bailin QC, 'Opinion on Conservatives' Proposals for Changing Britain's Human Rights Laws', Doughty Street Chambers, 3 October 2014.

263 These questions are discussed in F. Klug, '"Solidity or Wind?" What's on the Menu in the Bill of Rights Debate?' *The Political Quarterly* 80, no. 3 (2009): 420–26. See also F. Klug 'Do We Need a Bill of Rights or Do We Already Have One?' *Public Law* (Winter 2007): 701–19.

264 David Cameron, 'Balancing Freedom and Security – A Modern British Bill of Rights', speech to the Centre for Policy Studies, London, 26 June 2006, and 'Rebuilding Trust in Politics', speech at University of East London, 8 February 2010.

265 David Cameron, Prime Minister's Questions, House of Commons, 16 February 2011.

266 Conservative Party, 'Protecting Human Rights in the UK', 5–6.

267 'Boris Johnson's Father Calls for "Popular Uprising" against HS2', *The Guardian*, 24 January 2014.

268 Conservative Party, 'Protecting Human Rights in the UK', 3.

269 *Tyrer v the UK* (1978) 2 EHRR 1.

270 Ibid., at para 31.

271 Judge Robert Spano, 'How Does the European Court of Human Rights Seek to Discharge Its Mandate and What Lies behind its Reform Process?' unpublished paper, Chatham House, Monday, 13 October 2014.

272 Conservative Party, 'Protecting Human Rights in the UK', 5.

273 Sir Nicolas Bratza, 'Living Instrument or Dead Letter – The Future of the ECHR', *European Human Rights Law Review* 2 (2014): 116–28.

274 *Dudgeon v UK* (1981) 4 EHRR 149.

275 *Goodwin v UK* (1996) 22 EHRR 123.

276 *Buckley v UK* (1996) 23 EHRR 101.

277 *Price v UK* (2001) 34 EHRR 1285.

278 *Guerra and Others v Italy* (1998) 26 EHRR 357; *Hatton v UK* (2003) 37 EHRR 611.

279 *National Westminster Bank v Spectrum Plus* [2005] 2 AC 680 at para 32.

280 *DSD and NBV v The Commissioner of Police for the Metropolis* [2014] EWHC 436 (QB). The Metropolitan Police was held liable for its failure to properly investigate and for any damage attributable to this failure.

281 *ZH v Commissioner of Police for Metropolis* [2012] EWHC 604 (Admin). The court held that the teenager's right to liberty (Article 5), his right not to be subject to inhuman or degrading treatment (Article 3) and his right to respect for his private life (Article 8) were all violated.

282 The case of Patience Asuquo, who was assaulted in 2007 – judicial review proceedings were issued in January 2009. See http://www.liberty-human-rights.org.uk/human-rights/victims/forced-labour/index.php. After Liberty took judicial review proceedings

under the HRA, the police agreed to reopen the investigation and the employer was found guilty of assault. The case led to legislation to outlaw modern-day slavery with the creation of a new serious offence attracting a maximum sentence of fourteen years imprisonment.

283 *Paton v Poole Borough Council*, decided by the Investigatory Powers Tribunal, (IPT/09/01/C), 2 August 2010.

284 *Cowl et al v Plymouth City Council* [2001] EWCA Civ 1935 and *R (Madden) v Bury MBC* [2002] EWHC 1882.

285 *Ahmad Raja Ghaidan v Antonio Mendoza* [2004] UKHL 30, para 2, Schedule 1 of the Rent Act.

286 *Elizabeth Warren v Care Fertility (Northampton) Limited and Human Fertilisation and Embryology Authority* [2014] EWHC 602 (Fam).

287 *Blood and Tarbuck v Secretary of State for Health*, 2003, unreported.

288 *Pharmacists' Defence Association Union v Boots Management Services Ltd* [2013] IRLR 262; Upheld by the Administrative Court in *R (on the application of Boots Management Services Ltd) v Central Arbitration Committee* [2014] EWHC 65 (Admin).

289 *R (Amin) v Secretary of State for the Home Department* [2003] UKHL 51. Following this case the Prison Service introduced changes to its policy and procedures relating to cell-sharing risks, allowing information-sharing to identify high-risk factors.

290 'We'll End This Human Rights Madness, Pledges David Cameron', *Daily Express*, 30 September 2013.

291 Mark Elliot, 'My Analysis of the Conservative Party's Proposals for a British Bill of Rights', publiclawforeveryone.com, 3 October 2014.

292 Conservative Party press release, 'Conservatives Publish Plan for Radical Human Rights Reform', October 2014.

293 Conservative Party, 'Protecting Human Rights in the UK', 7.

294 *R (Smith) v Oxfordshire Assistant Deputy Coroner and Secretary of State for Defence* [2010] UKSC 29.

295 *Smith and Others v The Ministry of Defence* [2013] UKSC 41.

296 *R (Long) v Secretary of State for Defence* [2014] EWHC 2391 (Admin).

297 *Al-Skeini v UK* (2011) 53 EHRR 589, para 149. See also *Al-Jedda v the United Kingdom* (2011) 53 EHRR 23; *Hassan v the United Kingdom*, ECtHR, Application no. 29750/09 (16 September 2014).

298 Conservative Party, 'Protecting Human Rights in the UK', 6.

299 Sir William Gage, 'Baha Mousa Inquiry Report', MoD, 8 September 2011.

300 Described by Chakrabarti, *On Liberty*, 108.

301 *Chahal v The United Kingdom* (1996) 23 EHRR 413 (see note 170).

302 For example, the International Covenant on Civil and Political Rights and the UN Convention against Torture ratified by the Thatcher government on 8 December 1988.

303 *Othman (Abu Qatada) v the UK* (2012) 55 EHRR 1.

304 Conservative Party, 'Protecting Human Rights in the UK', 6.

305 Paul Houston, 'The Memory of My Daughter Amy Houston Has Been Dishonoured', *The Guardian*, 9 May 2013.

306 *Beoku-Betts v Secretary of State for the Home Department* [2008] UKHL 39 at 20.

307 *ZH (Tanzania) v Secretary of State for the Home Department* [2011] UKSC 4 at 1.

308 Conservative Party, 'Protecting Human Rights in the UK', 5.

309 Torture (Article 3) and slavery (Article 4) being two exceptions.

310 Conservative Party, 'Protecting Human Rights in the UK', 6.

311 The late Lord Chief Justice Lord Bingham observed that there is 'inherent in the whole of the Convention . . . a search for balance between the rights of the individual and the wider rights of the society . . . neither enjoying an absolute right to prevail over each other', *Leeds City Council v Price and others* [2006] UKHL 140, para 181.

312 See Klug, 'The Human Rights Act: Basic Principles and Values'.

313 Lord Neuberger, 'Conkerton Memorial Lecture', reported by Frances Gibb in the *Times*, 11 October 2014.

314 Keir Starmer, 'The Tom Sargant Memorial Lecture', Justice, 15 October 2014.

315 Ibid.

316 See http://www.liberty-human-rights.org.uk/news-and-events/1-press-releases/2010/bryantinquest-abandoned.shtml.

317 See F. Klug, 'Human Rights and Victims', in *Reconcilable Rights? Analysing the Tension between Victims and Defendants* (London: Legal Action Group, 2004).

318 *Whiteside v UK* (1994) 76A DR80.

319 *X&Y v Netherlands* [1985] 8 EHRR 235.

320 For example, see the Libertarian online magazine *Spiked*, November 2014.

321 Raab, *The Assault on Liberty*, 125–6.

322 See Andrew Clapham, *Human Rights in the Private Sphere* (Oxford: Clarendon, 1996).

323 David Davies MP, who took the principled step as shadow Home Secretary of resigning his seat in June 2008 to fight a by-election in protest over the Labour government's attempt to extend detention without trial to forty-two days, has also expressed opposition to the HRA.

324 See Sir Geoffrey Bindman, 'Magna Carta: Is Cameron for or Against?' *Our Kingdom*, 8 September 2014, https://www.opendemorcay.

325 See note 55.

326 'So Will the Revolution Start in Haltemprice and Howden?' Paul Vallely (ed.) *The Independent*, 14 June 2008.

327 Sadiq Khan, 'Human Rights Protect the Poor and Voiceless, Cameron's Replacement for Them Is a Dangerous Sham', *The Independent*, 3 October 2014.

328 Of the forty-seven state parties to the ECHR, only seven have total bans on allowing convicted prisoners to vote: Armenia, Bulgaria, Estonia, Georgia, Hungary, Russia and the UK.

329 Lord Irvine, 'A British Interpretation of Convention Rights', speech to Bingham Centre UCL, 14 December 2011.

330 The Registrar predicts that by the end of 2016 the total backlog (i.e. pending cases which the Court has not processed) will be down to about 17,000 – compared to 160,000 in September 2011. See Alice Donald, 'The Remarkable Shrinking Backlog at the European Court of Human Rights', *UK Human Rights* (blog), 1 October 2014; see also Klug, 'The Disputed Parentage of the European Convention on Human Rights', for a description of the enlargement of the CoE after 1989.

331 Written Ministerial statement on Protocols 15 and 16, 28 October 2014.

332 Protocol 15, Council of Europe, opened for signature on 16 May 2013. The Margin of Appreciation Doctrine is briefly explained in Klug, 'The Human Rights Act: Basic Principles and Values'.

333 *Handyside v UK* (1976) 1 EHRR, 737. See Howard Yourow, *The Margin of Appreciation Doctrine in the Dynamics of European Human Rights Jurisprudence* (The Hague: Kluwer, 1996). The ECtHR interprets the MoA across states, regardless of their constitution. In Germany, for example, the ECHR has the rank of a statute over which the constitution is supreme. However, the ECtHR does not apply the margin of appreciation any differently to Germany than any other state.

334 This is the title of the policy document, Conservative Party, 'Protecting Human Rights in the UK'.

335 Ibid., 6.

336 See note 125.

337 For a full discussion of the different interpretations of HRA section 2 see Francesca Klug and Helen Wildbore, 'Follow or Lead? The Human Rights Act and the European Convention on Human Rights', *European Human Rights Law Review Special Issue*, ed. F. Klug and J. Gordon (2010).

338 For example, Lord Toulson, *Daily Telegraph*, 1 November 2014; Lord Judge, *Daily Telegraph*, 7 January 2014, and Lord Laws, Hamlyn Lecture, 27 November 2013, 12.

339 Lord Hoffman, 'The Universality of Human Rights', *Judicial Studies Board Annual Lecture*, 19 March 2009, 26.

340   For example, Neuberger, 'The Role of Judges in Human Rights Jurisprudence'. See note 161.

341   For example, *R (Animal Defenders International) v Secretary of State for Culture, Media and Sport* [2008] UKHL 15 at 44; *R v Horncastle* [2009] UKSC 14; *R v McLoughlin, R v Newell* [2014] EWCA Crim 188.

342   For example, *R (Aguilar Quila) v Secretary of State for the Home Department* [2011] UKSC 45, where the Supreme Court ruled that an immigration rule designed to frustrate forced marriages interfered far more with unforced marriages, disproportionately interfering with the right to family life.

343   Irvine, 'A British Interpretation of Convention Rights'. See note 329.

344   Lord Justice, Laws, Hamlyn Lecture, 27 November 2013, para 34. This is precisely what happened in, for example, *Vinter v UK* [2013] ECHR 645, on 'whole life orders' for murder, a decision which is inaccurately described in *Protecting Human Rights in the UK*, note 3.

345   Conservative Party, 'Protecting Human Rights in the UK', 4. At the time of writing, thirty DOIs have been issued of which twenty-two are still standing and eight overturned on appeal. In only one instance involving legislation has the government refused to introduce a 'corrective' measure, namely on the issue of prisoner votes. Fourteen of the nineteen Acts of Parliament concerned were enacted before the HRA.

346   Gearty, 'On Fantasy Island'. See note 81.

347   *F & Anor, R (on the application of) v Secretary of State for the Home Department* [2010] UKSC 17.

348   David Cameron MP, HC debate, 16 February 2011, c955.

349   Conservative Party, 'Protecting Human Rights in the UK', 5 (my emphasis).

350   Ibid., 4.

351   Ibid. The doctrine of proportionality is briefly explained in Klug 'The Human Rights Act: Basic Principles and Values', 43.

352   Dominic Grieve QC, 'Why Human Rights Should Matter to Conservatives', lecture given at University College London, 3 December 2014.

353   For that matter, the US Bill of Rights was not able to stop the introduction of the Patriot Act or the establishment of internment at Guantanamo Bay, and so forth. Most bills of rights only allow laws to be reviewed once individuals challenge them after they are passed.

354   See Angela Patrick, 'Reforming Judicial Review: Cutting Pointless Delay or Preventing Legitimate Challenge?' UK Human Rights Blog, 24 February 2014. See also Clive Coleman, 'Judicial Review Reform: An Attack on Our Legal Rights?' *BBC News*, 1 December 2014.

355   See notes 82 to 88.

356   Charles Moore, '"Human Rights" Have Fallen Into the Hands of the Eurotollahs', *Daily Telegraph,* 31 October 2014.

357   The European Social Charter is the companion treaty to the ECHR and was adopted by the Council of Europe in 1961. It has no equivalent enforcement mechanism to the ECtHR and is therefore far less well known.

358   René Cassin, Nobel lecture, Norway, 11 December 1968.

359   Research by Peter Neumann, Professor of Security Studies, King's College London, *BBC*, 11 December 2014.

360   Jacqueline Bhabha, *Child Migration and Human Rights in a Global Age* (Princeton, NJ: Princeton University Press, 2014), 2.

361   Stephen Hopgood, *The Endtimes of Human Rights* (Ithaca, NY: Cornell University Press, 2013), 13, 23.

362   Ibid., 12. For a somewhat different analysis see Costas Douzinas, *The End of Human Rights* (Oxford: Hart Publishing, 2000).

363   Hopgood, *The Endtimes of Human Rights.* In 1897 a journalist was sent to inquire after the American author Mark Twain's health, mistakenly thinking he was near death. Twain recounted the event in the *New York Journal,* 2 June 1897, including his famous words: 'The report of my death was an exaggeration.'

364   Reported in *The Observer,* 23 November 2014.

365   Aase Lionaes, chair of the Nobel Peace Prize Committee, Award Ceremony Speech, Norway, 1968 (my emphasis).

366 Kamal Elgizouli, 'Sovereignty No Defence against ICC Action in Sudan', *Open Democracy*, 20 November 2014.

367 *Ghaidan v Godin-Mendoza* [2004] UKHL 30, para 132.

368 See Costas Douzinas, 'Who Counts as "Human"?' *Guardian Comment Is Free*, 1 April, 2009. https://www.theguardian.com/UK/commentisfree.

369 Veena Vasista, 'Wise Fools for Love? Arts Activism and Social Transformation', *Open Democracy*, 14 November 2014.

370 See Nick Macwilliam, 'Migrants in the Mediterranean: Europe's New Disappeared', *Open Democracy*, 20 November 2014, and Alison Whyte, '#Don't Let Them Drown (It's All Right for Some, at Sea)', *Open Democracy*, 8 November 2014.https://www.opendemocracy.net.

371 'Jordan Feels the Strain of Outflow from Syrian Strife', *The Guardian*, 2 December 2014. On 10 December 2014 the UNHCR recorded 3,205,180 registered Syrian refugees.

372 *BBC News*, 27 November 2014.

373 ECHR Protocol 4, Article 4. The ECtHR also found a violation of Article 3 due to the exposure to ill treatment on their return to Libya and Article 13, the right to an effective remedy.

374 *HIrsi Jamaa and others v Italy* (2012) 55 EHRR 21.

375 'Discours de Rene Cassin', 9 December 1948, quoted in Jay Winter and Antoine Prost, *Renee Cassin and Human Rights: From the Great War to the Universal Declaration* (Cambridge: Cambridge University Press, 2013), 250.

376 UDHR, Article 1.

377 Richard Rorty, 'Human Rights, Rationality and Sentimentality', in *On Human Rights: The Oxford Amnesty Lectures*, ed. Susan Hurley and Stephen Shute (New York: Basic Books, 1993), 129.

378 Ibid.

379 For the most part the term '*man*-made' does not seem entirely inappropriate here.

380 Senate Select Committee on Intelligence, 'Committee Study of the Central Intelligence Agency's Detention and Interrogation Programme', declassified 3 December 2014, and reported in *The Guardian*, 10 December 2014. Pressure is mounting from UK human rights groups for the 'government' to establish a judge-led inquiry on the extent of UK involvement in secret 'renditions' of human beings and torture interrogation techniques.

SECTION II
Anthology

1

THE DISPUTED PARENTAGE OF THE EUROPEAN CONVENTION ON HUMAN RIGHTS

Origins and controversies

Unpublished lecture, LSE Centre for the Study of Human Rights, 2012

Introduction

Who was the 'true' author of the European Convention on Human Rights (ECHR): Eleanor Roosevelt or Winston Churchill?

This is not a question you're likely to find in any textbook and I don't mean it literally, of course. But it is a question intended to highlight the uncertainty and confusion over the genesis of the ECHR.

From one perspective, the ECHR is purely a *European* phenomenon, developed entirely in the context of attempts to strengthen European co-operation following World War Two and as a response to the developing Cold War.

From another perspective, the ECHR is a regional manifestation of a *global* phenomenon: the post-war international human rights framework kicked off by the UN's 1948 Universal Declaration of Human Rights (UDHR), which is referred to 3 times in its preamble.

Regional mechanisms

The European human rights framework is only one of a number of regional mechanisms that has been established over the last 60 years, with varying effect. Along with the equivalent in the Americas, it is generally regarded as the most effective and influential, not least because of the case law or jurisprudence developed by the European Court of Human Rights (ECtHR).

The relationship between the United Nations (UN) and regional human rights mechanisms was initially somewhat ambivalent. Although chapter VIII of the UN charter makes provision for regional arrangements in relation to peace and security, there is no equivalent for human rights.

The international law theorist, Karel Vasak, has described the then tendency of the UN to regard regional human rights arrangements as "the expression of a breakaway movement," potentially threatening to the universal nature of human rights and the global reach of the UN.

This only really changed in 1977 after the long process of drafting and adopting the twin International Covenants came to fruition.[1] It was then that the General Assembly passed a resolution appealing to states in areas where regional human rights arrangements did not exist, to consider establishing them [*GA res 32/127*].

In fact the very first post-war human rights instrument – *the American Declaration of the Rights and Duties of Man* – was a regional one, adopted by the Organisation of American States, a few months before the UDHR. Like the Universal Declaration, it was not legally binding.

In 1978, two years after the UN's International Covenants came into force, the *American Convention on Human Rights* (ACHR) was ratified by many Latin American and Caribbean states, with an Inter-American Commission housed in Washington (although the US has signed but not ratified it) and an Inter-American Court based in Costa Rica. Through ratification, the Convention became legally binding on all the states that had both signed and ratified it. On 10 September 2012 the Venezuelan President, Hugo Chavez, formally announced that his country would withdraw from the ACHR following complaints about its impact on national sovereignty from his left wing government which resemble critiques of the ECHR by some senior politicians here in the UK.

Like the ECHR, the ACHR refers to the UDHR in its preamble but unlike the ECHR, it includes a chapter on economic and social rights. It has a distinctive framework of its own, with tasks and functions not mirrored in the European system. But there are also ways in which the ACHR and its enforcement structures are the closest to the European equivalent.

Four years after the 1977 UN resolution encouraging regional human rights mechanisms, the Organisation of African Unity adopted the innovative African Charter of Human and Peoples' Rights in 1981, with its own Commission to promote and protect human rights in the continent of Africa, and since 2004, its own Court. The Court's judgements are legally binding and execution of its judgments is monitored by the Council of Ministers of the African Union.

Other regional mechanisms continue to be developed. A Declaration of Human Rights is being drafted by the Association of Southeast Asian Nations Intergovernmental Commission on Human Rights and an Arab Charter on Human Rights came into force in 2008 when it was ratified by 7 states, with two more following suit. However there is no legal enforcement mechanism for either of these and it is fair to say they have not had the recognition, let alone impact, of their African, American, or European equivalents.

Background to the ECHR

In this lecture I am going to try to paint a picture of the world into which the ECHR was born, particularly here in the UK, to shed light on why the European Convention and European Court of Human Rights took the shape they did.

The adoption of the UDHR by the UN in 1948 had no initial impact on British domestic policy. There was little increased interest in human rights in the UK let alone pressure to introduce a bill of rights based on international human rights standards.

Adherence to international human rights in the UK was seen as primarily a product of international relations. It was the Foreign Office which led on the long and tortuous – although ultimately successful – negotiations at the UN to draft the International Covenants referred to above which were adopted in 1966 and came into force ten years later.

Despite this time lag, it is questionable whether the adoption of a legally enforceable *European* human rights convention, whose drafting began at a similar time to the UN efforts, would ever have been attempted were not similar endeavours already underway at the UN (this gives some weight to the Eleanor Roosevelt authorship theory, at least at a very indirect level).

A deep concern about national sovereignty and the legitimacy of a regional court dogged the negotiations over the drafting of the ECHR and its court from the outset.

It was high-powered European NGOs, in particular the British European Movement supported by the UK's war leader, Winston Churchill, and its French equivalent, which took the initiative towards creating some kind of pan-European body to promote human rights and democracy (providing evidence for the Churchill authorship theory). But there was a sharp distinction in perspective between what drove British support for such a body, ambiguous as it was, and that of countries which had experienced occupation in the very recently concluded war.

Many European citizens were aware, even if they preferred to forget it, that atrocities which took place outside conflict zones against majority and minority populations alike, were often inflicted by their own governments. In Britain (but not necessarily Northern Ireland) the state was much less likely to be viewed as a threat to its own citizens and was more likely to be seen as the champion of liberty, particularly in the period immediately after World War Two.

In a speech to the United Europe Movement on 17 May 1951 Sir David Maxwell Fyfe, a former member of Churchill's war time government who subsequently became Home Secretary and Lord Chancellor, and one of the most enthusiastic and prominent negotiators of the text of the ECHR, put it like this: "People in Britain are completely uninterested in human rights because, of course, they have never seen them go like some of the other nations who have adopted the convention."

If many British people were therefore indifferent to the European Convention at the time of its adoption in 1950, the government was wary precisely because Britain's tradition of liberty was not nearly as unblemished as patriotic sentiment suggested.

Developing restlessness and rebellions against the injustices and oppression of colonial rule within Britain's still extensive empire (now established to include torture) fed Britain's nervousness over proposals to establish a European-wide convention on human rights with a commission to supervise it, and a court to enforce it.

Council of Europe and the European Court

A Congress of Europe attended by 663 delegates from 16 countries, including 20 Prime Ministers or former Prime Ministers, met in May 1947, just as the drafting committee established by the United Nations Human Rights Commission was meeting, chaired by Eleanor Roosevelt, to draw up the UDHR. The legal historian, Brian Simpson, explains that "human rights were much in the air at this time" and "Churchill would have been well aware" of the corresponding activities at the UN.[2]

In his opening speech to the Congress, Churchill proclaimed his profound support both for greater European co-operation and for human rights protection as a core constituent of this project:

"The Movement or European Unity must be a positive force, deriving its strength from our sense of common spiritual values. It is a dynamic expression of democratic faith based upon moral conceptions and inspired by a sense of mission. In the centre of our movement stands the idea of a Charter of Human Rights, guarded by freedom and sustained by law."

Commenting on the "closer political unity" he was proposing, Churchill continued: "it is said, with truth, that this involves some sacrifice or merger of national sovereignty."[3]

This was an honest and interesting assertion, revealing that from the outset the prominent promoters of the ECHR were aware that a quid pro quo for greater European unity and common European standards on human rights would be some reduction in 'national sovereignty.' Given that this came from the most widely revered Conservative Prime Minister of all time it is a recognition which the current Conservative Party is not too keen to recall.

The Congress accepted two proposals. One was to establish a European Parliamentary Assembly and the other was to produce a European Charter of Human Rights. The Council of Europe was finally established by statute on 5 May 1949 as an organ of intergovernmental co-operation to promote democracy, the rule of law and greater unity amongst western European countries, in the context of the developing cold war.

The drafting of a human rights charter immediately became a high priority for the new Council. Much of the original draft of what became the ECHR was derivative of the text of the UDHR (again pointing the finger at Roosevelt authorship). What was entirely new was the the idea of establishing a European Court of Human Rights, a development strongly supported by the independent European Movement. This was an anathema to the post-war Labour government which, along with most of the civil servants who advised them, viewed it as an incursion into both parliamentary and national sovereignty.

This concern went to the heart of Britain's famously 'unwritten constitution' (or at least not written down in one place) in which rights are said to be protected by a combination of the common law developed by judges and statutes passed by a parliament which is said to be sovereign.

This means that in a reverse of systems associated with judicially entrenched bills of rights or written constitutions, judges under the UK common law system *cannot* overturn lawfully passed Acts of Parliament.

By the same token, there are no procedural or constitutional impediments to stop the UK Parliament from changing the common law as developed by judges, provided this is through lawful statutes. There is no 'higher' domestic law, in other words, which binds either parliament or the courts – or at least there wasn't back in 1948.

The proposed European Court of Human Rights not only appeared to threaten this system of *parliamentary* sovereignty, as Churchill implied, by empowering its judges to determine whether UK law and executive decisions were compatible with the ECHR but it seemed to involve a surrender of *national* sovereignty to a *European* Court to boot.

It is little wonder, then, that this proposal was so contentious although the contention largely remained within the political elite as there was little public awareness of the proposed new developments.

The negotiations within the council of Europe which produced the ECHR took place over a relatively short period of time from August 1949 to September 1950 (although the first protocol covering free and fair elections, property and education rights, which could not be agreed on in earlier inter-state discussions, was not signed until March 1952). Simpson tells us that the draft "comprised 33 Articles. Much of the text was derivative of the Geneva draft of the United Nations Declaration."[4]

The introduction to the published draft Convention took the line that since the UDHR had been adopted, there was no real need for a separate European charter as the rights had been established. What was missing was judicial enforcement of these rights.

Although there were initial fears within the UK government that it would be otherwise, the purpose of the court was not to act as a Supreme Court of Appeal from domestic courts in a Federal Europe on the American model. Whilst the ECtHR could build up its own human rights case law it would have no power to reverse domestic decisions, only to pronounce on them. Changes to the law or policy could only be undertaken by states themselves. Domestic courts would not be required to follow ECtHR rulings as they would a Supreme Court. However, having ratified the ECHR, governments would be bound to comply with the rulings of the Court, even if the means of doing so was of their own choosing.[5]

These assurances did little to pacify British anxieties initially. There were two main objections to these proposals expressed by the UK government which continue to echo in the rows in the British press and Parliament to this day.

The first concerned the nature of human rights law itself; the second, the powers of the proposed new Court.

There was considerable disagreement during the drafting stage between the Continental civil lawyers and British common law lawyers.[6] The former stemmed from legal traditions like that of France or Belgium where the courts were used to developing jurisprudence from broadly expressed norms like 'the right to life' or 'the right to free expression.' The latter were only comfortable with a legal tradition which revolved around judges developing case law from the interpretation of technical and detailed legislation, passed by Parliament, which trumped judge-made law.

The civil lawyers, largely from jurisdictions with written constitutions or bills of rights, were content for the proposed Convention to be loosely based on the rights in the UDHR, specified in very general terms, and to allow the proposed ECtHR to develop its own jurisprudence on these rights.

The common law lawyers, largely from the British Foreign Office, were distrustful of bills of rights and broad declarations. These were viewed as alien to the British legal culture despite the fact that the famous 1215 Magna Carta and the 1689 Bill of Rights are widely viewed as the precursors to subsequent rights documents around the world.

The British participants to the negotiations wanted to spell out in more detail only those rights in the UDHR they viewed as capable of being enforced by a court. To some degree they won out, when all the economic, social and cultural rights in the UDHR were deemed non-justiciable and not included in the draft.

The approach of the British Foreign Office was to support a minimal number of more tightly drafted rights accompanied by specific limitations which set out the scope of each right. The upshot was that this British scheme of drafting won out.

A cursory look at the ECHR reveals that amongst the substantive rights, only freedom of conscience and religion (but not their manifestation in religious and other practices) and the prohibitions on torture and slavery are expressed in more or less absolute terms.

Herein lies a basic difference between the text of the UDHR and the ECHR. It arguably gives weight to the 'Churchillian theory of authorship.' At the very least it is illustrative of the considerable British Foreign Office influence on a text which was clearly derivative of the UDHR.

As for the Court, whilst it continued to attract Churchill's support (although he was less enthusiastic about it when he was back in power), it was generally opposed by the UK Labour government. The Lord Chancellor, the minister representing the judiciary in government, wrote a draft Cabinet paper lamenting the proposal in terms remarkably similar to some of the less well informed comments by disenchanted press and politicians expressed today:

> "I cannot view with equanimity an . . . appeal to a secret court composed of persons of no legal training possessing the unfettered right to expound the meaning of 17 articles which may mean anything or – as I hope – nothing."[7]

Churchill took a contrary view: "A European assembly forbidden to discuss human rights would indeed have been a ludicrous proposition to put to the world."[8]

However, he also insisted that the proposed Court would have to rely on individual states for the enforcement of their judgements. This is the system that was effectively adopted with governments given considerable leeway as to how to comply.

Of the original ten members of the Council of Europe, only four were initially in support of the Court – Belgium, France, Ireland and Italy. The UK was opposed. The consequence was that acceptance of the Court, which sits in Strasbourg, France, was initially made optional under Article 46.

The strongest opposition from the UK was to the proposition that it would not just be states that would be able to take a case against other states. In addition individuals, having exhausted all legal remedies in their home countries, would be able to take their case to the European Commission on Human Rights. If it decided the case was 'admissible,' and deserving of 'merit,' the Commission could in turn take it further to the ECtHR whose judgements would be binding on the state concerned. There was nothing proposed for the UN machinery that came close to the powers of this Court.

In the end there was agreement to a Swedish compromise to include the right of individual petition but make it optional; in the UK this was not granted until the Labour government of 1966.

Colonialism and extra-territorial application

The fact that the right of individual petition was not originally available in the UK did not curb the concerns of the colonial office. It regretted that the Convention was ever produced and feared its extension to the colonies, whilst accepting that such a development was now inevitable.

In consequence, the British achieved the inclusion of Article 15 permitting derogations (or the power to bypass certain Articles) in times of "war or other public emergency threatening the life of the nation." This was considered an essential safeguard by the government to minimise the impact of the Convention on its increasingly restless colonies.

The UK also fought for an additional Article known as the "territorial application clause" which was effectively a 'colonial application clause.' What became Article 56 allowed states after ratifying the ECHR to *choose* whether or not to extend its provisions "to all or any of the territories for whose international relations it is responsible." The UK made such a declaration in relation to most of its remaining colonies but there was no automatic application in these territories when the ECHR was ratified in 1953.

This was despite the reference in Article 1 that the states which ratified the Convention "shall secure to everyone in their jurisdiction" the rights and freedoms it upholds.

The word 'everyone,' repeated in virtually every substantive article of the ECHR, is sometimes said to be the most important word in the Convention as this is what determines its universal application. This is distinct from most national legislation, even that devoted to ending discrimination or promoting equality, which usually defines which categories of people it applies to.

The reach of the ECHR continues to be controversial. Nowadays the ECtHR has extended its application to individuals in territories that states control, or where the court determines they are within their control, which has been interpreted to include both soldiers, and the detainees of UK forces, in Iraq.

This is the rub! It is this capacity of the Court to develop case law to extend protection to people and circumstances that could not have been envisaged at the time the ECHR was ratified that is causing such consternation to the UK Government, amongst others.

It is clear from the debates preceding the adoption of the ECHR that the British Government's greatest fear was that the human rights standards which it was very comfortable to use to condemn other countries, would come back to bite it and be applied to hold the UK to account. In these Iraqi cases this fear has materialised.[9]

The impact of the end of the Cold War

After the fall of the Berlin wall and the end of the cold war there was a rapid expansion of the Council of Europe (COE) in the 1990s. The COE statute (Article 3) requires its constituent states to "accept the principles of the rule of law and the enjoyment by all persons within its jurisdiction of human rights . . ."

Country after country from the former Soviet Union or its satellites were keen to demonstrate they were in a position to abide by these terms. There are now 47 member states stretching across the whole of Europe, including Russia, which have ratified the convention; Belarus being the only significant state to remain outside.

This increased membership has placed considerable strains on the system leading to long delays in the processing of cases which are only recently starting to recede. Initially this backlog was to the European Commission which considered whether an application was admissible. A case would then proceed to the Court or, in specific circumstances, the Committee of Ministers for a final determination. Unlike the Commission and the Court, the Committee of Ministers was not set up by the ECHR but was an already existing body of the COE, consisting of one ministerial representative from each member state. Together with the Parliamentary Assembly (composed of representatives of state parliaments) the Council of Ministers provide the political component of the body, and arguably an element of democratic legitimacy to it (although a very indirect one).

Various proposals were discussed to simplify and speed up this system culminating in Protocol 11 in 1998. This abolished the two tier system of Commission and Court and ushered in a single full-time court which it is no longer possible for states which have ratified the ECHR to opt out of.

Since then individuals, NGOs or groups who claim to be a victim of violations of the ECHR throughout Europe (or who live under European state jurisdiction), regardless of their citizenship, have had a mandatory right to complain directly to the Court.

States can still take cases against other states for Convention violations under Article 33 although this provision has only rarely been used.[10] This is typical of all the regional human rights mechanisms, including the Inter-American and African systems, where states are reluctant to police each other lest the tables are turned against them.

As a result of a continuing backlog, further changes to the European court system were introduced by protocol 14 adopted in May 2004 (its enforcement was delayed until 2010 because of initial obstruction by Russia).

The Court can now sit in various formations. The most important cases may be relinquished by a chamber of 7 judges to the so called Grand Chamber of 17 judges provided both parties consent to this.

Despite ongoing concerns about the backlog of cases, which only now shows signs of diminishing, the ECHR is often described in international law books as the most successful regional or international human rights framework in the world.

I asked at the beginning of the lecture who was the main drafter of the ECHR, Churchill or Roosevelt? Perhaps the fairest answer is that they can both claim credit for it. They themselves would probably have argued that they stood on the shoulders of those who drafted the great human rights charters that preceded them as well as the human beings whose life experiences are reflected in the aspirations of every Article.

Notes

1 The International Covenant on Civil and Political Rights and the International Covenant on Economic, Social and Cultural Rights, both ratified in 1976.
2 W. Brian Simpson, *Human Rights and the End of Empire, Britain and the genesis of the European Convention*, Oxford: OUP 2001, p605.
3 Winston S. Churchill, *His Complete Speeches, 1897–1963*, R.R James (ed) New York, 1974 p7635–9.
4 Simpson op cit note 2, p611.
5 See Simpson op cit note 2, p655.
6 Ibid, p658.
7 Quoted in Ibid, p742.
8 Ibid, p668.
9 E.g. *Al-Skeini v UK* (2011) 53 EHRR 589.
10 E.g. *Cyprus v Turkey* in 1975, *Ireland v UK* 1978 and *Georgia v Russia* in 2007.

2

A BILL OF RIGHTS FOR THE UNITED KINGDOM

A comparative summary

European Human Rights Law Review 5 (1997): 501–7

This text is a revised and annotated version of a lecture delivered by Francesca Klug at a conference on the Bill of Rights for the United Kingdom held at University College, London, on 4 July 1997, sponsored by Bindman and Partners. She compares the approaches of different States (notably Canada and New Zealand) to the conundrum of limiting the power of the executive without preventing a democratically elected Government from carrying out key popular reforms in areas where there is no settled human rights answer. She assesses what we can learn from other Bills of Rights when considering what form the British model should take, and argues for wide consultation and debate on any model involving significant constitutional change before it is enforced.

I recently had a discussion with a longstanding member of the American Civil Liberties Union. I asked him if the United Kingdom were still the occupiers of the United States and if there were an equally successful war of independence would he, as a founding father of a new constitution, approach the drafting of the Bill of Rights with the same vision as his predecessors. To my surprise he answered "no." He would, he said, not view the executive solely as a body from which to seek protection but one from which protection is sometimes derived; he would want to provide an impetus for the legislature and executive to take responsibility – along with the courts – for upholding the values in the Bill of Rights; he would, he maintained, be aware that rights frequently need to be balanced against each other in what sometimes involves finely nuanced judgments. He would, in short, want to engage with the debates which have emerged from the variety of Bills of Rights models developed over the last 200 years.

From my understanding, the Lord Chancellor is urging us to engage in such debates when he says that "our task is to find a distinctively British approach" to incorporation of the European Convention on Human Rights into U.K. law. I was involved in such an exercise on a modest scale when I was charged with the task of drafting a Bill of Rights for Liberty seven years ago. It is not widely known today that at the time there was considerable opposition within what was formerly the National Council of Civil Liberties to the very idea of a Bill of Rights. I learnt then to distinguish between Bills of Rights sceptics who are wary of any dilution of the exercise of parliamentary sovereignty and those who have no objection in principle but are unconvinced that armed with a Bill of Rights the courts can be relied upon to protect the rights of individuals and minorities any more than governments can.

I learnt, too, that virtually every country that has introduced a Bill of Rights in recent years has been faced with the same dilemma. How can a Bill of Rights limit the power of the executive without preventing a democratically elected government from carrying out key popular reforms in areas where there is no settled human rights answer? Examples of the latter include abortion laws (tightened in Germany but liberalised in Canada) and tobacco advertising restrictions (struck down in Canada but on the basis of current jurisprudence unlikely to be ruled as a breach of the ECHR by the European Court of Human Rights). The courts do not very often overturn statutes on such hotly disputed issues – perhaps once or twice an administration – but when they do they have the potential to discredit the very idea of Bills of Rights by the ousting of the democratic process from what many would see as legitimate democratic debate.

Each state had addressed this conundrum in different ways. In Sweden, which incorporated the ECHR in 1995, the courts are only empowered to overturn "manifest breaches" of the human rights treaty, making them less likely to cross into what many regard as the legitimate terrain of the legislature. In Hong Kong, whose 1991 Bill was introduced at the behest of the last British Government, the courts could overturn Acts of Parliament already in force (in line with the doctrine of implied repeal) but not new ones (although this was complicated by Hong Kong's unique constitutional status at the time). In Ireland the courts can strike down both preexisting and future legislation, but a referendum called by a simple majority of the Dail can overturn the impact of Supreme Court rulings, as happened when the Court imposed travel restrictions on women seeking an abortion.

Today's conference has largely focused on what are generally presented as the polar Bill of Rights models of New Zealand and Canada. As these have come to represent the parameters of the debate about the appropriate model for the United Kingdom it is worth considering what their salient features are and how these might be relevant for the British model.

It is fashionable to describe the Canadian model as a strong protector of rights and the New Zealand model as scarcely protecting rights at all. Rather than embracing one model wholesale and dismissing the other model outright it is more useful, I think, to understand why the two came to be adopted and what they set out to achieve.

The Canadian Charter of Rights and Freedoms is part of Canada's entrenched constitution (it can only be amended by special parliamentary majorities). It is from the latter that it derives its status as "supreme law." It was preceded by the 1960 Bill of Rights which was largely a dead duck for over 20 years. Conventional wisdom has it that this was because it did not allow the courts to overturn Acts of Parliament. In fact, as the courts established in the one case where the Supreme Court did overturn a statute (*R. v. Drybones*)[1] the Bill did confer the power to strike down both new and current legislation. The reluctance of the courts was related to the Bill's unentrenched status in a country with a written constitution – they were hesitant to use a non-constitutional instrument for a constitutional role – and the fact that the Bill did not apply to provincial legislatures in a country with a federal system.

The Charter was introduced in the context of a broader constitutional settlement. The extensive and lengthy consultation process which preceded it, together with its new constitutional status, gave the courts the signal that they were expected to enforce the Charter generously and purposefully. They have risen to the task: they have "read in," "read down," "severed" and "struck down". To avoid confusion they have also developed a procedure to suspend declarations of invalidity to allow the legislature to take the appropriate action. This was employed (although in the event it did not have to be used) in the landmark case of *Schacter v. R.*,[2] where the Supreme Court declared that a disparity in benefits between natural and adoptive parents was discriminatory. The people of Canada have unquestionably benefited enormously from this judicial activism. The vision behind this model – similar in essence to the classical American Bill of Rights – is that rights are inherently anti-majoritarian and the courts are therefore best placed to be their prime trustee.

The booby prize for the legislature was the "notwithstanding clause." Originally included in the 1960 Bill, this is a procedure to allow the federal and provincial parliaments to derogate from certain Charter Articles (subject to five-yearly renewal) by expressly acknowledging the fact within the offending statute; a kind of legislative "health warning." In practice no government is eager to acknowledge that they have breached their own charter of rights. Hence Acts which many might consider protected rights – like the "rape shield" laws protecting alleged rape victims from questioning about their sexual history and tobacco advertising restrictions – were felled alongside those statutes which did not involve such fine balances between conflicting rights. In fact the federal parliament has not used the "notwithstanding clause" once in 15 years; its use has almost entirely been by the Quebec Parliament in the context of a partition dispute which does not (as yet) have direct relevance here.

The vision behind the New Zealand Bill was arguably slightly different from the outset. In the words of Geoffrey Palmer, the former Prime Minister who championed the New Zealand Bill of Rights, its stated purpose was to act as "a set of navigation lights for the whole process of Government to observe." The White Paper which presented the New Zealand Government's original proposal to allow courts to strike down Acts of Parliament – a proposal that proved so unpopular during the Government's travelling road show to consult on the issue that it was dropped – acknowledged that "in a great many cases where controversial issues arise for determination there is no 'right' answer."

It is with these twin considerations in mind that the New Zealand *Bill of Rights* should be assessed. In line with this approach the Attorney General is required, under section 7, to notify Parliament of "any provision in [any] Bill that appears to be inconsistent with any of the rights and freedoms contained in the Bill of Rights." There is evidence that this function has led to a more thorough and nuanced consideration of the human rights implications of policy and legislation within government and parliament than existed prior to the Bill or is characteristic of the Canadian executive and legislature.

The Bill has been on the statute book only a few years but the number of reports issued by the Attorney-General warning Parliament that government or back-bench legislation might breach the Bill of Rights is in double figures. The tabled reports can be several pages long providing detailed consideration of the jurisprudence on an issue (mainly from Canada, interestingly). It could be said that they go some way towards providing the transparency sought by the "notwithstanding clause" but in a way which takes credence of the complexity of the issues involved. The fact that Parliament does not always agree with the advice of the Attorney-General, for example, does not necessarily mean that MPs are hell bent on breaching the Bill of Rights, but that – at the margins if you like – there is not necessarily one correct human rights answer, as the White Paper acknowledged.

Two examples will illustrate the point which I present only because the more interesting aspects of the New Zealand model tend to be buried along with its negative features. In 1991 the Attorney General tabled a report declaring that he considered the introduction of random breath testing to be a breach of the search and seizure provision of the Bill of Rights and of the right to liberty. After a considered review by the appropriate select committee on whether the tests were a "justified limit" to protect the right to life, the House voted to maintain it (on a free vote).

In a second example, a requirement that certain categories of workers responsible for the care of children (such as teachers or social workers) must report child abuse in particular circumstances was again said to be a breach of the (free expression) provisions of the Bill of Rights by the Attorney General. The Legislative Advisory Committee and the appropriate select committee disagreed. The provision fell for other reasons but if it had not, would it have been appropriate for Parliament to insert a "notwithstanding clause" in the legislation to protect it from judicial repeal? Would such a requirement enhance public understanding – or, more important, acceptance – of human rights values if the people are told that a

Bill of Rights has to be bypassed before the legislature can act to protect children in this way?

The greatest problem with the New Zealand model is section 4, which directly ousts the doctrine of implied repeal and states that the courts cannot refuse to apply any provision of any Act "by reason only that the provision is inconsistent with" the Bill of Rights. There is no denying that the New Zealand model fails to provide an effective remedy through the courts where to do so would strain the meaning of words in an Act or override the intention of Parliament in passing a statute. When, for example, Bennet, a convicted prisoner, claimed that his civil rights were violated because he was denied the vote, the courts could do nothing for him as to do so would be to overturn the clearly stated wording and intention of an Act.[3]

At the same time, the weakness of this approach should not be exaggerated. The courts can strike down subordinate legislation, discretionary powers under judicial review procedures and the common law where they breach the Bill. It is sometimes claimed that when it comes to statutes, however, the courts are required to follow the letter of the law. This is simply wrong. The New Zealand Bill uses an interpretative approach. Under section 6 "wherever an enactment can be given a meaning that is consistent with the rights and freedoms contained in the Bill of Rights that meaning shall be preferred." To everyone's surprise – and in contrast with the experience under the old Canadian Bill – the courts have by and large seen this clause as the green light to "read in" rights or "read down" breaches wherever they can. Thus in the famous case of *Mot v. Noort* and *Police v. Curran*[4] the courts "read in" the right to consult a lawyer when breathalysed under the 1962 *Transport Act*. Their reasoning was that as the 1962 Act did not expressly oust this right, and as consultation by telephone would not substantially impair the purposes or administration of the Act, the two convictions for drink driving which were the subject of the case should be quashed.

So what can we learn from other Bills of Rights as we take the Lord Chancellor at his word and consider what form the British model should take?

- A Preamble to the Act incorporating the Convention emphasising its scope and lofty aims could encourage the courts to give it a "generous" and "purposive" interpretation.[5]
- Assuming that the courts are only given the power to *interpret* Acts in conformity with the ECHR, why should this involve ousting the doctrine of implied repeal as the New Zealand model does? Why should the courts not be permitted to overturn provisions which breach the ECHR in legislation already on the statute book? So that no misunderstanding can arise on the grounds that a general statute cannot be assumed to implicitly repeal an earlier more specific one (the *generalia specialibus non derogant* principle) this power should be clearly spelt out in the incorporating statute (as under the Hong Kong Bill).
- As Lord Lester demonstrated in his 1997 Human Rights Bill, there is no need to replicate section 4 of the New Zealand Bill in drafting an interpretative Act. Indeed, I would go further. If the courts are not to be empowered to

strike down new legislation they should still be explicitly mandated to *declare* whether or not a breach has occurred. Lord Cooke has expressed the view that this would alleviate some of the criticisms levelled at the New Zealand model where it is not clear whether the prime duty of the courts is to uphold parliamentary sovereignty or uphold the rights and freedoms in the Bill of Rights. It should be remembered that the European Court of Human Rights cannot *directly* strike down Acts in the manner of the Canadian Supreme Court either.

- The ECHR already has a derogation procedure attached to it (Article 15) but it is more circumscribed than the Canadian "notwithstanding clause"; it can only be applied in times of war or public emergency. Should we not require that any derogations under Article 15, including current ones, be approved (perhaps annually) by Parliament rather than adopt Canada's more open-ended version?

- The strongest attraction of the "notwithstanding clause" – transparency – could largely be achieved through a system of ministerial certification (which is operated reasonably well by the New Zealand Attorney General). As Lord Lester argued during the debate on his 1997 Bill, where ministers (or Parliament) have not *expressly* declared that an Act is intended to breach the ECHR the courts can assume the legislation is intended to comply with it and "read in" or "read down" rights up to the point of frustrating the purposes of the Act. What Parliament cannot do is violate or amend the ECHR by implication. Proposed legislation to curb child pornography on the internet, for example, which was recently struck down as unconstitutional by the U.S. Supreme Court, could not be overturned under this model but could have all sorts of safeguards built into it by the U.K. courts unless Parliament were to expressly declare that the Act breached the ECHR.

- Assuming, as a bare minimum, that the courts are empowered to strike down subordinate legislation (along with the common law and discretionary powers) as indeed they can under both the Canadian and New Zealand models, there will be more pressure on Parliament to legislate through primary legislation in relation to civil and political rights. Appropriate and imaginative scrutiny mechanisms for Whitehall, Government and Parliament (both Houses) become more vital the less scope the courts have.

- The same case applies to the establishment of an effective Human Rights Commission which, in addition to providing independent advice to backbench MPs on compliance with the ECHR, could issue codes of practice to local government officers, immigration officials, the police, etc., as well as carry out an essential public education function (including working with education authorities on curriculum implications).

- There may well be different considerations for Northern Ireland (or even Scotland). It is already well recognised that the ECHR is an inadequate treaty as far as minority rights in Northern Ireland is concerned and that in the light of any future settlement the appropriateness of incorporating other ratified treaties – like the ICCPR – will be considered. A stronger role for the courts may also be more appropriate in those circumstances.

- On the issue of remedies the Act should be closer to the Canadian model; it should allow a court or tribunal to grant the appropriate remedy (as again proposed by Lord Lester). On the question of liability, on the other hand, the Act could be closer to the New Zealand model whose scope is wider than the Canadian Bill in this respect; the latter does not include the common law as it operates between private individuals which would exclude the libel laws, for example, from its operation.

In short the British model that I envisage would allow Parliament to proceed with democratically mandated reforms currently in the pipeline where there is no unequivocal breach of the ECHR (gun controls, tobacco advertising bans, political party funding controls, to name but three). It is extremely unlikely that the Strasbourg courts would in the foreseeable future wish to take a view on these "philosophical" or "political" issues to which they invariably give a wide "margin of appreciation" to domestic organs. Many would argue that the case has not yet convincingly been made for the domestic courts to be given a free reign to strike down legislation of this kind either.

On the other hand, where there is a clear breach of the ECHR, whether or not this is acknowledged by Parliament before legislating, it is highly unlikely that any government would defy the express view of the domestic courts when it is clear that the Strasbourg Court will mandate a change to the law. Lord Irvine's suggestion today that his Government is looking at fast-track procedures to amend legislation in the face of such declarations by the domestic courts is extremely encouraging (though consideration has to be given to the downside of a spate of significant amendments through statutory instrument; could the proposed parliamentary scrutiny mechanisms have a role here?).

Whichever model is adopted, this should not, in my view, be seen as the end of the road but the beginning. The Government has left the door open for consultation on what other ratified human rights instruments – or aspects of them – should be incorporated in a British Bill of Rights. It is up to people like us to create the momentum.

Once incorporation of the ECHR has bedded down – and people start to understand what it means to embrace a set of principles as a quasi-higher law – that may be the time to revisit the debate about the appropriate role of the courts *vis à vis* the legislature. My personal anxiety is not so much over *which* model is chosen but that any model which involves significant constitutional change – as the Canadian one does – should be widely consulted upon and debated before it is enforced. I do not want to be responsible for the shock women experienced in Canada when the "rape shield" provisions were overturned by the Supreme Court and they realised that the only option open to them was to work on a weaker version of the law; campaigning and lobbying to retain the stronger version was pointless. If constitutional changes of this nature do not acquire sufficient legitimacy, there is the danger of a significant backlash.

For now, let us welcome this crucial reform which some of you have spent a lifetime campaigning for. After half a century of debate, the European Convention on Human Rights is to be incorporated into our law. It will soon be time to start working towards, in Robin Cook's terms, placing human rights at the centre of public life. Two hundred years since Tom Paine set this debate rolling, human rights should soon be understood by the British people not only as something many foreigners apparently lack, but as something to which each and every one of us in the United Kingdom can lay claim.

Notes

1 [1970] S.C.R. 282.
2 1–93 D.L.R. (4th) [1982].
3 *Re Bennett* [1994] 2 H.R.N.Z. 358.
4 [1992] 3 N.Z.L.R. 260.
5 *Flickinger v. Hong Kong* [1991] 1 N.Z.L.R. 439.

3

THE HUMAN RIGHTS ACT

Origins and intentions

Confronting the Human Rights Act: Contemporary themes and perspectives,
Nicolas Kang-Riou et al. (eds) (Routledge, 2012)

Former US President Ronald Regan once said 'in America, our origins matter less
than our destination'.[1] The point about the Human Rights Act (HRA) is that its
not possible to understand its destination without *some* knowledge of its origins,
which contrary to tabloid legend, was neither an edict from Brussels nor an
ultimatum from Strasbourg.

Beginnings

Like the origin of the species, the HRA's precise evolutionary history is open
to some debate. Its gestation can be traced to 1968, a time when the sometimes
authoritarian chickens of the British Parliament came home to roost. The 1968
Commonwealth Immigrants Act was passed with all-party support by a panicky
Parliament, led by a Labour Government, in three days. Its sole purpose was to deny
British Asians expelled from East Africa entry to the UK, at the precise moment
when they sought to rely on their UK citizen status to protect them.[2]

A slumbering consciousness began to stir. The renowned lawyers Anthony Lester and John MacDonald produced pamphlets calling for a bill of rights to establish
some bottom-line principles and standards which would frame UK law.[3] Commentators and academics began to debate in earnest whether the famed UK doctrine
of parliamentary sovereignty could ever adequately protect minorities whose voting
power would forever be minimal; in so far as it existed at all. Under this doctrine,
Acts of Parliament not only trumped the common law, but were largely safe from
judicial review.[4]

In 1974, this nascent debate took a further leap when Sir Leslie Scarman, the
esteemed judge and subsequent law lord, chose to devote the first of his Hamlyn

Lectures to the question of a bill of rights. In a famous passage harking back to the 1968 Immigrants Act he said:

> 'when times are normal and fear is not stalking the land, English law sturdily protects the freedom of the individual . . . but when times are abnormally alive with fear and prejudice, the common law is at a disadvantage; it cannot resist the will . . . of parliament.'[5]

Surprisingly to modern audiences (in the light of the Tory Party's 2010 manifesto to scrap the HRA), it was the Society of *Conservative* Lawyers (SCL) who were amongst the first to link this call for a bill of rights with incorporation of the 1950 European Convention on Human Rights (ECHR) into UK law. The SCL recommended in their 1976 report *Another Bill of Rights?* that 'the ECHR should be given statutory force as an over-riding domestic law'.

Although inspired by the Universal Declaration of Human Rights, promoted by Winston Churchill and largely drafted by UK lawyers, Britain was one of the few countries in Europe that had not incorporated the ECHR into domestic law – only the government was bound by its terms following ratification in 1951.[6] Parliament, the courts and other public authorities were not. Most people in the UK were barely aware of the rights they were entitled to under the ECHR, except when the government lost a case at Strasbourg and the tabloids invariably protested at what they would characterise as rule by foreign judges.

Two years after the SCL report, the Conservative Lord Chancellor, Lord Hailsham, pronounced that 'in this armoury of weapons against elective dictatorship' – which is how he famously described the then Labour Government – 'a bill of rights, embodying and entrenching the European Convention, might well have a valuable . . . part to play'.[7]

Seeds of change

In the 1980s, the next push came from the perceived failure of Parliament to brook virtually any successful challenges to a now Conservative Government which, on the basis of three elections on a minority vote, could bring in almost any measure it wished. A legislature thoroughly dominated by the executive offered very little protection against a government determined to push through unpopular laws like the Poll Tax – or less unpopular, but in the view of civil libertarians just as troubling – measures like the Public Order Act 1986, the Official Secrets Act 1989, successive Prevention of Terrorism Acts[8] and the removal of the ancient right to silence.[9]

Although they sometimes strained to apply human rights principles like proportionality and necessity,[10] judges faced considerable restrictions when seeking to hold the executive to account, compared to many of their European counterparts and jurisdictions with constitutional bills of rights. The decisions or actions of the government or other public bodies could only be overturned if illegal or beyond the range of responses open to a so-called 'reasonable decision maker'.[11] Demonstrating that an interference with a fundamental human right is 'proportionate' and 'necessary' – the post-HRA test – requires a *much* higher level of justification than whether an interference is merely 'reasonable'. Sometimes it seemed as if public officials had to be so 'irrational' as to be virtually certifiable before their *decisions* would be quashed. Pre-HRA, the courts were effectively barred from reviewing primary *legislation* altogether.

The frustration of the judiciary came to a head in the case of *Smith* in 1996 over the ban on gay men and women serving in the military. Sir Thomas Bingham, then Master of the Rolls, strongly signalled his regret that he could not ask whether this measure was 'proportionate' or 'necessary'; only whether it was 'reasonable'.[12]

To the further embarrassment of our courts, the European Court of Human Rights (ECtHR), which subsequently overturned the ban when our courts could not, subtly damned the British constitutional system for effectively excluding any consideration of the human rights of the sacked personnel.[13]

The formation of Charter 88 in 1988 had placed support for a bill of rights firmly on the political agenda. This elite, but growing, campaign provided the impetus for the HRA. In those days, the marriage between calls for a bill of rights and incorporation of the ECHR into UK law seemed as self-evident as that of David Cameron and Nick Clegg today.

Whilst some pressure groups and think tanks – including Liberty and the Institute for Public Policy Research[14] – produced model bills of rights that went further than the ECHR, incorporation of a human rights treaty that the UK government was already bound by, was generally agreed to be the simplest and most logical way to introduce a bill of rights in the modern world. Canada – and subsequently New Zealand – did something broadly similar in basing their bills of rights on the International Covenant on Civil and Political Rights.[15]

After Labour lost the fourth election in a row in 1992 the new leader, John Smith, a Scottish lawyer who had a long-term personal interest in devolution and constitutional reform, committed his Party to support a British bill of rights as part of a package of proposals for democratic renewal. Echoing the former Tory Lord Chancellor, Lord Hailsham, he maintained that 'what we have in this country at the moment is not real democracy; it is elective dictatorship'.[16] In a watershed speech to Charter 88, Smith affirmed, like others before him, that 'the quickest and simplest way' of introducing 'a substantial package of human rights' would be to pass a Human Rights Act 'incorporating into British law the European Convention on Human Rights'.[17]

The 1993 Labour Party conference adopted a National Executive Committee statement, introduced by Home Affairs spokesperson Tony Blair, supporting an all-party commission to 'draft our own bill of rights' which would go further than the ECHR and was presumed to include social and economic rights.[18] In contemporary jargon, this second stage was to be unambiguously 'HRA plus'.

Support for a bill of rights was not uniform on the left – far from it. There was considerable opposition within the Labour party and amongst some radical lawyers.[19] The first Labour Party document to propose the incorporation of the ECHR into UK law, *A Charter of Human Rights*, was published in 1976. The National Executive Committee would not allow the paper to be presented as official policy but only as an issue for debate. This bill of rights scepticism was more political than constitutional, revolving round the feared impact on a democratically elected, centre-left government of public school, Oxbridge-educated judges overturning laws they disagreed with, under the guise of a bill of rights.[20]

New Labour triangulation

New Labour's scepticism about the HRA, which developed over time, was of a different kind. When Tony Blair stood as leader of the Labour Party after John Smith's untimely death in May 1994, he signalled continuity with his predecessor's agenda by including support for a bill of rights in a candidate statement not overburdened with policies. This was important for Blair politically as in most other ways the birth of New Labour represented discontinuity with even the immediate past.

Only two years later, as the general election was approaching, this pledge for a bill of rights was trimmed to a more technical-sounding commitment to incorporate the ECHR into UK law. It was no longer presented as a bill of rights *based* on the European Convention but as simply the logical next stage for complying with an international treaty which the government was *already* bound by.

Yet at the same time, constitutional reform as a *package* had become one of the badges of New Labour; a set of measures to signal that it still had a distinct radical programme whilst it was fast distancing itself from its socialist past. But there was little attempt to link different aspects of this programme into a coherent whole, let alone tie it into the party's traditional agenda for social justice.

This triangulated message – in which the HRA was simultaneously presented as both a radical departure on the one hand and a technical, tidying up exercise on the other, depending on the audience and the minister – seeped into the parliamentary debate and extra-parliamentary lectures and interviews which greeted the introduction of the HRA.

From this time onwards, ministers presented contrasting purposes for the Act.

On the one hand, it was introduced to 'bring rights home' – in the well-worn phrase and title of the White Paper which ushered it in – so that individuals could claim the ECHR rights they were entitled in the domestic courts.[21] The purpose was to 'enable people to enforce their human rights in the courts of the United Kingdom rather than having to take their case to Strasbourg . . . [to provide] better and easier access to rights which already exist'.[22]

On the other hand, the intentions behind the Act were apparently far more ambitious and fundamental. Ministers declared that the HRA was designed as a constitutional measure[23] to modernise and democratise the political system[24] and lead to cultural change beyond the courts.[25] The late Lord Williams, speaking as a Home Office Minister in the House of Lords debate on the HRA, specifically *contradicted* the 'bringing rights home' mantra when he said:

'[this] is not, as the Lord Chancellor pointed out, simply "you will be able to get your rights enforced quickly and cheaply because you will not have to make the journey to Strasbourg". *It is much more important than that.* Every public authority will know that its behaviour, its structure, its conclusions and its executive actions will be subject to this culture.'[26]

The then Home Secretary, Jack Straw, described the HRA as 'the first major bill on human rights for more than 300 years'[27] and 'the first bill of rights this country has seen for three centuries'.[28] This was then a fairly standard description of the HRA including by the eminent judge Lord Steyn,[29] the *New York Times*[30] and legal academics.[31] But if the *political* rhetoric as to the HRA's purpose was deliberately ambiguous – the better to court different audiences – the *legal* scheme adopted was much clearer as to the *intentions* behind the Act.

The British model

Sometimes referred to by Jack Straw, as 'the British model', it is possible to summarise – in very broad terms – the legal and constitutional intentions of the HRA as follows:

1) The primary purpose was *not* the technical incorporation of a human rights treaty, but the adoption of the rights in the ECHR as the basis for a specifically *UK* bill of rights, in response to years of lobbying for such a measure (*HRA s2*).

2) Almost without precedence in UK domestic law, the HRA would be a *higher law* whose broad principles would set the parameters of all other legislation and policy – past, present and future – except where Parliament explicitly, or by strong implication, had contrary intentions (*HRA s3*).

3) With no judicial strike-down power, the model would not fundamentally disturb the doctrine of parliamentary sovereignty, which there was no general appetite, let alone consensus, to overturn. Parliament would be given an explicit role in overseeing the operation of the HRA (through the establishment of the proposed Joint Committee on Human Rights).[32] Should the courts issue a Declaration that an Act of Parliament was incompatible with the fundamental rights in the HRA there would be no legal obligation on the executive or legislature to change the law in question, or even necessarily to respond to it. Nevertheless, the courts were empowered to hold the executive to account where they were impeded before (*HRA ss4, 6 and 19*).

Despite contemporary political and media commentary that the HRA was designed not just to incorporate most of the rights in the ECHR but the *totality* of its case law, there was no original intention to require UK judges to slavishly follow Strasbourg jurisprudence. Quite the contrary.[33] The parliamentary debate reveals that the language of the relevant section (2) was purposefully drafted to avoid the domestic courts from being bound by Strasbourg jurisprudence, whilst still requiring them to 'take [it] into account.' The 'distinctly British contribution'[34] our courts would make to developing European human rights jurisprudence was emphasised in the parliamentary debates on the Human Rights Bill and the accompanying White Paper:

> 'The Convention is often described as a "living instrument" . . . In future our judges will be able to contribute to this dynamic and evolving interpretation of the Convention.'[35]

Jack Straw explained when piloting the Bill through the House of Commons:

> 'Through incorporation we are giving a profound margin of appreciation to British courts to interpret the Convention in accordance with British jurisprudence as well as European jurisprudence.'[36]

Interestingly, given the vocal concerns of the current Prime Minister about the impact of European Court of Human Rights jurisprudence on British law,[37] the then Labour government rejected an amendment by the Shadow Lord Chancellor, Lord Kingsland, to make our courts 'bound by' Strasbourg jurisprudence.[38] The Lord Chancellor, Lord Irvine, said it would be 'strange' to require our courts to be bound by all European Court decisions when the UK is not bound in international law to follow that Court's judgments in non-UK cases. The Bill would 'of course' permit domestic courts to depart from Strasbourg decisions and 'upon occasion it might be appropriate to do so.' The Tory amendment, he said, would risk 'putting the courts in some kind of straitjacket where flexibility is what is required . . . our courts must be free to try to give a lead to Europe as well as to be led.'[39]

Lord Irvine addressed the question which has subsequently occupied the domestic courts; the extent to which they should *mirror* Strasbourg:[40]

> 'Should a United Kingdom court ever have a case before it which is a precise mirror of one that has been previously considered by the European Court of Human Rights, which I doubt, it may be appropriate for it to apply the European court's findings directly to that case; but in real life cases are rarely as neat and tidy . . . The courts will often be faced with cases that involve factors perhaps specific to the United Kingdom . . . it is important that our courts have the scope to apply that discretion so as to aid in the development of human rights law.'[41]

Differing in his approach to interpreting the HRA (s2) from a number of his fellow judges, Justice Laws, who determined that 'the English court is not a Strasbourg surrogate,' summed up the original intentions behind the HRA fairly when he said in 2002:

> '. . . the court's task under the HRA . . . is not simply to add on the Strasbourg learning to the corpus of English law, as if it were a compulsory adjunct taken

from an alien source, but to develop a *municipal law of human rights* . . . case by case, *taking account* of the Strasbourg jurisprudence as s2 [of the] HRA enjoins us to do.'[42]

Lord Scott developed this 'municipal approach,' in a more recent House of Lords case maintaining:

'. . . [Under s2] the judgments of the European Court . . . constitute material, very important material, that must be taken into account, but domestic courts are nonetheless not bound by the European Court's interpretation of an incorporated article.'[43]

He also said that the 'possibility of a divergence' between the opinion of the European Court as to the application of a right and the opinion of the House of Lords is 'contemplated, implicitly at least, by the [HRA]'.[44]

Commenting on the relationship between domestic and European human rights law under the HRA, the legal scholar, Andrew Clapham, has suggested that the 'challenge' for 'national courts' is to 'treat international human rights as part of the national heritage' whilst interpreting such rights 'in the national context to give them the appropriate maximum protection at the national level.'[45]

Conclusion

Since the HRA came into force it has had some significant impacts both inside and outside the courts. Whilst the profound cultural change amongst public authorities that some had predicted in the HRA's early days has not materialised, an Equality and Human Rights Commission Inquiry report documented policies and practices that were a direct consequence of the Act.[46] For some commentators the legal and extra-legal effects of the HRA have been much too extensive, for others they have not gone far enough. Depending who you believe, the HRA is either a wolf masquerading as a sheep, or a sheep masquerading as a wolf.

Following the atrocities of 9/11 and 7/7[47] there were, of course, well-documented erosions of rights and freedoms here and elsewhere. But this also occurred in the USA, with its famed bill of rights and powerful judicial strike down powers, as much as in the UK. The Patriot Act, the Military Commissions Acts, the Real ID Act and the Detainee Treatment Act were all passed by the US Congress after 2001. Lord Mac-Donald, the former Director of Public Prosecutions, has estimated that, in his words, the HRA 'has stood up to the buffeting' more effectively than the US Bill of Rights, in the post 9/11 era.[48] The reality is that with very few exceptions,[49] bills of rights *only* allow the courts to review laws once they have been passed, not stop their introduction.

Now, just over a decade since the HRA came into force, the coalition government is establishing a Commission to consider replacing the HRA with a British bill of rights.[50] It is, of course, possible to draft a bill that builds on the HRA and is stronger in enforcement powers and broader in scope. There are many good examples to draw from.[51] But, unusually in the history of bills of rights worldwide, most of the pressure for a 'British Bill of Rights' comes from those who wish to *reduce* the scope of the judiciary because, in the words of the Prime Minister, David Cameron, 'it is about time we ensured that decisions are made in this Parliament rather than in the courts'.[52] This is despite the fact the HRA already leaves *the last word* with parliament and does not require the legislature to change the law, even when judges declare that statutes breach fundamental human rights. The Director of Liberty, Shami Chakrabarti, has asked, 'are [the government] not prepared to accept even this gentle model of constitutional protection for the people against our rulers?'[53]

There are, additionally, growing demands to decouple the HRA, or any subsequent bill of rights, from Strasbourg jurisprudence entirely.[54] Some of the same sources have welcomed high profile examples where the European Court of Human Rights has come to a different conclusion from the domestic courts, for example on the retention of the DNA of innocent suspects[55] or the use of anti-terrorism legislation to search peaceful protesters.[56] Both of these judgements will lead to changes in the law flagged for inclusion in the coalition government's Protection of Freedoms Bill.[57] In the meantime UK judges, whilst not bound by such decisions,[58] are now required to '*take into account*' this case law in subsequent similar fact cases, which they either could not, or would not, do prior to the HRA. It is difficult to see how rights will be enhanced by watering down or removing this link with Strasbourg jurisprudence, even if it were *possible* to ordain to judges – who already frequently cite the common law in interpreting the HRA – which sources of authority they should consult in a subsequent British Bill of Rights.

The eminent QC Rabinder Singh, who has frequently acted on behalf of governments, has described the HRA as 'a success story from a legal perspective. It has not been a damp squib. Nor has it overwhelmed the legal system.'[59] Although most of the cases where the HRA has been cited would have been taken anyway, many of them would not have achieved the same results. The Prime Minister maintains he is committed to 'proper rights,' but that 'they should be written down here in this country', signalling that for the first time since the second world war a mature democracy may seek to introduce a bill of rights in order to distance its legal system from international human rights law.[60] This could mark a new departure in the history of bills of rights and lead in a direction that the prominent Conservatives who once called for a UK bill of rights, based on the European Convention on Human Rights, could scarcely have contemplated.

Notes

1 Address to the Republican National Convention, Houston, 17 August 1992.
2 See David Steel MP, *No Entry, the background and implications of the Commonwealth Immigrants Act 1968*, Hurst, 1969.
3 Anthony Lester, *Democracy and Individual Rights*, Fabian Society, 1968; John MacDonald, *Bill of Rights*, Liberal Party, 1969.
4 Outside the context of EU law.
5 Sir Leslie Scarman, *English Law – the New Dimension*, Hamlyn Lectures, 1974.

6 The ratification took effect from 1953 and in 1966 individuals were given the right to take cases to the European Court of Human Rights (EctHR). See 'Churchill's Legacy: The Conservative Case for the Human Rights Act', Jesse Norman and Peter Oborne, Liberty, 2009 and 'Common Sense: Reflections on the Human Rights Act', Francesca Klug et al, Liberty, 2010, chapter 2.

7 *The Dilemma of Democracy*, Colins, 1978.

8 1984; 1989.

9 In the Criminal Justice and Public Order Act 1994.

10 These principles set the parameters within which most rights can be legitimately limited under the ECHR. *Handyside v UK* (1976) 1 EHRR 737. A restriction will be 'proportionate' only if the objective behind the restriction justifies interference with a Convention right, there is a rational connection between the objective and the restriction in question and the means employed are not more than is necessary to achieve the objective. See Francesca Klug and Keir Starmer, 'Incorporation through the back door?' *Public Law,* Summer 1997.

11 Under the so-called doctrine of Wednesbury unreasonableness.

12 *R v Ministry of Defence ex p. Smith* [1996] 1 All ER 257.

13 *Smith v Grady v UK* (1999).

14 See *A British Bill of Rights*, The Institute for Public Policy Research, 1990; *A People's Charter*, Liberty, 1991.

15 Canadian Charter of Rights and Freedoms 1982 and New Zealand Bill of Rights 1990, respectively.

16 'A New Way Forward', Speech, John Smith, Leader of the Labour Party, Bournemouth, 7 February 1993.

17 *A Citizen's Democracy,* Charter 88, March 1993.

18 See Francesca Klug, 'A bill of rights-what for?' *Towards a New Constitutional Settlement*, Smith Institute, pp130–145, 2007.

19 See, K. D. Ewing and C. A. Gearty, *Democracy or a Bill of Rights,* Society of Labour Lawyers, 1991.

20 See John Griffiths, *Politics of the Judiciary*, Fontana, 1977.

21 'Our aim is a straightforward one. It is to make more directly accessible the rights which the British people already enjoy under the Convention'. *Rights Brought Home, White Paper*, para 1.19, October 1997.

22 Lord Chancellor, Lord Irvine, Hansard, HL vol.585, col.755 (5 February 1998).

23 See Francesca Klug, 'The Human Rights Act 1998, *Pepper v. Hart* and All That' [1999] *Public Law* 246.

24 Jack Straw, then Home Secretary, said on introducing the Human Rights Bill: 'The Bill falls squarely within [our] constitutional programme. It is a key component of our drive to modernise our society and refresh our democracy . . . to bring about a better balance between rights and responsibilities, between the powers of the state and the freedom of the individual.' Hansard, HC vol.306, col.782–3 (16 February 1998).

25 Lord Irvine made many statements to the effect that: 'Our courts will develop human rights throughout society. A culture of awareness of human rights will develop.' Hansard, HL Vol.582, col.1228 (3 November 1997).

26 582 HL AT 1308. My emphasis.

27 Above, n.24 at col.769.

28 Speech, IPPR, 13 January 2000.

29 '. . . the Human Rights Act 1998 which is our Bill of Rights'. 'Democracy, the Rule of Law and the Role of Judges' [2006] *EHRLR* 243 at p246.

30 'Britain Quietly Says It's Time To Adopt a Bill of Rights', *New York Times*, 3 October 1999.

31 Keith Ewing, 'The Human Rights Act and Parliamentary Democracy' [1999] 62 *Modern Law Review* 79.

32 See 'The Klug Report: Report on the Working Practices of the JCHR', Francesca Klug, published in 'The Committee's Future Working Practices', Twenty-third Report of Session 2005–06.

33 See Francesca Klug and Helen Wildbore, 'Follow or lead? The Human Rights Act and the European Court of Human Rights' [2010] 6 *European Human Rights Law Review* 621.

34 *Rights Brought Home*, para.1.14. The consultation document which preceded the White Paper makes no reference to domestic courts having to take into account Strasbourg jurisprudence. It said that the failure to incorporate the ECHR meant that 'British judges are denied the opportunity of building a body of case law on the Convention which is properly sensitive to British legal and constitutional traditions' and that the European Court 'has not been able to benefit from the experience of the UK legal system or to develop an appreciation of British legal principles and traditions.' See *Bringing Rights Home: Labour's plans to incorporate the European Convention on Human Rights into UK law*, Jack Straw and Paul Boateng, December 1996.

35 *Rights Brought Home*, para.2.5.

36 Hansard, HC vol.313, col.424 (3 June 1998).

37 Cameron said 'It makes me physically ill even to contemplate having to give the vote to anyone who is in prison,' House of Commons Hansard, 3 November 2010. This was in response to the ECtHR judgment that the blanket ban on convicted prisoners voting breached Protocol 1 Article 3 ECHR in *Hirst v UK* (2005).

38 Hansard, HL Vol.583, col. 511 (18 November 1997).

39 Ibid. at col. 514–5.

40 The eminent former Law Lord and Lord Chief Justice Lord Bingham controversially affirmed that 'The duty of national courts is to keep pace with the Strasbourg jurisprudence as it evolves over time: no more, but certainly no less.' *R (Ullah) v Secretary of State for the Home Department* [2004] UKHL 26, para 20.

41 Hansard, HL vol.584, col.1270–1 (18 January 1998).

42 *Runa Begum v Tower Hamlets* [2002] 2 All ER 668 para 17 (my emphasis). Justice Laws also determined that 'our duty is to develop, by the common law's incremental method, a coherent and principled *domestic* law of human rights,' *R (Pro-life Alliance) v BBC* [2002] 2 All ER 668.

43 *R (Animal Defenders International) v Secretary of State for Culture, Media and Sport* [2008] UKHL 15, para 44.

44 Ibid.

45 Andrew Clapham, 'The ECHR in the British Courts: problems associated with the Incorporation of International Human Rights', in *Promoting Human Rights through Bills of Rights*, OUP, 1999, pp134–5.

46 'Human Rights Inquiry', Report of the Equality and Human Rights Commission, 2009.

47 The terrorist atrocities in New York on 11 September 2001 and London on 7 July 2005.

48 Liberty's 75th Anniversary Conference, June 2009.

49 The French constitutional council provides pre-enactment judicial review.

50 The Coalition Programme for Government in May 2010 stated: 'We will establish a Commission to investigate the creation of a British Bill of Rights that incorporates and builds on all our obligations under the European Convention on Human Rights, ensures that these rights continue to be enshrined in British law, and protects and extends British liberties.'

51 See 'A Bill of Rights for the UK?', Joint Committee on Human Rights, 29th Report of Session 2007–08; *Repairing British Politics: A Blueprint for Constitutional Change*, Richard Gordon QC, Hart (2010); 'A Bill of Rights for Northern Ireland', Northern Ireland Human Rights Commission, 2008.

52 Prime Minister's Questions, HC, 16 February 2011.

53 'Warning: anti-justice stomach bug spreading', Shami Chakrabarti, *The Times*, 21 February 2011.

54 Attorney General Dominic Grieve said at a Politeia event on 14 February 2011: 'The [ECtHR] doesn't have the last word. It only has the last word so far as parliament has decided that it should. We could, if we wanted to, undo that . . .' quoted in the guardian. co.uk, 14 February 2011.

55 *Marper v UK*, ECtHR Grand Chamber, 4 December 2008.

56 Gillan and Quinton v UK, ECtHR 12 January 2010.

57 The Bill proposes the removal of DNA from the database of those arrested or charged but not convicted of minor offences, but the retention of DNA for three years for those arrested but not convicted of a serious or sexual offence. For stop and search, the Bill proposes to narrow searches in place and time and to be linked to a 'reasonably suspected' act of terrorism.

58 Only the government is bound to follow European Court of Human Rights judgments, even when they involve the UK.

59 'The HRA and the Courts: a practitioner's perspective,' *European Human Rights Law Review, Special Issue on 10th Anniversary of the HRA*, Francesca Klug and Jane Gordon (eds) Issue 6, 2010.

60 Prime Minister's Questions, HC, 1 December 2010.

4

THE HUMAN RIGHTS ACT

Basic principles and values[1]

Journal of Local Government Law (2001)

In these early days of the life of the Human Rights Act (HRA) there is, inevitably, a struggle for its soul. Three alternative descriptions of the HRA are currently competing for attention, of which the first two are the most familiar.

First, there is the caricature promoted by a large section of the media and increasingly (as a general election beckons) the front bench of the Conservative Party. This portrays the Act as a "crackpots' Charter" forced on the British people by the ever-expanding powers of Europe designed to benefit the BCDs only – barristers, criminals and deviants. The minimum wage will be introduced in prisons, uniforms outlawed in schools, polygamous marriages recognised – even though, in each instance, cases along these lines have been dismissed or struck out as manifestly ill-founded by the European Commission or Court of Human Rights.

Second, there is the view favoured by a number of lawyers who are generally sympathetic to the HRA. This presents the Act as a highly complex technical piece of law whose consequences – although difficult to predict – are far-reaching and likely to lead to a complete overhaul of the way some public authorities operate. From this perspective, the Act is not so much a challenge to legal culture as to the Government and public officials. Its broad effect will be to enhance individual liberties at the expense of public authorities. Stories about school uniforms and sex on school premises are loony, but the Act does introduce a whole range of freedoms never available before in this country. The focus is on the precise meaning of the words in the European Convention on Human Rights (ECHR) rather than its purpose. The message is: Public officials don't move without consulting a legal specialist.

Third, there is a vision of the HRA that predictably receives less public attention but which is being promoted not only by many human rights activists but by judges themselves in their first major rulings under the Act. From this standpoint human rights are essentially a set of ethical values for a pluralist and democratic society that – through the Human Rights Act – are now infiltrating our law. It is not that new rights have suddenly entered our legal system but that we did not have access to them before except through the European Court of Human Rights in Strasbourg – a long and expensive journey. What has entered our legal system is a moral code which places the liberties of the individual in the context of the legitimate needs of a democratic society. Although the ECHR has some overlap with British common law (which was in fact a major source of some of its principles such as fair trial rights) never before have we had a set of written values that effectively act as a higher law influencing all other laws and policies, past present and future. In the recent landmark case of *Brown* which confirmed the compatibility of section 172 of the Road Traffic Act 1988 with the HRA Lord Steyn said:

> "The fundamental rights of individuals are of supreme importance but those rights are not unlimited: we live in communities of individuals who also have rights. The direct lineage of this ancient idea is clear: the European Convention (1950) is the descendant of the Universal Declaration of Human Rights (1948) which in article 29 expressly recognised the duties of everyone to the community and the limitations on rights in order to secure and protect respect for the rights of others."[2]

If we are to accept this third characterisation that views the Human Rights Act as fundamentally a code of values for the public sector what kind of values are they, where do they come from and how should they be applied? To answer this we need to look at both the principles that drive the ECHR and the main characteristics of the HRA.

The evolution of rights

The idea of inalienable rights did not emerge fully clothed out of the minds of the great philosophers to be handed over to judges and legal theorists for interpretation. Its evolution has been a complex process in which large numbers of people have played a central role fuelled by the major events of their day.

The simple but powerful idea that individuals have inalienable rights just because they are human and that no government has the legitimacy to take these fundamental rights away, remains the enduring principle that binds all fundamental rights charters from the late eighteenth century to the present day.

What I call the "first wave of rights",[3] emerged in the context of the American War of Independence and the French Revolution, fuelled by the experience of tyrannical regimes and religious dogma. Liberty, autonomy and justice were the predominant values that characterised rights at this time. The state and all public officials were portrayed as potential oppressors. The idea of fundamental human rights was – at its simplest – aimed at reducing their power.

But the Second World War – and the events which led up to it – brought a new context to the idea of fundamental rights. The brutality that individuals and groups were capable of visiting on each other was exposed. The Nuremberg trials established that individuals as well as states could bear legal responsibility for the heinous crimes committed.

It was with this backdrop that the 1948 Universal Declaration of Human Rights (UDHR) was drafted. It was as much an attempt to establish a set of universal ethics for diverse societies as a declaration of individual rights. The task was not just to set the people free but to find common values in which the liberties of individuals would be respected without weakening the bonds necessary for a society to flourish. It was a different understanding of the concept of freedom.

> "All human beings . . . should act towards one another in a spirit of brotherhood." Bellowed Article 1.

> "Everyone has duties to the community in which alone the free and full development of his personality is possible." Commanded Article 29.

This "second wave rights" vision does not begin and end with isolated individuals pitted against mighty states; individuals who, in the words of the 1789 French Declaration of Rights, should have the power "to do whatever is not injurious to others". Instead it is a vision in which the "personality" of individuals can only effectively develop in community with others. Likewise, states were no longer only viewed as potential oppressors but had a responsibility to take the lead in developing a "moral code" that would make a reality of the phrase *"never again"*.[4]

Since the UDHR was "adopted the struggle for human rights has largely been a quest to create a better world for everyone. The drafters of international human rights treaties, including the ECHR, have sought to establish a framework of values driven not just by the ideals of liberty, autonomy and justice but also by such concepts as community, equality and dignity.

Increasingly, more and more people world-wide are relating to the great debates about fundamental rights, wresting control through the web and other modern communications from the well-intentioned international standard setters and jurists who have monopolised the human rights project since the Second World War. Because of this – and because rights are increasingly presented as more than just claims against governments but also as a set of obligations that individuals owe to each other – I would argue that a new value of mutuality can be said to characterise an emerging third wave of rights.

The ECHR

What has all this to do with the HRA? Well, once the philosophical underpinning of human rights is appreciated, the legal principles which have developed as a consequence are much easier to understand.

The ECHR is of course a child of the 1948 UDHR as acknowledged in its preamble. More specifically, it is a regional treaty drafted in 1950 to provide legal enforcement through the European Court of Human Rights of most of the civil and political rights in the UDHR.

Other than the most fundamental rights of all – to life, to freedom from slavery and torture, and to no punishment outside the rule of law – all the rights in the ECHR are qualified in particular circumstances or limited in general terms to protect the rights of others or the wider community in a democratic society. These limits on rights establish their scope and by implication the obligations individuals have to others and the wider society. If my right to privacy can be limited to protect your right to health, for example, then what is signposted to me is that there are legitimate limits to my claim to autonomy when it comes to spreading contagious diseases or smoking in public places. In this sense it is true to say that the Human Rights Act establishes the broad responsibilities as well as the fundamental rights of the individual.

It is entirely wrong, therefore, to view the new Act as a purely libertarian character. If it were, why aren't hormonally-driven teenagers going at it like rabbits on the premises of schools in the 40 other European states which have incorporated the ECHR into their domestic law? According to our press there would be nothing head teachers could do to stop this now the HRA is in force.

Nor is the ECHR a technical piece of law like any other where its meaning can be found only in the precise terms that it uses. If this were the case how could you make sense of the following?

> "Everyone has the right to freedom of expression . . . the exercise of these freedoms, since it carries with it duties and responsibilities, may be subject to such formalities, conditions, restrictions or penalties as are prescribed by law and are necessary in a democratic society, in the interests of: national security, territorial integrity, public safety, for the prevention of disorder or crime, for the protection of health or morals, for the protection of the reputation or rights of others, for preventing the disclosure of information received in confidence, or for maintaining the authority and impartiality of the judiciary."[5]

As many people have commented when looking at that list: *what human rights treaties give with one hand they take away with another.* Many lawyers and legal academics who assumed a literal reading of the ECHR in the past were opposed to its incorporation into our law for that reason.

To make sense of this apparent conundrum the European Court of Human Rights in Strasbourg has developed 5 *major principles for interpreting the ECHR.* Through the Human Rights Act our judges, magistrates and tribunal chairs are now bound to take account of – if not directly apply – these principles when enforcing domestic law.[6]

1. *The twin doctrines of legality and proportionality.* This is the bridge between a right and its qualifications or limitations. Any limits on rights must be:

    (a) *"prescribed by law"*. This does not mean just any old law. A law restricting freedoms must not only be accessible enough for you to know that it exists but it must be formulated with sufficient precision to enable you to regulate your behaviour accordingly. It's no good arresting someone for leaving their mobile phone on during a conference under a law prohibiting "irresponsible behaviour" when no-one could have reasonably known they were committing a criminal offence in the first place!

(b) *proportionate.* This is the defining approach to balancing conflicting rights with each other and with the interests of the wider society. Even where there is a legitimate reason for restricting rights which falls into one of the grounds listed above (public health, national security, etc.) officials must still show that such restrictions do not go beyond what is strictly "necessary" to achieve that legitimate purpose "in a democratic society".

It is important to note that where a fundamental right is limited the burden falls on the public body concerned to demonstrate that the particular measure involved is proportionate. It is not for the citizen to prove that an official has acted "unreasonably", as has been the case until now. Through the vehicle of the HRA, the ECHR has killed Wednesbury reasonableness stone dead with the sword of proportionality (at least as far as cases involving civil and political rights is concerned).

So, for example, when a German teacher was dismissed for membership of the Communist Party, the European Court of Human Rights ruled in 1996 that this was an extreme measure because teaching does not intrinsically involve any security risks – some teachers may beg to differ – and membership of the CP was lawful.

2.   The second major ECHR principle that our courts will now have to take account of is its *"purposive" value-laden nature.* The ECHR is not a technical piece of law and it requires a non-technical approach to interpretation. In a relatively early case the European Court of Human Rights established that under the ECHR "it is necessary to seek the interpretation that is most appropriate in order to realise the aim and achieve the objects of the treaty."[7] And what are these objects? In addition to the broad philosophical approach borrowed from the UDHR referred to above, the European Court of Human Rights has singled out promotion of "the ideals and values of a democratic society" characterised by "pluralism, tolerance and broadmindedness".

Adopting this purposive approach, the European Court of Human Rights has "read rights into" the Convention in order to fulfil its overall aim. It has held, for example, that the right to a fair trial involves a right of access to a court even though this was not written into the treaty itself. It has also found that the right to a fair trial involves protecting witnesses and victims in the conduct of that trial as well as the interests of defendants. Again these rights are nowhere to be found in the body of the text.

This purposive approach can be a real cultural shock to United Kingdom lawyers who are generally not used to straying from the literal meaning of a text when interpreting a law let alone looking at its overall aim. Predictably it will take a while before the required cultural shift from a technical to a purposive or teleological principle of interpretation has taken place.

3. The third major principle developed by the European Court of Human Rights is intended to guarantee rights that are *practical and effective,* not illusory or theo-retical. This principle is a descendant of the last. It has led directly to a related concept – that governments and public bodies must not only refrain from abus-ing rights but have "positive obligations" in certain circumstances to prevent violations from occurring even when it is individuals abusing each other (note the direct lineage from the UDHR here). It is not much use having a right to life, for example, unless the Government has some obligation in law to protect you from contagious diseases or violent murderers.

    This approach can have significant implications for public authorities. It inevita-bly means that public bodies need to review their policies and procedures to ensure that they have in place sufficient measures to prevent rights abuses. It is not enough for public authorities to satisfy themselves that they are not breaking the law.

    The European Court of Human Rights has explicitly ruled, for example, that governments have a 'positive obligation' to put in place "effective criminal law pro-visions" to deter offenders as well as "law enforcement machinery" to deal with the perpetrators of violent crime.[8] This duty can extend to the adequate investigation of suspicious deaths or other serious offences.

    This could have implications for law enforcement agencies, from the police to the CPS. It could also have consequences for local authorities. So, for example, a group of tenants plagued by serious anti-social behaviour on their housing estate may be able to argue that their council has failed to protect them adequately. They may try to use the Human Rights Act to force their local housing depart-ment to bring proceedings for anti-social behaviour orders against a particularly troublesome gang of youths. In such circumstances the Human Rights Act would not impose any additional burdens on local authorities but could help to ensure that their current powers are appropriately applied. In most cases, hopefully, this could be resolved without anyone having to resort to the law courts.

4. The fourth major ECHR principle is known as the *living instrument* principle. When interpreting the Convention, the European Court of Human Rights has adopted a dynamic and forward-looking approach which takes account of "present day conditions" rather than a static and historical one. Again this stems from the purposive and value-laden nature of the law.

    In many ways this is almost a mirror image of the classical common law approach. Instead of the oldest law having the greatest weight as under English law, the newest case law tends to be the most persuasive for the European Court of Human Rights. Instead of a doctrine of precedent the Strasbourg court has operated a doctrine of evolutionary law. This is likely to pose a major challenge to our judges' traditional way of doing things.

    In adopting this "living instrument" approach the European Court of Human Rights has declared, for example, that although distinctions between "legitimate" and "illegitimate" children may have seemed acceptable in the 1950s this was not so in the late 1970s.[9] Now in the twenty first century the Court is edging close to establishing transsexual rights; something the shadow Home Secretary, Anne Widdicombe, would be quite right to point out was not in the mind of the original drafters.[10] But then by now it should be clear that that is the whole point of purposive law.

5.   Finally, the European Court of Human Rights has developed a doctrine which it has called the *margin of appreciation* to distinguish between those cases where it is the "domestic authorities" that should determine the appropriate limitations on a right and those where it is appropriate for a regional human rights court to do so. Truth be told, this doctrine has as much to do with diplomacy as any fundamental principle. The Court has always known that to maintain its legitimacy among a growing number of Council of Europe member states it is better not to encroach on national sovereignty too often, especially where social and economic or moral and philosophical issues (which have been extended to include our blasphemy laws, for example) are at stake. It is because of this doctrine that ECHR case law is comparatively underdeveloped in a whole range of areas (*e.g.* planning and tax law). When our courts – being a "domestic authority" – come to rule on these areas they will be operating in relatively virgin territory.

The HRA

Finally, there is the Human Rights Act itself. Once the underlying philosophy and principles behind human rights law in general, and the ECHR in particular, is understood the main features of the HRA fall easily into place. *There are really only three essential principles to grasp about the new Act.*

First, it is a higher law. It is, in this sense, different from all others laws on the statute book in that it influences all relevant legislation and policies whenever they were introduced. (The only close parallel is EU law but that of course only applies to areas where the EU has "competence"). Even the equalities legislation only applies to the specific areas covered like employment and goods and services. *The HRA is, in other words, our first modern bill of rights.*

*   *The HRA qualifies for the description of a bill of rights because under section 3 all laws and regulations must be interpreted to comply with the rights in the HRA "so far as it is possible to do so".* A slightly weaker clause in the New Zealand bill of rights allowed judges to effectively "read in" rights to statutes with invisible ink or narrow down breaches of rights. For example, in the well-known case of MOT *v. Noort*, the courts "read in" the right of individuals to consult a lawyer, at least over the telephone, when they are being breathalysed even though not a word of this was contained in the New Zealand Transport Act 1962. In the first case under the HRA involving section 3 to re-interpret legislation, the Court of Appeal ruled that section 2 of the Crimes (Sentences) Act 1997 (otherwise

known as the "two strikes and you're out provision") had hitherto been applied in a disproportionate manner.[11]

- *The HRA is a bill of rights because the courts themselves are directly required not to act incompatibly with the HRA* which means they must develop their own law – the common law – to conform with the rights in the HRA. This should also mean that any case which comes before the courts, even a divorce or custody case involving two private individuals, must conform with the HRA, affecting private as well as public law.

- *The HRA is a bill of rights because under section 19 ministers are required to give new legislation a human rights health check.* When introducing a new bill to Parliament the minister in charge must make a statement before second reading that the legislation complies with the HRA or otherwise. As ritualistic as this has become – all bills have been found to comply so far – this provision not only gives backbenchers who are willing to stray from their pagers the opportunity to quiz ministers about their statement but gives the green light to judges to assume that new laws must be able to be interpreted to comply with Convention rights.

- *The HRA is a bill of rights because it goes much further than incorporating a human rights treaty into our law.* Under Section 2 of the Act judges, while required to "take account of ECHR case law" are not bound by it. This means that although the substantive rights in the HRA come from the ECHR, our courts will not merely parrot the European Court of Human Rights. Where the jurisprudence on an issue is very outdated or effectively non-existent because of the "margin of appreciation" doctrine explained above, United Kingdom judges can cite case law from other bills of rights in Canada, New Zealand, South Africa or America, for example, or indeed from other international human rights instruments. Early cases under the HRA suggests the courts are willing to do this where appropriate.

The second essential principle is that the HRA may be a bill of rights but it is a bill of rights with a difference. For the first time ever the courts are required to import the rights in the ECHR into their interpretation of legislation and for the first time ever judges have the authority to review Acts of Parliament – something they were constitutionally barred from doing before now. But unlike most bills of rights – *e.g.* America, Germany and South Africa – the courts cannot overturn statutes or strike them down as unconstitutional. To this extent our courts have less power under the HRA than they do under EU law. What the higher courts can do instead when they cannot interpret a law to comply with the HRA without effectively overturning it, is to make a declaration that the Act in question breaches the HRA – what is called a "declaration of incompatibility" under section 4. Where there are "compelling reasons" to do so, the Government can use a special fast-track procedure to introduce legislation to comply with the court's ruling under section 10.

We have seen how this is likely to work in the recent series of planning cases which led to one of the first notices that the courts intend to issue a "declaration of incompatibility". The Divisional Court held that the processes by which the

Secretary of State for the Environment made planning decisions and compulsory purchase and other orders were incompatible with Article 6(1) of the ECHR (the right to a fair hearing). In each case the minister's policy was at issue rendering him an adjudicator in his own cause. However the court did not find that the Secretary of State had acted unlawfully. Primary legislation required him to act the way he did. Under section 6(2) of the HRA it is not unlawful for a public authority to act incompatibly with a Convention right if an Act of Parliament so stipulates. The only course open to the court, therefore, is to issue a "declaration of incompatibility".[12]

This fetter on the courts' power to overturn Acts is another reason why the more sensational press reports on how civilisation as we know it is about to come crashing down as a result of the HRA is utter rubbish. If the Government of the day opposed the policy implications of a judicial ruling it could re-instate it by a clearly-worded Act of Parliament which could neither be re-interpreted to comply with the ECHR nor overturned.

Opposition to the courts having the kind of legislative power they effectively have in the US and elsewhere was one of the reasons why many commentators across the political spectrum opposed a bill of rights for this country for decades. In the end a unique British model was adopted which aims to set up a dialogue between the executive, legislature and the courts with the Government (through Parliament) having the final say. But the hostile press ignores this for the most part and rants and raves about judicial powers they don't actually have.

The third essential principle is that the HRA is a purposive piece of legislation just like the ECHR and every interpretation given through it, legally or otherwise, must fall within its purpose. *There are several layers to the purposes of the HRA:*

- It is clearly aimed at making the public (and to a more limited extent the private) sector more accountable for its actions according to internationally agreed human rights standards. That is why section 6 of the HRA explicitly requires public authorities – defined to include privately owned bodies which carry out public functions like Railtrack, as well as the courts themselves – not to act incompatibly with the HRA. This is a cultural as well as a legal requirement, leading inevitably to the kinds of audits of policy and procedure that have flown from the equalities legislation. The consequence could be that even if there is an initial burst of costly and time-consuming litigation public bodies should get into the swing of taking preventive actions – like reviewing their planning or care procedures – which might well prevent human rights cases from ever coming to court. In the first few months since the Act has been in force there has been no increase in civil cases and no evidence to suggest that a flood of human rights inspired cases are in the pipeline. Most of the cases where the Act has been cited would have been taken anyway.
- The other side of the coin, of course, is that the HRA is aimed at providing a mechanism by which individuals who have allegedly suffered human rights abuses (defined as victims under section 7) can challenge public bodies and receive an appropriate remedy where their claim is upheld. In line with

human rights philosophy as it has existed for 200 years, all individuals (not only citizens) in the United Kingdom now have positive rights. This means that individuals who have been prevented from challenging decisions in the courts in the past on so-called "public policy" grounds should find that they are no longer barred from making such claims. It also means that it is for officials to justify why fundamental rights to liberty or family life, etc., have to be restricted, that such restrictions are necessary in a democratic society and are proportionate to the legitimate aim sought (in accordance with the doctrine of proportionality described above).

• But the third purpose of the HRA is probably least understood. It is the facilitating of a decent democratic society in which the rights of the individual are appropriately balanced against the needs of others and the common good. There is a vision in the HRA of society as a whole. Everyone – from judges to officials, from ministers to individuals – are encouraged to be part of the enterprise of creating a fair and tolerant society. Just as for the first time we all have written, positive rights that we can all understand, so we now effectively have written limitations on those rights that broadly establish the appropriate boundaries of our freedoms. We can speak freely but not incite racial hatred, we can demonstrate but not cause others injury or severe harm, we are entitled to our autonomy but not to risk the health of others and so on and so forth.

These are the human rights values which have now entered our law through the Human Rights Act. In the end their survival will depend not only on the courts or government but on the extent to which they make sense of the perennial quest to find a way in which we can all live together in a diverse society. It is public authorities which are given a special responsibility under the Act to translate these ethical values into practical policies.

Notes

1 This is an edited and updated version of a speech given by Francesca Klug to the Harrogate Management Centre Conference, *The New Human Rights Act – Implications for Health & Social Care*, London, 2000.

2 *Procurator Fiscal & Advocate General v. Brown*, [2001] S.L.T. 59.

3 See Francesca Klug, *Values for a Godless Age: The story of the United Kingdom's new bill of rights*, Penguin, 2000.

4 See Johannes Morsink, *The Universal Declaration of Human Rights, origins, drafting and intent*, University of Pennsylvania Press, 1999.

5 ECHR, Article 10.

6 HRA, s.2(1).

7 *Wemhoff v. Germany*, [1979–1980] 1 E.H.R.R. 55.

8 *Osman v. UK*, [1999] 1 F.L.R. 193.

9 *Marckx v. Belgium*, [1979] 2 E.H.R.R. 330.

10 Most recently in *Sheffield and Horsham v. UK* [1999] 27 E.H.R.R. 163.

11 *R. v. Offen et al* [2001] Crim.L.R. 63.

12 *R. (on the application of Holdings & Barnes plc) v. Secretary of State for the Environment, Transport and Regions and other applications* [2001] E.G. 170.

5

THE PRESS, PRIVACY AND THE PRACTICAL VALUES OF THE HUMAN RIGHTS ACT

Justice Journal (December 2011)

*This is the speech that Professor Klug gave to Justice's joint fringe meeting with the Society of Labour Lawyers at the Labour Party Conference in September 2011. This was one of three meetings at each of the conferences of the major national political parties.**

Introduction

Responsibility is the word of the moment, isn't it? The well-worn phrase of preference under New Labour used to be 'rights and responsibilities' but lately these words have been decoupled. 'A decline in responsibility' was to blame for the riots, David Cameron told us. 'The twisting and misrepresenting of human rights . . . has undermined personal responsibility,' he said.[1] Was the Human Rights Act (HRA) responsible for the riots? It gives a whole new meaning to the phrase 'reading the riot act', doesn't it? Ed Miliband has also concurred that it was 'greed, selfishness, immorality and, above all, gross irresponsibility,' that drove the riots.[2]

Now there is nothing wrong with labouring the importance of responsibility. I personally *agree* that emphasising personal responsibility is *vital* in a fair and just society – provided that it is not license for punishing *most* those who have the *least*. The tabloids and Tory-supporting press also emphasise the theme of responsibility of course. In fact, they make a living out of it! They are particularly prone to do so to hammer the HRA as the source of a rights–obsessed, selfish, alien litigation culture. They do this every day in fact.

Responsibilities

What you can virtually guarantee they will *omit*, of course, is that the theme of responsibility is woven into the European Convention on Human Rights (ECHR),

* With special thanks to Helen Wildbore, Research Officer for the LSE's Human Rights Futures Project, who provided most of the background research for this speech.

most of whose rights were incorporated into our law through the HRA. Whilst a few of these rights are absolute (like freedom from torture and slavery), most are qualified or limited. This is usually to protect the rights of others and the common good.

As the late, great former Lord Chief Justice Lord Bingham put it: there is 'inherent in the whole of the ECHR . . . a search for balance between the rights of the individual and the rights of the wider society.'[3] For the press to mention this inherent approach would not only spoil a good story, it could draw attention to an inconvenient truth: that Article 10 ECHR, the right to free expression, explicitly states that free speech comes with 'duties and responsibilities'. This is not a very popular statement with many journalists. But, I suppose – with notable exceptions – the press is hardly alone in thinking that responsibilities apply to everyone but themselves.

Media hostility to HRA

We all cherish a free press and people all over the world risk prison, torture and even death to be able to speak their minds and criticise their governments. These days, many newspapers in our country are feeling the pinch as the new media and digital revolution threaten their long-term survival – something that should concern us all.

In light of this, perhaps it's not surprising that even before the HRA was introduced some sections of the press – and the tabloids in particular – opposed it vehemently. (I mean it when I *say not* all the press – *The Guardian* campaigned *for* the HRA for years.)

The now relentless campaign by the right wing and tabloid press to *repeal* the HRA cannot be understood outside their commercial vested interests. Why?

The answer lies in the legal framework that existed before the Act came into force in October 2000. At that time, our only legal remedy against press intrusion were torts such as breach of confidence, libel or malicious falsehood, none of which protected us from long-lens cameras or door-stepping journalists. They were pretty much free to be as feral as they liked.

Right to privacy

Despite the sometimes inflated boasts about the wonders of the common law, privacy was *not* a so-called 'basic interest' recognised by the common law before the HRA. The impact of this hit home in 1991 when the actor Gordon Kaye, star of the TV series *Allo Allo*, was involved in a car accident. Whilst recovering in hospital with head injuries, two journalists from the *Sunday Sport* entered his room without permission, photographed and interviewed him. Because of his injuries, Kaye had no recollection of this afterwards, but the journalists' article gave the impression he'd consented. Kaye tried unsuccessfully to get an injunction to stop publication. As Lord Justice Bingham stated in his judgment, the case highlighted 'yet again, the failure of both the common law of England and statute to protect in an effective way the personal privacy of individual citizens.'[4]

Interception of communications

In reality, the *practical* value of the HRA goes far deeper than introducing a gradually developing right to sue for breach of privacy. It is not an exaggeration to say that the entire phone hacking scandal would not have come to light were it not for a combination of the ECHR and the HRA. Without them, hacking would probably have remained legal, if not moral, and there would have arguably been no scandal to exploit.

'Was it human rights wot won the phone hacking scandal?' the lawyer Adam Wagner asked on his blog last July. He concluded that 'in a way it *was* the HRA which won a right of redress for the general public.' So, what's the back story? It is often forgotten now that there was no statutory regulation of interceptions of communications at all until the mid-1980s – the state could tap our phones and we had no means of stopping it.[5]

Regulation was only introduced by Margaret Thatcher's government because the UK fell foul of the ECHR. A few years earlier, antiques dealer James Malone learnt his phone had been tapped when he was wrongly suspected of handling stolen goods. He had to take his case to the European Court of Human Rights (ECtHR) in Strasbourg where the court ruled that the lack of *any* legal regulation of state interceptions of communications in the UK was a breach of the right to respect for private life under Article 8 ECHR.[6]

As a result, the UK passed the *Interception of Communications Act 1985*, regulating mail and phone interceptions. As was not unusual following Strasbourg judgments – then and now – this was a *minimal* response by the government to the court's findings. The 1985 Act only covered communications made on the *public* telecommunications system. So, in 1997, the UK government was found in breach of Article 8 once again when the calls of Assistant Chief Constable, Merseyside Police, Alison Halford were hacked on the *internal* phone system at her place of work; an interception which was not covered by the 1985 Act.[7]

By then, Labour was in power and pledging to introduce the HRA. As part of the preparation for its implementation, and following the *Halford* case, the government introduced the Regulation of Investigatory Powers Act (RIPA) shortly before the HRA came into force in October 2000.

RIPA and phone hacking

RIPA went well beyond the requirement in *Halford* to regulate interception of internal phones at work. It regulated interception of communications on *all* private networks, including mobile phones.

I cannot envisage any government doing *more* than Strasbourg requires now, but this was before 9/11 and the heyday of New Labour's support for constitutional reform, of which the HRA was a central part.

Although the HRA does not bind our courts to follow ECtHR case law (whatever you read in the press), they must now take Strasbourg rulings into account.

RIPA was passed in anticipation that our courts would declare the unregulated mobile phone networks in breach of the ECHR.

So without the HRA and without the Labour government introducing RIPA to comply with it and the ECHR:

- there would have been no conviction of private investigator Glenn Mulcaire;
- no demise of the *News of the World*;
- no Murdochs appearing before British parliamentary select committees;
- no discovery that Hugh Grant is not just a pretty face; and
- no Leveson Inquiry.

Protecting sources

The importance of the HRA in this story doesn't end there. When the Metropolitan Police tried to use the Police and Criminal Evidence Act (PACE) and the Official Secrets Act (of all measures) to require *The Guardian* journalists to disclose the confidential sources they used to expose the hacking scandal – unbelievably the only attempted prosecution in the scandal so far – Geoffrey Robertson QC, former *Times* editor Harry Evans and the chief executive of the Society of Editors all queued up to argue that the Met would fall foul of the HRA.

Whilst it would be an overstatement to claim that it was the HRA that won it again, the protection of journalists' sources is another area where the HRA and ECHR have transformed UK law. The common law again failed to provide special protection for journalists and their sources. When an investigative journalist was recently under pressure to reveal the source of a *Mirror* story about the moors murderer Ian Brady, the Court of Appeal used the HRA to protect him.[8]

Though you wouldn't know it (unless you're a *The Guardian* or *The Independent* reader), this is far from the only free speech protection made possible through the HRA. Others include:

- journalists' public interest defence in libel cases has been bolstered;[9]
- the media has been granted access to court of protection[10] hearings[11];
- anonymity orders under terrorism legislation have been set aside;[12] and
- the right to receive information under Article 10 has also been expanded.[13]

Wakeham and s12 HRA

In fact, the HRA contains a section which goes further than the free speech protections in the ECHR, and was a direct result of press lobbying. As the Human Rights Bill was passing through Parliament, Lord Wakeham, then chair of the Press Complaints Commission, proposed an unsuccessful amendment to exclude the media from the HRA altogether. Following detailed negotiations with the then Home Secretary, Jack Straw, s12 HRA was inserted to require the courts to 'have particular regard to the *importance* of . . . freedom of expression' when considering granting a remedy, such as an injunction.[14] This free speech provision is illustrative as to why the HRA is *itself a British* bill of rights; it does *not* just incorporate the ECHR lock stock and barrel into our law.

Injunctions

For months and months, if you can remember that far back – before Libya, before the riots and before the phone hacking scandal – we were reading on a daily basis about 'super-injunctions' issued by courts hell bent on destroying our freedom of speech. Super injunctions are undoubtedly problematic. Not only do they prevent publication of information which is claimed to be private, but also the injunction itself is subject to secrecy. Lord Justice Sedley has fairly described them as 'anathema not only to the press but to any system of open justice' but he has also explained that the courts only developed them because the press kept thwarting less restrictive injunctions.[15]

The now infamous – and thoroughly discredited – super-injunction preventing *The Guardian* from publishing details about Trafigura dumping toxic waste in the Ivory Coast, was, thankfully, a rarity. There have been no more than a dozen in five years[16] and the outrage they inspired may well have killed them off. Super-injunctions are often confused with the less restrictive 'anonymised injunction', which keeps the *names* of one or both of the parties secret, but doesn't prevent reporting of the *fact* of the injunction. Some of these should also never have been made.

The anonymised injunction that Sir Fred (the shred) Goodwin obtained to prevent disclosure about an affair with a colleague at Royal Bank of Scotland (RBS), was obviously wrong in most people's eyes. But if the courts hadn't partly rectified this mistake we wouldn't be talking about it now.[17]

It is very difficult to obtain accurate data, but excluding injunctions to protect children or vulnerable adults, reports suggest there have been only 69 anonymised injunctions in five years. Some of these were to prevent criminal trials collapsing, as in the recently re-opened Stephen Lawrence murder trial. Others concerned blackmail. Only 28 are said to concern men involved in extra-marital affairs – the main source of controversy.[18]

Is it necessarily wrong that the courts have ruled time and again that the rights of wives and children should be considered when a privacy injunction by a philandering husband is applied for?

Is it a breach of free expression when a mistress loses her chance to kiss and tell? I've never known the tabloids to champion the rights of women as doggedly as they have when former mistresses (and it is usually mistresses) have been prevented from selling their stories by the courts.

It's a perfectly sensible *business* decision to try to sell papers on the back of such stories of course – especially when your very survival is at stake. Waging a relentless campaign against the HRA and its privacy rights is a logical extension of this self-interest. But, pretending that this is in the name of a noble cause like free expression? John Milton's campaign for free speech in the name of 'God's partially revealed truth' it is not!

The ECtHR has long distinguished between political speech and gossip. The first is given far more protection than the second. The limits of acceptable criticism of politicians in their public life are far wider than those applying to the rest of us.[19] But tawdry and lurid allegations about an individual's private life – even politicians – aimed more at titillation than education, do *not* attract the same robust protection under Article 10, the right to free expression.[20] If politicians of all parties approve of this distinction, the next time they attack the European Convention on Human Rights they should be careful what they wish for!

Useful for everyone

Part of the prosecution case against the HRA is that it's only celebrities who've benefitted from privacy rights. Obviously they have the funds to take these cases and the decimation of civil legal aid will only make matters worse. But this 'privacy for pin-ups only' claim is an exaggeration.

Injunctions have been granted to protect a member of the public who didn't want the press to report his sex change[21] and to protect a couple from defamatory statements about misappropriating money from a family trust fund.[22] Mr Peck was certainly not a celebrity when he found his suicide bid, which had been unknowingly captured on CCTV, reported in the *Brentwood Weekly News* in a feature on the benefits of CCTV! Mr Peck took his case to the ECtHR and won.[23]

Only this month we learnt that the High Court is to hear a civil claim for breach of privacy from a number of alleged phone hacking victims, including Sheila Henry, whose son was killed in the 7/7 bombings. This 'test case' would be a new development of privacy law, to award the victims 'exemplary damages', to deter future hackers.

The privacy rights in the HRA have also protected:

- a mother and her children who were 'snooped' on by their council to determine whether they lived within a school catchment area;[24]
- a media co-ordinator for Campaign Against the Arms Trade photographed by the police leaving a meeting;[25] and
- the bereaved family of a 12-year-old boy when a coroner refused to read out his suicide note, citing his mother's right to privacy under the HRA.[26]

Conclusion

In this age of responsibility all *most* of us want, of course, is not injunctions and court cases but responsible journalism. All that *many* of us want is responsible and ethical leadership from our politicians, not the Prime Minister condemning the 'twisting and misrepresenting of human rights' one day,[27] and giving misleading information himself another day, for example, that the HRA prevents publication of pictures of riot suspects to bring them to justice.[28]

Perhaps one of the most irresponsible things New Labour ever did was to take this massive step of passing a bill of rights called the HRA and then wishing it would go away, taking almost no steps to explain or promote it. Is Nick Clegg going to remain the only leader of a political party to defend it?

As *The Guardian* journalist Jackie Ashley wrote last week, the Conservatives aren't joking when they say the HRA has to go. Perhaps it's time we all took some responsibility to explain and defend it.

Notes

1 'I want to reclaim our society and restore people's pride in Britain', the *Sunday Express*, 21 August 2011.
2 Ed Milliband, 'National Conversation', speech at Haverstock School, 15 August 2011.
3 *Leeds City Council v Price and others* [2006] UKHL 10.
4 *Kaye v Robertson* (1991) FSR 62.
5 Except for some specific offences relating to postal employees and interference with mail.
6 *Malone v UK* ECtHR, 1984.
7 *Halford v UK* ECtHR, 1997.
8 *Mersey Care NHS Trust v Ackroyd* [2007] EWCA Civ 101.
9 *Jameel v Wall Street Journal Europe* [2006] UKHL 44.
10 Which adjudicates when people lack mental capacity to make decisions themselves.
11 *A v Independent News* [2009] EWHC 2858 (Fam).
12 *Ahmed et al v HM Treasury* [2010] UKSC 1.
13 *Szabadságjogokért v. Hungary* ECtHR, 2009.
14 Section 12 also asserts that temporary injunctions to restrain publication before trial should not be granted unless the court is satisfied that the applicant 'is likely to establish that publication should not be allowed'.
15 'The Goodwin and Giggs Show', Stephen Sedley, the *London Review of Books*, Vol. 33, No. 12, 16 June 2011. See also Hugh Tomlinson, evidence to the PM Privacy Commission, BBC Radio 4, 13 June 2011.
16 According to figures cited in the *Daily Telegraph*, 14 May 2011 and *The Independent*, 25 May 2011. See also 'Report of the Committee on Super-injunctions', Lord Neuberger et al, 2011.
17 *Goodwin v News Group Newspapers Ltd* [2011] EWHC 1437 (QB).
18 According to figures cited in *The Independent*, 25 May 2011.
19 *Lingens v Austria* 1986.
20 *Von Hannover v Germany* 2004; *Société Prisma Presse v. France* 2003.
21 *The Independent*, 25 May 2011.
22 ZAM v CFW [2011] EWHC 476.
23 Peck v UK, 2003.
24 Paton v Poole Borough Council, decided by the Investigatory Powers Tribunal, 2 August 2010.
25 *Wood v Commissioner of Police for the Metropolis* [2009] EWCA Civ 414.
26 Reported in the *York Press*, 10 June 2011.
27 See note 1.
28 PM statement following riots, 10 August 2011.

6

ISSUES IN COMMUNICATING HUMAN RIGHTS

Unpublished conference paper, 2001

"To think justly, we must understand what others mean: to know the value of thoughts, we must try their effect on other minds."

(Author William Hazlitt, *The Plain Speaker,* 1826)

I learnt that lesson the hard way.

It was during the Gulf War when a taxi driver asked where I worked – I answered for Liberty (formerly the National Council of Civil Liberties).

I momentarily forgot the pragmatic Yiddish folk saying I learnt as a child – *"If you want people to think you are wise, agree with them"* and launched into a full throated defence of the principles of liberty and natural justice.

I soon realised I had managed to present myself as a threat – all five foot of me – and he was genuinely scared.

The challenge of communicating human rights effectively has never been more difficult; and never been more essential.

Promoting human rights effectively involves perfecting the art of being listened to as well as being heard. Throughout its history the human rights community has often found it extremely difficult to be heard. In some regimes of course this is literally so as human rights promoters are barred from most media outlets, harassed and persecuted.

Here in the West where these conditions don't by and large exist it is easy to lay the blame on others for obscuring our message – a sound-bite obsessed media, malevolent politicians, an ignorant and prejudiced public. Indeed in Western democracies communicating – or promoting – human rights should in theory be as easy as selling candy to a baby, or Nike trainers to teenagers. Western governments pride themselves on their human rights record. Human rights are meant to be one of the defining characteristics of Western democracy.

So why should it be so difficult to have a grown-up, meaningful dialogue on our human rights record, either in this country or abroad?

Why when the Human Rights Act was introduced last year was the press full of crazy stories about how school uniforms would be abolished, sex in school showers would become rampant, the prison doors would be flung open, and how virtually no-one would be convicted of a crime? (That is, if their case ever came to the courts in the first place which would be clogged up with the litigious-hungry public braying for compensation.)

It was almost impossible to get any but a tiny number of media outlets to explain that this was the first modern bill of rights for the people of this country who were belatedly joining the ranks of almost all of the democratic world – a landmark in our history.

Why, for that matter, every time the ECtHR finds against the UK government is it so easy for the press to present this as a deranged judgement by a power-mad European court of ignorant judges ranged against a blameless regime which has exported the idea of liberty and justice to most of the rest of the world and needs no lessons from anyone?

Why does there appear to be little or no basic understanding of what human rights are in this country, other than 'something most foreigners lack'?

To answer this honestly we need to take a long hard look at ourselves.

Talking of my own experience and mistakes, can we deny the confusion that we in the domestic civil liberties community have got ourselves into at times? When it comes to crime, we have historically allied ourselves with suspects and prisoners except if the victims happen to be black victims of racial violence or female victims of domestic violence. In which case we sometimes come across as caring little for the safeguards we insist should apply to other suspects.

Listening to us, it has sometimes appeared that some victims' rights are more crucial than others. We describe prosecutions under the official secrets acts or anti-terrorism laws as flagrant abuses of human rights but do we say that about the hundred children every year in this country who die at the hands of their parents, often after years of abuse and torture? Listening to many of us, we appear more concerned with spooks than school kids.

We say the right to life is inviolate but we seem to confine our concerns to the relatively small number of deaths that occur at the hands of the police or prison service in this country. As shocking as these murders are, our voices are rarely heard in support of the state taking action to protect us from violence which is not state driven, even though it is fear of criminals or terrorists that preoccupy most people most in their lives. Listening to us it can appear that although every death is equal, some seem more equal than others.

And what vision do we create of a society where human rights are respected? We talk about human rights as laws which can be enforced in courts when most people never enter a court room in their lives and have no intention of doing so.

We argue that legally enforceable rights are a fundamental part of our democracy, but the vision we sometimes create can seem painfully lonely and eccentric where isolated individuals pursue their individual wants and needs. This is very different from the democratic community most people aspire to where common sense dictates that the rights of individuals inevitably conflict, and have to be balanced at times with the needs of the community as a whole.

Many of these stances taken by the human rights community are completely understandable. In fact they can be more than that. They can be brave and they are often right. But they are nearly always partial. They are rarely enough.

Historically the human rights project has been driven by the mission of protecting the unpopular individual, the eccentric person or the minority group; those who cannot hope to be sufficiently protected by a system based on majority rule. From late 19th century America to modern Britain, politicians will always be seeking the popular mandate or the favourable headline.

This, of course, has been a major rationale for special laws safeguarding the human rights of every individual enforced by judges rather than elected politicians. (Although it should never be forgotten that the founding fathers of the American constitution apparently saw no contradiction between introducing a bill of rights to protect the minority from the majority whilst defining a slave as three fifths of a man.)

But human rights thinking has evolved substantially since the heady days of the Enlightenment which saw the French and American revolutions propel the idea of the 'fundamental rights of man' onto the world at large. This is only occasionally appreciated here in the UK, causing confusion and misunderstandings. As the author Lillian Helman once said: *"People change and forget to tell each other. Too bad. Causes so many mistakes."* Well it's a bit like that with human rights.

The post-war human rights framework promoted through the vehicle of the Universal Declaration on Human Rights – and the many treaties and declarations which have flowed from it – took human rights thinking a long way from the earlier 'first wave' model of the late Enlightenment of isolated individuals seeking protection from oppressive states.

This is not surprising. The UDHR was drafted by Muslims as well as Christians, by Confucians as well as Liberals, by Communists as well as Social Democrats. It was written in the aftermath of atrocities before and during the Second World War which were carried out not so just by states against their citizens but by states *and* citizens against those who were defined as 'outsiders,' as 'untermechen' – Jews, gypsies, gays and lesbians, disabled people.

Reflected in the UDHR is the realisation that for a human rights culture to sustain itself laws to protect individuals from tyrannical states, whilst essential, are not enough. What was needed, the drafters decided, was to establish a set of universal values based largely on the common ethical principles of the world's major religions and belief systems, suffused – so far as it was possible – with the old Enlightenment ideals of free speech, freedom of religion etc. Only if these values were widely accepted and understood would the peoples of the world hold their rulers sufficiently in check to guarantee human rights. Judges and courts could not be expected to do it alone.

The importance attached to the promotion of human rights values by individuals is reflected in the *preambles* to both of the legally binding treaties which flowed from the UDHR – the *ICCPR* & the *ICESCR* – which also emphasise the shift in 2nd wave rights thinking from a focus on liberty to a vision which embraces communitarian values as well:

> the individual, having duties to other individuals and to the community to which he belongs, is under a responsibility to strive of the promotion and observance of the rights recognised in the present Covenant.

So if our duty is to promote human rights, how do we do it? Well we don't go on replicating the same approach regardless of how many taxi drivers we enjoy infuriating on the grounds that our cause is bound to be unpopular, standing as we do for the unrepresented minority. As Spinoza said *"If you want the present to be different from the past, study the past."* We need to learn from our mistakes.

- We need to proclaim the obligation on states to protect us from the crime and violence of others every bit as loudly as we demand natural justice for the accused.
- We need to talk about the appalling abuse of children's human rights by their carers as one of the biggest human rights scandals of the modern world; we need to shift the terrain so that people associate us with *school kids more than spooks.*
- We need to liberate human rights from lawyers and return them to their rightful home – the people.
- We need to learn to talk of human rights as a set of values which influence law rather than 'black let laws' which you have to pay legal advisors to explain.
- And we need to draw from the richness of human rights thinking, as reflected in the UDHR – and its successor treaties – to explain what those values are. We need to repeat over and over again that outside those absolute rights like freedom from torture or slavery, the search for a fair and principled balance between the rights of the individual and the needs of the wider community underlines the whole of post-war (or 2nd wave) human rights thinking.

None of this means you've got to 'sell out' on the original goal of protecting the unpopular cause or unprotected minority.

In promoting human rights as universal values there is one dangerous trap of which we have to beware: we can sound like latter day missionaries.

How can we claim that human rights are universal when clearly they are disputed by so many groups of people world-wide?

How can we claim human rights are universal when parts of the world dismiss them as another form of Western imperialism, unevenly applied by Western government in furtherance of their foreign policy?

How can we claim human rights are universal when clearly most of the world experience tyranny and oppression in their daily lives?

How can we claim human rights are universal when social and economic rights – given equal significance in the UDHR – are barely recognised as such by any government in the world, West or East, North or South?

The only response I can muster is that human rights are universal in one sense only – they are applicable to every human being by virtue of their equal humanity.

But they are not universally accepted. Of course they are not. Nor are they ever likely to be. It is not enough to proclaim that human rights are universal for them to become so.

Universality can never be more than an aspiration. The struggle for human rights can never be won, even at an ideological level. The debate will never end, nor should it if the spirit of openness and enquiry which underlines human rights thinking is fully understood and respected.

But on the other hand this is a uniquely propitious time to be having such debates, not just in the UK but in the wider world. After a century of failed utopias there is an openness to fresh ideas most of us have not seen in our lifetime. The tightly drawn ideological battles which drowned out most of the subtleties of the human rights project since its inception no longer dominate the world. Human rights arguments seem fresh and appealing in many quarters where once they sounded week and stale.

There *is*, moreover, a way in which the universality of human rights is gradually being realised. It is through the developing conversation which is taking place on a global scale and is growing in volume and scope. Where once virtually every major national or international event was presented within the terms of a debate which pitted capital against labour, or socialism against free enterprise, an additional discourse is taking hold.[1] Through this global conversation the values and language of human rights are reaching more and more people who judge the merits or otherwise of state actions increasingly in human rights terms.

It is only by keeping the quest for human rights sufficiently attuned to *both* the anguished cries *and* cultural norms of those who need rights most that the aspiration for universal acceptance can hope to be sustained long term. Human rights are nothing if they do not inspire the imagination and give hope to those for whom hope has been previously denied.

No-one has expressed this better than Nelson Mandela who has eloquently made the point that despite the fact that the UDHR was adopted only a few months after the Apartheid regime formally took power, its resounding endorsement of equality proved inspirational:

> "For all the opponents of this pernicious system, the simple and noble words of the Universal Declaration were a sudden ray of hope at one of our darkest moments. During the many years that followed, this document . . . served as a shining beacon and an inspiration to many millions of South Africans. It was proof that they were not alone, but part of a global movement against racism and colonialism, for human rights and peace and justice."[2]

This, I suspect, is how to promote the moral power of human rights.

Notes

1 Following the recent elections in Iran, for example, there is evidence of an emerging Iranian democracy that respects human rights, drawing on values that are Islamic and Iranian as well as from international human rights norms.
2 Mary Robinson, 'The Universal Declaration of Human Rights: the international keystone of human dignity', p256, in *Reflections on the Universal Declaration of Human Rights*, B. van der Heijden and B. Tahzib-Lie, eds (The Hague: Kluwer, 1998).

SELECT BIBLIOGRAPHY

Arlidge, Anthony and Judge, Igor, *Magna Carta Uncovered*, Hart Publishing, 2014.

Benhabib, Seyla, *Dignity in Adversity: Human Rights in Troubled Times*, Polity, 2011.

Bhabha, Jacqueline, *Child Migration and Human Rights in a Global Age*, Princeton University Press, 2014.

Brownlie, Ian, *Principles of Public International Law*, 7th ed., Oxford University Press, 2008.

Bucar, Elizabeth M. and Barnett, Barbra, eds, *Does Human Rights Need God?* Eerdmans Publishing, 2005.

Chakrabarti, Shami, *On Liberty*, Penguin, 2014.

Clapham, Andrew, *Human Rights in the Private Sphere*, Clarendon Press, 1996.

Douzinas, Costas, *The End of Human Rights*, Hart Publishing, 2000.

Douzinas, Costas and Gearty, Conor, eds, *The Meanings of Rights: The Philosophy and Social Theory of Human Rights*, Cambridge University Press, 2014.

Finnis, John, *Human Rights and the Common Good: Collected Essays*, Oxford University Press, 2011.

Gearty, Conor, *Can Human Rights Survive?* Hamlyn Lectures, Cambridge University Press, 2006.

Gearty, Conor, *Principles of Human Rights Adjudication*, Oxford University Press, 2004.

Gearty, Conor and Douzinas, Costas, eds, *The Cambridge Companion to Human Rights Law*, Cambridge University Press, 2012.

Gerwith, Alan, *The Community of Rights*, University of Chicago Press, 1996.

Gilbert, Geoff, Hampson, Francoise, and Sandoval, Clara, eds, *Strategic Visions for Human Rights: Essays in Honour of Professor Kevin Boyle*, Routledge, 2011.

Gray, John, *Enlightenment's Wake*, Routledge, 2007.

Heijden, B. van der and Tahzib-Lei, B., eds, *Reflections on the Universal Declaration of Human Rights: A 50th Anniversary Anthology*, Kluwer, 1998.

Hodgson, Douglas, *The Protection of Individual Duty within the Human Rights System*, Ashgate, 2003.

Hopgood, Stephen, *The Endtimes of Human Rights*, Cornell University Press, 2013.

Hurley, Susan and Shute, Stephen, eds, *On Human Rights: The Oxford Amnesty Lectures*, Basic Books, 1993.

Ishay, Micheline R., *The History of Human Rights from Ancient Times to Globalisation*, University of California Press, 2004.

Kang-Riou, Nicolas, Milner, Jo, and Nayak, Suryia, eds, *Confronting the Human Rights Act: Contemporary Themes and Perspectives*, Routledge, 2012.

Malik, Habib C., ed., *The Challenge of Human Rights: Charles Malik and the Universal Declaration*, Charles Malik Foundation and the Centre for Lebanese Studies, 2000.

Morsink, Johannes, *Inherent Human Rights: Philosophical Roots of the Universal Declaration*, University of Pennsylvania Press, 2009.

Morsink, Johannes, *The Universal Declaration of Human Rights, Origins, Drafting and Intent*, University of Pennsylvania Press, 1999.

Moyn, Samuel, *The Last Utopia: Human Rights in History*, Belknap Press, 2010.

Nino, Carlos Santiago, *The Ethics of Human Rights*, Clarendon, 1993.

Quataert, Jean H., *Advocating Dignity: Human Rights Mobilisation in Global Politics*, Penn Press, 2009.

Schabas, William A., *UDHR Travaux Preparatoires*, Cambridge University Press, 2013.

Sellars, Kirsten, *The Rise and Rise of Human Rights*, Sutton, 2002.

Simpson, A. W. Brian, *Human Rights and the End of Empire: Britain and the Genesis of the European Convention*, Oxford University Press, 2001.

Starmer, Keir, *European Human Rights Law: The Human Rights Act 1998 and the European Convention on Human Rights*, Legal Action Group, 1999.

Sutcliffe, Adam, *Judaism and Enlightenment*, Cambridge University Press, 2003.

Vincent, Nicolas, ed., *Magna Carta: The Foundation of Freedom 1215–2015*, Law Society and Bar Council, Third Millennium Publishing, 2014.

Wadham, John, Mountfield, Helen, Edmundson, Anna, and Gallagher, Caoilfhionn, eds, *Blackstone's Guide to the Human Rights Act*, 4th ed., Oxford University Press, 2007.

Wellman, Carl, *The Moral Dimension of Human Rights*, Oxford University Press, 2011.

Winter, Jay and Prost, Antoine, *Renee Cassin and Human Rights: From the Great War to the Universal Declaration*, Cambridge University Press, 2013.

Selected published works by the author

Publications included in this book are excluded here.

'A Bill of Rights as Secular Ethics', in *Human Rights in the UK*, ed. Richard Gordon QC and Richard Wilmot-Smith QC, Clarendon, 1996.

'The Choice Before Us? The Report of the Commission on a Bill of Rights', with Amy Williams, *Public Law*, July, 2013.

Common Sense: Reflections on the Human Rights Act, Liberty, 2010.

'The "Democratic" Entrenchment of a Bill of Rights', with John Wadham, *Public Law*, Winter 1993.

'Follow or Lead? The Human Rights Act and the European Convention on Human Rights', with Helen Wildbore, *Special Issue of the European Human Rights Law Review*, 2010.

'The Human Rights Act: A "Third Way" or "Third Wave" Bill of Rights?' *European Human Rights Law Review* 4, 2001.

'The Human Rights Act: The First Two Years', with Claire O'Brien, *Public Law*, Winter 2002.

'The Human Rights Act 1998: *Pepper v Hart* and All That', *Public Law*, Summer 1999.

'Human Rights and Victims', in *Reconcilable Rights? Analysing the Tension between Victims and Defendants*, Legal Action Group, 2004.

'Incorporation through the Back Door?', with Keir Starmer, *Public Law*, Summer 1997.

'Judicial Deference under the Human Rights Act', *European Human Rights Law Review*, 2003.

Klug Report on the Working Practices of the Joint Committee on Human Rights, Joint Committee on Human Rights, 2006.

'New Labour and the Distribution of Power', in *Reassessing New Labour*, Patrick Diamond and Michael Kenny, eds, Wiley-Blackwell with Political Quarterly, 2011.

'"Solidity or Wind?" What's on the Menu in the Bill of Rights Debate?' *The Political Quarterly*, 80(3), 2009.

Special Issue of the European Human Rights Law Review, with Jane Gordon, eds, to mark the 10th anniversary of the HRA, 2010.

The Three Pillars of Liberty: Political Rights and Freedoms in the UK, with Keir Starmer and Stuart Weir, Routledge, 1996.

'The UK's 1998 Human Rights Act: Clarity and Confusion', with Amy Williams, in *Ireland and the European Convention on Human Rights: 60 Years and Beyond*, eds. Suzanne Egan, Liam Thornton, and Judy Walsh, Bloomsbury, 2014.

Values for a Godless Age: The Story of the UK's New Bill of Rights, Penguin, 2000.

SUBJECT INDEX

CASE INDEX